The Challenge of International Business

Also by Peter J. Buckley

CANADA–UK BILATERAL TRADE AND INVESTMENT RELATIONS (*with Christopher L. Paes and Kate Prescott*)

THE CHANGING GLOBAL CONTEXT OF INTERNATIONAL BUSINESS

FOREIGN DIRECT INVESTMENT AND MULTINATIONAL ENTERPRISES

INTERNATIONAL STRATEGIC MANAGEMENT AND GOVERNMENT POLICY

THE FUTURE OF MULTINATIONAL ENTERPRISE (*with Mark Casson*)

INTERNATIONAL TECHNOLOGY TRANSFER BY SMALL AND MEDIUM-SIZED ENTERPRISES (*co-edited with Jaime Campos and Eduardo White*)

MULTINATIONAL ENTERPRISES IN LESS DEVELOPED COUNTRIES (*co-edited with Jeremy Clegg*)

MULTINATIONAL FIRMS, COOPERATION AND COMPETITION IN THE WORLD ECONOMY

THE STRATEGY AND ORGANIZATION OF INTERNATIONAL BUSINESS (*co-edited with Fred Burton and Hafiz Mirza*)

STUDIES IN INTERNATIONAL BUSINESS

INTERNATIONAL BUSINESS: Economics and Anthropology, Theory and Method

The Challenge of International Business

Peter J. Buckley
Centre for International Business
University of Leeds
UK

palgrave
macmillan

First published 2004 by
PALGRAVE MACMILLAN
Houndmills, Basingstoke, Hampshire RG21 6XS and
175 Fifth Avenue, New York, N.Y. 10010
Companies and representatives throughout the world

PALGRAVE MACMILLAN is the global academic imprint of the Palgrave Macmillan division of St. Martin's Press, LLC and of Palgrave Macmillan Ltd. Macmillan® is a registered trademark in the United States, United Kingdom and other countries. Palgrave is a registered trademark in the European Union and other countries.

ISBN 1–4039–1306–4

This book is printed on paper suitable for recycling and made from fully managed and sustained forest sources.

A catalogue record for this book is available from the British Library.

Library of Congress cataloging-in-Publication Data
Buckley, Peter J., 1949–
The challenge of international business / Peter J. Buckley.
p. cm.
Includes bibliographical references and index.
ISBN 1–4039–1306–4 (cloth)
1. International business enterprises—Management. 2. Knowledge management. 3. Joint ventures. 4. Investments, Foreign. 5. Transfer pricing. 6. Competition, International. 7. International business enterprises—Developing countries. I. Title

HD62.4.B828 2004
658′.049—dc22

2004046494

10 9 8 7 6 5 4 3 2 1
13 12 11 10 09 08 07 06 05 04

Printed and bound in Great Britain by
Antony Rowe Ltd, Chippenham and Eastbourne

To current and future members of the Institute for Research on Contemporary China (IRCC), University of Leeds

Contents

Foreword by Stephen J. Kobrin ix

Acknowledgements xi

Notes on the Contributors xii

1 Introduction 1

Part I The Challenge

2 Is the International Business Research Agenda Running out of Steam? 7

Part II The Response

3 Strategic Complexity in International Business (*with Mark Casson*) 19

4 Internationalization – Real Options, Knowledge Management and the Uppsala Approach (*with Mark Casson and Mohammed Azzim Gulamhussen*) 54

5 Globalization and the End of Competition: a Critical Review of Rent-seeking Multinationals (*with Pervez N. Ghauri*) 83

6 Trust in International Joint Venture Relationships (*with Margreet F. Boersma and Pervez N. Ghauri*) 101

7 The Challenges of the New Economy for Multinational Firms: Lessons for South-East Asia 124

Part III Knowledge Management in Multinational Firms

8 Process and Structure in Knowledge Management Practices of British and US Multinational Enterprises (*with Martin J. Carter*) 145

9 Governing Knowledge Sharing in Multinational Enterprises (*with Martin J. Carter*) 167

Part IV Empirics

10 Evolution of FDI in the United States in the Context of Trade Liberalization and Regionalization (*with Jeremy Clegg, Nicolas Forsans and Kevin T. Reilly*) 189

11 The Impact of Inward FDI on the Performance of Chinese Manufacturing Firms (*with Jeremy Clegg and Chengqi Wang*) 198

12 FDI, Regional Differences and Economic Growth: Panel Data Evidence from China (*with Jeremy Clegg, Chengqi Wang and Adam R. Cross*) 220

13 Incentives to Transfer Profits: a Japanese Perspective (*with Jane Frecknall Hughes*) 242

14 A Survey-based Investigation of the Determinants of FDI in Portugal (*with Francisco B. Castro*) 254

Index 290

Foreword

In some respects international business is a relatively new field of scholarly research. Many of those who were 'present at the creation' such as John Dunning, Stefan Roebock and Jean Boddewyn are still active participants in academic meetings. On the other hand it has been over 40 years since two events occurred in 1960 which can be taken as marking the separation of international business from international economics: the completion of Stephen Hymer's seminal dissertation arguing that foreign direct investment (FDI) could not be explained as an international capital flow, and the first use of the term 'multinational corporation' by David Lillienthal at a conference at what is now Carnegie Mellon University.

One can only assume that the arguments about whether or not international business was a separate discipline started immediately! That somewhat hoary question aside, there is no question that the first few decades of international business research were dynamic, productive and exciting. Great strides were made in explaining FDI phenomenologically, developing systematic and empirically based analyses of the strategy and structure of multinational firms, understanding the motives for and sequence of international expansion, entry strategy and the management of joint ventures and alliances.

I suspect that many of us in the field feel that the flow of new knowledge has slowed considerably in the last decade. While international business researchers continue to be productive and there have been a large number of interesting new papers and books published, it is hard to think of many major breakthroughs since the last 1980s and early 1990s.

To some extent, this is a natural consequence of the maturity of any academic discipline. As a discipline ages the initial burst of new knowledge is replaced by deeper, more sophisticated and more empirically rigorous studies of a necessarily more limited scope. On the other hand, it may reflect the approaching exhaustion of the current paradigm (or paradigms): it may result from diminishing returns from current approaches to scholarship.

Peter Buckley hurls such a challenge at the outset of this volume, suggesting that 'the international business research agenda is running out of steam after a period of vibrancy'. Buckley argues that at this point international business lacks a 'big research question', an important confrontation with empirical reality that the scholars in the field can deal with collaboratively.

In the chapters that follow Buckley and his co-authors and contributors suggest some directions for international business research, some 'big problems' that will re-energize and reinvigorate the field and they provide some examples of methodologies and approaches to problems that will certainly be useful to other scholars. It would be unusual if every reader of this volume agreed with the challenge that Buckley poses, or indeed agrees that international business research is 'running out of steam'. That be as it may, every reader will find much of interest in this book: the problems posed; arguments and theories suggested; and the methodologies explored will serve to help stimulate a wide variety of research programmes.

Peter Buckley has never been known for avoiding controversy. In the chapters that follow he asks a much needed question and attempts to provide, at least an outline of, an answer. The challenge he puts forth should be taken up and considered seriously by all international business academics.

STEPHEN J. KOBRIN
Philadelphia

Acknowledgements

Chapter 2 first appeared in *Journal of International Business Studies*, vol. 33, no. 2, 2002, pp. 365–73. Chapter 3: Alan M. Rugman and Thomas L. Brewer (eds) *The Oxford Handbook of International Business*, Oxford University Press, 2003, pp. 88–126. Chapters 4 and 5: Virpi Havila, Mats Forsgren and Hakan Hakansson (eds) *Critical Perspectives on Internationalisation*, Elsevier Science, Oxford, 2002, pp. 229–61 and 7–28. Chapter 6: *Journal of Business Research*, xxxx. Chapter 7: N. Freeman and F. Bartels (eds) *The Future of Foreign Investment in Southeast Asia*, Routledge Curzon, London, 2004. Chapter 8: *Journal of International Management*, vol. 8, 2002, pp. 29–48. Chapter 9: *Management International Review*, vol. 43, Special issue 3, 2003, pp. 7–25. Chapter 10: *Journal of Business Research*, vol. 56, no. 10, 2003, pp. 853–57. Chapter 11: *Journal of International Business Studies*, vol. 33, no. 4, 2002, pp. 637–55. Chapter 12: *Transnational Corporations*, vol. 11, no. 1, 2002, pp. 1–28. Chapter 13: *Applied Economics*, vol. 33, 2001, pp. 2009–15. Chapter 14: James H. Taggart, Maureen Berry and Michael McDermott (eds) *Multinationals in a New Era*, Palgrave, London, pp. 226–58.

Notes on the Contributors

Margreet F. Boersma is consultant with Price Waterhouse Coopers.

Martin J. Carter is Lecturer in Economics, Leeds University Business School.

Mark Casson is Professor of Economics, University of Reading.

Francisco B. Castro is Professor Auxiliar at Universidade do Porto, Portugal.

Jeremy Clegg is Jean Monnet Professor of European Integration and International Business Management, Leeds University Business School.

Adam R. Cross is Senior Lecturer in International Business, Leeds University Business School.

Nicolas Forsans is Lecturer in International Business and Strategic Management, Leeds University Business School.

Pervez N. Ghauri is Professor of International Business, Manchester School of Management, UMIST.

Mohammed Azzim Gulamhussen is Assistant Professor of Finance at INDEG/ISCTE Business School, Lisbon, Portugal.

Jane Frecknall Hughes is Lecturer in Accounting, Leeds University Business School.

Kevin T. Reilly is Senior Lecturer in Economics, Leeds University Business School.

Chengqi Wang is Senior Research Fellow in International Business, Leeds University Business School.

1
Introduction

This book appears at a time when the academic community of international business scholars is taking stock. Numerous pieces have appeared which examine, or question, the future of the discipline. Chapter 2 of this volume represents my contribution to this debate. It questions the current direction of research and suggests that international business needs 'a big question' to answer. It suggests that research in international business has been at its most successful when it has been a collective enterprise focused on a key empirical issue in the evolving global economy.

Needless to say, not all researchers accept this position and several ripostes and rebuttals are in preparation. I have set the remainder of this book up as an answer to my own question in the hope that those who read on will find that there is a great deal of vibrancy in research in international business.

Chapter 3, co-authored with Mark Casson, explores a rational action approach to the questions surrounding complexity in strategic decisions in multinational enterprises (MNEs). It posits a systems theory approach to foreign entry strategy and focuses on the firm's need to collect and to process information. It also takes on board the dynamics of strategy and incorporates a real option approach to strategy. The real option approach is developed further in Chapter 4 (co-authored with Mark Casson and Mohammed Gulamhussen) where it is combined with knowledge management issues and is shown to include the 'Uppsala approach' to foreign market entry as a special case. This chapter shows that international joint ventures (IJVs) can be analysed as real options for the firm.

Multinational enterprises are not without their critics. Chapter 5 (co-authored with Pervez Ghauri) examines the critical literature on the 1950s to 1970s and examines the impact of MNEs on developing countries. It finds concern in the decline of the state as a regulatory body and in the threats to the self-regulating role of competition. Distributional outcomes of globalization also show worrying signs. The chapter concludes with a view that a new research agenda needs to address the dark side of globalization.

Chapter 6 (co-authored with Margreet Boersma and Pervez Ghauri) examines the role of trust in IJV relationships. It develops a process model of trust, incorporating a transactions cost approach to the generation of trust and its development (or degeneration) into commitment (or distrust). This chapter uses a case study research method and puts forward a testable model.

The final chapter in Part II examines the challenges of the 'new economy' for multinational firms. It moves from the examination of MNE strategy in a single economy to more than one national market, dynamic entry and exit, to considerations of strategic choice where there are interactions between markets (global/local issues are to the fore here) and finally to a consideration of the meaning and impact of globalization, not least upon the internal organization of MNEs. Implications for the important region of South-East Asia are then drawn.

Part III of this book illustrates the important elements of an emerging research agenda in international business: a systems approach to strategy in the global economy, dynamic analysis including real options, attention to the increasing role of IJVs in global strategy and information as a crucial determinant of the outcomes of decision making. Both the positives and the negatives of globalization are part of this agenda.

The two chapters in Part III concern the role of knowledge management in MNEs and are co-authored with Martin Carter. The previous chapters have highlighted the crucial part that information plays in the strategy of MNEs. Chapter 8 unpacks the notions of 'global' and 'local' in knowledge management and investigates the spatial aspect of the process of knowledge management. This chapter pays particular attention to the part played by ('active') subsidiaries within the organizational structure of MNEs. The case studies employed illustrate the importance of spatial issues in knowledge management in the MNE. The chapter further moves the analysis from a conceptualization relying on a unidirectional flow of knowledge towards much more complex interactions within the firm in both space and time. Chapter 9 examines a series of propositions on knowledge-sharing processes within MNEs. These propositions concern the division of knowledge processes between firms and examine 'knowledge frontiers' within them. It identifies architectural forms designed as integration and partition to exploit knowledge exchange and remove, or work round, knowledge frontiers and it suggests that firms can employ both application and discovery strategies in pursuing knowledge management. These propositions are tested in cases of UK and US multinationals.

Chapter 2 argued that engagement with the business world is an essential feature of successful international business research. The final part of the book presents empirical research based on both quantitative and qualitative methods. The first three chapters employ econometric techniques to examine the impact of regionalization in the world economy (particularly NAFTA) on the evolution of FDI in the USA, and inward investment in China. The first chapter finds that North American regional economic integration has led to an increase in inward FDI in the USA. Chapter 11 shows that inward FDI into China has generated positive spillover benefits for Chinese firms but that this depends on the absorptive capacity of the Chinese recipients and that this is patchy and varies according to the ownership type of indigenous Chinese firms. Chapter 12, based on panel data, shows that spillover benefits also vary according to region in China and that spillovers are at their highest where competition in local markets is greatest.

Chapter 13 continues my investigations of transfer pricing by multinational firms (in cooperation with Jane Frecknall Hughes). This chapter finds that the internal transfer prices of Japanese multinational firms serve to transfer profits away from the subsidiaries back to Japan. This is not a tax–minimizing policy as taxes are generally higher in Japan than elsewhere. This policy arises from need for control and from business consciousness. A wider view of transfer pricing than heretofore is necessary, the chapter concludes. The final chapter is a survey-based investigation of FDI in Portugal co-authored with Francisco Castro. It finds that low costs, access to the home market, political stability and 'push' factors were the key determinants for manufacturing investment in Portugal. However, more export orientated industries saw access to the EU market from a low-cost base to be the primary attractors. Segments and clusters were found in the overall picture which presents a more nuanced view of motivations and this helps to suggest that Portuguese policy should focus on competition from Eastern Europe and Spain in these different segments.

Overall this book suggests that the challenge facing international business researchers can be met by a refinement of theoretical techniques, a focus on real issues in the globalizing world economy and a judicious selection of both quantitative and qualitative techniques to refine empirical analysis.

Part I

The Challenge

2

Is the International Business Research Agenda Running out of Steam?

Introduction

This research note suggests that the international business research agenda is running out of steam after a period of vibrancy. It suggests that 'the big research question' with which international business researchers are engaged is no longer clear cut and that, after three distinct periods where a definite research agenda was pursued, no distinctive topic has emerged to take the place of the issues previously, and largely successfully, tackled.

Previous research agenda

Three major topics have been successfully tackled by researchers in the international business field. These are shown in Table 2.1. The three key topics were:

1. explaining the flows of foreign direct investment (FDI);
2. explaining the existence, strategy and organization of multinational enterprises (MNEs);
3. understanding and predicting the development of the internationalization of firms and the new developments of globalization.

Each of these research epochs is examined below.

Explaining flows of foreign direct investment

Following World War II and the re-establishment of the international economy, the renewal and increase of international flows of direct investment were a key feature of the dynamism of Western economies. The key empirical problematic was the explanation of private flows of investment, controlled by individual corporations. Of particular importance were flows of capital from the USA to Western Europe.

Table 2.1 Past major topics in international business research

Research agenda	*Approximate dates*	*Topics*	*Country focus*
1. Explaining flows of FDI	Post-WWII–1970s	US FDI in Europe Managerial issues of investing abroad	Europe (US → Europe) Latin America Canada
2. Explanation of existence, strategy and organization of MNEs	1970s–1990	Theories of MNE Strategies of MNE Organization of MNE Foreign market servicing strategies Smaller firms in IB International economic integration	LDCS Japan (MNEs from LDCS) 4 Little Dragons
3. Internationalization to globalization 'New forms' of international business	Mid 1980s–2000	Joint ventures Alliances (M&A?) Competitiveness Meaning(s) of globalization 'Born globals'	Eastern Europe 'Asian Crisis' China

Traditional explanations of this surge were inadequate. International trade theory assumed immobile factors of production (labour and capital) and macro explanations of capital moving in response to differential rates of interest were not only infeasible, but failed to deal with important industrial differentials within these flows. (The steel industry remained largely national but automobile manufacturers quickly internationalized.)

The initial solution lay in moving the theory of FDI into the sphere of industrial economics. Although elements of this approach had been foreshadowed (Penrose, 1956; Byé, 1958),[1] it was the doctoral dissertation of Stephen Hymer (1960, published 1976) which achieved the breakthrough. Hymer's central proposition was that the international firm making the entry into a foreign market must possess an internally transferable 'advantage', the control of which gives it a quasi-monopolistic opportunity to outcompete local firms. Barriers to trade and barriers which prevent host-country firms from duplicating this advantage mean that FDI is frequently the preferred form of exploiting this advantage in foreign markets. The advantage enables the foreign entrant to overcome the innate advantage of knowledge of the local market and business conditions possessed by indigenous firms. Hymer's supervisor, Kindleberger (1969), in a popularising book, examined key areas where these internationally transferable advantages were likely to be important, thus providing a testable empirical agenda for research. Hymer was fortunate to be able to draw on John Dunning's (1958) meticulous analysis of US FDI in the UK and on Bain's (1956) analysis on barriers to entry into industries, later refined by Caves (1971) in a paper which first systematized the industrial economics of foreign direct investment.

The product cycle hypothesis, chiefly associated with Raymond Vernon (1966), was particularly successful in explaining the dynamics of US FDI in Europe by close attention to changes in both the supply and demand sides and their complex interaction. However, it proved difficult to stretch this framework to the cases of European and Japanese multinationals, whose presence was becoming more salient (Vernon, 1974) and the framework, but not the underlying concepts, became outdated (Vernon, 1979). A second stream of research on flows of FDI concerned investment in less developed countries (Lall and Streeten, 1977).

The role of the strategy of the firm at this stage took a back seat to economic determinants of FDI. However, several studies took an evolutionary, 'internationalization' view of the firm. Prominent among approaches deriving from a behavioural theory of the firm was Aharoni's (1966) work on the foreign direct investment decision process. This book, with its focus on uncertainty and information, links to the work of the Uppsala school whose 'stages' model of internationalization become the foundation for the gradualist step-by-step internationalization model (Carlson, 1974, 1975; Johanson and Wiedersheim-Paul, 1975; Johanson and Valne, 1977). These models suggested an incremental approach to international involvement, 'deepening involvement' or 'creeping incrementalism' as the firm is pulled by market (or cost) attraction and pushed by executive interest and learning. This is in contrast to later approaches of *planned* globalization. FDI was seen, at this stage, as driven by external circumstance, somewhat unplanned and the coordinating and planning role of the firm were not central to theorizing. That was about to change.

The multinational enterprise

The multinational enterprise as an entity, with problems of organization and a purposive strategy became central to the international business agenda in the 1970s. This impetus came from two directions and it is possible to argue that the two research thrusts have never been fully reconciled.

The first approach followed Alfred Chandler's review of the changes in business organizational form through multifunction operation to divisionalization (1962) and the growth and impact of managerial hierarchies (1977). This led to a group of empirical studies on the organization of MNEs of different origins,[2] illuminated also by the painstaking historical work of Mira Wilkins (1970, 1974). The problems of organizing a multinational firm were analysed in the context of the tensions in the firm and the external pressures on it. One issue is whether the firm should be divided into domestic and international divisions (in the era of globalization now a rather redundant debate) and second, the direction of managerial line responsibility – should the primary organizational principle be functional, product or geographical area? Further, there is the question of coordination with the other two variables and the issue of how this evolves over time (Stopford and Wells, 1972). The resource based theory of the firm has since had a major role in the explanation of MNEs and their strategy.

The second approach derives from the ideas of Ronald Coase (1937) and together with concepts related to the transaction cost economics approach of Williamson (1975) on 'markets and hierarchies', the internalization approach has become the dominant paradigm for the analysis of the MNE. Although preceded by McManus (1972) and closely followed by Hennart (1982) and Swedenborg (1976), the standard treatment is that of Buckley and Casson (1976). The basic approach is marginalist: by carefully specifying the transactional costs and benefits of internalizing the external markets which face particular firms in particular economic circumstances, predictions can be made between internally and externally organized markets which fix the growth of the firm. A firm will grow by internalizing imperfect external markets until it is bounded by markets in which the transactions benefits of further internalization are outweighed by the costs. The incidence of transactions costs in internal (agency costs) and external markets can thus be used to derive propositions on the speed and direction of the growth of the firm. Both locational determinants (exports versus foreign production) and ownership factors (direct investment versus licensing) specify the foreign market servicing network of the firm.

John Dunning undertook a major systematizing effort in the formulation of his eclectic (theory, later) paradigm (1977, 1979, 1980, 1988). This has the unintended effect of diverting attention from answering big empirical issues into attempting to fill the boxes suggested by the theory and to widen the scope of a pre-existing explanatory framework. The relationships between the three pillars of Dunning's explanatory framework (ownership, location and internalization 'advantages') led to some interesting academic exchanges and empirical developments but not to a new research agenda.

Internationalization to globalization

The rise of the global economy has been an important element in the international business agenda since the 1980s. The sporadic, unplanned, externally driven approaches to international strategic planning needed to be superseded by more formal models of global strategy and the myriad ways of doing international business, particularly strategic alliances and international joint ventures, had to be captured by a holistic theoretical approach. The more overt stance of national governments towards competing in a global market led to a focus on competitiveness and the opening of new markets in the former socialist countries led to studies of the 'transition' (integration into global capitalism).

The notion of competitiveness became prominent. Competitiveness often was taken to mean simply out-competing rivals in the global market. Plans to achieve this were formulated at national, industry, firm and sub-unit of the firm (Buckley et al., 1988). A national level formulation of this interpretation (how to do better than your rivals) was famously formulated by Porter (1990) and his 'diamond' framework and it attracted criticism and modification from international business scholars (Dunning, 1997; Rugman, 1993).

Prominent amongst new theorizing were concerns for the understanding of IJVs and alliances (Contractor and Lorange, 1988) and for studies of alliance capitalism (Dunning, 1997). There was also renewed concern in the form of organization able to cope with the new demands (Bartlett and Ghoshal, 1989). Models now had to deal with the extreme diversity and reorganization of activities and with firms which were already international in scope, rather than those seeking internationalization as a goal. The object of firm strategy became 'flexibility', in order to adjust to increases in volatility as the sources of change and threat multiplied (Buckley and Casson, 1998).

These challenges were largely met by a reconfiguration of concepts. For instance, the model of the transnational given by Bartlett and Ghoshal combines Vernon's three drivers (innovation, competing with rivals on cost and differentiation of product) but removes their temporal sequencing. Similarly, the micro analysis of IJVs covers performance and control but also relies on newer concepts such as trust to deal with issues of managing beyond the boundaries of the firm. The appearance of instant MNEs 'born globals' requires a rapid telescoping of time but still faces the firm with Aharoni/Penrose problems of knowledge assimilation and verification to combat extreme uncertainty and with the incorporation and acculturation of new executives. The new dot com companies have found this balance too challenging to cope with in the short term.

The role of culture

This threefold division ignores an important element in international business theorizing and empirical studies – the role of culture and in particular the impact of differing national cultures (Hofstede, 1983, 1991). The interplay of national cultures and organizational cultures, including the organizational culture of multinational organizations which might augment, transcend or conflict with particular national cultural traits, represents a research agenda with much life left in it. The whole question of 'comparative management' has been a strand of work parallel to and cross-fertilizing 'mainstream' international business research and frequently grouped with other (more managerialist) literature as 'international management'

(Buckley, 1996). These issues are perhaps best understood as exemplars of a particularly fruitful methodological approach – the comparative method, rather than as answering particular issues or confronting radically separate agendas and stylized facts.

What now? The current research agenda

The above, overly brief, review shows that strength of past epochs of international business research in its close engagement with empirical reality. International business research has been successful because of its adroit choice of concepts with which to confront and explain real changes in the world economy. It is not now clear that there is a big empirical question which requires explanation (Table 2.2).

Several potential topics may be suggested as candidates (Table 2.3). They include mergers and acquisitions (M&A), knowledge management, geography and location. In addition, further explanation (or deconstruction) of the concept of globalization, with predictions for its future (further integration or fragmentation) may be suggested. New institutions in the wake of globalization, such as the increasing role of NGOs (non-governmental organizations), too, might be candidates for important research agendas.

Unlike the above mixed bag, international business scholars often do have a fixed country focus. The entry of China as a major player in the global

Table 2.2 Current research agenda in international business

Research agenda	*Approximate dates*	*Topics*	*Country focus*
The big question? (Legacy issues only?)	2000 onwards	M&A? Knowledge management? Geography and location? Globalization? Fragmentation? New institutions (NGOs)?	China India?

Table 2.3 Research issues for 2000 onwards

1. Do we need a 'big question'?
2. Relationship with other functional areas – how distinctive is IB research?
3. Is the answer in methodology? (culture, comparative studies, distinctive methods)
4. Feedback to other disciplines? (Leader or follower?)
   Evidence?
5. Area of application – applied concepts from other areas?
   IB as empirical field – testing ground for concepts?

economy has given new impetus to single country studies of the market entry and development behaviour of foreign firms in China. The correspondingly disappointing role of India may, eventually, give rise to a new set of such studies.

The future of international business research

The above analysis has suggested that international business research has succeeded because it has focused on, in sequence, a number of big questions which arise from empirical developments in the world economy. The agenda is stalled because no such big question has currently been identified. This calls into question the separate existence of the subject area. It raises the old problem of the relationship between international business and other functional areas of management and social science.[3] Without a close interaction between theoretical development and empirical reality, international business could become merely an area of application for applied concepts from other disciplines.

The way forward is, paradoxically, to look back. The need is to look back to the successes of international business research. These successes were achieved by identifying the key empirical factors in the global economy which needed to be explained and then searching out a tractable means of explication within a coherent theoretical framework. The first step is to identify the most important stylized facts.

In its successful era, international business researchers not only imported concepts and paradigms, they also exported them to neighbouring areas. This does not seem to be occurring at the moment. One response is to argue that international business is defined by its distinctive methods, its attention to cultural differences and the comparative method, for instance. An alternative argument might be that no big research question is needed – there are lots of issues left over from the preceding research epochs (legacy issues). These seem to be inadequate responses to a keenly felt problem. Perhaps there is a need for international business researchers to discover a new 'big question'. If so, this back-to-basics agenda requires the collation of new stylized facts.

Among these may be the following issues:

1. Can we explain the sequence of entry of nations as major players in the world economy? (Great Britain, USA, Germany, Japan, Singapore, Korea, China).
2. Why are different forms of company organization characteristic of individual cultural backgrounds? Or is this an artefact?
3. In what empirical measures can we identify trends to (and away from) globalization?
4. Challenges to global capitalism.

Notes

1. A great deal more could be said of the research which predated and foreshadowed Hymer's analysis, but that is for another essay.
2. Pavan (1972) on Italy, Rumelt (1974) on the USA, Channon (1973) on the UK, Dyas and Thanheiser (1976) on France and Germany and Wrigley (1978) on Canada.
3. Many international business scholars would suggest that the main problem is the appropriation of IB topics by scholars from other disciplines. The concern of this chapter is not *who* does the research, but what that research should be.

References

Aharoni, Yair (1966) *The Foreign Investment Decision Process*. Cambridge, Mass.: Harvard Business School Press.

Bain, J. S. (1956) *Barriers to New Competition*. Cambridge, Mass.: Harvard University Press.

Bartlett, Christopher A. and Sumantra Ghoshal (1989) *Management across Borders: the Transnational Solution*. Boston: Hutchinson Business Books.

Buckley, Peter J. (1996) 'The Role of Management in International Business Theory'. *Management International Review*, vol. 35 (1.1 Special Issue), pp. 7–54.

Buckley, Peter J. and Mark Casson (1976) *The Future of the Multinational Enterprise*. London: Macmillan.

Buckley, Peter J. and Mark Casson (1998) 'Models of the Multinational Enterprise'. *Journal of International Business Studies*, vol. 29, no. 1, pp. 21–44.

Buckley, Peter J., C. L. Pass and Kate Prescott (1988) 'Measures of International Competitiveness: a Critical Survey'. *Journal of Marketing Management*, vol. 4, no. 2, pp. 175–200.

Byé, Maurice (1958) 'Self-Financed Multiterritorial Units and their Time Horizon'. *International Economic Papers*, No. 8. London: Macmillan.

Carlson, Sune (1974) *Investment in Knowledge and the Cost of Information*. Uppsala: Acta Academiae Regiae Scientiarum Upsaliensis.

Carlson, Sune (1975) *How Foreign is Foreign Trade*? Uppsala: University of Uppsala.

Caves, Richard E. (1971) 'International Corporations: the Industrial Economics of Foreign Investment'. *Economica* (New series), vol. 38, pp. 1–27.

Chandler, Alfred D. Jr (1962) *Strategy and Structure*. Cambridge, Mass.: MIT Press.

Chandler, Alfred D. Jr (1977) *The Visible Hand: the Managerial Revolution in American Business*. Cambridge, Mass.: Belknap Press of Harvard University.

Channon, Derek F. (1973) *The Strategy and Structure of British Enterprise*. Boston, Mass.: Graduate School of Business Administration, Harvard University.

Contractor, Farok and Peter Lorange (eds) (1988) *Cooperative Strategies in International Business*. Lexington, Mass.: Lexington Books.

Dunning, John H. (1958) *American Investment in British Manufacturing Industry*. London: George Allen & Unwin.

Dunning, John H. (1977) 'Trade, Location of Economic Activity and the Multinational Enterprise: a Search for an Eclectic Approach'. In B. Ohlin, P. O. Hesselborn and P. M. Wijkman (eds) *The International Allocation of Economic Activity*. London: Macmillan.

Dunning, John H. (1979) 'Explaining Changing Patterns of International Production: In Defence of the Eclectic Theory'. *Oxford Bulletin of Economics and Statistics*, vol. 41, pp. 269–96.

Dunning, John H. (1980) 'Toward an Eclectic Theory of International Production: Some Empirical Tests'. *Journal of International Business Studies*, vol. 11, pp. 9–31.
Dunning, John H. (1988) 'The Eclectic Paradigm of International Production: a Restatement and Some Possible Extensions'. *Journal of International Business Studies*, vol. 19, pp. 1–31.
Dunning, John H. (1997) *Alliance Capitalism and Global Capitalism*. London: Routledge.
Dyas, Gareth P. and Heinz T. Thanheiser (1976) *The Emerging European Enterprise: Strategy and Structure*. London: Macmillan.
Hennart, Jean-Francois (1982) *A Theory of Multinational Enterprise*. Ann Arbor: University of Michigan Press.
Hofstede, Geert (1980) *Culture's Consequences: International Differences in Work-Related Values*. Beverly Hills: Sage Publications.
Hofstede, Geert (1991) *Cultures and Organizations*. London: McGraw-Hill.
Hymer, Stephen H. (1976) *The International Operations of National Firms: a Study of Direct Foreign Investment*. Cambridge, Mass.: MIT Press (PhD thesis 1960).
Johanson, Jan and Jan-Erik Vahlne (1977) 'The Internationalization Process of the Firm – a Model of Knowledge Development and Increasing Market Commitments'. *Journal of International Business Studies*, vol. 8, no. 1, pp. 23–32.
Johanson, Jan and Finn Wiedersheim-Paul (1975) 'The Internationalization of the Firm, Four Swedish Case Studies'. *Journal of Management Studies*, vol. 12, no. 3, pp. 305–22.
Kindleberger, C. P. (1969) *American Business Abroad*. New Haven: Yale University Press.
Lall, Sanjaya and Paul Streeten (1977) *Foreign Investment, Transnationals and Developing Countries*. London: Macmillan.
McManus, J. C. (1972) 'The Theory of the International Firm'. In G. Paquet (ed.) *The Multinational Firm and the Nation State*. Toronto: Collier-Macmillan.
Pavan, Robert J. (1972) 'The Strategy and Structure of Italian Enterprise'. Unpublished DBA thesis, Graduate School of Business Administration, Harvard University.
Penrose, Edith. T. (1956) 'Foreign Investment and the Growth of the Firm'. *Economic Journal*, vol. 66, pp. 230–5.
Porter, Michael E. (1990) *The Competittive Advantage of Nations*. New York: Free Press.
Rugman, Alan M. and Joseph R. D'Cruz (1993) 'The "Double Diamond" Model of International Competitiveness: the Canadian Experience'. *Management International Review*, Special Issue 2, pp. 17–39.
Rumelt, Richard P. (1974) *Strategy, Structure and Economic Performance*. Boston, Mass.: Graduate School of Business Administration, Harvard University.
Stopford, John M. and Louis T. Wells (1972) *Managing the Multinational Enterprise*. New York: Basic Books.
Swedenborg, B. (1979) *The Multinational Operations of Swedish Firms: an Analysis of Determinants and Effects*. Stockholm: Almqvist and Wicksell.
Vernon, Raymond (1966) 'International Investment and International Trade in the Product Cycle'. *Quarterly Journal of Economics*, vol. 80, pp. 190–207.
Vernon, Raymond (1974) 'The Location of Economic Activity'. In John H. Dunning (ed.) *Economic Analysis and the Multinational Enterprise*. London: George Allen & Unwin.
Vernon, Raymond (1979) 'The Product Cycle Hypothesis in a New International Environment'. *Oxford Bulletin of Economics and Statistics*, vol. 41, pp. 255–67.
Wilkins, Mira (1970) *The Emergence of Multinational Enterprise: American Business Abroad from the Colonial Era to 1914*. Cambridge, Mass.: Harvard University Press.

Wilkins, Mira (1974) *The Maturing of Multinational Enterprise: American Business Abroad from 1914 to 1970*. Cambridge, Mass.: Harvard University Press.
Williamson, Oliver E. (1975) *Markets and Hierarchies: Analysis and Anti-Trust Implications*. New York: Free Press.
Wrigley, Leonard (1978) 'Conglomerate Growth in Canada'. Unpublished dissertation, School of Business Administration, Harvard University.

Part II

The Response

3
Strategic Complexity in International Business

with Mark Casson

The current challenges facing international business theory

Most contributions to a handbook are necessarily retrospective, but there is also scope for a prospective view of the kind offered in this chapter. In retrospect there have been significant theoretical achievements in international business (IB) over the past 40 years, but the prospects are not so good.

1. A comparison of the periods 1972–82 and 1990–2000 suggests a declining dynamic of theoretical innovation; developments in IB were once ahead of those in related areas, whereas now they seem to follow behind;
2. Every answer raises new questions: but many of the new questions raised in the 1970s literature remain unresolved;
3. The 'strategic alliances' literature exhibits the weaknesses as well as the strengths of a multi-disciplinary perspective; there are so many different propositions about different aspects of alliances, often based on different definitions, that it becomes unclear whether they are coherent or not;
4. The debate between transaction costs and resource-based theories has become increasingly sterile; and
5. Excessive dependence on case studies means that the 'strategic management' literature increasingly confuses consultancy with research, and equates the development of executive teaching materials with original contributions to knowledge.

If IB is to regain its influence within the social sciences as a whole, it is necessary to reintegrate it into mainstream intellectual debate. One way in which this can be done is to introduce more refined analytical techniques into IB theory. This chapter recommends that the rational action approach to modelling should be expanded in order to address a wider range of IB issues. It provides practical examples of how this can be done, based mainly on our own recent work.

The rational action approach has achieved its greatest successes in addressing economic issues, but it can also elucidate issues in strategic management and organizational behaviour. By working with formal models whose assumptions are explicit it is possible to eliminate ambiguity, and thereby foster informed criticism that serves to eliminate logical error (Elster, 1986; Hargreaves-Heap, 1989). Modern IB texts tend to present the subject as a multi-disciplinary field of research that addresses issues that are specific to international business operations. This was not the view of IB that prevailed at the time of its greatest intellectual vitality in the 1970s, however. Many scholars of that time perceived IB as a field of applied economics – a useful 'laboratory' in which to test general theories against newly gathered statistical evidence (Buckley and Casson, 1976).

Since the 1970s the methods of economics have been extended to other fields of social science, such as politics, law and sociology (Buckley and Casson, 1993). This has been made possible by the increasing power of rational action modelling techniques. As a result, it is possible to update the 1970s view: IB is now best regarded as a field of applied social science, rather than just a field of applied economics, as before. But in this context social science must be understood, not as a collection of different disciplines, each with its own tradition and methodology, but as an integrated social science based upon the rational action approach.

This chapter does not present a forecast of how the subject will evolve, but simply makes a proposal, with which others may well disagree. It begins with a critique of recent calls for the use of 'softer' theories in IB. In particular, it considers whether the increasing complexity of the IB environment makes formal modelling impractical. It concludes that it does not. Much of what is called complexity, it suggests, is subjective, and merely reflects the confusion of scholars who rely on softer theories. Such confusions can be dispelled by invoking the intellectual rigour of the rational action approach.

Two main sources of complexity are identified. One is the uncertainty involved in long-term planning. It reflects the 'strategic' nature of certain decisions, such as those concerned with irreversible investments. There is a distinctive set of rational action modelling techniques that is available for analysing such decisions.

Another source of complexity is connected with networks. Networks in IB take both physical and social forms. A physical network comprises a set of production plants, distribution centres, and retail outlets. These various facilities are connected by transport infrastructure. Several facilities may be owned by the same firm, depending upon where the boundaries of the firm are drawn. Boundaries of firms that span international boundaries lead to multinational firms. Formal models of IB networks are now available which determine simultaneously where all the boundaries of the different firms within a system are drawn. These models can also incorporate flows of knowledge generated by R&D and marketing activities, as explained below.

Social networks are concerned with communications between decision-makers. Networks can be high-trust or low-trust, and either formal or informal. Communication through social networks allows different decision-makers to coordinate their decisions. Coordination within a firm involves internal networks, which often take a hierarchical form, whereas coordination between firms involves external networks which typically take a 'flatter' form. Formal analysis of communication costs makes it possible to analyse what kind of networks will emerge to coordinate different types of activity.

Complexity or confusion?

It is often asserted that the modern global environment is so complex that it is impossible to capture reality with the aid of any formal model. As a result, a good deal of effort has gone into developing heuristic approaches that use analogy and metaphor, rather than formal theory, to articulate key ideas (Parkhe, 1993). For example, writers on joint ventures and strategic alliances have argued that as the boundaries of the firm become increasingly 'fuzzy', so theory must become 'fuzzy' too in order to handle the issue. Fuzzy theories are difficult to refute, however, because it is usually unclear what they mean, so that errors in these theories go undetected for a considerable time. Researchers who attempt to build on 'fuzzy' foundations can waste a good deal of time before the weaknesses of their foundations are properly exposed.

Another example of fuzzy thinking arises when people apply general systems theory to try to understand the complexity of the global economy. General systems theory talks a lot about 'complex systems', and so it seems intuitively reasonable that it should be invoked to explain the nature and causes of complex IB phenomena. The fact that the theory is opaque only adds to its credibility so far as the uninitiated are concerned.

But a lot of what is described as 'complexity' is often just confusion. When people do not understand something, they tend to assume that it must be 'complex', and so turn to 'complexity theory' for a solution. This theory introduces them to new jargon – such as 'chaos', 'catastrophe', 'emergent properties', and the like (Arthur, 1988; Coriat and Dosi, 1998). It is suggested that these concepts derive from advanced mathematics, or 'rocket science'. In fact, many of the terms are little more than labels applied to areas of ignorance. While it is true that the mathematical theory of non-linear systems can explain chaotic behaviour, for example, such behaviour has little or nothing to do with the kind of behaviour that is observed in the IB system. If there is some connection, then it has certainly not been spelled out rigorously so far.

Popular perceptions of complexity may also be a response to a quickening pace of change. The world economy of today appears to be radically different from what it was only 50 years ago. It can be argued that radical changes call for radically new theories to explain them. A new brand of IB theory must be developed to meet the intellectual challenges of the new millennium, it may be said. Complexity provides an impressive range of novel jargon for describing change in the international business system. 'The global economy is a dynamic self-organizing system based on co-evolving institutions' seems to be a profound statement, even though it says little more than that the global economy is undergoing change.

Radical changes in theory are very expensive, however, because a whole new set of concepts needs to be developed and disseminated. Investing in radically new theory is extremely wasteful if existing theory is perfectly adequate. This chapter argues that complexity can be addressed perfectly adequately using existing concepts derived from the rational action approach.

Two concepts of complexity

Systems theorists distinguish between combinatorial complexity and what may be termed organic complexity. Combinatorial complexity is created when a large number of different cases have to be analysed before a decision can be made, and in each case a large number of different factors have to be taken into account. Organic complexity arises because of numerous interdependencies and feedback loops within a system. Everything depends upon everything else in such a way that cause and effect are difficult to disentangle. Organic complexity, it is suggested, cannot be addressed through rational analysis. In organically complex systems agents cannot understand the system of which they form a part. As a result, they have to commit themselves arbitrarily to certain rules, and the interactions between different agents playing according to different rules then generates the very kind of complexity in the system that defies analysis.

The techniques illustrated in this chapter approach complexity as a combinatorial problem. They address combinatorial complexity using a range of simplifying techniques. This reflects a methodological stance that complexity is best addressed by simplifying the representation of reality, rather than by making theory itself more complex. The problem of organic complexity is not ignored altogether, however. Organic complexity is handled by the traditional method of focusing on an equilibrium. For more than a century, economists have tackled system interdependencies by analysing the mathematical properties of equilibrium. Systems theorists often ridicule this approach. The fact remains, however, that the qualitative features of a system's dynamic behaviour are largely determined by its equilibrium properties. All stable systems have a propensity tc converge to an equilibrium. Systems that exhibit localized instabilities usually do so because they have more than one equilibrium. The number of equilibria is therefore an important guide to the out-of-equilibrium behaviour of a complex system. Although an equilibrium model cannot track the out-of-equilibrium behaviour of a system over time, it can identify the equilibrium to which the system will tend to converge from any given initial condition. For many purposes, this is all that a satisfactory model is required to do.

Certain types of disequilibrium behaviour can also be modelled in mathematical terms. This is normally achieved by assuming that agents follow certain simple myopic rules: the agent makes little attempt to look far ahead (Nelson and Winter, 1982). This contrasts sharply with the situation in rational action modelling, where agents are far sighted. Similarly, in simple disequilibrium models agents do not adapt their rules to the environment in which they operate, as a rational agent would do. These extreme assumptions are relevant in certain special cases: they are useful, for example, in explaining the sudden build-up of traffic jams, the persistence of stock exchange 'bubbles', and the formation of crowds around sensational events. It is not at all clear that they are useful in explaining IB phenomena, however. A successful multinational enterprise is unlikely to be controlled by a myopic rule-driven manager who is unable to adapt his behaviour to the circumstances he is in. It is more likely to be managed by a successful entrepreneur who can take a long-term view of a situation, and can adapt his behaviour to different sets of conditions.

Nevertheless, it is often claimed that disequilibrium models with system effects can provide a more realistic account of the global economy than a rational action model can. One reason for this is that some disequilibrium models predict that almost anything can happen out of equilibrium. When behaviour is highly sensitive to certain parameter values, which are difficult to measure, then it can always be claimed that the model has explained reality because the parameters took on whatever values they needed to. This kind of explanation is vacuous, because as long as key parameter values cannot be independently measured the explanation is impossible to verify.

'Path-dependence' is a good example of this type of non-explanation. Almost any historical aspect of the IB system can be explained in path-dependent terms. Path-dependent explanations usually begin with unspecified initial conditions which have been lost way back in the mists of time. 'Given the way things began, and all the things that have happened since, things are bound to be the way they are', goes this kind of explanation. The problem is that data on how things began, and on many of the things that happened since, are usually incomplete. In many applications of path dependence, even the pattern of causation linking one step to the next is unclear. Path-dependence can be used to rationalize almost any sequence of events, and can give any simple narrative of events the appearance of a being a scientific test of systems theory.

This is not to deny that path-dependence occurs. Agents are 'locked in' by their actions whenever there are adjustment costs, because their actions cannot be costlessly reversed. But 'lock in' is only a serious problem under certain conditions, and rational action models explain what these conditions are. It is often suggested that 'lock in' is a direct consequence of myopic decision-making, but this is incorrect. Everyone is locked in by adjustment costs, whether they are rational or not. Rational agents may be locked in less than irrational ones, however, because when they realize that they still have much to learn about a situation they will choose a course of action which maximizes flexibility. To establish that agents are myopic it is necessary to show that they are worse off than a rational agent would have been, and not simply that they were locked in by a situation. Few systems theorists have addressed this crucial issue.

An important reason why 'lock in' is of limited importance in IB is that multinational firms have access to a wide range of factor and product markets. For example, a firm that has overextended its capacity at an upstream stage of production can use external intermediate products to sell off surplus output to independent downstream firms. Alternatively, the firm could sell off surplus plant and equipment in markets for second-hand assets, or even divest the entire upstream operation as a going concern. All of these strategies incur adjustment costs, of course, but the costs are nowhere near as large as they would be in the absence of the market system. While it highly desirable for IB theory to take account of adjustment costs, therefore, it is unnecessary to suppose that adjustment costs are a major source of instability in the IB system.

Rational action and international business strategy

During the 1980s and 1990s the concept of strategy came to occupy an important role in the IB literature, although the term was hardly used at all before then (Porter, 1991). None of the key theoretical developments of the 1970s invoked the concept of strategy at all. It is interesting to note that very few of the writers who use the concept of strategy most regularly ever bother to define the term. Sometimes they employ it simply as a synonym for 'chosen course of action', while in other cases they use it to signal that some particular decision is of crucial importance.

The rational action approach clearly implies that some decisions are more important than others, and indicates why this is the case. A strategic decision may be defined, in rational action terms, as a decision with the following characteristics:

1. Long-term perspective creates a need for inter-temporal planning;
2. Uncertain environment;
3. Information needs to be collected in the most efficient and reliable manner;
4. Irreversible commitment of resources;

5. Determines the context in which future tactical (short-term) decisions are taken: the implications for tactical decisions need to be considered before strategic decisions are made;
6. Interactions with other strategists: either competition, cooperation, or both.

There is now a 'critical mass' of rational action technique that can be used to analyse strategic issues. These techniques address strategic complexity through clarification and simplification of the decision problem (see for example Kreps, 1990). The repertoire includes the following:

Information costs
- decision theory: rational choice under uncertainty
- sequential analysis
- search theory.

Dynamic optimization
- optimal timing of investment
- irreversibility and switching costs.

Real option theory
- deferring decisions to avoid mistakes
- valuing flexibility.

Game theory
- Nash equilibria of a non-cooperative game
- sequential games
- repeated games.

There is insufficient space to review all of the relevant techniques at this stage. This chapter focuses on the first three sets of techniques, as these have achieved the widest acceptance in IB theory (see, for example, Allen and Pantzalis, 1996; Buckley and Casson, 1981; Casson, 1995; DeMeza and van der Ploeg, 1987). The final set of techniques – game theory – affords major opportunities for IB which have so far been exploited to only a limited extent (Graham, 1990).

Example: analysing foreign market entry

The application of these new techniques is best illustrated by means of an example. One of the classic issues in IB is foreign market entry strategy (Buckley and Casson, 1981, 1998a). This is a decision by a firm in a home country (country 1) to supply the market in a foreign country (country 2). Foreign market entry involves uncertainty, relating to either demand side factors, such as the size of the foreign market, or supply side factors, such as foreign costs of production.

The simplest way of introducing uncertainty into the rational action approach is to assume that decision-makers partition the state of the environment into a number of different categories, or 'states of the world', and then assign a subjective probability to each. A sophisticated decision-maker may distinguish a large number of different states, whereas a naïve decision-maker may distinguish just a few. The simplest categorization of states is a binary one (Hirshleifer and Riley, 1992).

For the sake of simplicity, it is assumed that uncertainty relates to the supply side only, and that the decision-maker distinguishes just two states of the world: state 1, in which foreign cost conditions are bad, and state 2, in which they are good. The key issue is whether the foreign market is served by domestic production or foreign production. Under domestic production the foreign market is supplied through exports (strategy 1) whilst under foreign production (strategy 2) the firm undertakes foreign direct investment (FDI).

Suppose that the firm is already committed to serving the market, and that market size is fixed, so that the revenue obtained is the same for either strategy. Thus only the costs of the two strategies are different. Production takes place under constant returns to scale, with a unit cost of production c_0 in country 1. Unit cost is c_1 in country 2 when conditions are bad, and c_2 when conditions are good, where $c_1 > c_0 > c_2$. It follows that the firm should export when foreign cost conditions are bad and invest abroad when they are good. The probability that conditions are good is p $(0 \leq p \leq 1)$.

The firm's objective, it is assumed, is to maximize expected profit. This is a reasonable objective for a firm with a large number of shareholders who hold well-diversified portfolios. With given revenues, this translates into minimizing expected unit costs. The expected cost of foreign production is $E(c) = (1 - p)\ c_1 + pc_2$ while the unit cost of domestic production is already known to be c_0. Comparing the expected unit cost of foreign production with the cost of domestic production shows that the firm should produce abroad when $p > p^* = (c_1 - c_0)/(c_1 - c_2)$. In other words, the firm should produce abroad when the probability of good production conditions exceeds a critical level p^*.

A simple way of understanding this result is to recognize that there are two types of error that the firm can make. The first is to reject the export strategy when it is correct (a Type I) error, and the second is to accept the export strategy when foreign production is appropriate instead (a Type II error). The nature of these errors, and the costs associated with them, are set out in Table 3.1. The cost of a Type I error is $c_1 - c_0$, and the cost of a Type II error is $c_0 - c_2$. It follows that the critical probability value may be expressed as

$$p^* = \text{Cost of Type I error/Total cost of both errors}$$

Table 3.1 Two possible errors in strategic choice under uncertainty

	State 1: foreign cost conditions bad	*State 2: foreign cost conditions good*
Strategy 1 Produce at home: Exporting	0	*Type II error* $c_0 - c_2$
Strategy 2 Produce abroad: FDI	*Type I error* $c_1 - c_0$	0

The solution is illustrated in Figure 3.1. The horizontal axis measures the probability that foreign cost conditions are good and the vertical axis measures corresponding expected unit cost. The horizontal schedule C_1C_1' indicates that domestic costs are constant, independently of foreign costs, whilst the downward-sloping schedule C_2C_2' shows that expected foreign costs decrease as the probability of good conditions increases. The minimum attainable expected unit cost is indicated by the thick line C_1EC_2', which is the lower envelope of the two schedules, and has a kink at the switch-point E. The rational decision-maker minimizes expected costs by choosing to

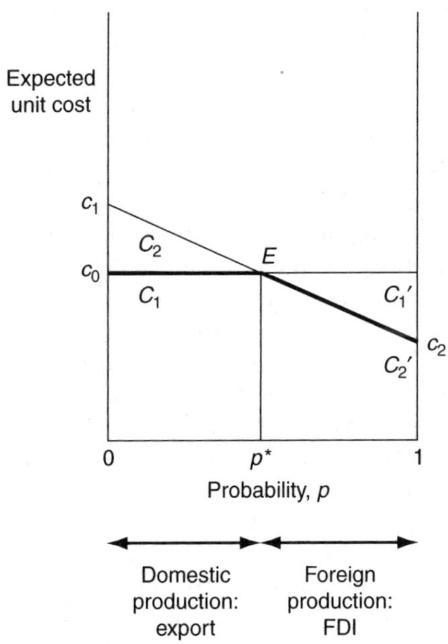

Figure 3.1 Diagrammatic solution of the entry strategy under uncertainty

export for low probabilities, to the left of E, and to produce abroad for high probabilities, to the right of E.

The economic implications of the analysis may be summarized as follows:

1. Optimists undertake FDI; pessimists export;
2. The greater the cost of Type I error relative to the cost of a Type II error, the more optimistic an investor needs to be;
3. The costs of a Type I error are greater, the higher the cost of foreign production under bad conditions relative to domestic costs; and
4. The costs of a Type II error are greater, the lower the cost of foreign production under good conditions relative to domestic costs.

Collecting information

It is often suggested that uncertainty is a basic 'fact of life', but this is not quite correct. Uncertainty can be dispelled by collecting information. Even if it cannot be dispelled entirely, its impact can be reduced by narrowing down the margin for error. It is therefore irrational to always passively accept uncertainty.

But how is it possible to know how much information is worth collecting? Rational action modelling provides an answer to this question. All that is required is that the decision-maker can estimate the cost of collecting relevant items of information, and attach subjective probabilities to what the results of investigation will turn out to be. This allows the decision-maker to estimate both the costs and the benefits of collecting information, and therefore to arrive at a rational information strategy (Casson, 2000a, chs 4, 7).

Decision-making becomes a two-stage procedure: in the first stage the decision-maker decides how much information to collect, and in the second stage he uses the information he has collected to take the decision. These two stages are interdependent, and the rational decision-maker arrives at his strategy by considering them in reverse order. He knows that it would be a waste of time collecting information that would not influence his decision. He therefore needs to determine in advance how he would use any item of information if he had it. If he would not use it whatever it turned out to be, then it is a waste of time collecting it. Only once he has decided how he would use it is he in a position to decide whether he wants to collect it or not.

Suppose, for example, that the decision-maker could research the costs of foreign production at a cost q. Once he has collected the cost information, he can avoid both the Type I and Type II errors shown in Table 3.1. If he discovers that the conditions are good then he can commit to invest abroad, while if he discovers that conditions are bad then he can export instead. As a result, the expected cost of market entry is $(1-p)c_0+pc_2$, which is always lower than the expected cost of either the ordinary export strategy or the ordinary foreign investment strategy, except when the decision-maker is certain at the outset what the conditions will be ($p=0, 1$).

The expected cost of market entry using information on foreign costs is illustrated by the line C_1C_2' in Figure 3.2. This figure is similar to Figure 3.1, but with the addition of the research strategy. To evaluate the total cost of the research strategy, the cost q must be added to the cost of market entry. Since this cost is independent of what the information turns out to be, its effect is simply to shift the schedule C_1C_2' in parallel fashion up to C_3C_3'. If the cost of research is suitably low, this will determine two new critical values, p_1^*, p_2^*, at which the decision-maker switches into and out of the information-gathering strategy. These critical points are determined by constructing the lower envelope $C_1E_1E_2C_2'$ of the three schedules, and identifying the kinks E_1 and E_2.

The following results may be derived from the figure:

1. Research is most efficient when uncertainty is high, i.e. the probability p is in the mid range $p_1^* < p < p_2^*$;
2. Research is most valuable when the variability of foreign production costs, $c_1 - c_2$, is large; and
3. The range of probability values for which research is efficient is greater, the lower the research cost, q.

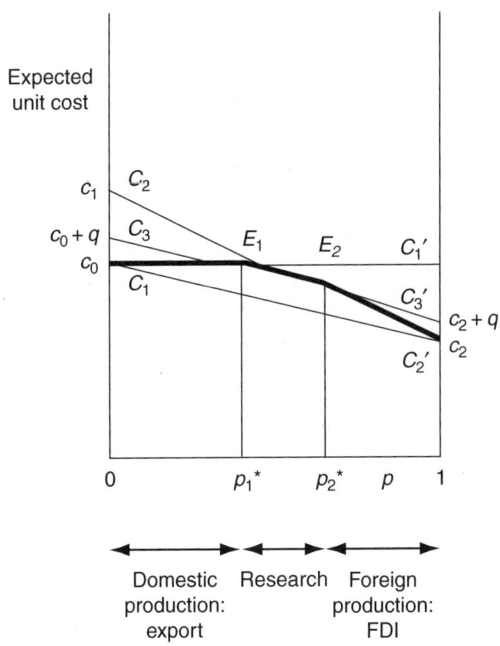

Figure 3.2 Strategy for information gathering

Using decision trees

The fundamental point about research is that it alters the information set available to the decision-maker at the time of the decision. The easiest way to appreciate the significance of this is with the aid of a decision tree. Figure 3.3 uses a decision tree to compare decision-making with and without research. Without research, the decision-maker acts first and the true situation reveals itself later, whereas with research the situation is revealed before the decision-maker acts.

A complete description of a research strategy involves specifying not only what information will be collected but also what the decision-maker will do with the information once it has been collected. In the previous example there are only two ways in which it could be used. Once of these – to invest if foreign cost conditions are good, and otherwise to export – is obviously sensible, whilst the alternative – to invest if foreign cost conditions are bad, is obviously absurd. The use of the information is indicated by the thick vertical lines in the bottom half of the figure.

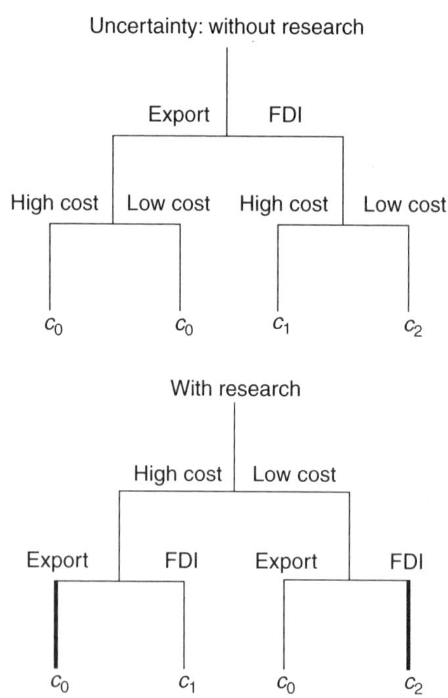

Figure 3.3 Comparison of decision trees with and without research

The gist of this discussion so far may be summarized as follows:

1. Research strategies enlarge the information set available to the decision-maker and thereby reduce the risk of error;
2. Research strategies involve rules for using the information that has been collected in the course of the research; and
3. As new strategies are introduced, new critical points are introduced at which switching between strategies occurs.

Deferring decisions: real options

Research is not the only way of augmenting the information set. If a decision-maker waits long enough, the information he/she requires may reveal itself anyway. Deferring a decision may save the cost of collecting the information at the outset. The reason why firms do not delay decisions is because there is a cost involved. For example, if market entry will be profitable right away, profits will be lost if entry is deferred. Furthermore, there is a risk that another firm may enter the market and pre-empt the profit opportunity. Comparing deferment with research, therefore, there is a trade-off between saving information costs on the one hand, and losing revenue on the other.

If market entry decisions were fully reversible then there would be no need to defer a decision at all. A provisional decision would be made on the basis of the information that was freely available at the outset, and when additional information became available this decision would be changed as appropriate. The revenue stream would therefore commence immediately, and the cost of information would be avoided altogether. The only losses would relate to errors made at the outset, and corrected later.

In practice, of course, most decisions are not reversible. If the firm invests in a foreign production plant, for example, it will not be able to sell it off for as much as it cost to build. The 'illiquidity' of the plant means that the firm incurs a capital loss. Similarly, if the firm adapts the plant to some alternative use then adjustment costs will be incurred. Some investments are more readily reversed than others. Strategies that involve reversible investments afford more flexibility than those which do not. High levels of uncertainty favour the selection of flexible strategies, since mistakes are easier to put right (Buckley and Casson, 1998b).

Example: optimizing the dynamics of foreign market entry using research, deferment, and switching strategies

The demand for flexibility can be analysed using real option theory (Dixit and Pindyck, 1994; Kogut, 1991; Kogut and Kulatilaka, 1994; Rivoli and Salorio, 1996). The specific approach followed here is based on Casson

(2000a, Ch. 7). Continuing with the previous example, suppose that there are now two periods, 1 and 2, and that the overall market entry strategy must be set at the beginning of period 1. The first period is short – of unit length, in fact – while the second period is of infinite length. The firm now maximizes expected net present value rather than expected profit; it discounts future costs and revenues at a fixed interest rate, r.

Entry into the foreign market is profitable right away, but information about the state of foreign cost conditions is not available until the end of period 1. Both exporting and foreign investment incur a fixed set-up cost, f, which is the same whether it is incurred in period 1 or period 2. An investment in foreign production is much more difficult to liquidate than an equivalent investment in export production: it can be sold off for only h_1 instead of h_2, where $h_1 < h_2 < f$.

At the beginning of period 1 the firm decides whether to carry out research to discover foreign production costs. It also decides whether to invest in foreign production right away, to commit itself to exporting right away, or to defer the decision on the method of market entry until period 2. If it carries out research then it will produce abroad only if it discovers that foreign costs are low; otherwise it will export instead. These commitments will be made right away since with the information at its disposal it has no reason to defer a decision.

In period 2 the firm can reverse any commitments it made in period 1 in the light of new information. Alternatively, if the firm deferred its decision, then it can decide its entry strategy unconstrained by the legacy of previous decisions.

The decision tree is shown in Figure 3.4. There are six dominant entry strategies, which are listed in Table 3.2. If the firm could costlessly obtain all the information it required at the outset then its profit would be

$$v = s(1+r)/r - f - pc_2 - (1-p)c_0$$

In practice none of the available strategies can achieve this level of profit, but they can be ranked by their shortfalls compared to this norm. The shortfalls are shown in the right-hand column of the table.

The number of strategies that need to be considered can be reduced using one or more of the following conditions:

1. If the firm exports initially then it will switch to foreign investment when cost conditions turn out to be good (i.e. strategy 5 is preferred to strategy 1) if and only if the sunk costs are lower than the capitalized savings on subsequent production costs:

$$f - h_1 < r(c_0 - c_2)/(1+r)$$

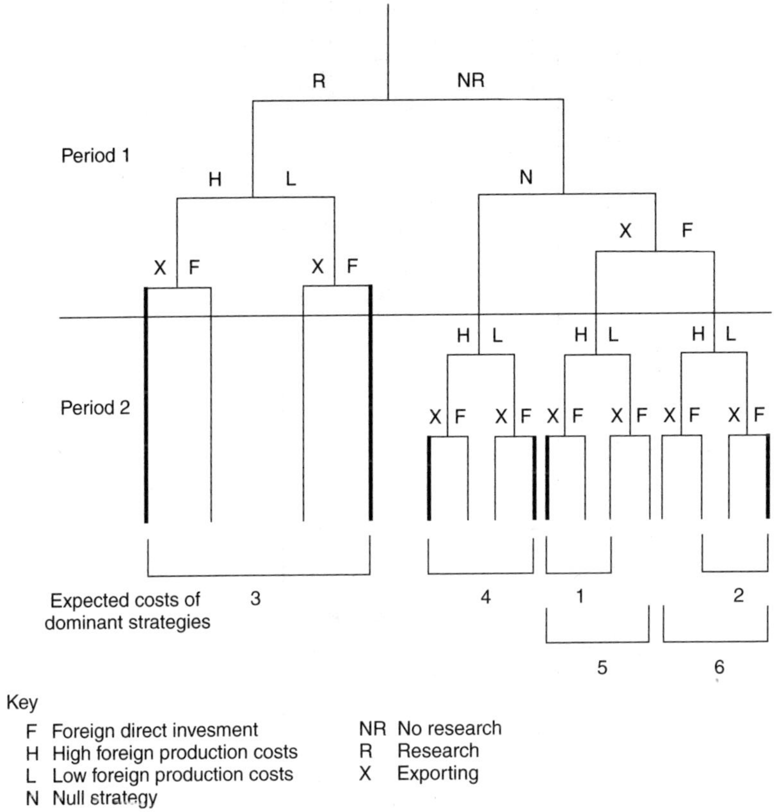

Figure 3.4 Decision tree for integrated research/waiting/switching problem

2. If the firm invests abroad initially then it will switch to exporting when cost conditions turn out to be bad (i.e. strategy 6 is preferred to strategy 2) if and only if

$$f - h_2 < r(c_1 - c_0)/(1 + r)$$

3. Deferment is preferred to research (i.e. strategy 4 is preferred to strategy 3) if and only if the expected profit lost from the first period trading is less than the costs of research:

$$s < q + c_0 - p(c_0 - c_2) + (fr/(1 + r))$$

The overall solution can be determined using a four-way comparison: this involves the cheapest from each of the two pairs of strategies (1, 5), (2, 6),

Table 3.2 Foreign entry strategy set encompassing research, deferment, and switching, assuming that it is always profitable to serve the market

Strategies	*Research?*	*Entry under uncertainty*	*If cost high*	*If cost low*	*Expected cost relative to norm*
1. Commit to X	NR	X	X	X	$p(c_0 - c_2)(1+r)/r$
2. Commit to F	NR	F	F	F	$(1-p)(c_1 - c_0)(1+r)/r$
3. Research	R		X	F	q
4. Defer	NR	N	X	F	$s - c_0 + p(c_0 - c_2) - fr/(1+r)$
5. Conditional switch from X to F	NR	X	X	F	$p((c_0 - c_0) + (f - h_1)/(1+r))$
6. Conditional switch from F to X	NR	F	X	F	$(1-p)((c_1 - c_0) + (f - h_2)/(1+r))$

Key: F Foreign direct investment
N Null strategy
NR No research
R Research
X Exporting

together with the research strategy (3) and the deferment strategy (4). The solution is illustrated graphically in Figure 3.5. In contrast to Figure 3.2, which plotted the absolute costs of each strategy, Figure 3.5 plots the costs of each strategy relative to the full-information norm as defined above. The schedule C_1C_1' shows the costs associated with the cheapest of strategies 1 and 5; the schedule C_2C_2' shows the costs associated with the cheapest of the strategies 2 and 6, while C_3C_3' and C_4C_4' show respectively the costs associated with strategies 3 and 4.

Because of the way that costs are defined, the horizontal axis represents the baseline performance of the full-information strategy. The figure shows that none of the strategies attains baseline performance except at the two ends of the axis, where the decision-maker is subjectively certain about the level of foreign production costs ($p=0, 1$). The figure has been drawn to illustrate the case where both research costs and the profits generated by foreign sales are relatively modest. This means that both research and deferment are optimal strategies for certain values of p. There are now three critical probability values at which the firm switches strategies: $p_1{}^*$, where the firm switches

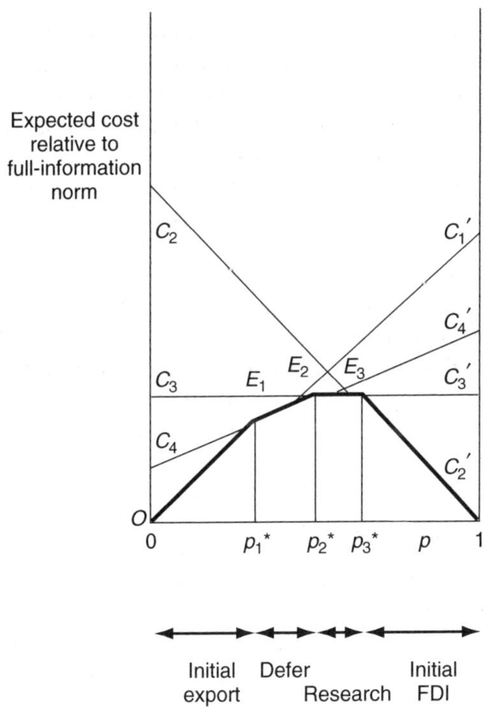

Figure 3.5 Diagrammatic solution of an entry problem encompassing research, deferment, and switching

from initial exporting to deferment; p_2^*, where it switches from deferment to research; and p_3^* where it switches from research to initial FDI.

A selection of the results that can be obtained (in addition to the previous results) is given below:

1. As the decision-maker becomes more optimistic, the chosen strategy switches in turn from exporting to deferment to research to FDI; some of the steps may be omitted when one of the strategies is completely dominated by the others, but the basic sequence is never reversed;
2. Deferment is preferred when uncertainty is high, the costs of error are high, set-up costs are high, the interest rate is high, and the cost of research is high;
3. Switching is more likely to take place, the lower are the losses incurred by liquidating a fixed investment; and
4. Switching is more likely to take place when foreign costs are highly variable.

Further extensions of the real options approach to strategy

This approach to modelling strategy is extremely versatile and can be extended in many different ways. The costs of research may depend on the ownership and location of facilities. For example, FDI may generate information about the foreign market as a by-product of the foreign location of production; this may provide a reason for undertaking FDI from the outset – but in a flexible form, so that it can be divested if the market turns out to be poor. Similarly a foreign-owned plant may be more useful in capturing information than a plant operated by a licensee, because ownership gives more effective access to information by-products. Hence not only does information-gathering affect ownership and location strategy, but ownership and location strategies affect information-gathering too. Ownership issues are considered in more detail below.

So long as there remains just a single source of uncertainty, most problems of this type can be solved using the graphical technique described above. The following properties of Figure 3.5 are common to all graphical solutions:

1. The envelope of minimum expected cost, indicated by the thick line, is (weakly) convex;
2. The convex envelope is constructed from a series of straight-line graphs representing the expected costs of the various dominant strategies;
3. There are critical probabilities defining the switch-points between strategies;
4. Changes in the parameters – such as costs, sales revenues, and interest rates – cause the straight-line graphs to shift and/or rotate, and thereby lead to previously efficient strategies becoming inefficient, and vice versa. This generates a wide range of interrelated hypotheses about the effects of various parameters on the dynamics of foreign market entry under uncertainty.

Additional sources of uncertainty can also be introduced: for example, the reactions of established foreign firms in the foreign market, or the reactions of other potential foreign entrants into that market. In this context, it is important to distinguish two types of situation:

1. The initial entrant wins customer loyalty, and subsequent entrants can only access the 'residual' market that was not captured by the initial entrant; and
2. There is no customer loyalty, so an initial entrant must subsequently defend their market share through price warfare, or other competitive weapons. The initial entrant can deter followers by making an irreversible commitment to the foreign market, which means that it will always pay him to 'stay and fight' rather than 'quit the market'. The method of entry then becomes important in determining the strength of this threat.

These issues (especially the second) can be analysed using game-theoretic techniques.

The IB system as a global network

As noted earlier, the rational action approach emphasizes combinatorial complexity rather than analytical complexity. An important source of combinatorial complexity in the IB system lies in its network structure. This network structure was only implicit in the previous analysis, and it now needs to be made explicit.

A simple network structure is represented schematically in Figure 3.6, using a set of conventions established in earlier work (Casson, 1995, 1997, 2000a, b). The figure illustrates a two-country world, comprising a home country (country 1) and a foreign country (country 2). It focuses on a single industry, assumed, for convenience, to be a manufacturing industry. Physical processes, such as production and distribution, are represented by square boxes. Each box indicates a facility, such as a factory or warehouse, at a specific location. Flows of tangible products are represented by black lines: thus factory output awaiting distribution flows from production, *P*, to distribution, *D*, and onwards from distribution to the final customer, *C*; the customer may be household consumers, the government, or firms in some other industry. The direction of flow is indicated by an arrow.

Intangible flows such as knowledge are represented by grey lines. Two types of knowledge are identified: technological know-how, produced by R&D, and local market knowledge, accumulated through experience in distribution of the product. Technological know-how is generated in scientific laboratories, *R*, indicated by a triangle, whilst marketing expertise is accumulated by a marketing department, *M*, indicated by a circle. Unlike product

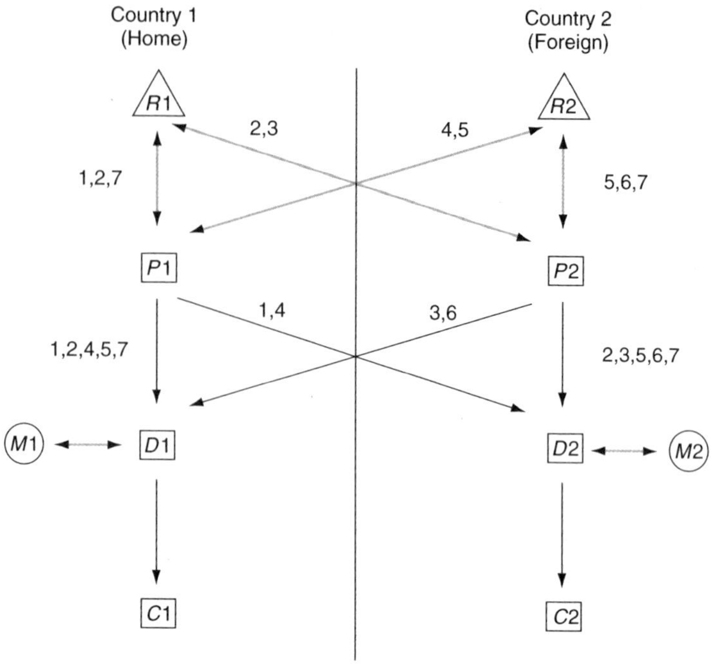

Figure 3.6 Schematic representation of a simple international business system

Note: The letter indentifying a facility denotes the type of the facility, as described in the text. The number indentifies the country in which the facility is located.
The numbers associated with the flows indentify the location strategies that involve these flows. The strategies concerned are described in Table 3.5.

flows, which are one-way, knowledge flows are two-way, as indicated by the two arrows on each grey line.

In principle any configuration of production plants, distribution facilities, research laboratories, and marketing offices located in any number of different countries can be represented in this way. Mapping out the entire IB system would, of course, prove extremely complex, and generate a very complicated diagram (Isard, 1956). However, the network structure of the IB system can also be conveniently summarized in tabular form, as indicated in Table 3.3; this tabular form can be more readily expanded to accommodate additional detail as required.

Levels of aggregation

The IB system can be represented at different levels of aggregation. For example, when discussing international trade and investment flows at a macroeconomic level it may be sufficient to analyse the system in terms of

Table 3.3 Tabular representation of flows illustrated in Figure 3.6

From/to	*R1*	*R2*	*M1*	*M2*	*P1*	*P2*	*D1*	*D2*	*C1*	*C2*
*R*1					Know-how	Know-how				
*R*2					Know-how	Know-how				
*M*1							Experience			
*M*2								Experience		
*P*1	Feedback	Feedback					Wholesale product	Wholesale product		
*P*2	Feedback	Feedback					Wholesale product	Wholesale product		
*D*1			Feedback	Feedback					Retail product	
*D*2			Feedback	Feedback						Retail product
*C*1										
*C*2										

a single representative plant in each country. In this case each of the boxes, triangles, or circles indicates a single representative facility of a given type. The number of facilities of that type in a given country may be indicated by placing a number adjacent to the corresponding box; thus a number 'three' placed adjacent to the box *P*2 would indicate that there are three production plants in country 2.

By contrast, a microeconomic view of a particular industry in a particular country might require different regional locations to be identified, and the transport infrastructure linking these locations to be mapped out, including ports, airports, railway junctions, and major road hubs. In general, the existence of specialized nodes where traffic is switched between linkages is fully apparent only with disaggregation.

The extreme of disaggregation occurs when individual workspaces are identified within each plant, and the roles of separate individuals are identified. This level of disaggregation is extremely useful for discussing the organizational structure of the firm, as explained below.

Each element identified at a high level of aggregation appears as a system in its own right when viewed at a lower level of aggregation. There is a hierarchy of subsystems within the system as a whole. The representation of a system using a high level of aggregation is analogous to the 'desk top' on a computer screen, whilst a representation using a low level of aggregation opens up the 'windows' to reveal the contents of the drives or files.

Different variants of IB work with different levels of aggregation:

- the individual person
- the firm
- the industry
- the global economy
- the socio-political–ecological system.

Economic theories of IB – such as internalization theory, and theories of international business strategy – operate at the firm and industry level, and these are the levels on which this chapter focuses.

Scholars working at one level of aggregation often criticize others for making unwarranted assumptions. This sometimes leads to unnecessary controversy. Typically those who work at low levels of aggregation criticize those working at higher levels of aggregation for making sweeping assumptions, whilst those who work at high levels of aggregation tend to criticize those working at lower levels of aggregation for cluttering their analysis with irrelevant detail, and being 'unable to see the wood for the trees'. It is important for those working at one level of aggregation to bear in mind that other scholars work at other levels of aggregation and that considerable care is needed in reconciling work at adjacent levels of aggregation.

It is not only the level of aggregation that is important when describing a system. There is an important distinction between short-run and long-run analysis too. In the short run the IB system comprises a fixed number of facilities which have been inherited from the past. In the long run, by contrast, the number of facilities is variable because new facilities can be created and established facilities may be closed down. In a long-run context it is therefore important to distinguish between actual and potential facilities.

Implementing the network research agenda

The network view of the IB system is well suited to addressing two of the major issues in IB: the issue of where IB facilities will be *located* and the issue of who will *own* them. These questions can be considered separately or together. It is possible to analyse, for a given pattern of ownership, where facilities will be located. Similarly, for a given pattern of location, it is possible to analyse the structure of ownership. Finally, it is also possible to determine simultaneously what the patterns of location and ownership within the system will be.

Issues of location, considered in isolation from issues of ownership, are addressed by theories of geography and trade. Relevant theories include the the Ricardian theory of comparative advantage, the Heckscher–Ohlin–Stopler–Samuelson theory of factor intensities, and theories of transport costs and economies of scale (Krugman, 1995).

IB theory has tended to concentrate on issues of ownership: in particular, internalization theory, as developed in the 1970s, focused on the question of why a firm that owned facilities in one country would wish to own facilities in another country, and how it could survive against international competition if it did so. The theory emphasized the gains from internalizing knowledge flow, and allowed for gains from internalizing intermediate flows of material product too – e.g. components and raw materials.

A major justification for distinguishing IB as a special field of study is that pattern of ownership used to coordinate international linkages in a network are different from those used to coordinate purely domestic ones. If there were no substantial difference then the international dimension would be of limited significance so far as the interaction of ownership and location is concerned. A key feature of an IB system is that the costs and benefits of internalization vary according to whether an international or domestic linkage is involved. This cost differential can impact on both ownership and location decisions. Thus a firm may license internationally a technology that it exploits internally in the domestic market; similarly, it may produce at home instead of abroad because it can only afford to produce abroad by licensing its technology and it is reluctant to do so because of the costs involved.

To illustrate this point, it is useful to consider the structure of costs within an IB network. Consider first location strategy. Suppose that in the previous example both the national markets have to be served, and that both are of fixed size. Market sizes are normalized to unity for simplicity. Since the markets cannot be served without distribution facilities, nor without market knowledge, the costs incurred by marketing and distribution activities are sunk costs, and so can be omitted from the analysis. This leaves just the costs that are shown in Table 3.4. The key elements in this table are the production costs in the two countries, c_1, c_2, R&D costs in the two countries, a_1, a_2, costs of transferring technology internationally, m, and the cost of transporting the product internationally, z. All of these costs are assumed to be known for certain; the analysis can be extended to allow for uncertainty by using the techniques described in the earlier part of this chapter.

It is easy to deduce that:

1. It is never efficient to carry out research in both countries unless there is production in both countries;
2. When there is research in both countries, it is never efficient to 'cross-haul' research by linking R&D in country 1 to production in country 2, and vice versa; and
3. When there is production in both countries it is never efficient to 'cross-haul' the product by exporting from country 1 to country 2 at the same time as exporting from country 2 to country 1.

It follows that just seven location strategies need to be distinguished. These seven strategies dominate all other conceivable strategies, in the sense that one of these seven strategies will always afford the lowest overall system cost. The dominant strategies are listed in Table 3.5. Note that because of locational specialization, strategies 1–6 utilize only some, and not all, of the available facilities.

The optimal location strategy is derived by comparing the costs set out in the final column of the table and identifying the strategy associated with the lowest cost. The following principles characterize an efficient location strategy in general terms:

1. Produce in both countries if and only if international transport costs exceed the savings from concentrating all production in the lower-cost country:

   $$z > \max[c_1 c_2] - \min[c_1, c_2]$$

2. Research in both countries if and only if producing in both countries, and if the cost of transferring technology exceeds the cost of researching in the higher-cost country:

   $$m > \max[a_1 a_2]$$

Table 3.4 Structure of location costs for the flows illustrated in Figure 3.1 (excluding sunk costs of marketing and distribution)

From/to	*R1*	*R2*	*P1*	*P2*	*D1*	*D2*
R1	Domestic R&D cost; fixed cost a_1		Domestic transfer cost (zero)	International transfer cost; fixed cost: m		
R2		Foreign R&D cost; fixed cost: a_2	International transfer cost; fixed cost: m	Domestic transfer cost (zero)		
P1			Domestic production cost; unit cost: c_1		Domestic transport cost (zero)	International transport cost; unit cost: z
P2				Foreign production cost; unit cost: c_2	International transport cost; unit cost: z	Domestic transport cost (zero)

Table 3.5 Dominant locational strategies

Location strategy	*Description*	*Active facilities*	*Cost*
	Research in country 1 only		
1	Export from country 1	*R*1, *P*1	$a_1 + 2c_1 + z$
2	Produce in both countries	*R*1, *P*1, *P*2	$a_1 + m + c_1 + c_2$
3	Export from country 2	*R*1, *P*2	$a_1 + m + 2c_2 + z$
	Research in country 2 only		
4	Export from country 1	*R*2, *P*1	$a_2 + m + 2c_1 + z$
5	Produce in both countries	*R*2, *P*1, *P*2	$a_2 + m + c_1 + c_2$
6	Export from country 2	*R*2, *P*2	$a_2 + 2c_2 + z$
	Research in both countries		
7	Produce in both countries	*R*1, *R*2, *P*1, *P*2	$a_1 + a_2 + c_1 + c_2$

Note: All the strategies utilize both distribution facilities *D*1, *D*2; these are omitted from the third column for reasons of simplicity.

3. Produce and research in different countries if and only if the cost of transferring technology is less than the smaller of the savings in research costs and production costs achieved by switching one of the locations:

$$m < \min[|a_2 - a_1|, |c_2 - c_1|]$$

4. If producing and researching in the same country, choose the country for which the sum of research and production costs is lowest:

choose country 1 if $(a_2 - a_1) + (c_2 - c_1) > 0$, and otherwise choose country 2

5. Similarly, if producing and researching in different countries, choose the combination for which the sum of research and production costs is lowest:

choose to research in 1 and produce in 2 if $(a_2 - a_1) - (c_2 - c_1) > 0$, and otherwise choose the opposite combination

Transaction costs: optimizing ownership patterns

From a network perspective, ownership patterns are driven by the need to minimize the costs of coordinating the system. Each facility is allocated an owner. Since no two owners can own the same facility outright, the ownership strategies of different firms constrain each other: what is owned by one firm cannot be owned by other firms as well. Although ownership can be shared through joint ventures, the partners must still harmonize their strategies, so that their shares add to 100 per cent. The interdependence of ownership strategies is missing from conventional expositions of internalization theory, which focus on the strategies of a single firm. This weakness is often mitigated by assuming that the firm invests in new facilities, such as a greenfield production plant, but the problem remains when discussing take-overs, where several firms may be competing to acquire the same facility, and only one of them can succeed. In general, the internalization strategies of all firms in a system need to be analysed simultaneously, and this can only be done using a network approach.

The pattern of ownership that emerges in an IB system depends crucially on the structure of transaction costs (Coase, 1937). For present purposes transaction costs may be equated with the costs of coordinating linkages, although a more refined analysis would distinguish different aspects of transaction costs (Casson, 2000a, chs 3, 5). The transaction costs associated with any given linkage in a network depend, in general, upon three main factors:

1. The nature of the flow along the linkage and, in particular, whether the flow is an intangible flow of knowledge ($i=1$) or an tangible flow of product ($i=2$);
2. Whether the flow is internal to a firm ($j=1$), or external, connecting two independent firms ($j=2$); and
3. Whether the flow is domestic ($k=1$) or international ($k=2$).

The transaction costs incurred by the IB system are the sum of the transaction costs associated with the individual linkages utilized by the system. The linkages that are active at any one time depend on the location strategy that is being used. Thus different location strategies, when applied in conjunction with a given pattern of ownership, are liable to generate different transaction costs, as well as different location costs.

The total cost of the system is the sum of the transaction costs and the location costs. In general, there is a trade-off between location costs and transaction costs, because economizing on location costs through the international rationalization of research and production locations will tend to increase the number of international linkages, and international linkages typically incur higher transaction costs than purely domestic ones. In order to mitigate the increase in transaction costs patterns of ownership may change. In this way, changes in the system driven by location factors may induce a change in patterns of ownership; conversely, changes in ownership patterns may induce changes in location strategies, although in practice this effect appears to be less common.

When all the different location strategies are permuted with all the different ownership patterns, a very large number of possible system structures emerge.

All of these structures can, however, be ranked in terms of their overall system costs, and so in principle the least-cost configuration of the system can always be ascertained. Although it is complex, the problem remains finite.

The solution of this problem determines how many different firms will exist within the system, and where their individual boundaries will lie. Firms must be large enough to internalize all the linkages that benefit from internalization, but small enough to allow other linkages to be external instead. The importance of internalizing knowledge flows means that a higher proportion of knowledge flows will be internal to firms than will flows of ordinary products. It follows that the boundaries of firms will be determined mainly by the structure of knowledge flows, and only secondarily by the structure of product flows. This highlights a major difference between the IB literature and some of the other literature on transaction costs (e.g. Williamson, 1985) where the emphasis of internalization is erroneously placed on ordinary product flows.

For many purposes, however, it is unnecessary to consider all of the permutations referred to above. IB scholars are typically interested in more specific issues which can be 'projected out' of the network model. For example, they are primarily concerned with the coordination of international linkages rather than domestic linkages. They also tend to be concerned with the choice between a subset of all the possible location strategies discussed above.

Consider, for example, the issue of foreign market entry strategy, as discussed in the first part of this chapter. Before internalization theory was developed it was normally assumed that FDI was the natural form of the local production strategy. Internalization theory pointed out that licensing was also an option. The network model presented above indicates that there are other options too. Foreign market servicing involves establishing a link between the R&D carried out in the home country (country 1) and the marketing and distribution of the product carried out in the foreign country (country 2). This involves two separate linkages: a flow of knowledge between R&D and production, and a flow of product between production and R&D. Either of these flows can be internal or external to the firm (see Table 3.6). Under the export strategy the flow of knowledge is domestic but the flow of product is international, whereas under local production the converse applies: the flow of knowledge is international and the flow of product is domestic. As a result, different location strategies generate different patterns of transactions costs, and the resulting differences in transactions costs can influence the choice of location strategy. They also determine the form of ownership structure used to implement the chosen location strategy.

Suppose, for example, that internalization of knowledge flow is always cheaper than external knowledge flow, but that the internalization of

Table 3.6 Alternative contractual arrangements for linking domestic R&D to foreign distribution

	Domestic production	*Foreign production*
Internalize knowledge flow		
Internalize product flow	(1) FDI in distribution $t_{111}+t_{212}$	(2) FDI in production and distribution $t_{112}+t_{211}$
Externalize product flow	(3) Export to independent foreign sales agent $t_{111}+t_{222}$	(4) FDI in production; sell through an independent foreign sales agent $t_{112}+t_{221}$
Externalize knowledge flow		
Internalize product flow	(5) License a firm that undertakes FDI in distribution $t_{121}+t_{212}$	(6) License a foreign producer that integrates forward into distribution $t_{122}+t_{211}$
Externalize product flow	(7) License an exporter that sells through an independent foreign sales agent $t_{121}+t_{222}$	(8) License a foreign producer that sells through an independent local agent $t_{122}+t_{221}$

Note: It is assumed that the domestic market is always supplied through domestic production. Domestic distribution is either integrated with domestic production, or undertaken by an independent agent, whichever affords the lower transaction costs. This decision can be made independently of all other decisions and, since it does not bear directly on IB strategy, is omitted from the analysis.

product flow is only cheaper where domestic rather than international linkages are concerned. Under these conditions it always pays to internalize the linkage between production and R&D. The structure of transaction costs for knowledge flow implies that the cheapest foreign production strategy involves FDI rather than licensing. The structure of transaction costs for product flow implies that foreign production will be integrated with foreign distribution, so that FDI in production implies FDI in distribution too. It also implies, however, that exporting will be carried out at arm's length, so that domestic production will be sold to an independent distributor in the foreign market. So far as the domestic situation is concerned, domestic production will be integrated with domestic distribution, so that the firm will be vertically integrated in both countries.

The actual choice between exporting and FDI depends on the structure of both location costs and transaction costs. The costs of domestic R&D are common to both strategies. The exporting strategy derived above incurs transaction costs

$$t_1 = t_{111} + t_{222}$$

while the FDI strategy incurs transaction costs

$$t_2 = t_{112} + t_{211}$$

where t_{ijk} is the transaction cost associated with a flow of type i through a market of type j along a linkage of geographical type k (as defined above). Combining these expressions with the expressions for location costs in Table 3.5 shows that FDI is preferred to exporting when

$$z + c_1 - c_2 > m + t_2 - t_1$$

This condition states that the savings in international transport costs *plus* any savings in production costs effected by FDI must exceed the costs of international technology transfer *plus* any additional transaction costs that stem from internationalizing internal technology transfer *less* any savings in distribution costs that arise from using an internal domestic market rather than an external international one. This result demonstrates how embedding an analysis of foreign market entry within a network view can enrich understanding of the issue.

The distribution of information within a global system

In the first part of this chapter foreign market entry was discussed from the standpoint of an individual firm, whereas in the second part it has been discussed from the standpoint of the overall system. In the first part the existence of the firm was given, whereas in the second part the structure of the firm emerged from an analysis of internalization. The first part also assumed uncertainty, whereas the second did not. Intuitively, the system perspective is that of an all-knowing planner who controls the whole system, while the firm perspective is that of a decision-maker who only understands a part of the system – specifically, that part of the system to which their personal knowledge and experience relates. Another difference is that the planner begins from scratch, and moves directly to the optimal configuration, whereas the individual decision-maker is constrained by the legacy of their previous decisions.

The link between the system-wide view of the planner and the partial view of the individual firm is that in a private enterprise economy, where individual entrepreneurs compete to establish firms, competition between them will tend to drive the system towards the planner's system-wide optimum (Hayek, 1937; Richardson, 1960). Different entrepreneurs will select different locations for their facilities, and choose to operate with different boundaries for their firms. They will compete to own facilities in highly desirable locations. The entrepreneurs with the most efficient strategies will be able to outbid those with less efficient strategies, and so competition for the ownership and control of scarce resources will reward those entrepreneurs whose partial plans are most closely aligned with the system-wide optimum.

In practice, of course, there is no planner who possesses all the information of the kind required to fully optimize the system. Planning has encountered numerous problems at national level, and these would only be further compounded if planning were attempted at the global level. This does not mean that the network view is irrelevant, however, because for reasons already noted a well-functioning private enterprise economy will tend to converge on the optimum through incremental trial and error. Competition between individual entrepreneurs within the system leads to a pooling of local knowledge – the knowledge being encoded in the prices that the entrepreneurs quote when bidding for the use of facilities and when competing for customers. So long as the competitive system remains stable, therefore, the network approach will successfully identify the long-run tendencies in the system by identifying the equilibrium to which it is converging through localized iterations.

Because an individual entrepreneur perceives only a small part of the global system, he faces considerable uncertainty regarding the consequences of his decisions. He cannot track the full implications of any decision that he makes. Conversely, because decision-making has been decentralized to many different entrepreneurs like himself, he is continuously exposed to unexpected changes caused by decisions made by other people – notably his customers and his competitors. The efficiency with which the global system works will therefore depend on the skill of entrepreneurs in handling uncertainties of this kind.

Social networks and organizations

An important strategy for handling uncertainty is to construct a network of contacts that act as sources of information (Ebers, 1997). An entrepreneur can develop two main types of network for this purpose. First, he can build a network involving other entrepreneurs, who own independent firms, and secondly he can turn his own firm into a networking organization. External networks may encompass not only other firms, but governments, banks, and opinion-leaders too. Internal networking may involve a hierarchical structure of reporting based on authority relations, or a flatter structure where people of similar status consult with each other.

There is insufficient space to describe in detail how social networks can be analysed using the rational action approach. It is sufficient to note that the rational action approach explains very simply why people are motivated to join social networks in order to gain access to information. Networks generate efficiency gains by exploiting the 'public good' property of knowledge and information. The rational action approach also explains how social and physical networks interact. Social networks are used to coordinate physical networks – for example by planning the flow of product along the linkages between facilities. At the same time, social networks utilize physical networks as inputs – as, for example, when people travel to face-to-face meetings by road, rail, or air.

It is worth noting that the rational action approach to social networks has significant implications for the modelling of organizational behaviour within multinational firms (Egelhoff, 1991). Where a large amount of information on the global environment needs to be routinely collected, a division of labour may be introduced that allows different members of an internal network to specialize in collecting different sorts of information. Where multiple sources of uncertainty are involved, multiple sources of information are normally required. The information obtained from these various sources needs to be synthesized for decision-making purposes. This requires communication between the specialists involved. Some of the communication may be 'intermediated' by other specialists, and these intermediators may sometimes take overall responsibility for the decisions. Thus the nature of the division of labour applied to information processing determines the organization of the multinational firm.

The efficiency of internal communication is a major factor in the overall cost of decision-making, and hence a major determinant of the performance of the firm. The 'entrepreneurial' qualities of the firm's key decision-makers govern its ability to synthesize information successfully. This in turn affects the overall quality of decisions (e.g. the frequency with which potential mistakes are avoided) and so determines overall performance.

The organization of decision-making can be introduced into the previous model of foreign market entry under uncertainty by formally splitting the final period into an infinite number of sub-periods, and allowing new information of a particular type to become available each period. Foreign costs of production fluctuate from one period to the next, and foreign output each period therefore needs to be adjusted in response. This encourages the firm to invest in information systems for predicting changes in cost. It also encourages the firm to invest in highly versatile capital equipment, thereby establishing a link between the structure of the organization and the type of physical capital that it employs (Capel, 1992).

Conclusion

All of these research avenues need to be fully explored before any claim that the challenge of complexity warrants the introduction of more radical or unorthodox techniques into IB theory can be accepted. It is only sensible to follow the simplest and most straightforward path of theoretical development before investing too heavily in untried concepts and techniques. This chapter has suggested that the most productive theoretical developments in IB over the next ten years or so are likely to be those that build upon the rational action approach.

When the rational action approach is along the lines described above, many of the notions found in systems theory emerge in their proper light. Rule-driven behaviour, of the kind assumed in systems theory, is shown to be a rational response to information costs (Baumol and Quandt, 1964). It is only rational in certain types of environment, however: in other environments, entrepreneurial improvisation is shown to be the order of the day.

Economy of coordination calls for a division of labour in information processing, and this in turn calls for cooperative behaviour of a social nature. It is rational to adapt the rules governing social behaviour to the long-term features of the environment within which decisions have to be made. The environment differs between locations, and it is therefore to be expected that there will be differences between locations in the kinds of rules that are used. In other words, social interactions will follow different rules in different places.

It is not expected that everyone will agree with these recommendations. But the onus is on those who disagree to set out their own agenda with a similar degree of analytical rigour, and to demonstrate that their favoured approach can deliver practical results. Talking about 'strategy' or 'complexity' in non-specific ways may be adequate for consultancy assignments, or for teaching certain types of courses, but it is not an adequate response to the research challenges that currently face IB.

References

Allen, Linda and Pantzalis, Christos (1996) 'Valuation of the Operating Flexibility of Multinational Corporations'. *Journal of International Business Studies*, vol. 27, no. 4, pp. 633–53.

Arthur, Brian W. (1988) 'Competing Technologies: an Overview'. In Giovanni Dosi, C. Freeman, R. Nelson, G. Silverberg and L. Soete (eds), *Technical Change and Economic Theory*. London: Francis Pinter.

Baumol, William J. and Quandt, Richard E. (1964) 'Rules of Thumb and Optimally Imperfect Decisions'. *American Economic Review*, vol. 54, no. 1, pp. 23–46.

Buckley, Peter J. and Casson, Mark C. (1976) *The Future of the Multinational Enterprise*. London: Macmillan.

Buckley, Peter J. and Casson, Mark C. (1981) 'The Optimal Timing of a Foreign Direct Investment'. *Economic Journal*, vol. 91, pp. 75–87.

Buckley, Peter J. and Casson, Mark C. (1993) 'Economics as an Imperialist Social Science'. *Human Relations*, vol. 46, no. 9, pp. 1035–52.

Buckley, Peter J. and Casson, Mark C. (1998a) 'Analysing Foreign Market Entry Strategies: Extending the Internalisation Approach'. *Journal of International Business Studies*, vol. 29, no. 3, pp. 539–61.
Buckley, Peter J. and Casson, Mark C. (1998b) 'Models of the Multinational Enterprise'. *Journal of International Business Studies*, vol. 29, no. 1, pp. 21–44.
Capel, Jeanette (1992) 'How to Service a Foreign Market under Uncertainty: a Real Option Approach'. *European Journal of Political Economy*, vol. 8, pp. 455–75.
Casson, Mark C. (1995) *Organization of International Business*. Aldershot: Edward Elgar.
Casson, Mark C. (1997) *Information and Organisation: a New Perspective on the Theory of the Firm*. Oxford: Clarendon Press.
Casson, Mark C. (2000a) *Economics of International Business: a New Research Agenda*. Cheltenham: Edward Elgar.
Casson, Mark C. (2000b) *Enterprise and Leadership: Studies on Firms, Networks and Institutions*. Cheltenham: Edward Elgar.
Coase, Ronald H. (1937) 'The Nature of the Firm'. *Economica*, NS, vol. 4, pp. 386–405.
Coriat, B. and Dosi, Giovanni (1998) 'The Institutional Embeddedness of Economic Change: an Appraisal of the "Evolutionist" and "Regulationist" Research Programmes'. In K. Nielsen and E. J. Johnson (eds), *Institutions and Economic Change*. Cheltenham: Edward Elgar.
DeMeza, David and van der Ploeg, Frederick (1987) 'Production Flexibility as a Motive for Multinationality'. *Journal of Industrial Economics*, vol. 35, no. 3, pp. 343–51.
Dixit, Avrinash and Pindyck, Robert S. (1994). *Investments under Uncertainty*. Princeton, NJ: Princeton University Press.
Ebers, Mark (ed.) (1997) *The Formation of Inter-Organizational Networks*. Oxford: Clarendon Press.
Egelhoff, William G. (1991) 'Information-processing Theory and the Multinational Enterprise'. *Journal of International Business Studies*, vol. 22, no. 3, pp. 341–68.
Elster, John (ed.) (1986) *Rational Choice*. Oxford: Blackwell.
Graham, E. M. (1990) 'Exchange of Threat between Multinational Firms as an Infinitely Repeated Game'. *International Trade Journal*, vol. 4, pp. 259–77.
Hargreaves-Heap, Shaun (1989) *Rationality in Economics*. Oxford: Blackwell.
Hayek, Friedrich von A. (1937) 'Economics and Knowledge'. *Economica*, NS, vol. 4, pp. 33–54.
Hirshleifer, Jack and Riley, John G. (1992) *The Analytics of Uncertainty and Information*. Cambridge: Cambridge University Press.
Isard, Walter (1956) *Location and Space Economy*. Cambridge, Mass.: MIT Press.
Kogut, Bruce (1991) 'Joint Ventures and the Option to Expand and Acquire'. *Management Science*, vol. 37, no. 1, pp. 19–33.
Kogut, Bruce and Kulatilaka, Nalin (1994) 'Operating Flexibility, Global Manufacturing, and the Option Value of a Multinational Network'. *Management Science*, vol. 40, no. 1, pp. 123–39.
Kreps, David M. (1990) *Game Theory and Economic Modelling*. Oxford: Oxford University Press.
Krugman, Paul (1995) *Development, Geography and Economic Theory*. Cambridge, Mass.: MIT Press.
Nelson, Richard and Winter, Sidney G. (1982) *An Evolutionary Theory of Economic Change*. Cambridge, Mass.: Harvard University Press.
Parkhe, Avind (1993) '"Messy" Research, Methodological Predispositions, and Theory Development in International Joint Ventures'. *Academy of Management Review*, vol. 18, pp. 227–68.

Porter, Michael E. (1991) 'Towards a Dynamic Theory of Strategy'. *Strategic Management Journal*, vol. 12 (Special Issue), pp. 95–117.
Richardson, George B. (1960) *Information and Investment*. Oxford: Oxford University Press.
Rivoli, Pietra and Salorio, Eugene (1996) 'Foreign Direct Investment under Uncertainty'. *Journal of International Business Studies*, vol. 27, no. 2, pp. 335–54.
Williamson, Oliver E. (1985) *The Economic Institutions of Capitalism*. New York: Free Press.

4

Internationalization – Real Options, Knowledge Management and the Uppsala Approach

with Mark Casson and Mohammed Azzim Gulamhussen[1]

Introduction

Scandinavian literature on the internationalization strategy of a firm emphasizes the incremental and sequential nature of both the export process and the foreign direct investment process (see, for example, Johanson and Vahlne, 1977; Johanson and Wiedersheim-Paul, 1975; Strandskov, 1986). Firms acquire experience of one foreign market before entering the next: they do not enter all major markets at the outset. In this way they benefit from the lessons learnt in the early stages of expansion and avoid making too many big mistakes. There are two other theories, however – namely internalization and globalization – which seem to imply that, on the contrary, firms will internationalize in a single discrete step involving simultaneous entry into all markets. This conflict between the theories is more apparent than real, however. This chapter shows that the theory of organizational learning implicit in the Scandinavian approach in fact complements these other approaches, by highlighting factors which they omit. A formal model is presented which clarifies these complementarities and so enriches all three areas of theory. This chapter is an attempt to show the relevance of the real option analysis in the internationalization process.

It turns out that this model includes, as a special case, an international analogue of Penrose's (1959) theory of the growth of the firm. This is because it embodies, in addition to Scandinavian insights, one of Penrose's key ideas, namely that it is prohibitively costly for any team of managers to diversify in several directions at once. It touches on an even more fundamental issue too: the scope of the rational actor model in analysing managerial behaviour.

It is widely believed that rational action implies that managers do not make mistakes. It is claimed that, in consequence, behavioural models of learning may provide a better account of managerial behaviour than does the rational action approach.

This argument ignores the possibility that rational managers will take account of information costs, however. The model presented here shows that, when information is costly, rational managers will make mistakes because the optimal frequency of mistakes is greater than zero. Because the model assumes rationality it can actually predict the kind of mistakes that will be made and the frequency with which they will occur. It shows that the entire internationalization strategy of a firm can be interpreted as a strategy designed to reduce, but not eliminate, the incidence of mistakes in individual market entry strategies. This illustrates one of the main strengths of the rational action approach: it facilitates simple mathematical modelling which not only captures existing insights in parsimonious terms, but deepens these insights and reveals new ones as well.

Real options

Real options reduce risk by providing the flexibility to respond to new information as it becomes available. The key to the successful exploitation of real options is to foresee the kind of information that is likely to become available and to plan the options in order to exploit this information at an early stage. Its use in internationalization theory puts the Uppsala approach into a wider context.

Almost everyone has heard about financial options – in particular 'put' and 'call' options based upon stock market prices (for a review see Dempster and Pliska, 1997). These options involve a contract between two parties. This contract creates a right to buy or sell an asset at a future time at a prespecified price – either a fixed price, or a price specified by some agreed rule. This right can be traded: it can be bought and sold, just like the underlying asset to which it relates. The main object of option theory, as developed in finance, is to price such options correctly.

There is a good deal of confusion about the relation between real options and financial options. There are two opposing views that can be found in the popular literature, and both of them are wrong. The first is that real options and financial options are basically the same thing – that real options relate to real assets, and financial options relate to financial assets, but that the underlying principles are the same. The second view is that real options and financial options are fundamentally different: real options are about the timing of irreversible investment decisions, whilst financial option theory is about the valuation of 'derivative' contractual instruments. Those who take the second view believe that those who take the first view are misled by the use of the same term – option – to describe two different phenomena. In fact, the first view is closer to the truth than the second, in the sense that financial options are simply a special case of real options, and the same principles – as described above – apply to both. The mistake of the first view is to suppose that the difference lies simply in whether the asset is real or monetary. The nature of the asset is important, but the key issue is whether the asset is tradable or not, rather than whether it takes a real or monetary form. In practice, almost all monetary assets are tradable, but the converse does not apply: not all real assets are non-tradable. Because some real assets are tradable, tradability is a separate issue from whether the asset is a real or monetary one.

The nature of the option is also important. Some options are contractual, and others reflect the physical properties of the asset. For example, some options are exercised by buying and selling an asset, whereas others are exercised by retaining ownership of the asset and reallocating it to an alternative use. The importance of distinguishing between contractual and non-contractual options is reflected in the second view described above. Where this view goes wrong is to suppose that different principles apply to the valuation of contractual options and non-contractual options. In fact they do not. The principles are the same. This is fortunate, because it means that there is, in fact, just one body of option theory, and not two. Financial option theory is just a special case of a more general theory of options which is based on the principles set out above. Real option theory is the body of theory that has applied these general principles to non-contractual options on non-tradable assets, and neglected their applications to financial options. The applications of real option theory given below clearly demonstrate that the principles commonly ascribed to real option theory apply to financial options as well.

These remarks are elaborated in Table 4.1. The table classifies different types of options using two main dimensions. The first dimension, indicated by the columns, specifies whether the asset is tradable or not. A tradable asset is an asset which can always be bought and sold. When there are no transaction costs or other 'market imperfections', the purchase price of a tradable asset is equal to its selling price. This is a crucial property used in standard option pricing models in the theory of finance. The columns also identify a secondary distinction between real and monetary assets, but as indicated above, this is of no real significance. It is of no significance because, as emphasized above, it is the economic value of the asset that matters in option theory, and the physical form that the asset takes is of no consequence unless it affects some other more relevant aspect of the problem too.

The second dimension, indicated by the rows, specifies whether the option takes a contractual form or not. This distinction is not important for the mathematical structure of the models, but it is important in understanding how an option model is applied. The distinction shows that

Table 4.1 Classification of options by type of option and type of asset, with examples

Type of option	*Type of asset*		
	Monetary	*Tradable Real*	*Non-tradable Real*
Contractual			
Formal	Bond or currency option	Commodity option Equity option	Option to purchase land or building Option to acquire a non-quoted firm
Informal			'First refusal' option to acquire a firm in which a minority stake is held
Non-contractual	Holding money as a source of liquidity		Option to upsize, downsize or relocate a factory: see also Table 4.2

option theory can be used to value the flexibility provided both by contractual arrangements and by the physical properties of an asset. A minor distinction is between contractual arrangements of a formal and an informal kind. Whilst formal arrangements are the most conspicuous, informal arrangements may be of greater consequence where long-term corporate strategies are concerned – for example, informal options agreed with partner firms to acquire or divest joint venture companies.

The options of greatest relevance to IB theory appear in the bottom right-hand corner of the table. They are real options rather than financial options. They include options to vary the size, location, timing and utilization of an investment project once the initial phase of it is complete. These are non-contractual options, which are highly relevant to location issues in IB. Another important set of options discussed above are contractual options to acquire or divest assets owned wholly or partly by other firms. These contractual options are highly relevant to ownership issues in IB. Between them, these two issues – ownership and location – dominate the modern economic theory of IB (Buckley and Casson, 1976, 1998). It follows that real options have a key role in generating a dynamic version of IB theory.

Techniques of analysis

Much of the technical difficulty in contemporary financial option theory stems from the commitment to continuous time models. Continuous time is a reasonable approximation to reality in stock markets and currency markets where trading is virtually instantaneous, but it is a poor approximation to the circumstances under which non-contractual decisions relating to the deployment of real assets are made. Here, discrete time models, based on dividing up time into a finite number of periods, are generally more realistic. Since discrete time models are much simpler to solve than continuous time models, there is much to be gained from studying options from the outset in terms of discrete time. This is the approach adopted in this chapter.

The discrete time models used in this chapter involve rational intertemporal decision-making under uncertainty. All the models can be solved by explicit analytical methods, although for certain types of model approximations are useful. The general method of solution is a recursive technique. This technique solves for the rational choices in the final period, conditional on the choices made in the previous periods, and then uses these results to determine the optimal choices in preceding period. This method is repeated until the initial period is reached. Initial decisions are optimized on the assumption that, in the light of these decisions, the most appropriate choices in subsequent periods will then be made. This determines a comprehensive contingent plan of action covering every period.

Most of the models are presented in numerical rather than algebraic form. This is the most convenient way of expounding models like the present ones, which involve choices between discrete strategies over discrete periods of time. It is straightforward to reformulate the models in algebraic form, and interested readers may like to do this for themselves. The only difficulty is that the derivation of solutions is relatively tedious, and the algebraic inequalities that characterize the optimum strategy are cumbersome to write down. Because the present chapter has a mainly expository role, numerical examples are preferable because they are much quicker to present and are more readily understood.

To illustrate the discrete time approach, consider the following numerical example, which places a standard financial option problem in a discrete time framework. Because the example involves a tradable financial asset, it possesses the special feature that the purchase price of the asset is always equal to its selling price. The decision-maker has to decide whether to purchase a contractual option which will allow him to buy the asset in the future at a pre-specified price, if he wishes to.

Example 1. Consider a single indivisible asset whose future value may be either 20 or 10, depending on whether conditions are good ($s = 1$) or bad ($s = 0$). Conditions are good with probability p. The asset can be purchased today ($t = 0$) for 15 units, or purchase can be deferred until tomorrow ($t = 1$), when tomorrow's price will be known. A call option can be purchased today for two units, which gives the right to purchase the asset tomorrow for 15 units, i.e. for the same price as today. The objective of the risk-neutral decision-maker is to maximize the expected profit v. Because of the short period of time elapsing between today and tomorrow, discounting is ignored.

There is an element of irreversibility in today's purchase because a purchaser cannot guarantee to sell the asset tomorrow for the price at which he bought it. Such a guarantee can only be acquired through the separate purchase of a 'put' option, which allows him to sell the asset at a pre-specified price, such as the price at which he bought it. To keep the model simple, the put option is ignored.

The problem is represented using a decision tree in Figure 4.1. Starting from the top of the figure, the decision maker has three initial alternatives:

1. To purchase the asset immediately;
2. To purchase the call option instead;
3. To defer a decision on purchasing until later.

Once conditions have been revealed, the decision-maker faces further decisions. If he has purchased the option then he must decide whether to exercise it or not. The net rewards, derived from the data given above, are indicated by the numbers along the bottom of the figure. If conditions are good then it pays to exercise the option, whereas if conditions are bad then it pays not to exercise it. The optimal choices are indicated by the thicker branches in the figure. If the decision-maker has deferred a decision then he can decide whether to purchase the asset the following day. However, the special conditions assumed in this problem mean that this decision is of no

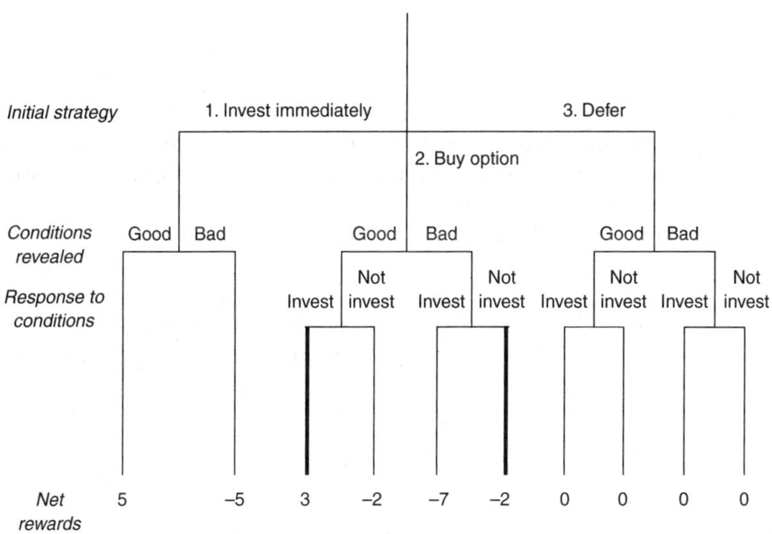

Figure 4.1 Decision tree for appraisal of option purchase

consequence. Since the purchase price is always equal to the value of the asset, the decision-maker is indifferent to purchase, whatever conditions prevail. It is assumed for simplicity that in these circumstances the decision-maker will choose not to make a purchase.

It follows from this discussion that three main strategies need to be considered: Let v_i be the expected value of the ith strategy; then

$$v_1 = (20p + 10(1-p)) - 15 = -5 + 10p \tag{4.1}$$

$$v_2 = ((20-15)p + 0(1-p)) - 2 = -2 + 5p \tag{4.2}$$

$$v_3 = 0 \tag{4.3}$$

The first term in equation (4.1) is the expected revenue from an initial investment when it is sold in the following period, whilst the second term is today's purchase price. The first term in equation (4.2) is the value of the option when exercised, weighted by the probability that conditions are good. The second term is its value (zero) when conditions are bad, and the third term is its purchase price.

Selecting the highest value of v for any given value of p gives the solution:

$$i = \begin{matrix} 1 & \text{if } p > 0.6 \\ 2 & \text{if } 0.4 < p < 0.6 \\ 3 & \text{if } p < 0.4 \end{matrix} \tag{4.4}$$

Thus as the probability of good conditions increases from zero to one, the decision-maker switches from no purchase to option purchase, to immediate purchase, illustrating his growing confidence that conditions will be good. The inequalities specified here assume that when two strategies are of equal value, the strategy with the lower number is always chosen; this convention is used throughout the chapter.

The solution is illustrated graphically in Figure 4.2. The vertical axis measures the expected profit and the horizontal axis measures the probability of good conditions. The schedule V_1V_1' indicates the expected value of the initial purchase strategy. The relatively low intercept and steep slope show that this is the riskiest strategy. The investor is exposed to a serious risk of capital loss if conditions turn out to be bad. The schedule V_2V_2' indicates the value of the option strategy. Holding an option eliminates the risk of capital loss, whilst offering the prospect of a capital gain by preserving the right to purchase the asset at a pre-specified price equal to the initial price. The option therefore provides a speculative opportunity whilst controlling the risk involved. The horizontal axis represents the null value of the third strategy.

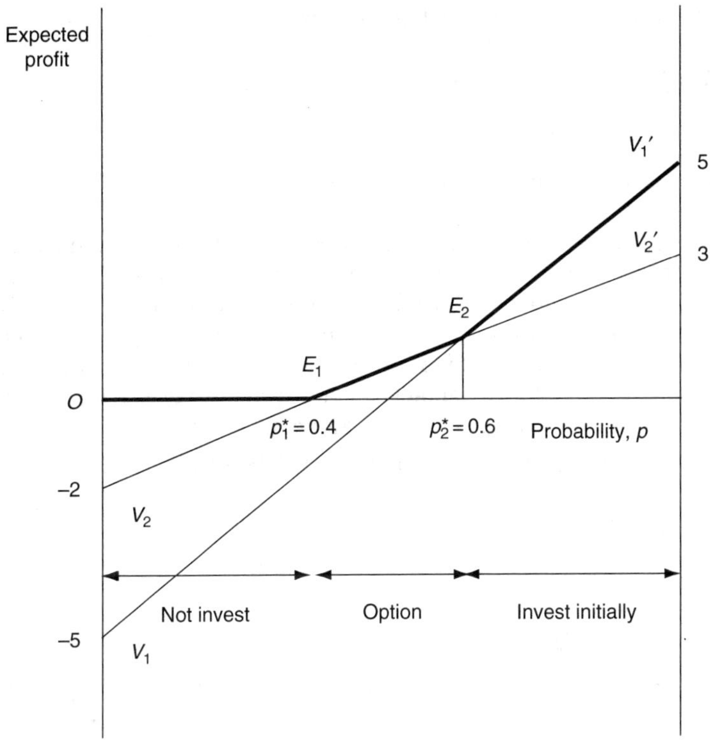

Figure 4.2 Graphical solution of the financial option problem

To maximize expected profit it is necessary to identify the upper envelope of the three schedules. This is the schedule $OE_1E_2V_1'$, which has kinks at the points E_1, E_2, where some pair of strategies has equal value. For any given value of p, the optimal strategy is the one that forms the portion of the envelope at the relevant point along the horizontal axis. The kinks E_1, E_2 correspond to the two critical values of probability $p_1^* = 0.4$, $p_2^* = 0.6$, where switches of strategy take place. At the first switch point, the no purchase strategy and the option strategy are of equal value, whilst at the second switch point the option strategy and the immediate purchase strategy are of equal value.

The same diagrammatic technique can also be used to measure the value of an option. Suppose that the decision-maker does not know that an option can be purchased for two units. A decision rule is required to determine when to purchase an option. Let a be the unknown value of the option. Equation (4.2) then becomes

$$v_2 = -a + 5p \qquad (4.5)$$

and the decision rule is to purchase the option if

$$v_2 > \max[v_1,\ v_3]$$

i.e. if

$$a < \max[-5 + 10p,\ 0] + 5p$$

The determination of the value of the option for $p = 0.5$ is shown in Figure 4.3. This involves a two-stage procedure. In the first stage the maximum expected value obtainable from the two alternative strategies is determined by constructing the envelope OE_3V_1' from the higher of V_1V_1' (representing strategy 1) and the horizontal axis (representing strategy 3). In the second stage, a line WW' is drawn parallel to V_2V_2' through the envelope OE_3V_1' so that it touches the envelope at the lowest possible point. Given the assumed value for p, this happens to be the point E_3 where the line V_1V_1' intersects the

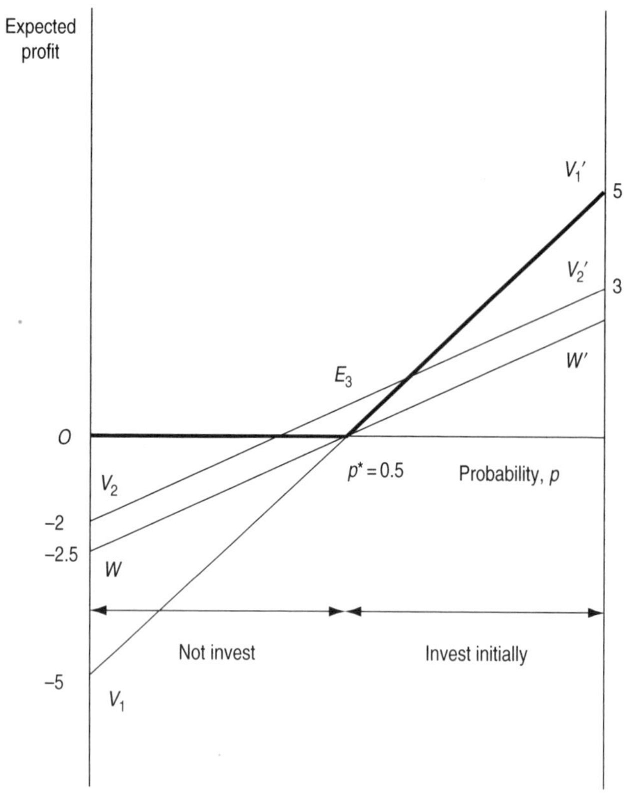

Figure 4.3 Valuation of a financial option

horizontal axis. The vertical distance between V_2V_2' and WW' is a measure of the value of the option. The decision rule is to purchase the option only if this distance is a positive one. The distance in the figure can be measured by comparing the intercepts V_1 and W on the left-hand vertical axis. The value of the option is 2.5. Since its purchase price is only 2, the option should be acquired when $p = 0.5$. This agrees with the result obtained in Figure 4.2, which showed that the option should be purchased whenever p was in the range between 0.4 and 0.6.

The timing of a real investment: a simple role for contractual options in international business

Consider a firm contemplating entry into a foreign market. The firm has identified an investment opportunity which it alone can exploit. Exploitation of the opportunity begins in period 2, but the investment expenditure can be incurred in either period 1 or period 2; the problem is to determine which is best. It is convenient to assume that the second period, beginning tomorrow, is very much longer than the first. Because the period is much longer, it is difficult to justify ignoring issues relating to the discount rate. However, to keep the model simple it is convenient to take the rate of discount as fixed and specify the entire problem in terms of discounted values. Discounting is introduced explicitly below.

The opportunity generates a known flow of income with present value 20 units. To appropriate this income stream, the firm needs to acquire a site for the erection of a factory. Conditions in the local market for industrial property are very uncertain, however (as they are in many transitional economies). At the moment, a site is available at a price of 15 units, but in the following period a similar site could be become available for either 10 units or 20 units, depending upon whether supply conditions in the property market are good or bad. Conditions are good (the price is 10 units) with probability p.

Once the site has been bought, the factory must be erected immediately, and once this has occurred, the site has no alternative use, and no resale value. The owner of the site is willing to fix the price for a sale tomorrow at 17 units, provided that a non-refundable deposit of two units is paid. The reservation on the site can be cancelled tomorrow if desired. Cancelling the reservation would allow the firm to make a spot purchase at a price of 10 units if conditions were good.

This example has been chosen to illustrate the close connection between real options and financial options, as described earlier. The situation closely resembles the financial option problem discussed above. The principal change is that the asset in which the firm invests is no longer tradable. The future value of the asset depends not upon what it can be sold for, but only upon what it can be used for. The purchase is technically irreversible, but economically it incurs little risk because the owner is certain that the asset is worth 18 units from the outset. The only risk is that the owner may pay more for the asset than is really necessary.

Because the asset is not tradable, a wedge can be driven between its purchase price and its value to the firm. This is reflected in the fact that, whether it is purchased for 10, 15 or 20 units, it is still worth 20 units to the firm. By contrast, above, the asset was always worth what it was purchased for at the time.

There are three dominant strategies, each of which corresponds to one of the strategies in example 1:

1. Invest at the outset;
2. Place a deposit (the call option) and exercise it if the spot price is high; cancel the order and purchase spot if the price is low;
3. Defer the decision, and invest only if the price is low.

The expected profits generated by these strategies are:

$$v_1 = 20 - 15 = 5 \tag{4.7}$$

$$v_2 = 20 - 2 - 10p - 15(1 - p) = 3 + 5p \tag{4.8}$$

$$v_3 = (20 - 10)p = 10p \tag{4.9}$$

Equation (4.7) shows that initial purchase carries no risk, since both the value of the asset (18 units) and the purchase price (15 units) are known at the outset. Equation (4.8) shows that the option will not be exercised if conditions are good – a cost of 10 units is incurred with probability p – but will be exercised if conditions are bad – a cost of 15 units is incurred with probability $(1 - p)$. Equation (4.9) shows the profit to be made by deferring the decision when conditions turn out to be good.

Expected profit is maximized by setting

$$i = \begin{cases} 1) & \text{if } p < 0.4 \\ 2) & \text{if } 0.4 < p < 0.6 \\ 3) & \text{if } p > 0.6 \end{cases} \tag{4.10}$$

The solution is illustrated in Figure 4.4. The conventions are the same as for Figure 4.1. The expected values of the three strategies are represented respectively by the schedules V_1V_1', V_2V_2' and OV_3'. The maximum attainable value of profit for a given value of p is indicated by the height of the envelope $V_1E_1E_2V_3'$. The figure shows that when the future purchase price of the asset is expected to be very high (p is low) the investment will be made at the outset (when strategy 1) is chosen), whilst if it is expected to be very low (p is

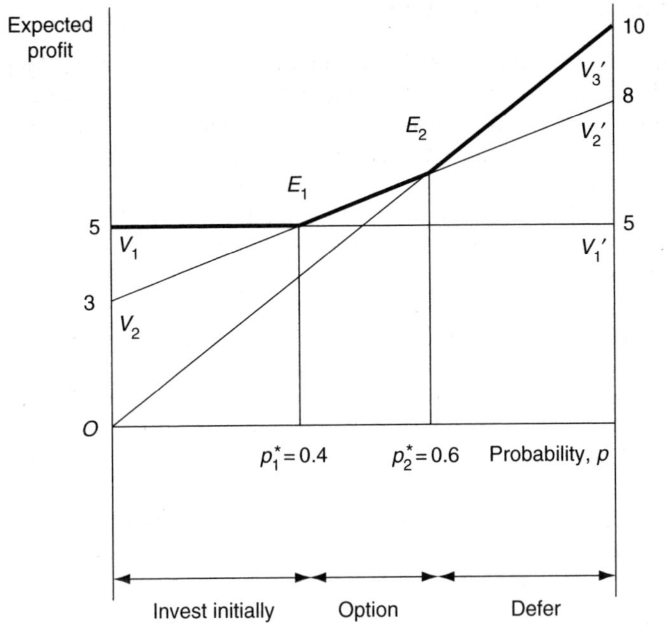

Figure 4.4 Option to purchase a real asset with an uncertain future price but known value in use

high) the investment will be deferred (when strategy 3) is chosen). A deposit will be placed on the asset (strategy 2)) if the firm believes that a high or low price will occur a probability in the mid-range of values between 0.4 and 0.6. Indeed, it is readily established, using the method described in the previous section, that the option is most valuable when the uncertainty is greatest, i.e. when $p=0.5$.

The similarity between this example and the previous one is illustrated by the appearance of the same critical probability values, $p_1^* = 0.4$, $p_2^* = 0.6$. Indeed, a comparison of Figure 4.4 with Figure 4.2 shows that the two figures are almost identical except for the fact that all the schedules have been pushed upwards by five units. This explains why the critical values are the same. The only substantial difference arises from the fact that the role of the strategy 1) in the previous example has now been taken over by strategy 3), and vice versa. The role of strategy 2) – the option strategy – remains exactly the same. The interchange of the roles of strategies 1) and 3) is explained by the fact that in the previous example risk was eliminated by not purchasing the asset, whilst in the present example it is eliminated by purchasing the asset at the outset. Although the new model relates to a real asset rather than a financial asset, it is still driven by the same kind of speculative forces as before.

Uncertain demand conditions

The previous section discussed a contractual option governing the purchase of a real asset. This is only one of several types of option relating to real assets, and it is certainly not the most important one so far as IB is concerned. When real options were introduced (Casson, 1999), the emphasis was on their role in coping with uncertainty about demand for the asset's services – and specifically with uncertainty about the foreign demand for the product from which the demand for these services is derived. The previous example, by contrast, focused on uncertainty about the supply of the asset instead.

Both demand and supply are potential sources of uncertainty, and the relation between them is illustrated in Table 4.2. The columns of the table distinguish three sources of uncertainty: supply, demand, and a combination of the two. The rows of the table distinguish two types of option: contractual and non-contractual. The most important type of contractual option is the IJV, which is useful in coping with uncertainty in both demand and supply. Non-contractual options involve issues such as the size, timing, location and versatility of investments. Both contractual and non-contractual options can take numerous forms – indeed, there are far too many to do justice to them all in a single chapter.

The remaining sections of this chapter concentrate on a few important cases, beginning with some simple cases relating to non-contractual options that reduce the risks relating to uncertainty in demand. By switching attention from uncertainty about supply to uncertainty about demand some classic examples of real option models are obtained.

Demand uncertainty is an important factor in foreign market entry decisions. Entry is often deferred, even when it would be profitable to go ahead immediately, because it would be even more profitable to wait until later.

Table 4.2 Classification of non-tradable real options by source of uncertainty and type of asset, with examples

Type of option	*Source of uncertainty*		
	Cost of supply	*Intensity of demand*	*Either supply or demand, or both*
Contractual	Option to purchase land or building		IJV
Non-contractual	Build flexibility into sources of input supply	Build flexibility into range of demands that can be satisfied	Build in potential to upsize, downsize or relocate plant at low cost

The strategy of deferring foreign market entry was discussed by Buckley and Casson (1981), but only under conditions of certainty. Under these conditions, the main motive for deferring entry is to await further growth in the market. Once uncertainty is introduced, another motive for waiting is introduced – namely, to dispel uncertainty about whether the market is likely to grow or not. Entry is postponed until some crucial information relating to the prospective size of the market has become available. This is the gist of the example that follows.

Consider an initial investment in a foreign market. This could be an investment in marketing and distribution facilities, or it could involve investment in production facilities as well. As before, there are two periods, with the second period being very long. Investment today generates a revenue of two units today, and a revenue of 20 units tomorrow if conditions are good and 10 units if they are bad. Demand conditions are good with probability p. If the asset is not purchased until tomorrow then only tomorrow's revenues are obtained. The purchase price of the asset is 15 units in both periods. The advantage of purchasing tomorrow is that the purchase decision can be made when the state of demand is known. An asset purchased today cannot be sold off again tomorrow: the entire purchase price is a sunk cost.

By deferring the entry decision, the firm can guarantee that it will not make a loss. When the decision is deferred, the optimal strategy is to enter if and only if demand conditions are good. This generates an expected profit of $5p$. It follows that deferred investment with conditional entry dominates a strategy of not investing at all.

As a result of this, there are only two strategies worth distinguishing:

1. Invest at the outset;
2. Defer the investment decision, and invest tomorrow only if demand conditions are good.

The expected profits generated by these strategies are:

$$v_1 = 10(1-p) + 20p + 2 - 15 = -3 + 10p \tag{4.11}$$

$$v_2 = (20 - 15)p = 5p \tag{4.12}$$

The first two terms in equation (4.11) express expected revenue in period 2): namely, 10 units when demand conditions are bad, and 20 units when they are good. The third term captures the revenue generated in period 1), while the final term is the outlay on the investment. The derivation of equation (4.12) has already been explained. There is no revenue stream and no outlay when demand conditions are bad, because the firm does not invest in this case. There is no revenue from period 1) either, because investment does not take place until period 2).

Expected profit is maximized by setting:

$$i = \begin{matrix} 1 & \text{if } p > 0.6 \\ 2 & \text{if } p < 0.6 \end{matrix} \qquad (4.13)$$

The solution is illustrated in Figure 4.5. The expected profit generated by immediate investment is indicated by the height of the schedule V_1V_1', while the expected profit generated by deferral is indicated by the height of the schedule OV_2'. The maximum attainable profit is indicated by the envelope OEV_1', which has a kink at E. The point E identifies the critical probability $p^* = 0.6$ at which the firm switches from deferral to immediate entry. Thus for low values of p, where the firm is pessimistic about demand conditions, entry is deferred, whilst for high values of p, where the firm is optimistic about demand conditions, entry is immediate because the firm is so confident that conditions will be good.

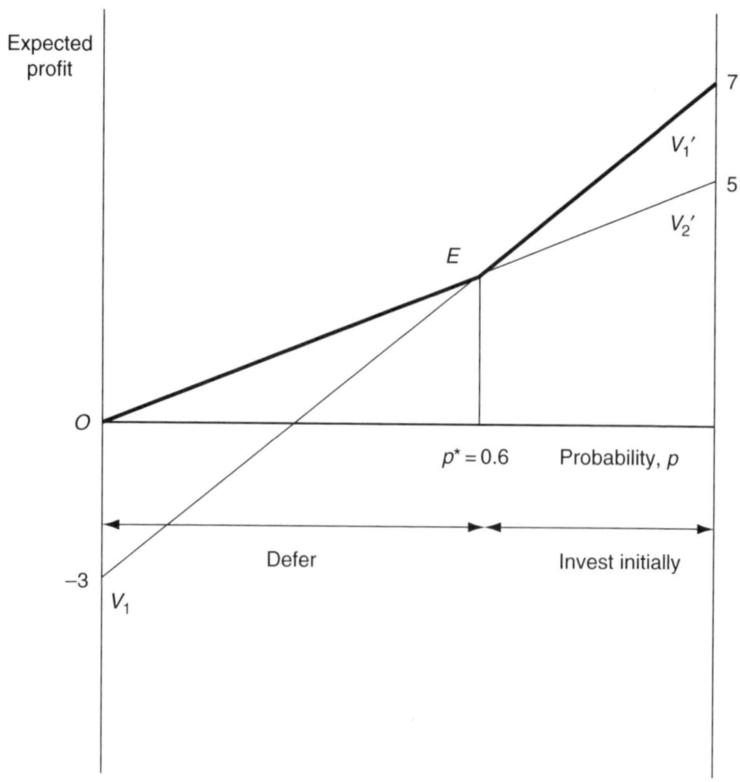

Figure 4.5 Decision to defer investment when future demand is uncertain

Scale and reversibility of investments

In the previous example the only strategy conferring option value was deferment. In practice, however, real option value is often generated by choosing an alternative, more flexible, form of investment. This section examines a variant of this strategy which is particularly relevant to foreign market entry (for a similar application to corporate growth see Kulatilaka and Perotti, 1998).

Suppose that there is an alternative to the irreversible investment described in the previous section, in the form of a smaller investment which is partially reversible. This small investment can be upgraded to a full investment the following period if desired. It involves an initial outlay of 10 units, 7 units of which can be recovered if the investment is abandoned the following period. The cost of an upgrade is assumed to be 6 units. The small investment yields the same revenue as the large investment in the initial period – namely 2 units. This is because the market is initially small, and can be served just as adequately from a small investment as from a large one. However, the small investment is much less effective in the second period. Because of its small scale it can generate an income of only 5 units whatever the size of the market.

The obvious way to exploit the small investment is to use it for initial entry and then either scale it up, if demand is strong, or liquidate it if demand is weak. The alternative to scaling up is to liquidate the investment in the second period and put the proceeds towards a purchase of the larger asset. This is uneconomic, however, because the cost is $15 - 7 = 8$ units, as against 6 units for the upgrade. The alternative to liquidation is to keep the asset in use, but this is uneconomic because the income from use is 5 units whereas the proceeds from liquidation are 7 units.

It follows that there is only one additional strategy which is worth considering:

1. Invest on a small scale with a view to scaling up if demand is buoyant and liquidating if demand is weak.

The expected value of the new strategy is

$$v_3 = -10 + 2 + (20 - 6)p + 7(1 - p) = -1 + 7p \qquad (4.14)$$

The first term in (4.14) is the initial outlay, and the second term the revenue from period 1); the third term is the expected profit from an upgrade when demand conditions are good, and the final term is the expected proceeds from liquidation when conditions are bad.

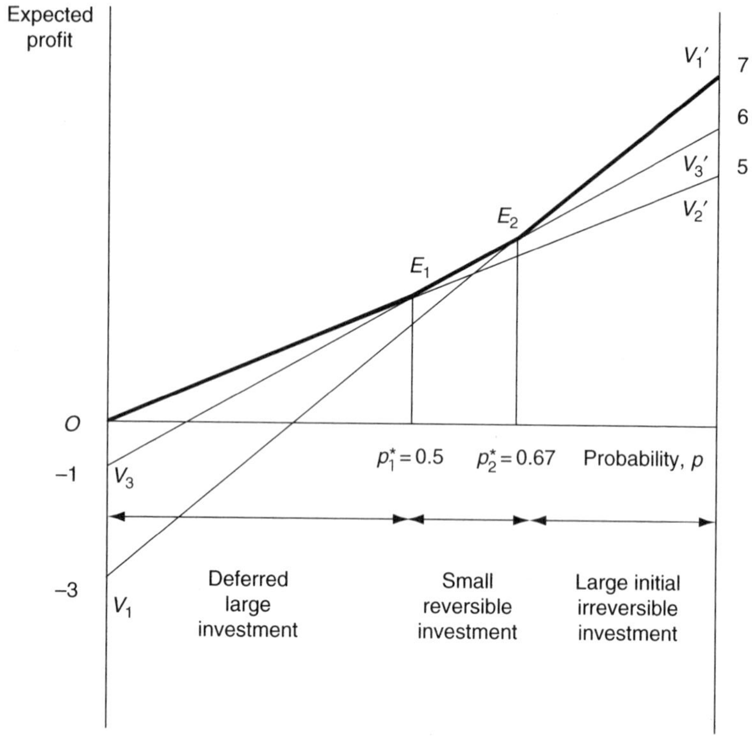

Figure 4.6 Advantages of a small-scale reversible initial investment when future demand is uncertain

The new solution is

$$i = \begin{cases} 1 & \text{if } p > 0.67 \\ 2 & \text{if } p < 0.5 \\ 3 & \text{if } 0.5 < p < 0.67 \end{cases} \tag{4.15}$$

The solution is illustrated in Figure 4.6. The value of the new strategy 3), is indicated by the height of the schedule $V_3V_3{}'$. This intersects $OV_2{}'$ at E_1 and $V_1V_1{}'$ at E_2, determining the critical probabilities $p_1^* = 0.5$, $p_2^* = 0.67$ between which the small-scale investment is preferred. This is a good example of the way that small flexible investments are preferred when future demand conditions are highly uncertain.

Investment in information-gathering as a real option

While the previous example clearly demonstrated the advantages of small reversible investments, the value of the option that was generated was not sufficiently large to make the strategy dominant. It was efficient only when there was a high degree of uncertainty. Given the prevalence of such investments in real-world market entry situations, this suggests that something important may have been omitted from the model.

The obvious omission is investment in the collection of information. So far it has been assumed that information about the state of demand is automatically revealed in the second period whether the firm has invested in the first period or not. Under these conditions, deferred investment is very attractive when market prospects are poor because investing at the outset confers no information advantage. On the other hand, the problem with making an irreversible investment at the outset is that it is too late to do anything useful with the information once it has been obtained.

Suppose now that information on demand conditions can only be obtained in the second period if an investment has been made in the first period. While the values of both of the initial entry strategies remain unchanged, the value of the deferred entry strategy is dramatically reduced. Because it now confers no information advantage, the value of the deferred investment strategy falls to

$$v_2 = 10(1 - p) + 20p - 15 = -5 + 10p \tag{4.16}$$

It is now totally dominated by the initial full-scale investment strategy, because the only remaining difference between them is that the initial investment generates two units of profit from period 1) whereas the deferred investment does not.

The deferred investment strategy previously dominated the null strategy of no investment in either period, but as deferment is now less profitable, this is no longer the case. It is therefore necessary to reintroduce the null strategy explicitly into the strategy set. It is convenient to introduce it as a replacement for the deferred investment strategy. The new strategies that need to be evaluated are therefore:

1. Invest on a large scale at the outset;
2. Do not invest at all;
3. Invest on a small scale at the outset with a view to scaling up if demand is buoyant and liquidating if demand is weak.

The new solution is

$$i = \begin{array}{ll} 1 & \text{if } p > 0.67 \\ 2 & \text{if } p < 0.14 \\ 3 & \text{if } 0.14 < p < 0.67 \end{array} \tag{4.17}$$

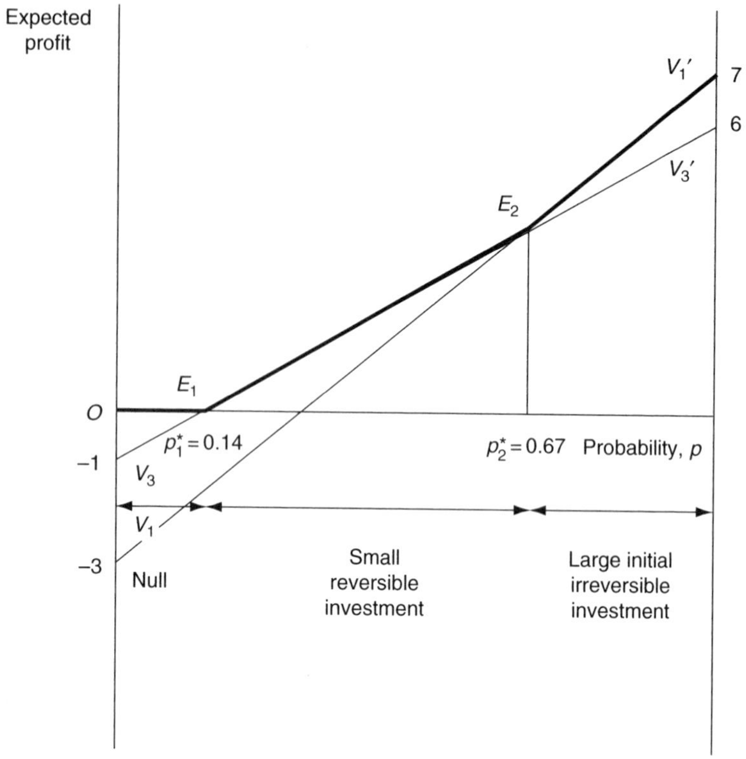

Figure 4.7 Role of a small-scale reversible investment for collecting information on demand conditions in a market

The modified solution is illustrated in Figure 4.7. The schedules V_1V_1', V_3V_3' remain in their previous positions (see Figure 4.6). The value of strategy 2), which is now the null strategy, is represented by the horizontal axis. V_3V_3' intersects the horizontal axis at E_1, corresponding to a critical probability $p_1^* = 0.14$. It intersects V_1V_1' at the same point, E_2, as before, corresponding to the critical probability $p_2^* = 0.67$. The range of probability values for which the small reversible strategy is chosen has therefore more than tripled as compared with the previous case.

This modified example shows very clearly why a small scale reversible investment is so often chosen as an initial entry strategy. It can act as a 'listening post', helping the investor to collect information on the future prospects of the market. Using another metaphor, it can be described as a 'toe in the water': it is an exercise in collecting important information which affords the option of a quick withdrawal if necessary. This metaphor is also consistent with the picture of FDI as a process of increasing commitment to the foreign market, as described in the Uppsala model of the internationalization of the firm (Johanson and Vahlne, 1977; Johanson and Wiedersheim-Paul, 1975).

Quality of judgement and the performance of the firm

When the present model 'rationalizes' marketing errors, however, it does not rationalize errors in the internationalization strategy itself. While management chooses, within the model, whether or not to improve its own subjective estimates of the state of each market, it does not choose whether to improve its estimates about the type of market in order to make a better choice about investigation or about the sequence of market entry. This is because of the focus of the model on the 'hands on' investigations that are carried out after a commitment to market entry has been made.

It would be possible, in principle, to extend the analysis back in time to a period before the management was required to make the internationalization decision. At this stage management could consider investing in information which would improve the quality of the subjective probabilities used to determine the internationalization strategy. Since the cost of additional information would itself be uncertain, however, this would introduce a third variety of uncertainty into the model. Indeed the process could be continued back even further until a time was reached in which the management had just a few simple theories about how information on various subjects might conceivably relate to this issue, and a small amount of initial information with which to prime the learning process. It would then be possible to impute subsequent successes and failures to the reliability of these early beliefs and their relevance to subsequent situations. With the regression of the quest for information further into the past, the cultural heritage of the management each would emerge as the key to its performance.

In the absence of such ambitious analysis, however, the present model does at least provide a simple basis for relating the accuracy of the subjective beliefs as inherited from culture and past experience, to the performance of the internationalization strategy (Buckley and Chapman, 1997). Generally speaking, the more accurate are the beliefs, the better will be the performance of the firm. The relation between accuracy and performance is not a continuous one, though, because, as noted earlier, errors in probabilities translate into errors in strategy only when critical probability thresholds are exceeded. This amplifies the earlier comparison between two firms in which it was just the relevance of the home country marketing experience which affected subsequent performance. It suggests that it is not just the firm's own experience in its home market that is important, but the culture it acquires from its domestic environment too.

To analyse the impact of beliefs upon performance the modeller must, of course, specify what the true situation – unknown to the management – really is. Suppose, for example, that each market is of a different type, so that correct beliefs are represented by $q_2 = q_3 = 1$, $p_2 = p_3 = 0$. Suppose also that there is no correlation, $k = 0$. Under these circumstances a simultaneous strategy is almost certainly preferable to a sequential strategy because, with both foreign markets being different, the sequential approach offers no economies of scope to information.

A very optimistic management might take the view that all the markets were of the same type, so that both foreign markets were exactly like the domestic market: that is, $q_2 = q_3 = 0$. With expected costs of internationalization well below their actual level, the firm could decide to internationalize when in fact the null strategy of remaining a domestic firm might be better. Moreover, being so confident in its beliefs, management may not investigate the states of individual markets either, so that costly errors may be perpetrated in marketing strategy too. Thus the firm will expand into the two foreign markets simultaneously without any investigation, and make losses as a result. Misguided subjective beliefs therefore provide a simple rationalization for impetuous globalization.

At the other extreme, so far as strategy is concerned, is the management that wrongly believes that both foreign markets, though different from the home market, are of the same type, but recognizes that it does not know what state this is. This firm will opt for the cautious strategy of sequential internationalization when in fact simultaneous internationalization with investigation at each stage would definitely be better. This kind of firm is typically commended in the internationalization literature, although, as this example makes clear, its strategy is inefficient in certain circumstances.

Evaluation of the Scandinavian approach

The preceding analysis has immediate relevance to the evaluation of alternative theories of the firm. To begin with, the analysis highlights the importance of subjective beliefs about the similarity and dissimilarity of different markets. It shows that the advantage of a sequential approach to expansion is greatest when foreign markets are believed to be different from the home one but are likely to be similar to each other. Given that they are indeed similar, the sequential approach maximizes the economies of scope that the first investigation affords. Conversely, the advantage of the simultaneous strategy is greatest when the foreign markets are believed to be similar to the home one, and, if different, to be different in their own particular way. This means that experience gained from any particular market will be of little relevance elsewhere.

The strategic management literature advocating globalization (Porter, 1980) clearly adopts this latter view. The markets of different industrialized countries are claimed to be basically similar – at least so far as the preferences of young high-income consumers are concerned – and any variation tends to be imputed to local factors peculiar to each market. Globalization therefore appears in the present model as a specific response to a particular configuration of the international market system.

Internationalization theory is often alleged to favour a rather similar strategy. This is because of the theory's emphasis on the public good properties of knowledge developed in the domestic market, and the advantage of exploiting these properties internally through expansion of the firm. In fact, however, most authors in this tradition have been very aware of the 'psychic costs' to the firm of entering foreign markets (Buckley and Casson, 1976). Internalization theorists have tended to assume that all markets are different, so that there is always a cost of entry. Because all markets are different, the scope economies of accrued experience of market entry have not been emphasized in the same way as in the Scandinavian literature. The internalization view has supported the simultaneous approach simply because there is little point in deferring entry if the costs cannot be reduced using experience gained in other markets first. Simultaneous entry is also promoted by the fact that, where technological knowledge is concerned, patents expire and trade secrets leak out, so that early entry into all markets is advisable before the potential monopoly rents are dissipated. Internalization theory, in other words, highlights a particular kind of pre-emptive advantage (see Table 4.3).

Where internalization theorists have argued for sequential entry has generally been in terms of the 'Penrose' effect – that simultaneous internationalization of the firm will overstretch its managerial resources. The Penrose argument is, however, quite distinct from the argument for sequential internationalization based on economies of scope available from the learning process. The two approaches are, in principle, rival explanations of the sequential expansion of the firm, although they can be regarded as complementary and mutually reinforcing within a synthetic view. While this chapter is committed to elaborating the learning approach, it has been useful, from the standpoint of practical application, to have incorporated the Penrose theory within the model as a special case.

The difference between the internalization approach and the globalization approach lies not, therefore, in the recommended internationalization

Table 4.3 Classification of theoretical approaches to internationalization

Foreign markets	*Home and foreign markets*	
	Same	*Different*
Same	Globalization	Scandinavian
Different	–	Internalization

Note: Because globalization assumes that foreign markets are essentially the same as the home market it follows that differences between foreign markets must be small. But in so far as these small differences are idiosyncratic to each market, the logic of simultaneous internationalization will be more secure.

strategy but rather in the perceived profitability of internationalization per se. Because internalization theory recognizes psychic costs that globalization theory discounts, it more often favours the null strategy of remaining at home and licensing the technology to other firms overseas. Licensing to foreign firms with local knowledge of market conditions is an important element of internalization theory precisely because the psychic costs of foreign market entry are fully recognized.

It can be seen that, by elimination, the Scandinavian approach focuses on those situations where foreign markets are unlike the home market but very similar to each other. The older Scandinavian literature associated with the Uppsala school emphasizes the need to expand in stages in a manner reminiscent of (but not coincident with) the product cycle model (Vernon, 1979). The more recent literature, on the other hand, emphasizes the importance of speeding up the learning process by improving communication between foreign subsidiaries.

Recall that the net advantage of the sequential approach depends on, amongst other things, the excess of the cost of investigation over the cost of communication between subsidiaries (Table 4.4). To encourage subsidiaries to learn from each other, it is desirable not only to improve headquarters–subsidiary communication but to encourage subsidiaries to communicate directly with each other. Organizational learning needs to be decentralized, in other words. This is an important aspect of the thinking underlying the 'heterarchy' or the 'network' firm (Chesnais, 1988; Hedlund, 1986). Whilst the discussion of the heterarchies tends to focus on the organizational restructuring of the mature multinational enterprise, the present model emphasizes the more general advantage to the firm of building up the heterarchy in stepwise fashion from the very start of the internationalization process.

As indicated earlier, learning by doing is a satisfactory alternative to systematic investigation if the costs of making a mistake are not too great. To control these costs, firms will tend to make small commitments to begin with, and only increase their commitments once experience has been gained. Thus sequential entry into markets is accompanied by incremental expansion in these markets over time. Because systematic investigation reduces the

Table 4.4 Information gathering versus investment deferral decisions

	Do not defer, commit resource time t	*Defer commitment of resource 'real options'*
Do not collect information (measure things you would otherwise not know)	1 Gung-ho investor	3 Cautious but uninformed investor
Do collect information research prudentially	2 Uninformed investor	4 Sophisticated investor

likelihood of mistakes (in the model above it eliminates it altogether – which is clearly a very extreme case) it supports a greater initial commitment. Thus sequential expansion will be associated with different degrees of initial commitment according to the way that knowledge of markets is acquired. This coincides with the general thrust of the Scandinavian approach.

International joint ventures as real options

International joint ventures (IJVs) are primarily contractual real options. Although an IJV's physical assets may embody a certain degree of flexibility, the distinctive feature of an IJV from an option perspective is the flexibility afforded by the joint ownership arrangement. There are many different types of IJV. This section presents an example which has been chosen to illustrate the option perspective on IJVs in the simplest possible way.

The basic idea is that a partner in an IJV possesses both a 'call option' to buy out the other partner, and a 'put' option to sell out to the other partner, depending upon how the IJV performs in the future (Chi and McGuire, 1996; Kogut and Zander, 1993). The question arises, however, as to why the other partner would be willing to trade on especially favourable terms. One reason is that transaction costs are lower between the partners than they are between ordinary firms because the partners have got to know and trust each other. They share the gains from this trust by trading equity with each other on mutually favourable terms. This means that the partners possess options to trade on these terms instead of on the terms that would prevail if there were no previous connection between them.

Another explanation is that one of the partners is better informed than the other. Their reputation for being better informed gives them an advantage in negotiations over equity purchase. As the IJV evolves, the more sophisticated partner makes offers to the less sophisticated partner which the latter is willing to accept. In this way information rents accrue to the partner that is better at valuing the joint venture, i.e. is better at forecasting the IJV's future stream of profits. This mechanism for appropriating information rents will only work, however, if the other partner receives no rival offers from third parties. One reason why they may not receive such offers is that other firms are not so well informed about the prospects for the IJV because they lack the 'inside knowledge' that is shared by the partner firms. They therefore lack the confidence to make rival offers. The other partner may not possess sufficiently tangible evidence to go out and solicit such offers to test the offers received from the more sophisticated firm. It is this case of asymmetric information which is the basis of the example that follows.

Consider two firms which can go into partnership by sharing ownership of equity on a 50 : 50 basis. One firm provides finance and the other provides the human capital, such as the ideas. The issue is analysed from the standpoint of the financial investor, which is the more sophisticated firm. This investor, it is assumed, has identified a small high-technology start-up venture which requires capital in order to fund further R&D. The owner of the start up will sell 50 per cent of his equity for five units, or sell out completely for 10 units. These sales must be effected at the outset (period 1)), before the outcome of the R&D is known.

In the future (period 2)) the outcome of the R&D is revealed to the owners of the firm. The financier knows that if the research is successful then the project will be worth 20 units, whereas if it is unsuccessful then it will be worthless. The partner, however, is not so good at valuing projects, and believes that if the outcome is successful then it will be worth only 12 units, whilst if it is unsuccessful, it will still be worth 7 units. These beliefs are reflected in negotiations between the firms, in which the sophisticated firm extracts maximum rents from the unsophisticated one. The unsophisticated partner is willing to sell his 50 per cent stake for $12 - 5 = 7$ units if the outcome is good, and to buy the financial investor's stake for $7 - 5 = 2$ units if the outcome is bad. The outcome does not become public knowledge, so these offers will not be affected by rival bids. The partners come to an informal understanding on these terms when they enter the IJV. Because of the trust between them, they both honour these terms in the following period, even though their initial contributions have been 'sunk' by the start of the second period.

The financial investor has three main alternatives:

1. Acquire the firm immediately;
2. Enter a joint venture immediately and review the situation in the next period;
3. Avoid the project altogether.

If he participates in the IJV then it always pays him to exercise the call option if the outcome is good because the unsophisticated partner undervalues the project. Thus instead of earning 50 per cent of 20 units, namely 10 units, the investor can pay out an additional seven units to obtain an additional 10 units, i.e. the entire 20 units, for himself. Similarly, it always pays to him exercise the put option when the outcome is bad. This is because the unsophisticated partner overvalues the project, since he is willing to pay two units to buy more of a project that is actually worthless. Thus the sophisticated partner will not continue with the IJV in its initial form, but will either take over the IJV, or divest his share of it, depending on the outcome of the R&D.

Let the probability of a successful outcome perceived at the outset by the sophisticated investor be p. Then the expected profits of the three strategies are:

$$v_1 = -10 + 20p \tag{4.18}$$

$$v_2 = -5 + (20 - 7)p + 2(1 - p) = -3 + 11p \tag{4.19}$$

$$v_3 = 0 \tag{4.20}$$

The first term in equation (4.18) is the purchase price for an outright acquisition, and the second term is the profit from the entire project when its outcome is good. The first term in equation (4.19) is the cost of buying a stake in the IJV. The second term is the expected profit generated by exercising the call option, and the third term is the expected profit generated by exercising the put option.

The solution is

$$i = \begin{matrix} 1 & \text{if } p > 0.78 \\ 2 & \text{if } 0.27 < p < 0.78 \\ 3 & \text{if } p < 0.27 \end{matrix} \tag{4.21}$$

The solution is illustrated in Figure 4.8. As before, the expected profit associated with the ith strategy ($i = 1, 2$) is indicated by the height of the schedule V_iV_i', with the horizontal axis indicating the expected profit of

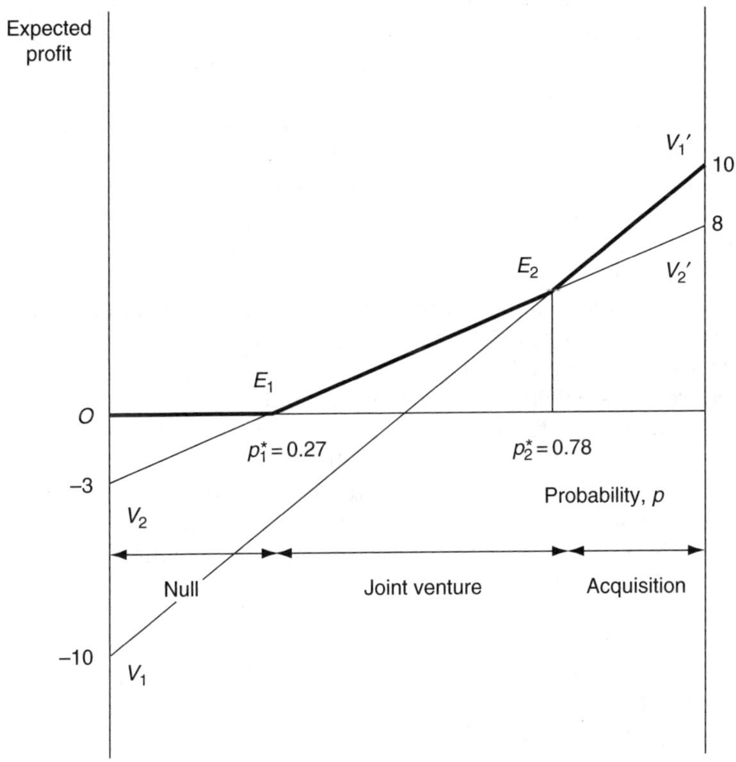

Figure 4.8 An international joint venture as a real option

the null strategy (strategy 3)). The envelope $OE_1E_2V_1'$ indicates the maximum attainable profit. The IJV is the preferred strategy between the critical values $p_1^* = 0.27$, $p_2^* = 0.78$, which correspond to the switch points E_1, E_2. The figure reveals the IJV as a classic option strategy – namely one that is pursued when the investor is highly uncertain about the outcome of a project.

It is possible to extend this model by taking the exercise of options as a repeated process but this is beyond the scope of this short chapter.

Conclusions

Real options provide a way of rationalizing many practical aspects of business behaviour which until recently defied analysis: the seeming irrationality of procrastination and delay in committing resources to new foreign markets, and the cautious incremental approach to investment that is so often pursued once the market is entered.

The application of real options to IB issues has been discouraged by confusions over the relation between real options and financial options. This chapter has sought to clear up some of this confusion by demonstrating that a single set of four key principles underlie both branches of options theory. The principal difference between the two branches of theory lies in the fact that one deals mainly with tradable assets and the other deals mainly with non-tradable ones.

Options reduce risk by providing the flexibility to respond to new information when it becomes available. The key to a successful exploitation of real options is to foresee the kind of information that is likely to become available, and plan the options to exploit this information from an early stage. Flexibility can take many forms: IJVs provide flexibility through contractual options, whereas small reversible investments in versatile assets provide flexibility in a non-contractual form. These forms of flexibility can be combined – for example, by holding a portfolio of IJVs, each of which operates versatile assets, and utilizes information by-products from other IJVs, as well as supplying its own information by-products to them.

This chapter has introduced and synthesized ideas rather than presented an exhaustive treatise on its subject. Much work remains to be done in producing algebraic versions of the numerical models presented above, and in simulating the algebraic models to determine the sensitivity of various option strategies to the parameters which govern them. This chapter has focused on applications to manufacturing, but real options also apply to marketing and R&D (see, for example, Huchzermeier and Loch, 1997). New models can be generated by modifying the assumptions of the models presented above. The new models can be made more realistic than the ones presented here – for example, by introducing oligopolistic rivalry (Lambrecht and Perraudin, 1996) – but they are also likely to be more complicated.

Insights from these models can be used to construct 'dynamic' versions of existing static theories. The real option perspective can be applied to standard IB theories, including classic theories such as the product cycle model and its variants (Vernon, 1966, 1974, 1979). The real option perspective can provide a formal analysis of the leads and lags in the internalization process which is missing from many orthodox accounts of the subject.

Note

1. This chapter relies heavily on three earlier pieces of work: Casson (1994), Buckley and Casson (1998) and particularly Casson (1999).

References

Buckley, P. J. and Casson, M. C. (1981) 'Optimal Timing of a Foreign Direct Investment'. *Economic Journal*, vol. 91, pp. 75–87.

Buckley, P. J. and Casson, M. C. (1998) 'Models of Multinational Enterprise'. *Journal of International Business Studies*, vol. 29, no. 1, pp. 21–44.

Buckley, P. J. and Chapman, M. (1997) 'The Perception and Measurement of Transaction Cost'. *Cambridge Journal of Economics*, vol. 21, no. 2, pp. 127–45.

Campa, J. M. (1994) 'Multinational Investment under Uncertainty in the Chemical Processing Industries'. *Journal of International Business Studies*, vol. 25, no. 3, pp. 557–78.

Capel, J. (1992) 'How to Service a Foreign Market under Uncertainty: a Real Option Approach'. *European Journal of Political Economy*, vol. 8, pp. 455–75.

Casson, M. (1996) 'Internationalisation as a Learning Process: a Model of Corporate Growth and Geographical Diversification'. In V. N. Balasubramanyan and D. Sapsford (eds), *The Economics of International Investment*. Cheltenham: Edward Elgar.

Chi, T. and McGuire, D. J. (1996) 'Collaborative Ventures and Value of Learning: Integrating the Transaction Cost and Strategic Option Perspectives on the Choice of Market Entry Modes'. *Journal of International Business Studies*, vol. 27, no. 2, pp. 285–307.

DeMeza, D. and van der Ploeg, F. (1987) 'Production Flexibility as a Motive for Multinationality'. *Journal of Industrial Economics*, vol. 35, no. 3, pp. 343–51.

Dempster, M. A. H. and Pliska, S. R. (eds) (1997) *Mathematics of Derivative Securities*. Cambridge: Cambridge University Press.

Dixit, A. and Pindyck, R. S. (1994) *Investments under Uncertainty*. Princeton, NJ: Princeton University Press.

Hirshleifer, J. and Riley, J. G. (1992) *The Analytics of Uncertainty and Information*. Cambridge: Cambridge University Press.

Huchzermeier, A. and Loch, C. H. (1997) 'Evaluating R&D Projects as Real Options: Why More Variability is not Always Better'. Fontainebleau: INSEAD, Working Paper 97/105/TM.

Johanson, J. and Vahlne, J.-E. (1977) 'The Internationalization Process of the Firm – a Model of Knowledge Development and Increasing Foreign Market Commitments. *Journal of International Business Studies*, vol. 8, no. 1, pp. 23–32.

Johanson, J. and Wiedersheim-Paul, F. (1975) 'The Internationalization of the Firm: Four Swedish Cases'. *Journal of Management Studies*, October, pp. 305–22.

Jorgenson, D. W. (1963) 'Capital Theory and Investment Behaviour'. *American Economic Review*, vol. 53, pp. 247–59.

Jorgenson, D. W. (1967) 'Investment Behaviour and the Production Function'. *Bell Journal of Economics and Management Science*, vol. 3, pp. 220–51.

Kogut, B. and Kulatilaka, N. (1994) 'Operating Flexibility, Global Manufacturing and the Option Value of a Multinational Network'. *Management Science*, vol. 40, no. 1, pp. 123–39.

Kogut, B. and Zander, U. (1993) 'Knowledge of the Firm and the Evolutionary Theory of the Multinational Corporation'. *Journal of International Business Studies*, vol. 24, no. 4, pp. 625–45.

Kulatilaka, N. and Perotti, E. C. (1998) 'Strategic Growth Options'. *Management Science*, vol. 44, no. 8, pp. 1021–31.

Lambrecht, B. and Perraudin, W. (1996) 'Real Options and Pre-emption'. Discussion Paper, Department of Economics, Birkbeck College, University of London.

Marschak, J. and Radner, R. (1972) *Economic Theory of Teams*. New Haven, Conn.: Yale University Press.

Mello, A. S., Parsons, J. E. and Triantis, A. J. (1995) 'An Integrated Model of Multinational Flexibility and Hedging Policies'. *Journal of International Economics*, vol. 39, pp. 27–51.

Rangan, S. (1997) 'Do Multinationals Shift Production in Response to Exchange Rate Changes? Do Their Responses Vary by Nationality? Evidence from 1977–1993'. Fontainebleau: INSEAD, Working Paper 97/84/SM.

Rivoli, P. and Salorio, E. (1996) 'Foreign Direct Investment under Uncertainty'. *Journal of International Business Studies*, vol. 27, no. 2, pp. 335–54.

Schmitzler, A. (1991) *Flexibility and Adjustment to Information in Sequential Decision Problems: a Systematic Approach*. Berlin: Springer-Verlag. Lecture Notes in Economics and Mathematical Systems, 371.

Shackle, G. L. S. (1970) *Expectation, Enterprise and Profit*. Cambridge: Cambridge University Press.

Van Mieghem (1998) 'Investment Strategies for Flexible Resources'. *Management Science*, vol. 44, no. 8, pp. 1071–7.

Vernon, R. (1966) 'International Investment and International Trade in the Product Cycle'. *Quarterly Journal of Economics*, vol. 80, pp. 190–207.

Vernon, R. (1974) 'The Location of Economic Activity'. In J. H. Dunning (ed.), *Economic Analysis and the Multinational Enterprise*. London: Allen & Unwin, pp. 89–114.

Vernon, R. (1979) 'The Product Cycle Hypothesis in a New International Environment. *Oxford Bulletin of Economics and Statistics*, vol. 41, pp. 255–67.

Wiseman, J. (1989) *Cost, Choice and Political Economy*. Aldershot: Edward Elgar.

5
Globalization and the End of Competition: a Critical Review of Rent-seeking Multinationals

with Pervez N. Ghauri

Introduction

This chapter suggests that, for a variety of reasons, there is likely to be a renaissance of critical writing on the multinational enterprises (MNEs) in the first decade of the new millennium. The chapter first revisits the critical literature on MNEs of the 1950s to 1970s, in order to refresh our minds on the basis for that criticism. It then suggests a number of areas on which criticism is likely to focus – the strategy of multinational firms, bargaining power of multinationals versus the state, development issues, the decline of competition, and distributional issues (affecting unskilled workers in particular). These are old concerns, but the problems are emerging in new ways because of the new configuration of the globalizing economy.

The chapter concentrates on issues in international political economy. It does not deal with issues of globalization that are related to the decline of local indigenous cultures, felt to be under attack from the homogenizing pressure of globalization. This is not because cultural issues are unimportant or intrinsically separable from political economy, it is simply for ease of focus of exposition.

Critical literature to the mid-1970s

Edith Penrose (1956) wrote a classic piece, which pointed out the controversial aspects of foreign investment where, in spite of the successful establishment of a subsidiary, the foreign capital and its possible benefits for the local economy may be largely transmitted out of the host country. It also explained why the returns on the initial investment could be exceptionally high. This illustrates the 'gambler's earnings hypothesis' (Barlow and Wender, 1955), which likens the foreign investor to a compulsive gambler who constantly reinvests his winnings in the game, until he makes a killing, then he withdraws a large amount (in comparison with the initial stake). Penrose's paper discussed the implications of this form of foreign investment for the economic policies of less industrialized host countries. It revealed that for the year ending 1954, GM earned a return of 590 per cent on its original dollar investment in Australia. The debate started by this incident led to Australian economists concluding that the country should use 'some caution in giving indiscriminate encouragement to foreign investment' and that the country should concentrate less on attracting American capital. The imputed behaviour of the multinational firm clearly has detrimental implications for the host country – in particular, the negative impact on the balance of payments in the withdrawal period and the associated instability. This is an interesting case, also because it is related to a typical 'import replacement' investment, as sought by most developing countries at that time.

This study evaluated a number of options the host country could have in such a situation, but concluded that once a foreign firm was established, it was not economically sound to limit its growth or to acquire it wholly or partly. From the firm's perspective, the establishment of a foreign subsidiary was no different from establishing a subsidiary in the domestic market. Other than that, it entailed higher risk and thus led to the fact that higher returns were expected through this growth. Moreover, even if the profitability in a particular industry declined due to increasing competition over the years, an MNE was able to diversify more easily and to move its capital to areas that ensured higher returns on the capital.

A second important study by Stephen Hymer (1991) examined 'two basic laws of development'; namely the law of uneven economic development and the law of increasing firm size. The study strove for a futuristic viewpoint and claimed to look towards the year 2000. Written in 1971, it opened with the statement that until then most MNEs came from the United States, where the firms had achieved the largest size and development. But now (i.e. 1971), European corporations were beginning to 'see the world as their Oyster'. It claimed that the multinationalization would continue through giant firms from both sides of the Atlantic. Moreover, although initially dominated by the US firms, eventually some kind of oligopolistic equilibrium will be achieved with a new structure of international industrial organization. It also suggested that while North Atlantic MNEs will dominate, a geographical division of labour and dependence relationship, with one being superior and the others being subordinate, would emerge. This situation would lead to tensions and conflicts and to further uneven development.

The study started with the evolution of MNEs, 'beasts' or 'the US corporate monsters'. It claimed that the Hudson Bay Company, or the British East India Company, or large mining and plantation enterprises were not the forerunners of MNEs. Instead, it was small-scale capitalist enterprises in manufacturing who were the forerunners of MNEs. The contributing factors were the industrial revolution and the railways, as suggested also by Chandler (1977), until we came to the stage where if a firm was to grow steadily, it had continuously to introduce new products. Thus product development and marketing replaced production as the factor dominating growth. A new divisionalized organizational form emerged, which also led to an increased outward FDI. In the 1950s and 1960s US FDI increased at a rate of 10 per cent per annum. The rapid growth in Europe and Japan was one of the major factors stimulating this growth in FDI.

Using the Chandler–Redlich (1961) scheme, it suggested that MNEs would spread their day-to-day, i.e. manufacturing, activities all over the globe, thus diffusing industrialization to developing countries and creating new centres of production. The other activities, i.e. coordination and communication, would stay closer to the head offices, which would be completely centralized. As a result, 'the best' highly skilled and highly paid manpower would concentrate in the major cities of the US and Europe, while lower level skills and manpower would remain in other parts and cities of the world. Most new products would be developed in the 'major' cities and, once accepted there, would travel to other countries. MNEs would thus be greatly interested in the markets of these less developed countries. This system would automatically force developing countries not to develop skilled manpower above a certain level, as there would be no market for their skills. The local governments would not even be able to invest in their infrastructure, communication, education and health, to achieve growth, as it would not be able to finance these investments. They would not be able to tax MNEs to acquire finance, due to the ability of these corporations to manipulate transfer prices or to move to low-tax countries, whereas the home countries of these MNEs would be able to tax these corporations as a whole, as well as through their highly paid manpower.

The relationship between MNEs and developing countries would also be of a superior and subordinate nature. The study concluded that if MNEs could solve the following four problems for developing countries, they could survive and have continued growth. The four issues were:

1. MNEs must break foreign exchange constraints and provide local governments with imported goods for capital formation and modernization;
2. They must help local governments in training labour and industrialization;
3. They must solve the urban food problems created by growth;
4. They must keep the excluded two-thirds of the population under control.

Hymer's vision represents a stark picture of opposition between the interests of multinational firms and those of the populations of developing countries.

Streeten (1974) dealt with the theory of development from the perspective of the 1970s. He started with the assumption that countries were poor because they were poor and thus needed large injections of foreign capital because they could not raise their own savings. The low investment ratio was considered both the cause and effect of poverty. While discussing MNEs and developing countries, he suggested that the bulk of FDI in developing countries consisted of the reinvestment of local earnings. The benefits of MNEs in terms of the training of local labour (investments in human capital), management, science and technology, and R&D depended largely upon the ability and willingness of the host government to pursue the 'right' policies. The policy issues thus became of prime importance and one could see MNEs filling in the 'gaps' in the policy that local governments could not achieve on their own, such as: savings, foreign exchange, tax revenues, and skills. There were some other contributions that MNEs could make, such as: appropriate technology, entrepreneurship, balance of bargaining power, and providing a network of relationships to local firms.

In a macro-economic sense, MNEs could contribute towards job creation, import substitution, and more efficient market structure. It was, however, very difficult to measure or assess the contribution of MNEs. Moreover, there were a number of contradictions in these contributions, for example, MNEs could improve foreign exchange earnings but at the same time could impose a foreign exchange burden. Another problem raised when assessing the contribution of MNEs was that many of the actions of an MNE were dependent on individuals responsible for its affairs or on host government policies. Moreover, it was suggested that a number of these activities could have been equally well or better done by other means than MNEs.

MNEs were often blamed for:

1. Uneven development, dualism and inequality;
2. A fragmented consumption pattern only for a small proportion of the population;
3. Local funds being wrongly allocated, not in accordance with social needs;
4. Influencing government policies, often unfavourable to development;
5. Creating political frictions by the suspicion that foreign capital controlled assets and jobs.

Streeten's analysis highlighted the problem of transfer pricing and the bargaining power of MNEs (often due to monopolistic or oligopolistic market structures). Because of these powers, MNEs often end up with very beneficial contracts while negotiating with host governments. Even if the specific contribution of the MNE is technical knowledge, and if this knowledge bestowed bargaining power, why had competition in the market not eroded this power? Why had there been so few inventions of low-cost, simple, appropriate products? Why did industrialized countries with a comparative advantage in manufacturing, protect, often at high cost, their agricultural and other sectors, instead of exchanging low-cost machinery and durable consumer goods for the agricultural exports of developing countries?

The analysis of Barnet and Muller (1975) was typical of the critical literature from the 1970s. It addressed the myth of development, 'the struggle of human beings to realize their full potential' and an evaluation of FDI. According to them, the 1960s were considered to be the 'decade of development' and the most important issue was to see whether the 'free world model' or the 'communist model' would survive. By the end of the 1960s, the gap between the rich and the poor world was widening. Moreover, the gap within countries was also widening, a small minority was becoming affluent but for a large majority the miseries were increasing. Yet, in absolute terms there has been growth in most countries. At the same time, global corporations proclaimed themselves to be the engines of growth. This could only be judged by understanding or defining 'development'. The positive impact of MNEs as regards job opportunities could be compared with the negative impact of maintaining and increasing poverty and having conflicting interests to those of developing countries.

The primary objective of MNEs was profit maximization, thus MNEs used all their resources and power to achieve that, which had an adverse effect on the distribution of income and employment levels in developing countries. The claim that MNEs supplied capital to poor countries was a metaphor and not reality. Most of the investments came from reinvested earnings derived from the local market, while most of the profits were generated from local resources with more than 50 per cent being repatriated back to developed countries. As a net result the capital or resources were moving from the developing to the developed world. It is a proven fact that where it was to their advantage, MNEs widely overvalued their imports into developing countries. By taking into consideration the overpricing of imports and the underpricing of exports, repatriated profits, royalties, and fees repatriated to head office, we could really evaluate the advantages or disadvantages of MNEs for developing countries. There was no doubt that the import of technology had a major impact on poor countries. In fact, the technology dependence was an obstacle to development, as when technology was controlled from abroad all funds for R&D also went abroad.

After these critical studies most of the literature of late 1970s, and of the 1980s and 1990s, has presented MNEs and FDI as positive factors and essential for economic development and the well-being of societies, rich or poor. Recent literature, as we show below, is beginning to highlight certain problems in the relationship between states and MNEs and a new dissatisfaction with the new world order is beginning to appear as the riots against the World Trade Organization (WTO) meeting in Seattle (December 1999) illustrate.

The strategy of multinational firms

Buckley and Casson (1998) and Ghauri (1999) suggest that internal and external pressures on the multinational enterprise in the 1990s are producing a new strategic imperative – flexibility. The search for flexibility is a reaction to external volatility (e.g. in exchange rates) and to attempts to reduce monopolistic 'pinch-points' (e.g. single supply sources, tie-in to particular locations). The search for flexibility leads to (vertical) disintegration and foreign direct investments being seen as 'real options'. This results in a new ownership strategy with networks of joint ventures and a new location strategy based on 'hub and spoke' operations where central facilities (e.g. manufacturing) are augmented by decentralized activities (e.g. distribution). These two strategies can be combined so that wholly owned central facilities such as finance, production and R&D are combined with dispersed joint ventures in marketing, distribution and warehousing. The existence of increasingly integrated regional economic unions (EU, NAFTA) facilitates this strategy.

The ability of multinational firms to appropriate rent by adjusting their foreign market servicing strategies, partly in response to national governmental policies (Buckley, 1996), enhances their flexibility and their bargaining power. Buckley shows that the range of policies open to multinational firms makes broadbrush policies untenable, because in each policy cell (exporting, licensing, foreign direct investment), government policies will have both positive and negative effects. Targeted policies, moreover, are difficult to design, given the dynamics of the firm's evolving foreign market servicing strategies and the links between the different elements in the firm's global value chains.

The result of these strategies is to create uncertainty for the host countries. Locational policies create difficulties in that multinationals are becoming more 'footloose' and are liable to move 'offshore plants' in response to changing incentives, demand and supply conditions. The search for flexibility also means that multinationals may engineer internal competition between competing plants within the same firm, with weaker plants being winnowed out by failures in internal tendering.

The arguments for policy intervention are weakening. Krugman (1994), in reviewing the arguments for interventionist policies based on externalities and strategic trade considerations, concluded that the optimal policy set is so sensitive to technological and behavioural parameters that the results of intervention are uncertain, even in areas where externality and monopoly arguments abound. Further, the information available to government policy makers is likely to be partial, out of date and biased (not in the least by representations on the part of the rent-seekers). This analysis has important implications for bargaining power.

Bargaining power

Arguments about bargaining power between multinationals and governments have moved on in the decades since the 1970s. The move from confrontation to cooperation (Dunning, 1991) or from government policies as constraint to conflict and bargaining and then to cooperation (Boddewyn, 1992) is a commonplace. However, the nature of the interaction between governments and multinational firms is much more complex than a simple two-person game, be it competitive or cooperative. Stopford and Strange (1991) developed a view that multinationals and governments are colluding in order to acquire market share for 'their' firms. Strange (1997) went further and argued that 'globalisation by shifting power from states to firms, has allowed international bureaucracies to undermine that accountability'. This leads to dilemmas, not only economic, but also environmental (lacking countervailing power, corporations polluting the planet) and political (lack of accountability, transparency and greater insecurity for citizens because the safety net of the state is eroded). This 'retreat of the state' (Strange, 1996) leads to a vacuum of governance.

Host country policies that have changed in this period include the relaxing of controls, increasing incentives to inward FDI, privatization, provision of guarantees and arbitration. We have seen a trajectory of MNE–emerging market relations where tension increased during 1950–1975 and then reduced, whilst the host country gained bargaining strength in the first period, which relaxed as the MNE gained ascendancy (Dunning, 1992, 1994; Vernon, 1966; Wells, 1998). The reason for these shifts in bargaining power suggests three alternative scenarios for the future – 'more balanced', 'cyclical' and a continuation of present trends. Jenkins believes that it is most likely that a cyclical shift will occur, taking us back to an increase in host country bargaining power and increased tension. Even those who doubt this outcome will find much interest in these projections (Jenkins, 1999). Figure 5.1 illustrates the history of the balance in bargaining between MNEs and host countries from the 1950s to the millennium with projections

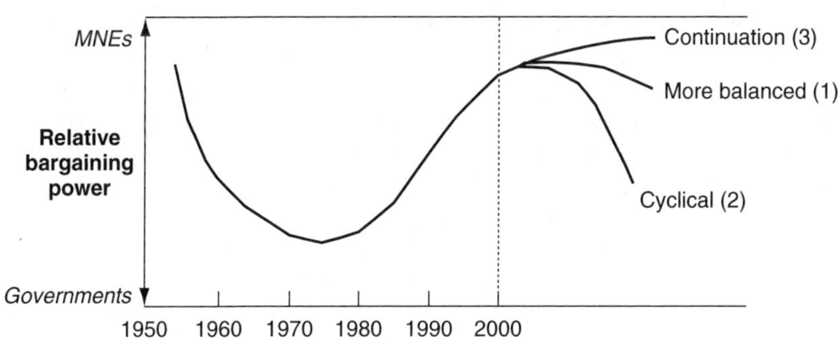

Figure 5.1 Bargaining power of governments versus MNEs: 1950 to the millennium, and three future scenarios

indicated after 2000. Recent developments suggest a continuation of current trends, the MNEs gradually accreting bargaining power.

If we re-examine some of the issues above in the light of the Asian crisis, we can see that the penetration of northern multinationals in the South will increase. As asset prices fall in developing economies, more of the firms denominated in these assets will be acquired by northern multinationals from strong currency countries. UNCTAD figures show this happening (1998). The symmetry of the relationship will be further distorted by the decline of southern multinationals in the North, which will be increasingly unable to fund outward FDI and which will be vulnerable to takeover, considering the increasing size and resources of northern MNEs due to a wave of big mergers and acquisitions. The balance of FDI will thus swing ever more decisively to the northern firms.

All of this, of course, is not without cost to the multinationals. Prahalad and Lieberthal (1998) say:

> In order to participate effectively in the big emerging markets, multinationals will increasingly have to reconfigure their resource base, rethink their cost structure, redesign their product development process, and challenge their assumptions about the cultural mix of their top managers. In short, they will have to develop a new mind-set and adopt new business models to achieve global competitiveness in the post imperialist age.

Prahalad and Lieberthal thus predict the end of corporate imperialism and a more 'accommodatory' stance by multinational firms in emerging markets. Their position approximates to the 'more balanced' scenario.

There are also grounds for believing that bargaining power will continue to move in the direction of multinational firms. They have a wider choice of investment locations as new 'emerging countries' put themselves forward as export platforms – usually on a tax-free basis. Their proprietary technology is widely sought after by host countries and their branded products sell at a premium to upscale consumers globally. Flexible manufacturing and production controlled by IT systems mean that more and more of the activities of MNEs are footloose. They can use the threat of switching locations to squeeze concessions from host countries. We thus have reasons to believe that MNE–government relationship is shifting towards MNEs gaining more power, as depicted in scenario (3) in Figure 5.1.

States are, however, not without recourse to new reserves of power. Domicile in national locations still requires state guarantees of security and underwriting of property rights. Indeed, it is the inability of the states in transition economies to underwrite such rights, which is a major cause of their failure to achieve secure growth (Buckley and Ghauri, 1994; see particularly Casson's chapter, 1994). Private appropriation of the rewards of entrepreneurial activity is a key driver of growth but achieving the legitimacy of this process is not easy to accomplish in many societies – notably where it contributes to the already huge inequalities and where private wealth has heretofore been discouraged by state institutions. The role of the state in preventing the growth of corruption (in its own long-term interests) is becoming a major location factor. These issues are far more prevalent in developing than in developed countries.

Developed versus developing countries

In the discussion of states versus firms, a special reference is always made to governments of developing countries. The role of the government and government bodies from developing countries is relatively more crucial than the role played by these bodies in developed countries. The government bodies in developing countries regulate their economies not only to secure the best interest of their population, but also to safeguard local firms. Governments aim to plan their economies to seek goals which they believe a purely market outcome will not secure. These actions thus take the stance of developing countries versus developed countries, or governments from developing countries versus MNEs. Thus, we can expect an inharmonious conjunction of the strategies of MNEs and governments' policies. However, we need to consider the fact that markets are not perfect and both firms and governments are attempting to appropriate rents in a world of imperfect markets (Buckley, 1996). This opens up the possibility of collusion between governments and MNEs in dividing rents and mitigating conflicts between them. The game is not a simple one and its rules are constantly changing. It is this game which is taking place in a globalizing world where markets are becoming increasingly interdependent, and this is critical in allocating the benefits of improving technology, communication, productivity and output.

In terms of strategic decision-making, firms undertake FDI to achieve three main objectives:

1. 'Market seeking': firms invest in countries where they see a large and/or rapidly growing market, for example, recent investments in China and India;
2. 'Efficiency seeking': firms invest in countries where they can achieve efficiency in cost reduction due to lower operating costs, for example, recent investment by Philips and other consumer electronic products companies in Singapore and Malaysia;
3. 'Resource seeking': firms invest in countries to get access to raw materials or other inputs, for example, investments by oil companies in the Middle East or textile companies in India and Pakistan.

Some investments may include more than one of the above elements and some of the motives are specific; for example, in banking a number of investments are made because banks follow their home country clients into the emerging markets. Firms in oligopolistic industries gain economies of scale and other advantages that enable them to be superior to local competitors in host countries (Hymer, 1976). Moreover, firms choose FDI when the transaction costs associated with other modes (such as licensing) are higher (Buckley and Casson, 1976). FDI thus enforces the internationalization of transactions.

For years, the absence of strong local competitors in most developing markets was one of the reasons that the FDI flow was predominantly from the industrialized countries of the North to the developing countries of the South. The import substitution and protectionist strategies of most emerging markets made FDI a more viable mode than trade to gain access to these markets. Now government-induced market imperfections are declining, there are some strong and competitive local firms that can beat off the entry of foreign firms. Moreover, as most of the countries are moving away from protectionist politics and are opening up their markets to all types of entry by foreign firms, the nature of the resource flow has thus changed. According to a UNCTC (now UNCTAD, Division on Transnationals) (1992) study, 26 developing countries had already changed over the period 1977 to 1987 towards more hospitable and less restrictive policies towards FDI. However, in the last decade macro-economic determinants rather than the micro-economic determinants mentioned above, have become more important. Factors such as: the investments or capital flow to countries where it can achieve highest returns, the market size or potential for local sales and benefits which can be achieved through local sourcing have become more important (Brewer, 1993; Contractor, 1991; Pfefferman and Madarassy, 1992).

In addition to the above, it has been suggested that the investments flow to the markets where a certain level of FDI is already in existence. This leads to synergetic effects such as foreign firms buying from each other. Moreover, the presence of a number of foreign firms helps to develop specialized know-how and skills with regard to the availability of skilled labour, suppliers and distribution networks. This also means that firms investing abroad go to countries with a good quality infrastructure, communications, transport, energy, and a certain degree of industrialization. Thus, it is not surprising that the stock of FDI in a given country is often a good predictor of future FDI. It has also been established that although relative cost is still important, direct labour costs in particular are not as important as previously. On the other hand, costs related to highly skilled labour and well-educated manpower have become more important (Pfefferman and Madrassy, 1992).

Privatization (the transfer of productive assets from public to private ownership) has been part of most structural adjustment policies in LDCs since the 1980s. It has been undertaken to achieve a variety of objectives, such as enhanced economic efficiency, reduction of financial deficits and reducing the role of the state. If we summarize experiences with privatization strategies showing that there is now a sufficient body of evidence to review its progress made and to assess what works and what does not, we end up with the cautionary point that privatization alone is unlikely to ease significantly the burden of the state-owned sector in many less developed countries.

The emergence of China as a major player in the world economy has already had an impact equal to that of Japan in earlier decades of the post-war world. An initial, almost blanket acceptance of FDI has now become more targeted in terms of priority sectors and regions. China represents a non-uniform environment for the inward investor and there are currently difficulties in the implementation and transparency of business law, contractual difficulties, regional differences and uncertainties about the direction of future economic policies. These challenges need to be addressed by careful adaptation of company strategies.

We are in a state where MNE–host country relations in middle-income countries have fully emerged onto the world stage, leaving behind a group of largely inert less developed countries which have so far been bypassed by globalization. Increasing location 'tournaments', to attract FDI, may have reduced the benefits to the host countries as have the increasing skill of the managers of MNEs in making their investments more 'footloose'. Corresponding skills on the part of host countries to make FDI sticky are not developing at the same rate. Differences within developing countries may lead to divergence between those which can develop the velocity to catch up and those which will fall behind as the world economy becomes more interdependent.

In both advanced and less developed countries, the period from the mid-1970s to the millennium has generally been one where the activist functions of the state have declined. This has been more true in equity-related policies (the right-hand side of Table 5.1) than in addressing market failure. Indeed, the role of the state at the turn of the millennium is much more related to market-enhancing policies than heretofore. On the left-hand side of Table 5.1, the state has become more active in addressing externalities, regulating monopoly and attempting to redress information imperfections than in previous decades. The prevailing fashion for 'competitiveness' has led to increasing attempts to go further than this in fostering 'dynamic comparative advantage' by subsidizing and otherwise encouraging clustering of industry (often in a fashion which is competitive with other states) – even within a customs unions (the EU is a prime example) and encouragement of 'indigenous' research and development (Cantwell, 1989).

These market-enhancing state policies, fuelled by the rhetoric of competitiveness (Porter, 1990), have encouraged competitive bidding for inward foreign direct investment and led to escalation in the effective locational subsidy for multinational firms. As the next section shows, there has been no effective international control, or even coordination, of the process.

Following the collapse of the state-dominated and centrally planned economies, the Asian crisis and firms increasingly gaining monopoly powers, there is a general feeling that the functions of state require reformulating and refocusing. The main problem in redefining the state's role is that the basic conditions are constantly changing. Market failure and the concern for equality provide for economic rationale for government intervention. However, there is no guarantee that any such intervention will benefit society. As we have seen in the Asian crisis, government failure is equally possible as market failure. Thus, the challenge is to see that the political process and institutional structures get the incentives right, so that the interventions actually improve social welfare (IBRD, 1997). The task of the state is first to match the state's role to its existing capability – to establish the institutional rules and norms that will enable the state to provide collective goods and services efficiently – and secondly, to reinvigorate the state's capability through rules, partnerships, competitive pressures, outside and within the state. According to IBRD, the functions of the state can be represented as a continuum from activities that should not be undertaken without state intervention, to activities in which the state plays an activist role in coordinating the market or redistributing assets, as illustrated in Table 5.1.

First, countries with low state capability need to focus first on minimal basic functions, such as: provision of public goods, such as property rights, macroeconomic stability and basic infrastructure. Second, there are intermediate functions such as the management of environment, regulation of monopolies and provision of social benefits. Again, in these functions it is not a question of whether the government should or should not intervene, but rather how best to intervene. In this case, government can work together with market and society. Third, states with strong capabilities should play a more active role in dealing with problems related to market imperfections. Experience from the Asian crisis has strengthened the view that states should play an active role in promoting markets through industrial and financial policy. Rethinking the role of the state also means that it has to explore alternative instruments and ways to enhance the effectiveness of its policies. The regulatory role of the state has become broader and more complex than before. The regulatory action needs to fit with the capabilities of state regulatory agencies and the sophistication of the market. The state's responsibility for providing basic services – education, health, etc. – has become doubtful. The state's responsibility has to be based on its capabilities and the relative strength of the market and society. To protect the weaker part of society and to improve equality it has to differentiate between insurance against the unexpected (unemployment, etc.) and providing a minimum level of living conditions for the poorest.

Table 5.1 Reinvigorating functions of state

State capabilities	*Handling market failure*	*Improving equality*
Minimal functions	Providing basic public goods and services	Protecting the poorest
Intermediate functions	Management of environment Regulating monopolies Providing social benefits	Providing social insurance
Activist functions	Coordinating markets and private activities	Redistribution of assets

Source: Based on IBRD (1997: 27).

Decline of competition

This scenario takes place against a world economy that exhibits strong signs that, in many markets, competition is decreasing. This exacerbates problems where little countervailing power exists. At least six factors may be adduced for the argument that globalization is associated with the decline of competition in many markets. These are:

1. The oligopolistic structure of markets and the associated strategic behaviour of multinational enterprises;
2. The emergence of alliance capitalism and the competition-reducing practices of alliances;
3. Regionalization and its associated internal consolidation and external protection;
4. The decline of anti-trust and anti-monopoly policy implementation;
5. The ability of multinational firms to become (or to be seen as) 'insiders' rather than 'outsiders' in national markets;
6. Control of information and knowledge management in multinational firms.

The culmination of these trends is to accent the political skills of lobbying and shelter seeking (insider status) over the economic value of activities. The result is that ineffective and imperfectly informed governments are unable to act to restore any kind of competitive equilibrium.

In a sense, the nature of global oligopolistic competition is 'old news'. Its effects were analysed by Knickerbocker back in 1973. The intensity of this behaviour has increased as cross-border entry, particularly by merger and takeover, has become more commonplace (Flowers, 1976; Ghauri, 1999). Threats to a global oligopolistic world market share may be met by a welfare suboptimal strategy of takeover or pre-emptive entry into a market where the oligopolist knows that profitable operation cannot take place. It is, however, preferable than allowing a rival player to have a sheltered base from which to mount a strategic attack (Lenway et al., 1996).

Such strategies are reinforced by alliances designed to 'regulate markets' or 'enforce conformity to industry standards'. Competition between alliances of firms, rather than unitary firms, has become the norm in industries such as airlines. Cooperation, rather than competition, may sound a good slogan, but alliances may have deleterious effects on those shut out of them, on those coerced into membership, and on suppliers and customers who become much more price takers.

Regionalization, the consolidation of national economies into trade and investment blocks, often implies increased concentration of industry. The EU is perhaps the best example of this.

The inability of individual nation states' laws to act against monopoly, oligopolistic practices and cartel-like behaviour in alliances, is of course exacerbated by the regional strategies of multinationals and despite the extraterritorial nature of some countries' laws (e.g. US anti-trust laws), globalization provides shelter from such legislation.

Eden and Molot (1993) examine the ways in which foreign-owned companies become insiders (in the case of the North American automobile industry). Insinuation, through lobbying and seeking government shelter, enables the companies to become insiders and raises the question 'Who is us?' (Reich, 1990).

The control of information within multinational firms and strategies to prevent its diffusion, whilst appropriating rents from proprietary knowledge, are a key focus for public policy and business strategy (Buckley and Carter, 2000). The privatization of public knowledge provides a real challenge in the new global economy.

However, there are countervailing trends. The entry of e-commerce as a major factor in global competition is breaking some existing monopolies and providing competition at crucial points in the value chain. This results in fragmentation of existing competitive structures and may well result in a new wave of consolidation. These effects are not confined to the developed world and may well have some direct effects on low-cost labour locations, extending the ability of firms to control 'offshore operations'.

The Asian crises might, in the short term, be regarded as increasing competition by breaking down sheltered domestic monopolies but, on a global scale, they may have removed independent (nascent) multinationals. The potential destruction of 'infant industry' competitors by takeovers of the newly cheap firms in emerging economies, may, in the longer run, have a detrimental effect on world competition.

Indeed, new circumstances force a reconsideration of the correct level of analysis of competition. Should it be assessed at global, regional or national levels? It is clear that large-scale consolidation of activities by multinationals at regional level within, for example, the EU and NAFTA, make this an appropriate analytical domain. In matters of international financial flows, the global market may well be the crucial one. Competition issues within individual markets have to be considered against this background.

Further, competition must be assessed in the dynamic context. The role of oligopolistic structures in fostering innovation was highlighted by Schumpeter and has been a feature of economic discourse for centuries, from Smith to Marx to Marshall and Schumpeter. The 'creative destruction' wrought by new combinations of factors of production is needed to push firms and industries on to new levels of attainment. The question of the reality of this picture and the extent to which there is a trade-off between innovation and market power remain matters of ideological dispute and contradictory evidence.

Distributional issues

The argument that trade and FDI in globalization damage the interest of workers mirrors the arguments in the 1970s of the detrimental effects of outward FDI on the USA and UK (Bergsten et al., 1978).

The argument now is that trade (and FDI) redistribute income away from unskilled workers, towards capital and skilled (knowledge) workers. Krugman (1994) has continually made a powerful argument that trade, based on comparative advantage, is a non-zero sum game. Partly this argument rests on the view that government policies are based on imperfect information. However, technological innovation may be the major culprit in eroding real wages for unskilled workers.

There is a further element of severe inequality in the world economy and that is the extent to which poorer nations attract inward foreign direct investment. The data in Table 5.2 show that:

1. FDI goes to a minority of less developed countries;
2. There is a very uneven distribution amongst less developed countries in the amounts they attract.

In 1999, China was the recipient of almost 5 per cent of world FDI and more than 20 per cent of FDI in developing countries.

Societies living with ineffective states have long suffered the consequences in terms of postponed growth and social development. There are great dangers of ineffective governments, such as political and social unrest, disintegration, loss in productive capacity and human misery. Well-functioning markets are considered the most efficient means to provide social justice. But it is not always true, as markets often undersupply a range of collective goods necessary for the benefits of society. These goods can include basic infrastructure, literacy, and employment opportunities.

Provisions for basic education, health and other social services can help achieve a better match between roles and capabilities. In the long run,

Table 5.2 Inflows of foreign direct investment by region, 1996–99 ($ billion)

	1996	*1997*	*1998*	*1999*
World of which:	363	468	660	827
Developed countries	212	276	468	609
• Western Europe	116	138	246	–
• European Union	109	128	237	269
• Other western Europe	8	9	9	–
• Japan	–	3	3	–
• United States	76	109	189	–
Developing countries	139	173	174	198
• Africa	6	8	9	10
• Latin America and the Caribbean	46	68	73	97
• Asia	85	96	90	91
West Asia	4	5	4	–
Central Asia	2	3	3	–
South, East and South-East Asia	80	88	83	84
of which China	40	44	43.5	40
• The Pacific	–	–	–	–
Central and eastern Europe	13	18	19	20

Note: Due to rounding, the sum of the subregions might not add up to the total.
Source: World Economic Situation and Prospects 2000, United Nations, New York, and *The Economist*, 8 April 2000.

investment in people will cut poverty and create basic living conditions for the most vulnerable. This can be achieved through social assistance programmes to help the poorest and through unemployment and other social insurance programmes to support the poorest or lowest level of workforce.

Some developing countries have experimented with social assistance measures for meeting the basic needs of the poorest, ranging from cash assistance to subsidization of labour-intensive public or private works. In many countries, however, these programmes have failed to achieve their objective of protecting the most vulnerable (IBRD, 1997).

Conclusion

There is likely to be an upsurge of critical material on globalization, and specifically on the role of MNEs' rent-seeking behaviour which fosters globalization. This literature will mirror the critical literature of the 1970s in some ways but will also have some new features. The revisiting of extant issues will include competitive issues, issues of bargaining and lobbying, and labour-related questions such as the export of jobs. Issues likely to have a renewed focus are those relating to regional integration, insecurity of tenure (both of multinationals in individual locations and workers within multinationals), questions of monopolistic practises, and a focus on environmental damage and cultural issues.

Our analysis suggests that a new research agenda is likely to emerge in the new millennium. This agenda concerns the external impact of the strategies of the leading multinational firms as they consolidate their hold on the global economy and as they accrete the power that comes from control of scarce knowledge resources. Combined with economic abundance, the new development raises threats such as economic insecurity, political instability and cultural decay leading to further imbalance in equality. The resulting insecurity felt by citizens is likely to be exacerbated by the declining ability of individual states to provide a safety net. Attention to the empirical reality of these issues, their extent and impact, is a key focal point for international business researchers.

References

Barnet, R. J. and Muller, R. E. (1975) *Global Reach: the Power of the Multinational Corporations*. London: Jonathan Cape.

Bergsten, C. F., Horst, T. and Moran, T. H. (1978) *American Multinationals and American Interests*. Washington, DC: Brookings Institution.

Boddewyn, J. J. (1992) 'Political Behaviour Research'. In P. J. Buckley (ed.), *New Directions in International Business*. Cheltenham: Edward Elgar.

Brewer, T. L. (1993) 'Foreign Direct Investment in Emerging Market Countries'. In L. Oxelheim (ed.), *The Global Race for Foreign Direct Investment*. Berlin: Springer-Verlag.

Buckley, P. J. (1996) 'Government Policy Responses to Strategic Rent-seeking Transnational Corporations'. *Transnational Corporations*, vol. 5, no. 2, pp. 1–17.

Buckley, P. J. and Carter, M. J. (2000) 'Capturing Value from Internationally Dispersed Knowledge in Multinational Firms'. *Long Range Planning* (forthcoming).

Buckley, P. J. and Casson, M. (1976) *The Future of the Multinational Corporation*. London: Macmillan.

Buckley, P. J. and Casson, M. (1991) 'Multinational Enterprises in Less Developed Countries: Cultural and Economic Interactions'. In P. J. Buckley and J. Clegg (eds), *Multinational Enterprises in Less Developed Countries*. London: Macmillan.

Buckley, P. J. and Ghauri, P. N. (1994) *The Economics of Change in East and Central Europe*. London: Academic Press.

Cantwell, J. A. (1989) *Technological Innovation and the Multinational Enterprise*. Oxford: Basil Blackwell.

Casson, M. (1994) 'Enterprise Culture and Institutional Change in Eastern Europe'. In P. J. Buckley and P. N. Ghauri, *The Economics of Change in East and Central Europe*. London: Academic Press.

Chandler, A. D. (1977) *The Visible Hand: the Management Revolution in American Business*. Cambridge, Mass.: Belknap Press of Harvard University Press.

Chandler, A. D. and Redlich, F. (1961) 'Recent Developments in American Business Administration and their Conceptualization'. *Business History Review*, Spring, pp. 103–28.

Contractor, F. (1991) 'Government Policies toward Foreign Investment: an Empirical Investigation of the Link between National Policies and FDI Flows'. Paper presented at the Annual meeting of Academy of International Business, Miami.

Dunning, J. H. (1991) 'Governments and Multinational Enterprises: from Confrontation to Cooperation'. *Millennium*, vol. 20, pp. 225–44.

Dunning, J. H. (1992) 'The Political Economy of International Production'. In P. J. Buckley (ed.), *New Directions in International Business*. Cheltenham: Edward Elgar.

Dunning, J. H. (1994) 'Re-evaluating the Benefits of Foreign Direct Investment'. *Transnational Corporations*, no. 1, pp. 23–51.

Eden, L. and Molot, M. A. (1993) 'Insiders and Outsiders: Defining "Who is Us" in the North American Automobile Industry'. *Transnational Corporations*, vol. 2, pp. 31–64.

Flowers, E. B. (1976) 'Oligopolistic Reaction in European and Canadian Direct Investment in the US'. *Journal of International Business Studies*, vol. 7, pp. 43–55.

Ghauri, P. N. (1999) 'Relationship Games: Creating Competitive Advantage through Cooperation'. In S. Urban (ed.), *Relations of Complex Organizational Systems*. Wiesbaden: Gabler, pp. 59–84.

Hymer, S. (1976) *The International Operations of National Firms: a Study of Direct Foreign Investment*. Cambridge, Mass.: MIT Press.

International Bank for Reconstruction and Development (IBRD) (1997) *The State in a Changing World: World Development Report 1997*. Washington: IBRD, p. iii.

Jenkins, R. (1999) 'The Changing Relationship between Emerging Markets and Multinational Enterprises'. In P. J. Buckley and P. N. Ghauri (eds), *Multinational Enterprises and Emerging Markets: Managing Increasing Interdependence*. Pergamon.

Knickerbocker, F. T. (1973) *Oligopolistic Reaction and Multinational Enterprise*. Boston: Harvard University.

Krugman, P. (1994) 'Does Third World Growth Hurt First World Prosperity?' *Harvard Business Review*, July–August, pp. 113–21.

Lenway, S., Morck, R. and Yeung, B. (1996) 'Rent-seeking, Protectionism and Innovation in the American Steel Industry'. *Economic Journal*, vol. 106, pp. 401–21.

Penrose, E. T. (1956) 'Foreign Investment and the Growth of the Firm'. *Economic Journal*, vol. 66, pp. 220–35.

Pfefferman, G. P. and Madarassy, A. (1992) 'Trends in Private Investments in Developing Countries'. International Finance Corporation, discussion paper No. 14. Washington, DC: The World Bank.

Porter, M. A. (1990) *The Competitive Advantage of Nations*. New York: Macmillan.

Prahalad, C. D. and Lieberthal, K. (1998) 'The End of Corporate Imperialism'. *Harvard Business Review*, vol. 76, no. 4, pp. 69–79.

Reich, R. (1990) 'Who is us?' *Harvard Business Review*, vol. 68, no. 1, pp. 53–65.

Stopford, J. M. and Strange, S. (1991) *Rival States, Rival Firms*. Cambridge: Cambridge University Press.

Strange, S. (1996) *The Retreat of the State: the Diffusion of Power in the World Economy*. Cambridge: Cambridge University Press.

Strange, S. (1997) 'The Erosion of the State'. *Current History*, November, pp. 365–9.

Streeten, P. (1974) 'The Theory of Development Policy'. In J. H. Dunning (ed.), *Economic Analysis and the Multinational Enterprise*. London: George Allen and Unwin.

UNCTC (1992) *The Determinants of Foreign Direct Investment: a Survey of Evidence*. London, New York: United Nations.

UNCTAD (1998) *World Investment Report*. Geneva: UNCTAD.

Vernon, R. (1966) 'International Investment and International Trade in the Product Cycle'. *Quarterly Journal of Economics*, vol. 80, pp. 190–207.

Wells, L. T. (1998) 'Multinational Enterprises and Developing Countries'. *Journal of International Business Studies*, vol. 29, no. 1, pp. 101–14.

6

Trust in International Joint Venture Relationships

with Margreet F. Boersma and Pervez N. Ghauri

Introduction

International joint ventures (IJVs) are frequently stated to be increasingly popular but with significant managerial dissatisfaction in their operations (Madhok, 1995a). Therefore, a great deal of attention has been paid to the performance of IJVs (e.g. Contractor and Lorange, 1988; special issue of *JIBS* no. 5, 1996; Hyder and Ghauri, 2000). Particular emphasis has been placed on the dynamic processes within IJVs, including conflict resolution strategies (Lin and Germain, 1997) and the development of trust between the partners (Parkhe, 1993b; Madhok, 1995b; Ariño and Torre, 1996).

This chapter examines the development of trust in IJVs over time. Many scholars have recognized trust as a key factor in improving the performance of IJVs (including Gabarro, 1978; Granovetter, 1985; Parkhe, 1993a; Ganesan, 1994; Ring and van de Ven, 1994; Nooteboom, 1996; Uzzi, 1997). Our approach is to formulate propositions based on transaction cost process analyses in which trust is seen as both an input and an output in various stages of development of the IJV. Trust reduces transaction costs because it 'economises on the specification and monitoring of contracts and material incentives for co-operation' (Nooteboom, 1996, p. 989). Buckley and Casson (1988, p. 32) argue that the firm essence of voluntary interfirm cooperation lies in 'coordination effected through mutual forbearance, which in turn becomes possible where there is reciprocal behaviour and mutual trust'. When trust is present, managers will find 'ways by which the two parties can work out difficulties such as a power conflict, low profitability and so forth' (Sullivan and Peterson, 1982 in Dwyer et al., 1987, p. 23).

The emergence of trust is a process. Every process has inputs and outputs. The process is likely to be recursive, not linear. However, it is useful as a first approximation to build a linear schema of the trust development process, and this we do below in developing our research propositions.

The following section explains the notion of trust, its dimensions and sources ending with a formal definition. We then examine a transaction cost approach to trust, and a process model is introduced. The four IJV cases are then examined, and the model is applied to their development. The conclusion presents refinements to the initial model.

Explaining trust

The first question is whether trust is simply a subset of risk taking (Corazzini, 1977; Gill and Butler, 1996; Luhmann, 1988) or whether it has a more moral basis (Hosmer, 1995; Craswell, 1993). In this discussion, trust is exemplified as an explanation of particular behaviour; for example 'X loaned some money to Y. What might explain X's behaviour?' (Craswell, 1993, p. 487). Deutsch (1962) argues that trust arises only when the expected loss is greater than the expected gain, otherwise 'trust would be a matter of simple economic rationality' (Hosmer, 1995, p. 381). This is in line with Williamson's (1993) presumption of opportunism and calculative behaviour. He believes that actors who seemingly take a leap of faith are mostly behaving in a self-interested way. Williamson thus argues that trust is not the right word to use in such cases. Craswell (1993), however, also recognises instances in which individuals take leaps of faith because they trust others. He thereby acknowledges that actors do not always act from calculative motives (see also Rempel et al., 1985; Luhmann, 1988). Some definitions only emphasize (an absence of) negative behaviour (e.g. Nooteboom, 1996), including cheating, while others focus on more positive conduct, such as doing more than is expected (e.g. Sako, 1992). Madhok's (1995b) explanation starts from a presumption of opportunism, but then goes on to observe (from four interviews) the growth of trust, while Das and Teng (1998) suggest that trust is strongly related with control.

Dimensions of trust

Authors have used different dimensions of trust and distrust (see e.g. Lewicki et al., 1998; Bigley and Pearce, 1998); however, in order to define trust, we follow Sako (1992) who makes clear distinctions between three different dimensions of trust in interfirm relationships. The dimensions she distinguishes are: contractual-based trust, competence-based trust (Ganesan, 1994 combines both promissory-based trust and competence-based trust into the label 'credibility') and goodwill-based trust (other labels for this type of trust are, amongst others, character-based trust (Gabarro, 1978), behavioural trust (Nooteboom, 1996) and benevolence (Ganesan, 1994)).

Promissory-based trust arises from the explicit written or oral agreements that partners make during the joint venture relationship. When making such agreements, a party should be relied upon to keep to that agreement. Our definition of *promissory-based trust* follows: 'an expectation that a party can be relied upon to carry out a verbal or written promise'. The second form, *competence-based trust,* refers to 'an expectation that a party will perform its role competently' (Barber, 1983, p. 15).

The third dimension, *goodwill-based trust,* is explained by Sako (1992, p. 39) in the following way: 'The key to understanding goodwill-based trust is that there are no explicit promises which are expected to be fulfilled, as in the case of contractual-based trust, nor fixed professional standards to be reached, as in the case of competence-based trust.' This, then, is a less self-interested, non-egotistic form of trust.

Sources of trust

Is it possible to use the term 'trust' when one person believes that the other is acting in a trustworthy fashion for other than moral reasons (Hosmer, 1995)? Cooperative behaviour can occur even when the motives are material advantage or fear of sanctions (Buckley and Casson, 1988). So X believes Y will keep a promise because X thinks that Y has a clear self-interest in being 'trustworthy'. Table 6.1 represents a schema examining the determinants of cooperative behaviour that classifies its determinants into micro/macro determinants and egotistic/non-egotistic motives (Williams, 1988). The range of motives underlying trust can range from material advantage and fear of sanctions to an ethical stance based on superordinate goals and personal emotions.

Our formal definition of trust thus is: 'on expectation that a party can be relied on to keep to agreements (promissory), will perform its role competently (competence) and that the party will behave honourably even where no explicit promises or performance guarantees have been made (goodwill)'. This is a wider definition and, as we shall see, it may be necessary to uplift the concept back into its component parts in practical situations.

The role of trust in IJVs: a transaction cost approach

The distinctive characteristic of a joint venture, which is shared ownership, is also its key problem (Killing, 1982; Beamish and Banks, 1987; Hennart,

Table 6.1 Determinants of cooperative behaviour/sources of trust

	Macro	*Micro*
Egotistic	Coercion or fear of sanctions from some authority (God, law)	Material advantage or 'interest'
Non-egotistic	Ethics: values/norms of proper conduct	Bonds of friendship, kinship or empathy; emotions

Source: Williams (1988).

1988; Geringer and Hebert, 1989). Shared control implies two or more companies deciding the strategic direction and operational issues of the joint subsidiary. Shared control brings with it increased transaction costs.

Transaction costs have both ex ante and ex post elements. Ex ante transaction costs include drafting, negotiating and safeguarding an agreement. They can be quantified by examining actual costs (mainly management time) of the agreement process and examining the insurance costs of default. Ex post transaction costs are more complex. They include:

1. The adaptation costs incurred when transactions drift out of alignment with the terms of the agreement;
2. The haggling costs incurred if bilateral efforts are made to correct ex post misalignments;
3. The set-up costs and running costs associated with the governance structures (either in the courts or outside them) to which any disputes are referred; and
4. The bonding costs of effecting secure commitments.

Ex post costs are not easily quantifiable prior to the implementation of the agreement because they include an element of uncertainty. (How likely is it that the partner will default on the agreement?) This implicit probability exists in the minds of the executives entering the agreement. It is difficult for the executives to articulate the complexity of these issues and, hence, 'The transaction costs that are really there, in the sense that they determine the outcome are those transaction costs that are perceived by the manager (or managers) who make the decisions' (Buckley and Chapman, 1997, p. 139).

The role of trust can now be seen in clear focus. Trust is a transaction-cost-reducing mechanism that lowers the subjective risk of entering into an agreement. Both ex ante and ex post elements are reduced by trust. Costs of negotiating are reduced (perhaps legal trappings are replaced by 'a gentleman's agreement') and the subjective probability of ex post transactions failure declines when the parties trust one another.

Buckley and Casson (1988, p. 32) approach the issue of trust by defining cooperation as 'co-ordination effected through mutual forbearance'. Forbearance is refraining from cheating (avoiding opportunism in Williamson's 1975 term). Cheating may take a weak form – failing to perform a beneficial act for the other party, or a strong form – committing a damaging act. The incentives for forbearance arise from the possibility of reciprocity, leading to mutual forbearance. Parties that are observed to forbear may gain a reputation for this behaviour, which makes them potentially attractive partners for others. The parties to a successful agreement may develop a commitment to mutual forbearance, which cements the partnership, and, in this way, mutual trust is created, which alters the preferences of the parties towards a mutually cooperative mode. Thus, short-term, self-interested behaviour becomes converted to cooperative trusting behaviour, with beneficial transaction-cost-reducing results. This analysis is suggestive of a process method of analysing the key issue of developing trust in intracompany relationships.

A process model of trust

The main problem is 'how can trust be developed between parties within IJV relationships?' Here, the development of trust is analysed within a process framework (illustrated in Figure 6.1), based on Ring and van de Ven (1994) and Larson (1992). The framework provides the basic concepts for our model, but it is further formalized into discrete stages of development.

The process framework indicates that trust in IJVs will develop through four different stages. The first stage is the *previous history*. This is the stage *before* the parties meet to negotiate the joint venture. During this stage, one party may construct an initial mental image of the other party with whom they will create the joint venture. The parties come together in order to negotiate the joint venture during the *negotiation stage*. 'In *the commitment stage*, the will of the parties meet, when they reach an agreement on the obligations and rules for future action in the relationship' (Ring and van de Ven, 1994, p. 98). 'In the execution phase, the commitments and rules of action are carried into effect' (Ring and van de Ven. 1994, p. 98). Renegotiations may take place after each period of execution during official board meetings. When one or both parties cannot maintain the commitment, the

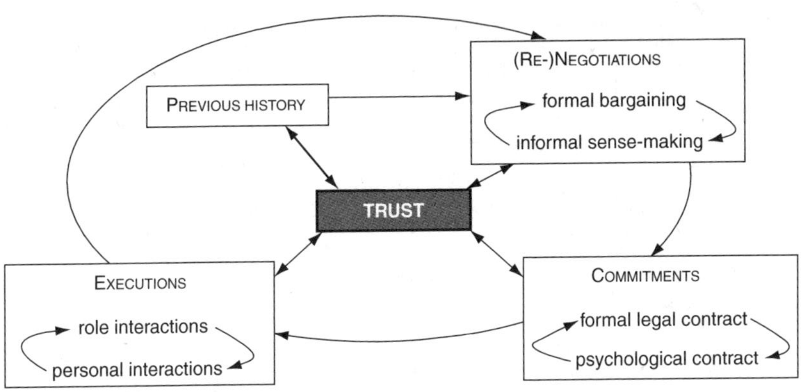

Figure 6.1 A process model of the development of trust in IJV relationships

Source: Based on Ring and van de Ven (1994) and Larson (1992).

IJV relationship will cease to exist. Having described these stages and the dimensions of trust, the following two subquestions arise:

- Do all three dimensions of trust develop in each stage or do different dimensions of trust develop in different stages?
- What are the sources of trust and do they change over time?

These questions are relevant to purely national joint ventures, as well as IJVs. However, there are purely international issues, which we highlight below.

The conceptual model that we derive for analysis is presented in Figure 6.2. It combines the concepts of Williams (1988), Ring and van de Ven (1994), Larson (1992) and Sako (1992). The model suggests a sequential process, arbitrarily broken into stages with each stage having both inputs and

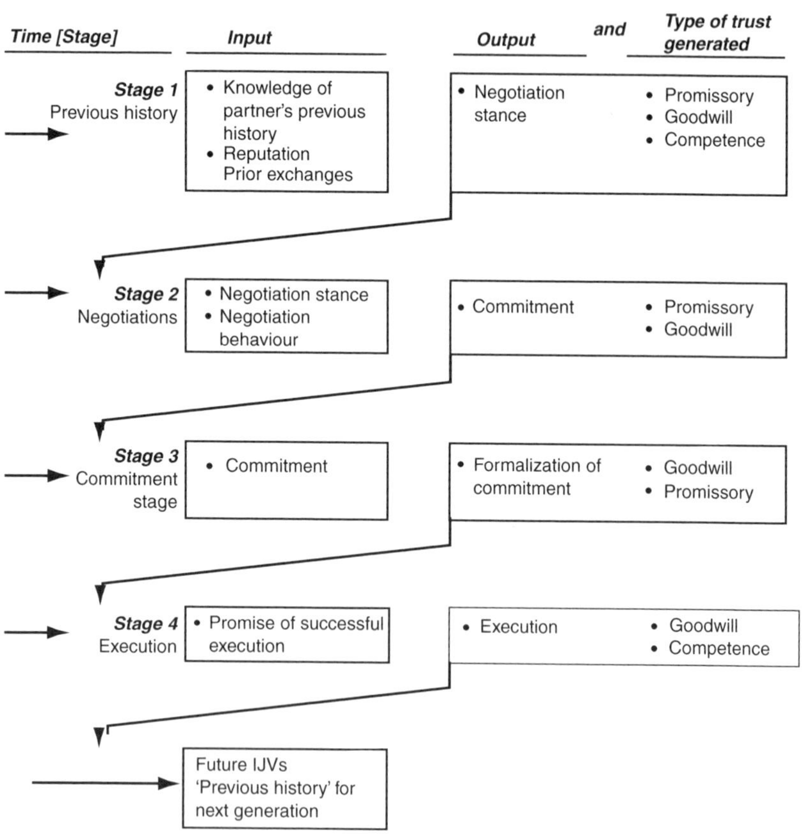

Figure 6.2 A process model of the development of trust in IJVs

outputs. Based on the literature, reviewed earlier, and our framework, we derive the following propositions:

Proposition 1: The development of trust can be examined as a sequential process. These inputs build on the previous stage and represent the generation of trust from interactions in the earlier stage. The output of trust feeds into the next stage of the process. Trust can either be generated *de novo* or can result as part of the ongoing process. It should be noted that at any stage mistrust (or distrust) can also be generated as an input into the next stage.

Proposition 2: The development of trust as a sequential process can be broken into stages where the output of a preceding stage can be regarded as an input into the next. The input of Stage 1 (Reputation) will be affected by the output of past joint ventures, and firms will build their reputation for successful joint venturing by generating trust from previous IJVs, which can be observed directly by their partners and indirectly by future, potential partners.

Proposition 3: The history of previous IJVs represents the final stage (input) of the process of building trust.

Proposition 4: The negotiations stage has an input from previous history of IJVs and generates on output 'commitment' to the next stage of trust building.

Proposition 5: The commitment stage has an input from negotiations and an output to the execution stage of the IJV.

Proposition 6: The execution stage has an input from the commitment stage and (observed) output to the next generation of IJVs (as the 'previous history' of the partners). These propositions are shown diagrammatically in Figure 6.2.

The four case studies

The case research method is appropriate to the study of the development of trust over time (Yin, 1989; Stafford, 1995; Parkhe, 1993b). The aim of this research is to study development over time, and so we wanted to examine joint ventures that varied in the length of time they had existed. Secondly, we were interested in international as opposed to national joint ventures. Hence, the joint ventures should have at least one foreign partner. However, in order to constrain cultural differences between the cases, and thus to reduce a major source of variation, we selected joint ventures with foreign partners from countries with similar cultures. All the partners are from EU member countries. The cases that we selected are (1) ABG, (2) Kemax, (3) LAP and (4) DSM–BASF. It was felt that relative cultural closeness would allow us to focus on issues of trust, which might be obscured if wide cultural differences were encountered. The limitations of the use of only four examples of IJVs needs to be borne in mind throughout the chapter. The cases are not chosen to be representative of the population of IJVs, but as illustrative material against which to demonstrate the testability of our propositions.

1. ABG is a joint venture between Gamma in Scandinavia and Alpha and Beta in The Netherlands. ABG was established in 1976, is located in The Netherlands and produces an intermediate chemical product. Alpha and Beta each hold 30 per cent of the joint venture's equity, Gamma holds 40 per cent. All the three parent companies are users of the output of the joint venture ABG. Each parent achieves security of supply, gains economies of scale in the production of the intermediate by ABG and shares risks (Figure 6.3). In addition, the venture reduces competitive bidding between the parents for the input and raises the possibility of collusion between them. This is a classic case of an indivisibility in part of the supply chain leading to an IJV solution.
2. Kemax is a joint venture between Kemira, Sweden and Akzo Nobel, The Netherlands. Kemax was established in 1993, is located in The Netherlands and also produces a chemical product. Kemira holds 51 per cent of the joint venture's equity, Akzo Nobel owns the remaining 49 per cent. The production processes of the joint venture and Akzo Nobel are connected to each other (see Figure 6.4). Akzo Nobel produces an intermediate product as a by-product of its main production process. The joint venture Kemax distillates this by-product from the main stream of waste and sells the product via the marketing channels of Kemira. The advantages for Akzo Nobel and Kemira of this joint venture are clearly not the same. Akzo Nobel gains extra profitability and environmental benefits from the recovery of the by-product (which was previously dumped at sea!). Kemira gains access to a production source without meeting all the

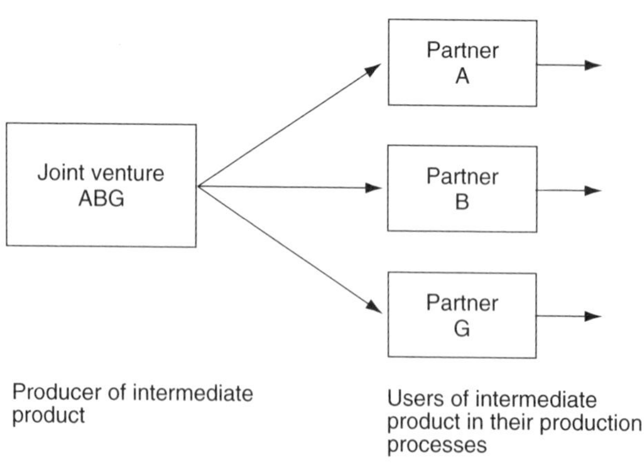

Figure 6.3 The physical structure of the joint venture ABG

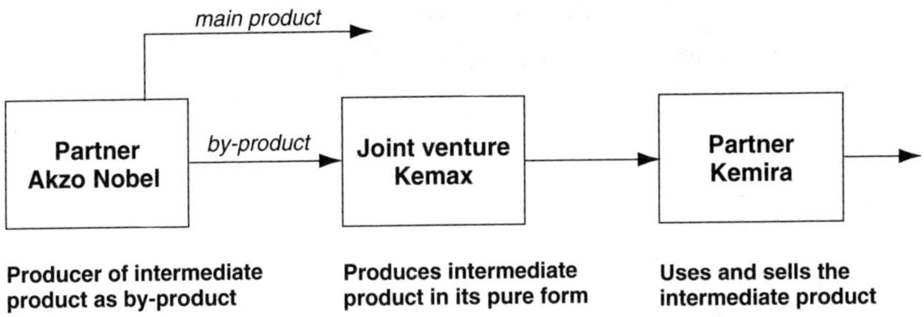

Figure 6.4 The physical structure of the joint venture Kemax

set up costs. Again, an important indivisibility (between Akzo Nobel's main product and the joint venture's by-product) is a key factor in the choice of an IJV.

3. The third case came about because of a complex privatization in Portugal where the joint venture LAP is located. The Dutch partner Hoogovens supplies a basic input to the (newly privatized) joint venture LAP, which it entered because it wished to secure supply of its output to the new company. The French partner Usinor operates at the same stage of production as the later stages of activity carried out by LAP, and it wished to ensure prices and quality at the output stage. The French and Dutch companies share ownership 50 : 50 (see Figure 6.5 and Table 6.2).
4. The fourth case is analogous in physical structure to Case 1. The joint venture DSM–BASF produces an intermediate product, which is supplied to the partner companies for further processing (Figure 6.6). The ownership is shared 60 per cent by the Dutch company DSM and 40 per cent by the German company BASF.

All IJVs present examples of barriers to full merger. In the first case, none of A, B or G wish to wholly own the joint venture production as they would have to ensure the sale of the excess production or run the plant at less than the optimal scale. In the second case, the joint venture Kemax is merely using a by-product of Akzo Nobel's main business, and it would be infeasible for Kemira to buy the whole of Akzo Nobel's production just to obtain access to the by-product. As Table 6.2 illustrates, only Case 3 is a completely symmetrical joint venture (Makino, 1995). It is a classic symmetrical case in that ownership is shared 50 : 50 and the physical structure is identical for the two partners (Figure 6.6). This presents a useful benchmark for the three non-symmetrical cases. The four cases thus have important commonalities. They are all IJVs with a Dutch partner. They are all structured so as to manage the flows of intermediate products linking the IJV with the parents

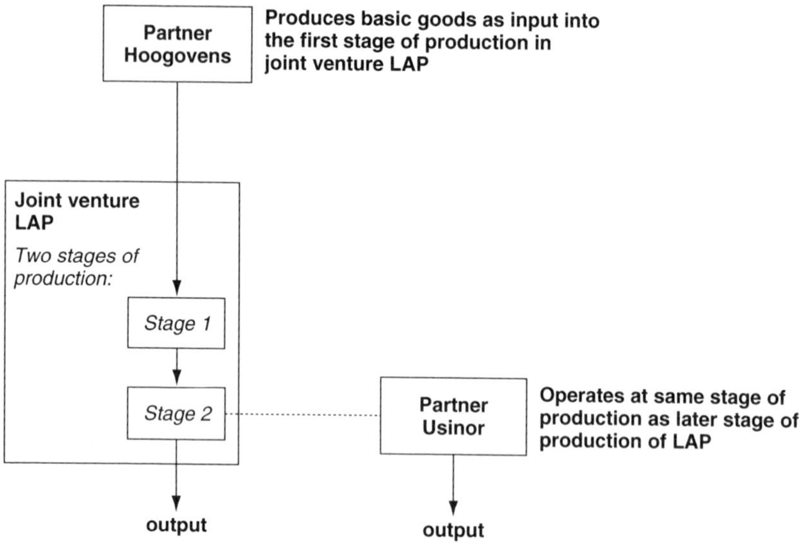

Figure 6.5 The physical structure of the joint venture LAP

(although in different configurations). They are all trans-EU ventures. From these basic commonalities, we are able to proceed with confidence to apply a focus on the long-term study of the development of trust.

The unit of analysis encompassed the board members and people from the management team of the IJV (MIJV). Tracking the joint venture in real time

Table 6.2 Ownership structure of the four IJVs

Joint venture name	*Ownership share*		
	The Netherlands 1	*The Netherlands 2*	*Foreign partner*
1. ABG	Alpha (30%)	Beta (30%)	Gamma, Scandinavia (40%)
2. Kemax	Akzo Nobel (49%)	–	Kemira, Sweden (51%)
3. LAP	Hoogovens (50%)	–	Usinor, France (50%)
4. DSM–BASF	DSM (60%)	–	BASF, Germany (40%)

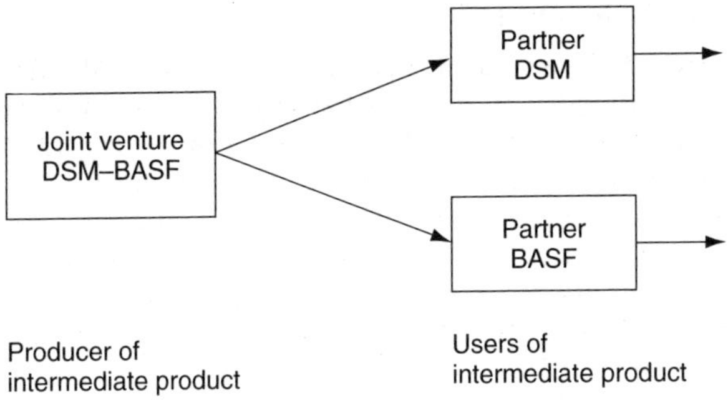

Figure 6.6 The physical structure of joint venture DSM–BASF

was not possible, so we collected retrospective data by interviewing most of the current board members and the MIJV, as well as former board members who were representing their company during the creation of the joint venture. A complementary advantage of interviewing delegates from the several parents was that the reliability of the stories was checked. The total amount of interviews was 16, which lasted, on average, one hour and a half. During the interviews, we used a semi-structured questionnaire. Following Ring and van de Ven (1994, p. 112), we let the respondents focus on critical events during the lifetime of the joint venture. In addition to these interviews, we obtained written documents on the history of the companies. Second, we were allowed to read the minutes of the board meetings. Third, we used public information such as annual reports, public relations material, press releases and information from the World Wide Web.

The interviews were tape-recorded and fully transcribed. The transcribed reports were sent back for factual data verification. The data were analysed in three steps (Miles and Huberman, 1994; Strauss and Corbin, 1990). Firstly, the transcribed interviews were broken into meaningful segments. Each segment brought out a major idea that was coded and summarized in a one- or two-line sentence. The interpretation of the quote was verified by sending the format back to the respondents. After the meaningful segments were coded, we grouped them into the dimensions of trust that were specified in the section above. The result of this second step was a convenient arrangement of the interview's segments. Based on this coding, we analysed the cases.

Test of the propositions

This section tests the propositions of the model using the four case studies as examples. The discussion of each stage examines the three dimensions of trust contained in our definition. Our more general propositions (Propositions 1 and 2) are examined in the concluding section.

Proposition 3: previous history

This stage proved to be a valuable period of time to learn about the prospective partner. We found three factors that established a basic level of trust, namely prior exchange between the companies on an organizational level (two cases); direct personal contact between the initiators (two cases); and the overall reputation of the company (four cases). Through prior exchange Akzo Nobel and Kemira had learnt about each other's competencies. It even happened that Kemira bid for a part of Akzo Nobel before Akzo Nobel acquired that part. Usinor bought raw materials from Hoogovens 'for years' before they began the IJV.

Direct personal contact between the initiators of Kemax and DSM–BASF gave an insight into their behaviour and character. Because they operated in the same industry, they had met each other before at trade fairs. During these meetings, it appeared that the people who had to set up the IJV could get along with each other and that they could be taken at their word.

The reputation of the company played a role in all cases. For example, Kemira's market position was a sign for Akzo Nobel that Kemira was a valuable partner. Gamma knew Alpha and Beta as 'leading companies in the petrochemical industry'. Alpha and Beta also believed that Gamma would become a strong partner. An example is Alpha's and Beta's reaction to Gamma's plans for building a plant near their plant: in order to prevent competition, they contacted Gamma for possible cooperation instead of competition. DSM regarded BASF as its 'best competitor'. 'They had particular resources that we liked to have. In this way, we gained an insight into their competencies' (DSM). Figure 6.7 presents the three factors that set an initial level of trust between the partners: direct personal contact, overall reputation and prior exchange. This is a more nuanced approach than the usual designation of reputation effects.

Proposition 4: negotiations

Most of the interviewees stressed the importance of mutual economic advantage. The conviction that the other party would benefit from a joint

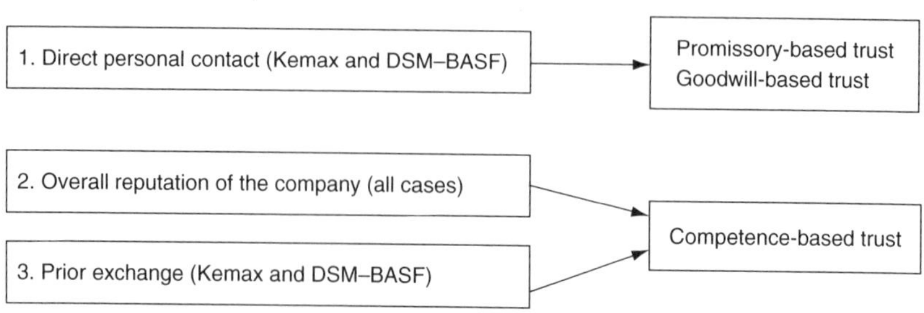

Figure 6.7 Factors affecting the development of trust from the firms' previous history

venture strengthened the belief that they would behave in a trustworthy fashion, because such behaviour would be in their self-interest. In addition to this key foundation of trust, we found a number of other ways by which trust developed. The managers of Kemax already started with a basic level of promissory-based trust. Therefore, the psychological process of constructing a perception about the other's trustworthiness took less time. Promissory-based trust was magnified through the actual behaviour of the other:

> When somebody says 'I will sell 100.000-ton,' you can only check that after three years. So maybe it starts in a very common way, that somebody says he will be somewhere at eight and he is there at eight. In this way somebody builds a reputation of 'a man a man, a word a word' (Kemira).

The parties of ABG started without any prior experience with each other before this joint venture. Only general knowledge about the company as a whole was available. Hence, promissory-based trust and goodwill-based trust between the people had to be built up. This was done in a variety of ways. The following quote illustrates how Gamma tried to assess whether the others could be taken at their word and whether they were sincere:

> You have to make up your mind whether the fellows on the other side of the table are just like yourself. I said to myself, I am open, what I am saying I can stand for, I am always truthful, not trying to put in some snares. We are like that, so why shouldn't the people on the other side of the table be of the same kind? And that you discover fairly quickly (Gamma).

Hence, the respondent used his own trustworthy behaviour as a reference point and trusted his partners until the opposite was proven. Stated differently, he started with trust instead of distrust. Such an attitude also emanated from the belief that only by acting in good faith could good business deals be made. The Alpha delegate also started with trust. His attitude resulted from considering himself as being naive, from lessons from other joint ventures and from the idea that the joint venture was a business opportunity and not a necessity. Hence, when people were not to be trusted (and he would use his own judgement and intuition in order to find this out), he would quit negotiations. In order to come to an opinion, social meetings (like dinners before the official meeting) played an important role. These meetings facilitated a setting in which the delegates could make up and adjust their perception about each other, thereby discovering that they could get along with each other that trust could be built. Competence-based trust already occurred in the former stage, but could not be proven during this phase. Keeping promises in situations of minor importance gradually leads to a reputation for trustworthiness. Competence in these minor matters leads to competence-based trust even where (as in the DSM–BASF case) openness was not assumed by either party at the outset. The solution here was effected by frequent face-to-face meetings, to which purely social meetings were added. This led to the building of common interest by the individuals involved and knowledge of more subtle details of each other, such as body language. Examples include:

> You get to know people better, including their body language. I am better able to understand the way the other person thinks and feels. The people know each other by now, and when mister X says something, you know that it is the truth (Gamma). And, what was very essential was that we liked each other a lot. We appreciated and respected each other, and when such a basis is lacking, you can simply forget about the whole thing (DSM).

> The whole process towards the joint venture has a strong influence on the development of personal relationships. Our process towards the establishment of the joint venture took a long time, so we grew close. And in such a process an important factor is that people get on with each other (LAP).

This personal friendship is both created and built on to progress the IJV through mutual trust. One case shows that getting along with each other on a personal basis is not a necessary condition for the development of trust. Two initiators could not really get along with each other, but because of high levels of professional skills, competence-based trust and promissory-based trust compensated for this deficiency in building goodwill-based trust. Figure 6.8 summarizes the factors that play an important role in the development of trust during the negotiation stage. Keeping promises, personal relationships and forbearance are important here.

Proposition 5: commitments

In the commitment stage, the wills of the parties meet (Ring and van de Ven, 1994). The formal legal contract gave the juridical security that both parties were committed to the joint venture. In addition to this formal contract, a number of psychological contracts also contributed to the development of trust. These were the additional investments to make the joint venture work and set the mode of cooperation. In all cases, it was necessary to make extra investments before the joint venture could start production. These investments were a signal for the partners that all parties were long-term oriented and that they were committed to the joint venture. Hence, financial investments reinforced goodwill-based trust. This accords with Ganesan (1994) who calls these investments 'credible commitments' (following Williamson, 1983). In addition to these investments, starting a joint venture instead of a

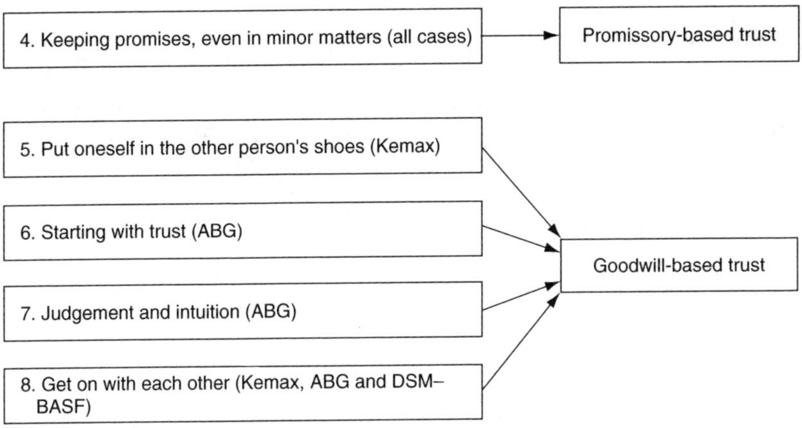

Figure 6.8 Factors affecting the development of trust during negotiation stage

non-equity agreement appeared to be a signal that the partner was to be trusted:

> We have started a joint venture because we wanted to create commitment towards both processes (production and marketing) ... Kemax has several production locations. Therefore, it would be relatively easy for them to drain this plant in case of a bad supply agreement and to deliver from their own production locations. And you never know how such things develop in the future (Akzo Nobel).

Hence, the creation of a joint venture aligned the interest of the parties, and, therefore, the parties trusted each other to do their best for the joint venture while they had a self-interest to do so.

However, a legal contract is seen as a last resort – something to fall back on. Partners work things out in other ways and will not often use the contract to enforce decisions. Using the contract in order to make the other party keep to the agreement is perceived to be damaging to the long-run relationship. Examples include:

> Putting things on paper is like a protection, normally legal. However, when things function you could discuss them over a cup of coffee as well as at a formal meeting. I feel it is more because of a lack of confidence, that you would like to have things on paper, because then you have your back covered. I don't have that need and I think that there is nothing wrong with a failure sometimes (Kemax).

> We never have to use our documents after we have signed them. But that is not unique for ABG, we have this in all our joint ventures. We are of the

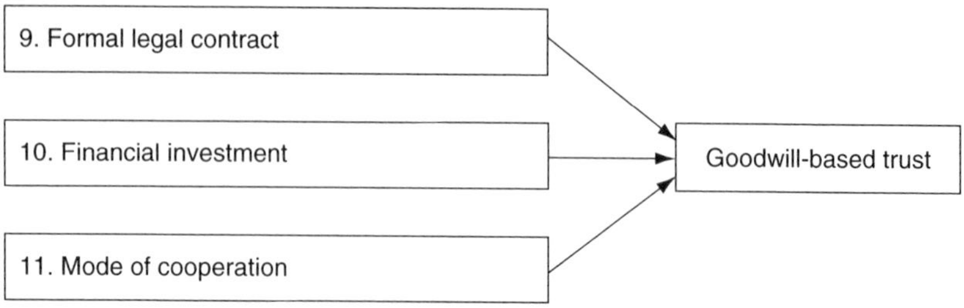

Figure 6.9 Factors affecting the development of trust during the commitment stage

> opinion that when a problem arises, we have to solve it in a friendly way, and to discuss it irrespective of what has been written in the legal documents (Alpha).

Figure 6.9 presents the factors that develop trust during the commitment stage. The formal legal contract and supporting investments reinforce ongoing cooperative behaviour.

Proposition 6: execution

During the execution stage, the expectations raised during the previous three stages are confirmed or confounded. Considering ABG, we conclude that trust between the parties only strengthened. Kemax showed a decrease in competence-based trust in time. However, after its performance improved, trust was restored. Trust between the people of ABG became stronger mainly due to a growing personal bond between most of the delegates, which resulted in friendship between some of the board members. This personal bond started during negotiations, when the participants found out that they could get along with each other very well. The bond stimulated cooperative behaviour (i.e. showing empathy and giving support) when ABG began to have financial problems. It happened that additional financing was needed in order to assure survival of the joint venture. One party was not able to make this extra investment, without bringing itself into severe financial problems. It turned out that both European partners were ready to solve ABG's problems on their own by financing Gamma's part as a loan to ABG. The following quote illustrates the motivation to do so:

> I felt such a sympathy for Gamma's delegate and his companion, that when we would have followed the rules of the game, they would have gone down the drain. So I put a lot of effort into finding all kinds of ways to help him, without betraying Alpha and Beta. I knew the joint venture was his baby so I did not want to let him down because I liked him too much for that . . . So, it was not self-interest but pity for the other partner (Alpha).

Hence, the social relationship between the people stimulated support, although it was not required economically. The bond was maintained through social events (such as dinners before the board meeting, weekends with spouses). Two board members kept visiting each other even after their retirement. The result of this growing bond was that although each delegate kept advocating their own firm's interests, the members actively looked for consensus when the interests were opposing. Such behaviour, in turn, reinforced trust.

Goodwill-based trust also results in acceptance of failure to perform according to expectations for a given period of time. The case of Kemax is an example of this. From the start, the intermediate product plant did not perform optimally. This was due to an ongoing failure of Akzo Nobel to solve a technical problem. Kemira, however, believed that Akzo Nobel made an effort to solve the problem because it was also in the interest of Akzo Nobel to solve it as quickly as possible. After all, low performance of the plant directly affected Akzo Nobel's performance as a whole (i.e. Akzo Nobel had a clear self-interest to solve the problem). Hence, goodwill-based trust had the effect that Kemira kept competence-based trust in Akzo Nobel for quite a period of time. Moreover, Kemira did not monitor Akzo Nobel's endeavours as they trusted the information that Akzo Nobel presented. This is a sign of Kemira's promissory-based trust in Akzo Nobel, which developed during the former stages. Yet, after 4 years, Kemira's tolerance for Akzo Nobel's failure decreased; they started to think that they would send their own people in order to investigate the problems. In addition, the partners arranged an extra board meeting to discuss the problem. However, before this happened, Akzo Nobel succeeded in resolving the problem, thereby taking away Kemira's worries and removing potential competence-based distrust.

An important mechanism in the execution stage is monitoring. However, in all four cases, monitoring was indirect rather than direct. Through indirect monitoring, the partners keep themselves posted on changes in their partner's behaviour, strategy or environment. Changes may be an indication of changing self-interest in the joint venture. Indirect signals are used to maintain mutual trust in the joint venture. Figure 6.10 summarizes the factors discussed in this section. In this stage, ongoing cooperative behaviour reinforces trust, while technical incompetence can damage trust.

Discussion

The chapter started with the observation that, although many scholars have stated that trust has a positive effect on IJV performance, only a few studies have investigated the development of trust over time. Specifically, it was found that competence-based trust develops before the parties come together. Moreover, this proved to be an important factor in selecting a partner. The data reveal that this dimension of trust is somewhat impersonal;

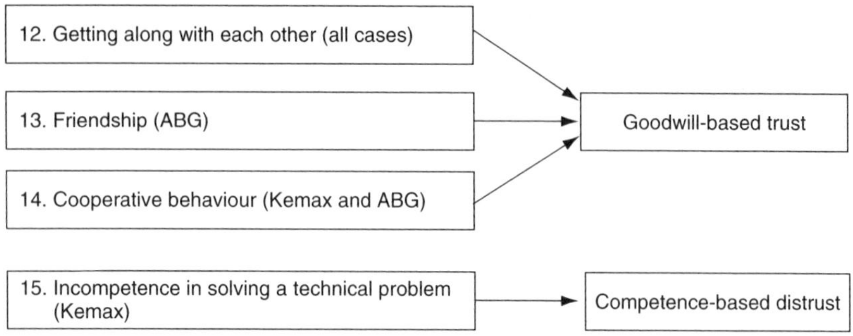

Figure 6.10 Factors affecting the development of trust during the execution stage

it is mainly based on company-specific characteristics. The facts that lead to such a perception are predominantly of a public nature. Hence, before the parties really meet to start a joint venture, competence-based trust develops mainly through the performance of a company. Promissory-based trust and goodwill-based trust are, however, more person oriented and based on individual knowledge. These two types of trust mainly develop through direct personal interaction. Congruent industries increase the likelihood of prior interaction, while delegates of similar industries may come together at trade fairs. Such prior interaction may also contribute to the creation of ties between firms. As one respondent noted: 'a lot of business is emerging from the fact that people know each other'. Having a trustworthy reputation is therefore extremely important.

The cases, however, show a difference in trust before negotiations. Whereas Kemax started with a positive initial level of all three dimensions of trust between the parties, ABG began with only a basic level of competence-based trust. The latter case showed, however, that promissory-based trust and goodwill-based trust can also be built during negotiations. On the other hand, as one respondent noted, it saves negotiation time when parties do not have to gather information on each other, when this has already been done before negotiations.

The commitment stage confirms the goodwill of the other party. The data suggest that trust is based mainly on the perceived economic self-interest of the other: contracts establish fear of coercion; choosing a joint venture aligns the material advantage of the partner. In other words, during this stage, perceived economic self-interest of the other party seems to be a main source of trust. We found that trust based on emotions may develop during the execution stage. In order to develop this trust, friendship between the delegates plays an important role. Bonds of friendship have the effect that people listen to each other more carefully, support each other when difficulties arise, are more open and direct in their communication and look for consensus when the interests are opposing. Such behaviour successively strengthens trust. The different cases show that time is important in order to let such bonds grow. While all cases start with people that can get along with each other, ABG shows that such a bond may transform itself into friendship. When personal bonds dominate the main source of trust shifts from perceived self-interest towards emotional commitment.

The investigation has thus highlighted 14 factors that the partners use to build and sustain trust in IJVs and one factor that leads to distrust. These are incorporated in Figures 6.7–6.10. Most of the factors establish goodwill-based trust in the partner, that is, the factors create an expectation that the other party will take care of the interests of ego (Hosmer, 1995) and may be willing to do more than is formally expected (Sako, 1992). We found that this goodwill-based trust is mainly based on the other's perceived economic self-interest. Most of the factors are particularly useful for assessing and confirming the other's economic self-interest. For example, partners put themselves into the other's shoes to understand the other's economic self-interest. The contract strengthens the belief that the other has indeed a self-interest (otherwise, they would not sign the contract). Trust is only based on emotions when bonds of friendship develop. ABG shows evidence for this proposition. Such a friendship is more than 'getting on with each other'. It includes feelings of affection and warmth, and the involved persons see each other also outside the joint venture relationship. In this case, the development of trust thus runs from the top line of Table 6.1 towards the bottom line – from egotistic to non-egotistic behaviour.

Conclusion

The case studies illustrate several key findings. First, we believe that trust can be seen both as an output and an input at various stages of the process. Propositions 1 and 2 are vindicated. It is possible to see the development of trust as a sequential process, and a linear form of this process, broken into stages, serves the analysis well. Second, we can observe forbearance (as defined above) both in its strong form (avoiding damage to the other party) and in its weak form (avoiding omitting actions which benefit the partner). A good example of the former is the forbearance shown by Kemira when Akzo Nobel was failing to correct a defect in the plant. The latter form is illustrated when Alpha helped to solve Gamma's financial problems. Third, reputation effects are important, as an appreciating asset brought to the table in the first stage and as an operating asset as promises are delivered or overfulfilled. Fourth, from a transaction cost point of view, the cases illustrate some very important advantages of joint ventures (Buckley and Casson, 1988). The joint venture ABG (1) allows hedging against changes in the price movement of the intermediate product; (2) sees to it that long-term supply is assured; (3) makes sure that operational integration between upstream and downstream activities is achieved; and (4) implements quality assurance in supplies. The joint venture Kemax (1) allows efficient utilization of a by-product of a separate process and (2) prevents competition from a (second) source of production. Through the LAP joint venture, Hoogovens secured its supply to the joint venture and Usinor prevented the growth of competition in the Iberian market. The risks of financing the takeover were shared. The joint operations of DSM–BASF provided economies of scale, but the attitude of key clients prevented a full merger – there was a strong chance that the acquiring party would lose customers when the business was sold. The cases illustrate a combination of internalization economies, indivisibilities and barriers to merger. In addition, the IJVs provide a context where the partners demonstrate mutual forbearance and therefore build up trust. A key thread, which runs through the exposition, is that trust reinforces self-interest and is often seen to be there when self-interest is clearly congruent with trusting behaviour.

In terms of our process model as presented in Figure 6.2, we can see from the summary of results (Figure 6.11) that it performs well. At every stage, we can identify outputs of trust, which become inputs into the next stage (see also the recursive model of Madhok, 1995b). Not all the assumptions in the conceptual model are justified, and we find one instance of an output of distrust. The research findings reveal a rich picture and suggest that the model is a useful one for the further examination of trust-building processes in IJVs. Indeed, the results are richer in many areas than the original conceptual model initially suggested. For instance, the personal elements of relationships and feelings (e.g. 'putting oneself in the other's shoes') are shown to be important. Moreover, it appears that promissory-based trust is important early in the process and competence-based trust later in the sequence of stages. Trust based on individual self-interest thus grows, through forbearance to a commitment to cooperate, which is self-reinforcing (Buckley and Casson, 1988). Goodwill is important throughout. These preliminary results provide an excellent basis for more research – and, in particular, for testing our model on a wider sample of firms.

Our research has limitations. It is based on only four case studies. These case studies cannot be considered representative of all IJVs because of their industrial and cultural biases. Generalization is only possible by applying our model to further examples. Because our model is longitudinal, it is necessary to test it against the behaviour of firms over time – a difficult, costly and time-consuming enterprise. It is not easy to transform our model to make it suitable for point-of-time cross-sectional postal questionnaire type approaches. However, we believe that longitudinal analysis is the correct way to proceed in IJV research. The next step is to confront our model with a richer, more widely dispersed set of cases, with more cultural and structural variety in the IJVs analysed in order to investigate its degree of robustness. It may also be possible in future research to move forward from our linear model to a more realistic, recursive flow schema.

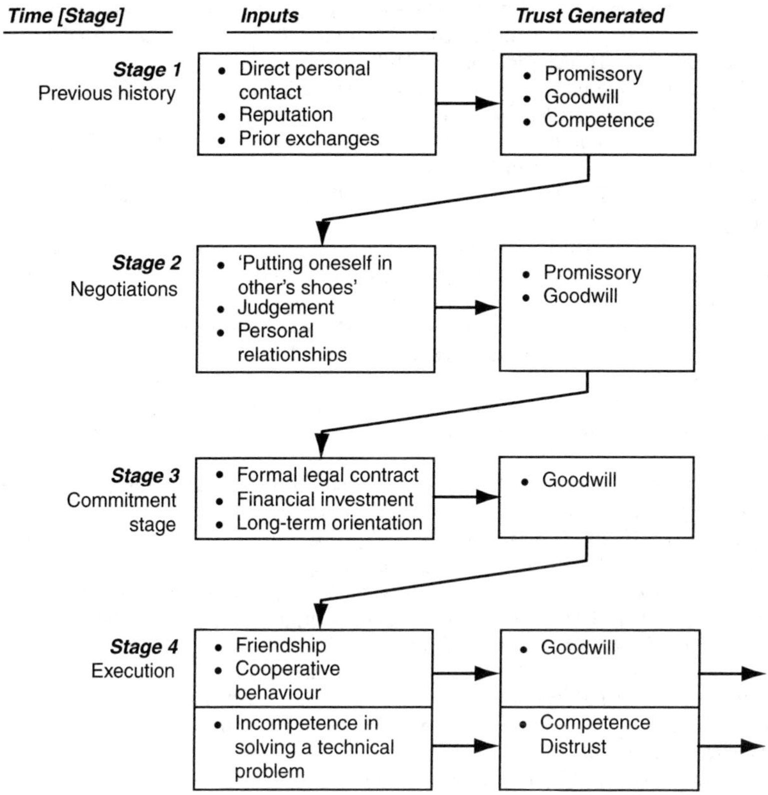

Figure 6.11 The research model: findings of the four illustrative cases

Acknowledgements

The authors thank Professor Wouter van Rossum, Rosalinde Klein Woolthuis and two anonymous referees for their helpful comments.

References

Ariño, A. and Torre, J. de la (1996) 'Learning from Failure: the Evolution of Co-operative Behaviour in Inter-firm Ventures'. Paper presented at the AOM Annual Meeting, Cincinnati.

Barber, B. (1983) *The Logic and Limits of Trust*. New Brunswick: Rutgers Univ. Press.

Beamish, P. and Banks, J. C. (1987) 'Equity Joint Ventures and the Theory of the Multinational Enterprise'. *Journal of International Business Studies*, vol. 18, no. 2, pp. 1–16.

Bigley, G. and Pearce, J. (1998) 'Straining for Shared Meaning in Organization Science: Problems of Trust and Distrust'. *Academic Management Review*, vol. 23, no. 3, pp. 405–21.

Buckley, P. and Casson, M. (1988) 'A Theory of Co-operation in International Business'. In F. J. Contractor and P. Lorange (eds), *Co-operative Strategies in International Business*. Lexington: D. C. Heath and Co., pp. 31–53.

Buckley, P. and Chapman, M. K. (1997) 'The Perception and Measurement of Transaction Costs'. *Cambridge Journal of Economy,* vol. 21, no. 2, pp. 127–45.

Contractor, F. and Lorange, P. (1988) *Co-operative Strategies in International Business*. Lexington: D. C. Heath and Co.

Corazzini, J. G. (1977) 'Trust as a Complex Multi-dimensional Construct'. *Psychology Reports,* vol. 40, pp. 75–80.

Craswell, R. (1993) 'On the Uses of Trust: Comment on Williamson's "Calculativeness, Trust and Economic Organization"'. *Journal of Law Economy,* vol. 36, pp. 487–500.

Das, T. K. and Teng, B. S. (1998) 'Between Trust and Control: Developing Confidence in Partner Cooperation in Alliances'. *Academic Management Review,* vol. 23, no. 3, pp. 491–512.

Deutsch, M. (1962) 'Co-operation and Trust: Some Theoretical Notes'. In Jones M. R., (ed.), *Nebraska Symposium on Motivation*. Lincoln: University of Nebraska Press, pp. 275–320.

Dwyer, F. R., Schurr, P. H. and Oh, S. (1987) 'Developing Buyer–Seller Relationships'. *Journal of Marketing,* pp. 11–27 (April).

Gabarro, J. J. (1978) 'The Development of Trust, Influence, and Expectations'. In Athos, A. G. and Gabarro, J. J. (eds), *Interpersonal Behaviour: Communication and Understanding in Relationships*. Englewood Cliffs, NJ: Prentice-Hall, pp. 290–303.

Ganesan, S. (1994) 'Determinants of Long-term Orientation in Buyer–Seller Relationships'. *Journal of Marketing,* vol. 58, pp. 1–19.

Geringer, J. M. and Hebert, L. (1989) 'Control and Performance of International Joint Ventures'. *Journal of International Business Studies,* pp. 235–54 (Summer).

Gill, J. and Butler, R. (1996) 'Cycles of Trust and Distrust in Joint Ventures. *European Management Journal,* vol. 14, no. 1, pp. 81–9.

Granovetter, M. (1985) 'Economic Action and Social Structure: the Problem of Embeddedness'. *American Journal of Sociology,* vol. 91, pp. 481–510.

Hennart, J. F. (1988) 'A Transaction Cost Theory of Equity Joint Ventures'. *Strategic Management Journal,* vol. 9, pp. 361–74.

Hosmer, L. T. (1995) 'Trust: the Connecting Link between Organizational Theory and Philosophical Ethics'. *Academic Management Review,* vol. 20, no. 2, pp. 379–403.

Hyder, A. and Ghauri, P. (2000) 'Managing International Joint Venture Relationships: a Longitudinal Perspective'. *Industrial Marketing Management,* vol. 29, no. 3, pp. 205–18.

Killing, J. P. (1982) 'How to Make a Global Joint Venture Work'. *Harvard Business Review,* vol. 61, no. 3, pp. 120–7.

Larson, A. (1992) 'Network Dyads in Entrepreneurial Settings: a Study of the Governance of Exchange Relationships'. *Administrative Science Quarterly,* vol. 37, pp. 76–104.

Lewicki, R. J., McAllister, D. J. and Bies, R. J. (1998) 'Trust and Distrust: New Relationships and Realities'. *Academic Management Review,* vol. 23, no. 3, pp. 438–58.

Lin, X. and Germain, R. (1997) 'Sustaining Satisfactory Joint Venture Relationships: the Role of Conflict Resolution Strategy'. *Journal of International Business Studies,* vol. 29, no. 1, pp. 179–98.

Luhmann, N. (1988) 'Familiarity, Confidence, Trust: Problems and Alternatives. In D. Gambetta (ed.), *Trust: Making and Breaking Co-operative Relations*. Oxford: Blackwell, pp. 101–7.

Madhok, A. (1995a) 'Revisiting Multinational Firms' Tolerance for Joint Ventures: a Trust-based Approach'. *Sound International Business Studies,* vol. 26, no. 1, pp. 117–37.
Madhok, A. (1995b) 'Opportunism and Trust in Joint Venture Relationships: an Exploratory Study and a Model'. *Scandinavian Journal of Management,* vol. 11, pp. 57–74.
Makino, S. (1995) 'Joint Venture Ownership Structure and Performance: Japanese Joint Ventures in Asia'. Unpublished PhD dissertation, University of Western Ontario.
Miles, M. B. and Huberman, A. M. (1994) *Qualitative Data Analysis*. Thousands Oaks: Sage Publications.
Nooteboom, B. (1996) 'Trust, Opportunism and Governance: a Process and Control Model'. *Organization Studies,* vol. 17, no. 6, pp. 985–1010.
Parkhe, A. (1993a) 'Trust in International Joint Ventures'. Paper presented at the Academy of International Business Meeting, Hawaii.
Parkhe, A. (1993b) 'Messy Research, Methodological Predispositions, and Theory Development in International Joint Ventures'. *Academic Management Review,* vol. 18, pp. 227–68.
Rempel, J. K., Holmes, J. G. and Zanna, M. P. (1985) 'Trust in Close Relationships'. *Journal of Personal Social Psychology,* vol. 49, no. 1, pp. 95–112.
Ring, P. S. and van de Ven, A. H. (1994) 'Developmental Processes of Co-operative Inter-organizational Relationships'. *Academic Management Review,* vol. 19, pp. 90–118.
Sako, M. (1992) *Prices, Quality and Trust: Inter-firm Relations in Britain and Japan.* Cambridge: Cambridge Univ. Press.
Stafford, E. R. (1995) 'Opportunities for Alliance Research in Marketing: an Argument for a Multi-method Case Research Strategy'. *American Marketing Association,* pp. 508–15 (Summer).
Strauss, A. and Corbin, J. (1990) *Basics of Qualitative Research.* Thousands Oaks: Sage Publications.
Uzzi, B. (1997) 'Social Structure and Competition in Interfirm Networks: the Paradox of Embeddedness'. *Administrative Science Quarterly,* vol. 42, no. 1, pp. 35–67.
Williams, B. (1988) 'Formal Structures and Social Reality'. In Gambetta D. (ed.), *Trust: Making and Breaking Co-operative Relations.* Oxford: Blackwell, pp. 3–13.
Williamson, O. E. (1975) *Markets and Hierarchies.* New York: Free Press.
Williamson, O. E. (1983) 'Credible Commitments: Using Hostages to Support Exchange'. *American Economic Review,* vol. 73, pp. 519–40.
Williamson, O. E. (1993) 'Calculativeness, Trust, and Economic Organization'. *Journal of Law Economy,* vol. 36, no. 1, pp. 453–86.
Yin, R. K. (1989) *Case Research: Design and Methods.* London: Sage Publications.

7
The Challenges of the New Economy for Multinational Firms: Lessons for South-East Asia[1]

Introduction

This chapter examines the impact of the 'new economy' on decision making in the multinational firm. Here, the new economy is taken to mean the technological revolution brought about by the widespread use of the Internet and electronic commerce (e-commerce), together with the political developments in the first years of a new millennium. These developments have brought a new volatility to international business and to the operations of multinational firms. The responses of firms to these pressures, and to 'globalization', which multinationals help to further, have resulted in important changes of strategy in the world's multinational firms, with widespread consequences for the world economy.

The chapter is structured in the following way. The second section examines the operations of multinational firms in a single market. This is an artificial situation, but it helps to clarify the importance of key decisions, and the impact on those decisions of changes brought by e-commerce. The third section then goes on to examine operations in more than one market, and the fourth section tackles the crucial issues of interaction between markets. The fifth section looks in detail at the meaning of globalization for multinational firms and shows the interaction between globalization and e-commerce. The sixth section concentrates on the internal effects of technological and socio-political change within multinational firms. Reactions to increased volatility are shown to have a profound impact on internal organization. The seventh section is a summary, and the eighth section draws out implications for South-East Asia and its investment attraction agencies.

Operations of multinational firms in a single market

Location and ownership strategies

The typical US MNE of the 'golden age' was a vertically, as well as horizontally, integrated firm. In consequence, each division of the firm was locked into linkages with other divisions of the same firm. As Asian competition intensified, there was growing recognition of the costs of integration of this kind. Figure 7.1 shows the complex network of a multinational firm involved in a single market. There are two critical decisions covering each of the activities displayed (production, stockholding, promotion, etc.). These are: (1) where should the activity be located, and (2) how should it be controlled? The control decision is whether to own and operate the function in-house or to subcontract, outsource or contract for the function outside the company. Joint ventures are a halfway house between ownership and contract. These two decisions determine the strategy of the company but need careful co-ordination. For instance, a promotional (advertising) strategy must be carefully coordinated with the product or service supply chain.

Commitment to a particular source of supply or demand of any product, intermediate good or service is relatively low-cost in a high-growth scenario, since it is unlikely that any investment will need to be reversed. It is much more costly in a low-growth scenario, where production may need to be switched to a cheaper source of supply, or sales diverted away from a depressed market. The desire for flexibility therefore discourages vertical integration – whether it is backward integration into production, or forward integration into distribution. It is better to subcontract production and to franchise sales instead. The subcontracting of production is similar in principle to a 'putting out' arrangement, but differs in the sense that the subcontractor is now a firm rather than just a single worker.

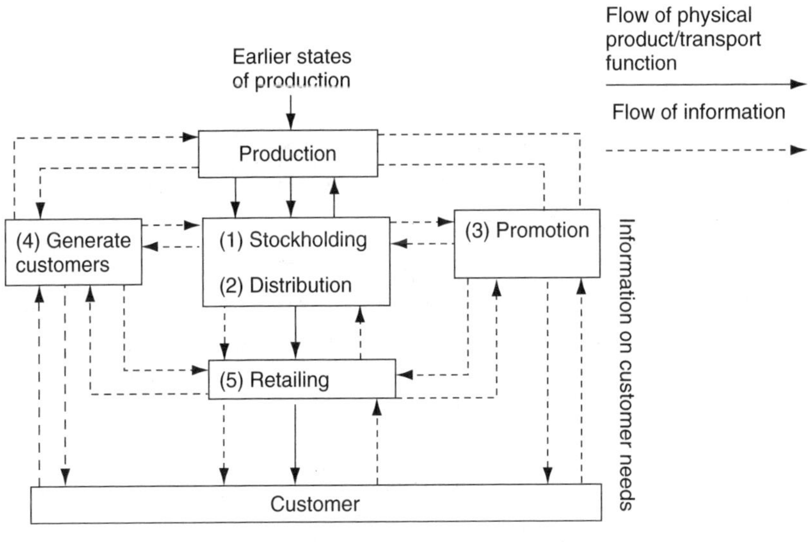

Figure 7.1 Linkages between the activities of the firm. Reproduced from Buckley et al. (1990)

Disintermediation and reintermediation

Dis-integration was also encouraged by a low-trust atmosphere that developed in many firms. Fear of internal monopoly became rife, including worries about the 'hold-up' problem, even when the single source of supply was an internal one. Production managers faced with falling demand wished that they did not have to sell all their output through a single sales manager. Sales managers resented the fact that had to obtain all their supplies from the same small set of plants. Each manager doubted the competence of the others, and ascribed the loss of corporate competitiveness to selfishness and inefficiency elsewhere in the firm. Divisions aspired to be spun off so that they could deal with other business units instead. On the other hand, managers were wary of the risks that would be involved if they severed their links with other divisions altogether. The result is that a much more complex strategy set faces decision makers in multinational firms.

B2B e-commerce

B2B transactions account for 80 per cent of all e-commerce. E-shopping accounts for only approximately 1 per cent of all retail sales in the US (or one-tenth of catalogue sales). However, it should be pointed out that usage of the net is greater than the number of transactions, because customers can use it to compare prices and to search for information. The new value chain is shown in Figure 7.2, which illustrates both the impact of disintermediation on the vertically integrated firm and the opportunities for reintermediation.

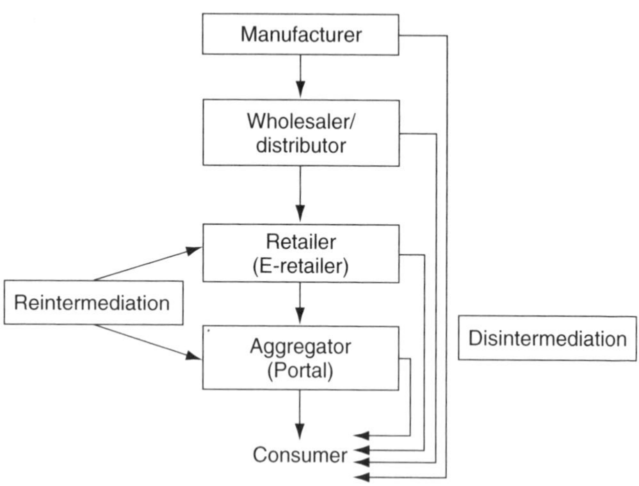

Figure 7.2 The new value chain

Source: *The Economist*, e-commerce survey, 26 February 2002.

Disintermediation by e-commerce reduces warehousing costs but increases the costs of maintaining a reliable website. It reduces stock holding cost and fixed capital but logistics and distribution requirements become more complex and costly. There are gains in economies of scale and scope by using e-commerce and the ease of data exploitation is a major benefit, allowing companies to reach customers and sources of supply more easily and to foster competition for supply contracts. These advantages can be summarized as 'reach' and 'richness'. Reach describes the size of the audience which can be accessed and the ease of connection. This measures the number of customers a business can service or how many products it can offer. Richness describes the customization of service, the depth and detail of information which can be given or collected. The degree of affiliation measures the attachment of customers to individual suppliers and reciprocally the company's responsiveness to customer needs. The argument is that global/local trade-offs (see fourth section) can be managed better on the web using e-commerce, so that integration and responsiveness are replaced by reach and richness.

Reintermediation using e-commerce

Figure 7.2 shows that as well as disintermediation e-commerce allows re-intermediation. A number of wholesalers/distributors can be aggregated by an e-retailer and on this reading a portal is equivalent to a shopping mall. Aggregators thus acquire considerable buying power. An example is the impact of e-commerce on travel agents. Many travel agents have been disintermediated but the response to this is a 'clicks and mortar' strategy integrating e-commerce with traditional business. Successful travel agents now manage a combined strategy. This is instructive for businesses facing such challenges. The advent of electronic commerce has also introduced new players such as 'navigators' who represent customers and fulfil their choices, and 'infomediaries' who take care of privacy issues and provide payment security.

The nature of the product and therefore of the industry remains important in e-commerce transactions. We can constrast 'high touch' versus 'low touch' goods and services (e.g. clothes and shoes versus books, computers and CD-ROMS). For the second group delivery over the Internet is a prime example of the impact of e-commerce in changing the competitive dynamics of an industry. E-commerce lowers barriers to entry to industries where electronic delivery is possible and provides opportunities for growth by reintermediation. However, firms still have to find the best location for all the activities in the value chain and to protect their market niche. Achieving optimum scale of each activity in the chain and consistency of product delivery and quality remain major competitive necessities.

Strategy, e-commerce and networks

These changes are challenges for 'old economy' companies – integrating online functions with existing brand and back office infrastructure. B2B, building online links with suppliers and customers, implies a redesign of the business processes network. Smaller companies may find it easier to operate internationally. It is therefore easier to reach customers but there are still information problems, logistics difficulties and the necessity to maintain management control. Products still have to be distributed and thus the firm has to take account not just of transport costs but also of regulatory differences between countries, cultural distance and other barriers.

A natural way to cope with these pressures is to allow each division to deal with external business units, as well as internal ones. In terms of internalization theory, internal markets become 'open' rather than 'closed'. This provides divisional managers with an opportunity to bypass weak or incompetent sections of the company. It also provides a competitive discipline on internal transfer prices, preventing their manipulation for internal political ends, and bringing them more into line with external prices. There are other advantages too. Opening up internal markets severs the link between the capacities operated at adjacent stages of production. The resulting opportunity to supply other firms facilitates the exploitation of scale economies because it permits the capacity of any individual plant to exceed internal demand. Conversely, it encourages the firm to buy in supplies from other firms that have installed capacity in excess of their own needs.

The alignment of internal prices with external prices increases the objectivity of profit measurement at the divisional level. This allows divisional managers to be rewarded by profit-related pay, based on divisional profit rather than firm-wide profit. Management may even buy out part of the company. Alternatively the firm may restructure by buying in a part of an independent firm. The net effect is the same in both cases. The firm becomes the hub of a network of interlocking joint ventures (Buckley and Casson, 1988, 1996). Each joint venture partner is responsible for the day-to-day management of the venture. The headquarters of the firm coordinates the links between the ventures. Internal trade is diverted away from the weaker ventures and towards the stronger ones, thereby providing price and profit signals to which the weaker partners need to respond. Unlike a pure external market situation, the partners are able to draw upon expertise at headquarters, which can in turn tap into expertise in other parts of the group.

A network does not have to be built around a single firm, of course. A network may consist of a group of independent firms instead. Sometimes these firms are neighbours, as in the regional industrial clusters described by Best (1990), Porter (1990) and Rugman et al. (1995). Industrial districts, such as 'Toyota city', have been hailed as an Asian innovation in flexible management, although the practice has been common in Europe for centuries

(Marshall, 1919). As tariffs and transport costs have fallen, networks have become more international and 'virtual'. This is demonstrated by the dramatic growth in intermediate product trade under long-term contracts. For example, an international trading company may operate a network of independent suppliers in different countries, substituting different sources of supply in response to both short-term exchange rate movements and long-term shifts in comparative advantage.

Flexibility is also needed in research and development. A firm cannot afford to become overcommitted to the refinement of any one technology, in case innovation elsewhere should render the entire technology obsolete. As technology has diffused in the post-war period, the range of countries with the competence to innovate has significantly increased. The pace of innovation has consequently risen, and the threat of rapid obsolescence is therefore higher as a result. The natural response for firms is to diversify their research portfolios. But the costs of maintaining a range of research and development projects are prohibitive, given the enormous fixed costs involved. The costs of basic research and development have escalated because of the increased range of specialist skills involved, while the costs of applied research and development have risen because of the need to develop global products which meet increasingly stringent consumer protection laws. Joint ventures are an appropriate solution once again. By establishing a network of joint ventures covering alternative technological trajectories, the firm can spread its costs whilst retaining a measure of proprietary control over new technologies.

The advantage of joint ventures is further reinforced by technological convergence, for example, the integration of computers, telecommunications and photography. This favours the creation of networks of joint ventures based on complementary technologies, rather than on the substitute technologies described above (Cantwell, 1995). Joint ventures are important because they afford a number of real options (Trigeorgis, 1996) which can be taken up or dropped, depending upon how the project turns out. The early phase of a joint venture provides important information which could not be obtained through investigation before the venture began. It affords an opportunity later on to buy more fully into a successful venture – an opportunity which is not available to those who have not taken any stake. It therefore provides greater flexibility than does either outright ownership or an alternative involving no equity stake.

Operations of multinational firms in more than one market

The new dynamic agenda focuses on: uncertainty and market volatility; flexibility and the value of options; cooperation through joint ventures and business networks; entrepreneurship, managerial competence and corporate culture; and organizational change, including the mandating of subsidiaries and the 'empowerment' of employees. Flexibility may be defined as the ability to reallocate resources quickly and smoothly in response to change. The greater are the amplitude and frequency of change in the environment, the greater is the need for flexibility. As far as multinational firms are concerned, the impact of change is captured by the volatility induced in the profit stream. The volatility of profit that would occur if the firm made no response to change summarizes the impact on the firm of volatility in its environment.

The international diffusion of modern production technology has increased the number of industrial powers, and hence increased the number of countries in which political and social disturbances can impact significantly on global supplies of manufactured products. The liberalization of trade and capital markets means that the 'ripple' effects of shock travel further and wider than before (Casson, 1995, ch. 4). Ripples are transmitted more quickly too: news travels almost instantaneously, thanks to modern telecommunications. Thus speculative bubbles in stock markets spread quickly around the world. Following the breakdown of the Bretton Woods exchange rate system, fluctuations have created a new dimension of financial volatility too.

As a result, any given national market is now affected by a much wider range of disturbances than ever before. Every national subsidiary of a multinational firm experiences a multiplicity of shocks from around the world. It is no longer the case that a national subsidiary has to respond to shocks originating in its national market alone. The shocks also come from new sources of import competition and new competitive threats in export markets. While most shocks reveal themselves to firms as competitive threats, new opportunities for cooperation may sometimes be presented as well. The awareness of this sustained increase in volatility has led to a search for more flexible forms of organization.

Increased volatility is not the only reason for greater interest in flexibility. Contemporary culture is very much opposed to building organizations around a single source of monopoly power. The nation state, for example, is under threat from advocates of regional government. The traditional role of the state, to supply defence, can in principle be effected through multilateral defence treaties in which politically independent regions club together for this specific purpose. The demise of the Soviet bloc, and the subsequent political realignment between its member states, may be seen as an example of this kind of cultural change at work. This distrust of monopoly power may be linked to an increase in other forms of distrust, as suggested below.

The aversion to internal monopoly is apparent amongst multinational firms as well. This movement began in the early 1980s when the powerful central research laboratories of high-technology multinational firms were either closed down, shifted to the divisions, or forced to operate as suppliers to 'internal customers' in competition with outside bodies, such as universities (Casson et al., 1991). Headquarters' bureaucracies came under attack shortly afterwards, as 'de-layering' got under way. The favoured form of firm has become a federal structure of operating divisions drawing on a common source of internal expertise, but where each division belonging to the federation is free to outsource expertise if it so desires. As with any trend, there has been a tendency for certain advocates to take it to extremes. Just as the 'golden age' was rife with suggestions that oligopolies of hierarchical multinational firms would come to dominate world markets, so the 1990s have spawned visions of the 'network firm' and the 'virtual firm'. A factor common to these visions is a 'fuzzy' boundary of the firm, where the firm fades into the market, through joint ventures, with declining proportional equity stakes. These arguments for fuzzy boundaries are, unfortunately, often based on equally fuzzy reasoning. Fuzzy boundaries can be configured in many different ways. The new research agenda outlined here places arguments for fuzzy boundaries on a rigorous basis, and predicts the specific form that fuzziness will take in each particular case.

Dynamic market entry (and exit)

Consider the problem of modelling market entry from a dynamic, rather than a static, point of view (Chi and McGuire, 1996). The most important new point to take into account is that the foreign market can decline as well as grow. Divestment or withdrawal must be considered as serious strategies. Clearly, these strategies do not apply until the market has been entered, but once it has been entered they may need to be used. Static models assume that the market will be constant, while very simple dynamic models, such as Buckley and Casson (1981), only suppose that the market will grow. In a volatile environment a market may grow to begin with, attracting investment, but then go into decline, requiring divestment instead. Such explicit recognition of adverse scenarios is a characteristic of the new research agenda.

Switching between strategies is costly, and the costs depend on both the strategy the firm is switching from, and the strategy the firm is switching to. In some cases, switching costs decompose neatly into a cost of exit from the old strategy and a cost of setting up the new strategy. Detailed modelling of such costs is a key element of the new research agenda.

To preserve flexibility, it is important for the firm to choose at the outset strategies whose exit costs are low. This tends to favour exporting over host-country production, and licensing over internalization. In other words, it reveals foreign direct investment as a high-risk strategy. Switching decisions can be mistaken, however, because the information upon which they are based is poor. Expected switching costs are reduced by avoiding unnecessary switches. Different strategies afford different opportunities for capturing information from the host environment and feeding it back to inform subsequent switching decisions. The new agenda involves explicit modelling of how the strategy chosen at one stage affects the information available at following stages.

Foreign direct investment offers better opportunities for information capture than either licensing or exporting, since ownership of assets confers ownership of information too. This means, for example, that if volatility caused the market to unexpectedly grow, then the foreign investor should recognize this quickly. Since it is often cheaper to expand existing capacity than to build from scratch, the foreign investor also faces lower cost of capacity expansion than does an exporter who decides to switch to foreign production at this stage. While exporting continues to confer more flexibility in response to market decline, therefore, foreign direct investment confers more flexibility in respect to market growth. Is it possible to find a strategy with a better combination of characteristics than either exporting, licensing or foreign direct investment? An international joint venture may provide the answer (Kogut, 1991). Investing in a 50 : 50 partnership with a host-country producer lays off some of the risks associated with wholly owned foreign direct investment. At the same time, information capture remains reasonably good. There is an option to expand capacity if there is unexpected market growth, and a further option to increase commitment by buying the partner out. There is also an easy option to withdraw by selling out to the partner. The partner provides a ready market for divested assets that an ordinary direct investor lacks. There is a downside, of course – an obvious problem is that the partners may themselves become a source of volatility. This is why trust is such an important element in an international joint venture. In this way the emphasis on risk management within the new research agenda leads to the emergence of new 'compromise strategies', which would be dominated by more conventional strategies, were it not for the 'option value' they possess within a volatile environment.

International joint venture options can only be exercised once, of course, unless the investor switches back to an international joint venture arrangement at a later date, when they can be exercised all over again. This explains international joint venture instability as a rational response to the role that international joint ventures fulfil. An international joint venture in which the options are never exercised is probably inferior to a wholly owned investment, while an international joint venture in which the options are exercised at the first available opportunity does not last for very long. When international joint ventures are chosen because of their option value, it is normally inefficient both to switch out right away, or to never switch at all. The optimal timing of a switch is one at which uncertainty about future market growth is dispelled for a reasonable period of time. This implies that the duration of an international joint venture is, on average, fairly short, and relatively variable. This new approach provides a simple means of deriving such hypotheses about the period of time for which a given strategy will be pursued.

Interaction between markets

Global/local operations

There has always been a tension between the pressures to globalize and the need to stay local and to serve individual customers, in the strategic decisions of multinational firms. The advantages of global operations are cost based, maximizing economies of scale and reducing duplication, thus achieving efficiency. The advantages of localization are revenue based, allowing differentiation to reach all customer niches and achieving responsiveness. The tension can be summed up in the phrase 'the cost advantages of standardisation versus the revenue advantages of adaptation'. (Global and local oppositions are shown in Figure 7.3.) Much of the strategy of the multinational firm can be explained by the attempts of management to reconcile these pressures. Over time, firms have (been advised to) switch their organization so as to balance these pressures – one example is the 'transnational' type of organization advocated by Bartlett and Ghoshal (1989). However, pressures in different industries push firms towards a strategic imperative (scale in electronics, local demand differences in consumer goods) and different functions require different balances of global/local orientation (finance, production, sales functions). The 'hub and spoke' model is a key method of attempting to reconcile these conflicts.

The globalization of markets has been a major factor in the growth of volatility, as explained above. A feature of many global markets is the use of regional production and distribution hubs, where several neighbouring countries are serviced from the same location. The regional hub, like the

GLOBAL	LOCAL
Cost	Revenue
Efficiency	Responsiveness
Centralization	Decentralization
Standardization	Adaptation
'GLOCAL'?	

Figure 7.3 Global and local oppositions

international joint venture, can be understood as a strategy that offers superior flexibility. Just as an international joint venture offers a compromise ownership strategy, a regional hub offers a compromise location strategy. Because the hub is nearer to each market than is the home location, it reduces transport costs, and offers better information capture too. Yet, because it is close to several markets, it avoids exclusive commitment to any one. If one market declines, production can be switched to other markets instead; provided the shocks affecting the national markets are independent (or less than perfectly correlated, at any rate), the hub provides gains from diversification. These are real gains that only the firm can achieve, as opposed to the financial gains from unrelated product diversification, which have proved disappointing in the past, because they are best exploited through the diversification of individual share portfolios instead.

Location and ownership strategies revisited: 'hub and spoke strategies'

The two strategies of IJV and hub can be combined (see Figure 7.4). Since one – the international joint venture – is an ownership strategy and the other a location strategy they can, if desired, be combined directly in an international joint venture production hub. Closer examination of the issue suggests that this is not normally the best approach, however. The model suggests that a combination of a wholly owned production hub supplying international joint venture distribution facilities in each national market is a better solution. A hub facility is too critical to global strategy to allow a partner to become involved, because the damage they could do is far too great. Even with a wholly owned hub facility, the combination still affords considerable flexibility to divest or withdraw from any single market. The

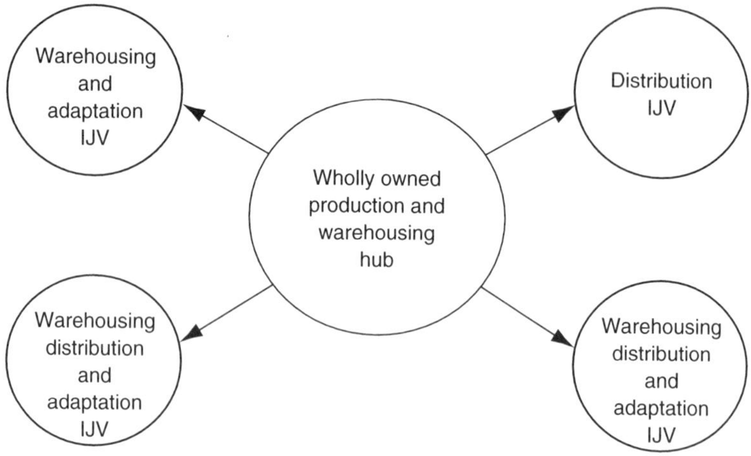

Figure 7.4 'Hub and spoke' strategies: an example

advantage of the combination is that when divesting, the distribution facility can be sold to the partner, while the production capacity can be diverted to markets elsewhere. These options for divestment are combined with useful options for expansion too. This example illustrates the crucial role that the concepts of flexibility and volatility play in analysing foreign market entry in the modern global economy. Without these concepts it is impossible to fully understand the rationale for international joint ventures and production hubs. It is also impossible to understand why these strategies have emerged at this particular historical juncture and not before.

While some of the insights of this model can certainly be expressed in terms of a framework, a framework is too crude to analyse the interplay of the different factors in a completely rigorous way. The concepts of adjustment costs and exit costs can already be found in the strategy literature, for example, but even this simple example is sufficient to show that the interplay of present entry and future exit cannot be properly understood without the aid of a fully specified model. This does not mean that the strategy literature is flawed. The new dynamic agenda is perfectly compatible with much of the existing strategy literature, but it goes beyond it by developing and refining the insights in a way that the strategy framework is unable to do.

Globalization

The differential speed of globalization

The impact of electronic communications and the increased skill of managers in deploying these resources is to allow de-duplication in the firm's international activities. Several authors on the development of multinational firms' organizational structures (Ohmae, 1990; Bartlett and Ghoshal, 1987; Doz and Prahalad, 1984) have commented that a period of replication of functions abroad (clone models, multi-domestic structures) are followed by more fully integrated structures (transnational structures, global organization). These more truly globally integrated forms are achieved by de-duplicating functions, often by coalescing them back to head office, or by having single locations for activities such as finance or divisional R&D. The advance of electronic communication has made this process more manageable.

There are a number of problems with globalization using e-commerce: delivery; taxation [electronic customs clearance and vertical warehousing]; language and currency differences [digital currencies?]; patenting of business processes; and privacy/data protection. There are also issues of trust, which arise particularly when face-to-face transactions are not the norm.

Mass customization

Mass customization is another important means of reconciling scale and differentiation (efficiency and responsiveness), e.g. in textiles – bespoke garments en masse from offshore sites with rapid delivery. Another example is 'lean retailing' – distribution and design centres linked to production centres by electronic means. Electronic ordering and automated distribution centres and inventory management systems linked to customers enable rapid response to customer needs. This combines information technology, speed and flexibility with low labour costs. So the custom versus bulk manufacture divide becomes fine. ('Cyber consumers expect to be able to customize everything.')

De-duplication of function becomes possible where electronic links allow single locations to service the whole firm's needs. Rather than a call centre for each division or country, a single one can serve all. There is also a tendency for reintegration of the supply chain from independents back to the major manufacturers, as e-commerce matures.

Internal effects on the multinational firm

Flexibility and internal organization

In a very volatile environment the level of uncertainty is likely to be high. Uncertainty can be reduced, however, by collecting information. Flexibility was defined above in terms of the ability to respond to change. The costs of response tend to be smaller when the period of adjustment is long. One way of 'buying time' to adjust is to forecast change. While no one can foresee the future perfectly, information on the present and the recent past may well improve forecasts by diagnosing underlying long-term trends. Collecting, storing and analysing information therefore enhances flexibility because by improving forecasts, it reduced the costs of change. Another way of buying time is to recognize change as early as possible. In this respect, continuous monitoring of the business environment is better than intermittent monitoring, because the potential lag before a change is recognized is eliminated. Continuous monitoring is more expensive than intermittent monitoring, though, because more management time is tied up.

Investments in better forecasts and speedier recognition highlight the trade-off between information cost and adjustment cost. This trade-off is particularly crucial when volatility is high. High volatility implies that more information should be collected to improve flexibility, which in turn implies that more managers need to be employed. This is the reverse of the usual recommendation to downsize management in order to reduce overhead costs. To improve flexibility whilst downsizing management, the trade-off between information cost and adjustment cost must be improved. There are two main ways of doing this. The first is to reduce the cost of information processing through new information technology (IT). The second is to reduce adjustment costs by building flexibility into plant and equipment, both through its design and its location. A combination of IT investment and flexible plant can reconcile greater flexibility with lower management overheads in the manner to which many multinational firms aspire.

The information required for strategic decision-making is likely to be distributed throughout the organization. It is no longer reasonable to assume that all the key information can be handled by a single chief executive, or even by the entire headquarters management team. It is difficult to know in advance where the really crucial information is likely to be found. Every manager therefore needs to have the competence to process information effectively. Managers need to be able to recognize the significance of strategic information that they acquire by chance, and to have the power of access to senior executives in order to pass it on. In other words, ordinary managers need to become internal entrepreneurs.

Few entrepreneurs have sufficient information to make a good decision without consulting other people, however. In a traditional hierarchical firm, the right to consult is the prerogative of top management. If ordinary managers are to have the power to initiate consultation, and act upon the results, then channels of communication within the firm need to be increased. Horizontal communication, as well as vertical communication, must be easy, so that lower-level managers can readily consult with their peers. A natural response is to 'flatten' the organization and encourage managers to 'network' with each other. This improves the trade-off between local responsiveness and strategic cohesion (Bartlett and Ghoshal, 1987; Hedlund, 1993). Unfortunately, though, there has been some confusion over whether flatter organizations remain hierarchies at all. However, as Casson (1994) shows, the efficient managerial processing of information normally requires a hierarchical structure of some kind. The key point is that the more diverse are the sources of volatility, the greater are the advantages of widespread consultation. The less predictable is the principal source of volatility on any given occasion, the greater is the incentive to allow consultation to be initiated anywhere in the organization. In practice this means that an increased demand for flexibility is best accommodated by flattening the organization, whilst maintaining basic elements of hierarchy.

If flexibility were costless, then all organizations could build in unlimited flexibility at the outset. In practice, the greater is flexibility, the higher transactions costs become. For example, the flexibility to switch between different sources of supply and demand (described above) means that relations with customers and suppliers become more transitory than before. Cheating becomes more likely, because the prospect of further transactions between the same two parties is more remote. Direct appeals to the other part's loyalty lose their credibility as well.

The same effect occurs when internal entrepreneurship is promoted. Internal entrepreneurs are given more discretion to act upon information that they have collected for themselves, and this increases their opportunity to cheat. Giving managers a direct stake in the business activities they help to build is one solution. The firm incubates new business units in which particular managers, or groups of managers, have equity stakes.

An alternative approach is to appeal to the integrity of managers instead. They are treated well, and in return are expected to be open and honest about what they know.

It is one of the ironies of the 1970s that at a time when personal integrity needed to be high in order to support more flexible organizations, it had been allowed to fall very low. The decline of traditional religion, the intellectual cynicism created by two world wars, and the rise of mass consumerism have all been blamed for this state of affairs. Communitarians argue correctly that moral values like integrity are most efficiently engineered at the societal level, through family, church and school. But when these institutions fail, they must be engineered to support specific economic relations instead (Fukuyama, 1996). Firms must engineer these values amongst their employees at their own expense instead (Kotter, 1996). Greater flexibility therefore implies greater costs in promoting a corporate culture that reinforces moral values.

Outsourcing and logistics

Many input functions are now viably outsourced – even human resources departments and procurement.[2] Digital delivery of product is analogous on the output side. The danger is the loss of core competences (outsourcing IT 'loses part of company's brain'). This development contributes to volatility and increases the mobility of activities internationally, as a great deal of outsourcing functions are competed for on a global basis. The policy of promoting linkages (forward as well as backward) followed by many agencies of national and local government needs to account for these changing decision-making parameters.

As is always the case, disintegration of established supply chains is followed by reintegration and consolidation. The trend to outsource (disinternalize) manufacturing by major multinationals led initially to subcontracting to independents – many of them located in South-East Asia (and Mexico). Contract manufacturing[3] has been growing by 20 per cent per year in the late 1990s and the early part of this century. However, contract manufacturers are rapidly consolidating, through mergers, and are expected to reach an oligopolistic equilibrium, with around six firms dominating the global market. These firms are becoming supply chain managers, sometimes even organizing distribution and repair. These links between customers and suppliers are, of course, facilitated by the use of the Internet.

Contract manufacturers, ensured of future contracts, are thus able to achieve economies of scale and to become more capital intensive, replacing unskilled labour by high-tech capital equipment. This trend is accelerated by the competitive imperative becoming speed to market, not cost. A linked supply of available factories in different national locations means that contract manufacturers can switch production lines between these units. Flexibility is achieved by using these 'shell' factories between principals – entire production lines can be flown in from another location. Vertical disintegration is thus accompanied by specialization. The principal concentrates on R&D, design and marketing, the contract manufacturer provides a service to the global supplier. Companies with a strong manufacturing culture, and a commitment to a fixed location, may be outcompeted by more agile 'virtual' firms owning no manufacturing facilities at all.

Summary

Multinational firms face a number of key challenges in the new millennium. Among these are:

- the management of electronic commerce, and its integration with conventional business firms
- reacting to increased volatility in the world economy by strategies based on flexibility of response
- *reassessing ownership and location factors* in:
  - relocation
  - international joint ventures and alliances
  - disintermediation
  - de-duplication
- revisiting market entry strategies:
  - sequential market entry
  - dynamic market entry
- the creation, renewal and maintenance of viable corporate cultures, to combine competence, honesty and entrepreneurship
- coping with uncertainty, notably the increased political uncertainty following the events of 11 September 2001

Implications for South-East Asia

There are a number of suggestions for South-East Asia and its investment agencies, which emerge from the above analysis.

Dynamic market entry

Investment attraction (and retention) requires attention to be paid to dynamic market entry. Investment agencies need to take a long-term view of the foreign market servicing strategies and sourcing strategies of multinational firms. This includes both locally owned firms and foreign investors. Foreign firms having only sales subsidiaries or subcontracting agreements, or indeed utilizing sales agencies, may (be induced to) expand into wholly owned production or service centres.

Hubs

Investment agencies should understand the 'hub and spoke' strategy, and monitor its development, particularly in an integrating area like the European Union. The appeal of hubs with higher-order activities (such as research and development or finance) is particularly attractive for locations like Singapore, but spokes may well develop into hubs or sub-hubs. This may involve supporting or fostering international joint ventures between local and foreign firms. Investment may not always be 'greenfield ventures' on a new site, but mixed forms with joint ventures and takeovers as key entry strategies. A more sophisticated attitude to takeovers is implied by this approach.

Expectations of South-East Asian economies

There is much more competition for 'footloose' foreign direct investment projects. The entry of China as a major location for labour-intensive projects has created substantial difficulties for those countries trying to compete as a location for export orientated projects. Many countries are engaged in attempting to upgrade their offer to potential inward investors. This may include direct cost competition or attempts to attract higher-order activities and skilled labour/knowledge-intensive projects.

The entry of China as a global economic superpower and super-location for inward foreign direct investment will be consolidated by its membership of the World Trade Organization and its policy of increasing openness. The competitive response of South-East Asian countries is less sure. China's range of exporting industries covers the spectrum from cheap labour-intensive products like toys to sophisticated ones like computer chips. Where is South-East Asia to find a niche? The response must be a flexible one. China may have areas of absolute advantage, but trade is based on comparative advantage. Further, as China's trade balance becomes increasingly positive, its exchange rate will rise. The growth of China's domestic purchasing power will also provide opportunities for export sales to this new consumer base.

The era of massive new greenfield projects designed for export may be passing. Much more likely are incremental changes in MNE configuration – the results of de-duplication, outsourcing, offshore production and reinvestment. The volatility of strategy increasingly makes foreign direct investment a two-way bet, unless strong investment retention policies are in place. The rationalization of facilities by MNEs is ongoing and relentless.

Networks and clusters

Establishing viable clusters – of subcontractors and suppliers – around an important principal plant has been fashionable. My analysis, and the impact of e-commerce, suggest that these clusters are becoming increasingly dispersed and virtual. It may be possible to build clusters *de novo*, but this is not the norm. A more detailed understanding of company networks is necessary. More sophisticated policies on 'promoting linkages' need to evolve.

The 'Asian crisis' and its aftermath has not only slowed inward foreign direct investment from outside South-East Asia, it has also disrupted intra-regional flows of foreign direct investment. Both of these factors, the decreasing share of world foreign direct investment attracted by South-East Asia, and disrupted intra-South-East Asian networks, have serious long-term effects. The switch of footloose foreign direct investment to China may have permanent repercussions, but the necessity to reconsolidate regional networks is vital in a region of small interdependent states.

E-commerce

The operations of small, fully internationalized companies are now much more viable. Many companies are alleged to be 'born global' and this means paying attention to start-ups and potential small global players in the domestic economy. There is a clear importance to the building and maintenance of state-of-the-art electronic infrastructure. Physical infrastructure quality still remains important in attracting and retaining investment. The attitude of investment attraction agencies must be like a venture capital company which expects only a few (perhaps 1 in 20?) projects to fully succeed.

Volatility

The key message of this chapter is that volatility in the global economy is increasing. International joint ventures, for instance, are likely in general to be short-lived but variable in longevity. There will *not* be massive 'successes' in the attraction of new greenfield investments or massive 'failures' in closure, but the search for flexibility will mean that incremental shifts will be many and cumulatively profound. In this context, there is no substitute for being close to the companies' thinking.

Impact of New Developments in Southeast Asia

Location	New locations Race to the bottom?
Ownership	Foreign direct investment in South-East Asia Networks of South-East Asian firms Entrepreneurship
Internalization	Vertical disintegration? De-duplication? Size of firms

Notes

1. The basic framework of this chapter is derived from Buckley and Casson (1998).
2. See 'Out of the Back Room', *The Economist*, 1 December 2001, pp. 75–6.
3. See 'Factories for Hire', *The Economist*, 12 February 2000, p. 81.

References

Bartlett, Christopher A. and Ghoshal, Sumantra (1987) 'Managing across Borders: New Strategic Requirements'. *Sloan Management Review*, Summer, pp. 6–17.

Bartlett, Christopher A. and Ghoshal, Sumantra (1989) *Managing across Borders: the Transnational Solution*. Boston: Hutchinson Business Books.

Best, Michael H. (1990) *The New Competition: Institutions of Industrial Restructuring*. Oxford: Polity Press.

Buckley, Peter J. and Casson, Mark C. (1981) 'The Optimal Timing of a Foreign Direct Investment'. *Economic Journal*, no. 91, pp. 75–87.

Buckley, Peter J. and Casson, Mark (1988) 'A Theory of Co-operation in International Business'. In Farok J. Contractor and Peter Lorange (eds), *Co-operative Strategies in International Business*. Lexington, Mass.: Lexington Books.

Buckley, Peter J. and Casson, Mark (1996) 'An Economic Model of International Joint Venture Strategy'. *Journal of International Business Studies*, vol. 27, no. 5, pp. 849–76.

Buckley, Peter J. and Casson, Mark (1998) 'Models of Multinational Enterprise'. *Journal of International Business Studies*, vol. 29, no. 1, pp. 29–44.

Buckley, Peter J., Pass L. Christopher and Prescott Kate (1988) 'Measures of International Competitiveness: a Critical Survey'. *Journal of Marketing Management*, vol. 4, no. 2, pp. 175–200.

Cantwell, John (ed.) (1995) *Multinational Enterprises and Innovatory Activities: Towards a New Evolutionary Approach*. Chur: Harwood Academic Publishers.

Casson, Mark (1994) 'Why are Firms Hierarchical?' *International Journal of the Economics of Business*, vol. 1, no. 1, pp. 3–40.

Casson, Mark (1995) *Organization of International Business*. Aldershot: Edward Elgar.

Casson, Mark, Pearce, Robert D. and Singh, Satwinder (1991) 'A Review of Recent Trends'. In M. Casson (ed.), *Global Research Strategy and International Competitiveness*. Oxford: Blackwell.

Chi, Tailan and McGuire, Donald J. (1996) 'Collaborative Ventures and Value of Learning: Integrating the Transaction Cost and Strategic Option Perspectives on the Choice of Market Entry Modes'. *Journal of International Business Studies*, vol. 27, no. 2, pp. 285–307.

Doz, Yves and Prahalad, C. K. (1984) 'Patterns of Strategic Control within Multinational Corporations'. *Journal of International Business Studies*, vol. 15, pp. 55–72.

Fukuyama, F. (1996) *Trust – the Social Virtues and the Creation of Prosperity*. Harmondsworth: Penguin.

Hedlund, Gunnar (1993) 'Assumptions of Hierarchy and Heterarchy: an Application to the Multinational Corporation'. In S. Ghoshal and E. Westney (eds), *Organization Theory and the Multinational Corporation*. London: Macmillan.

Kogut, Bruce (1991) 'Joint Ventures and the Option to Expand and Acquire'. *Management Science*, vol. 37, no. 1, pp. 19–33.

Kotter, John (1996) *Leading Change*. Cambridge, Mass.: Harvard Business School Press.

Marshall, Alfred (1919) *Industry and Trade*. London: Macmillan.

Ohmae, Kenichi (1990) *The Borderless World*. London: Collins.

Porter, Michael E. (1990) *The Competitive Advantage of Nations*. New York: Free Press.

Rugman, Alan M., Joseph R. D'Cruz and Alain, Verbeke (1995) 'Internalisation and De-internalisation: Will Business Networks Replace Multinationals?' In Boyd, G. (ed.), *Competitive and Cooperative Macromanagement: the Challenge of Structural Interdependence*. Aldershot: Edward Elgar.

Trigeorgis, Lenos (1996) *Real Options*. Cambridge, Mass.: MIT Press.

Part III

Knowledge Management in Multinational Firms

8

Process and Structure in Knowledge Management Practices of British and US Multinational Enterprises

with Martin J. Carter

Introduction

This chapter investigates three key issues:

1. What determines the *process* of knowledge management? This process involves creating value from localized knowledge by combining spatially separate sources of knowledge. The firm needs to know where its knowledge assets and sources are located, and it needs to find a means of combining specific knowledge.
2. What effect does the process of knowledge management have on the organizational *structure* of the firm? The organization structure can be investigated to show if it facilitates or inhibits the knowledge management process. The management imperative is to move towards structures that enhance knowledge combination.
3. How are process and structure affected by the key *local* competence versus centralized *global* management divide within the multinational firm? Can we envisage 'global' solutions to the management of knowledge? The case studies below show that spatial issues are important in knowledge management practices and in potential organizational solutions. It also appears that successful strategies to combat knowledge 'stickiness' will involve combinations of local and global configurations of knowledge.

There is a potential conflict between the process and the organizational structure of the firm, which depends on (1) the pre-existing alignment of process and structure (this is dynamic and interactive over time), (2) the critical sequencing of the knowledge management process and (3) boundaries in knowledge, which represent 'frontiers' across which management must operate to achieve integration. Our framework has two *drivers* (knowledge characteristics and the value from combining knowledge) and two *constraints* (the participants and the technology of knowledge transfer) and two *outcomes* – on the organizational structure of the firm and the performance characteristics of the process. The approach of the chapter synthesizes earlier papers and applies the resulting theoretical framework to the spatial issues driving the knowledge management practices of multinational enterprises using illustrative case studies.

It is apparent that these management practices have local versus central conflicts inherent in them. *Knowledge* characteristics may have a local flavour because of market conditions that are particular to geographical location, or they may be due to the historical localization of particular industrial specializations (Krugman, 1994). The *value from combining knowledge* may arise from geographical separation – this is the classic rationale for the existence of a multinational firm – internalizing externalities by putting together within an internal market attributes, resources or activities generating synergy, which can be exploited with profit (Buckley and Casson, 1976). The *participants* in the process will be separated by physical and cultural difference – the combination of previously distant activities yielding a return to the coordinator. The *technology of knowledge* transfer may reside in the firm, perhaps centrally, and may be an important factor in releasing and combining local competencies. The *organizational* structure of the firm may be a result of central management dictate, or may have evolved over time, but may well be in conflict at any given time with the needs of smooth knowledge transfer and efficient knowledge management. How far do firms transfer best practice from subsidiary to parent or parent to subsidiary in order to achieve greater success in knowledge management?

The chapter reports findings from three case studies in which firms are concerned with combining localized competencies, often from different source locations, into an overarching knowledge strategy, which will enable the application of these competencies within other (localized) markets. In these examples, while there is some degree of tension between the local needs of operating business units and the global requirements of each corporation as a whole, these needs are not in inevitable opposition to one another, but instead they are mutually supportive. The corporations we describe have endeavoured to 'think globally' in order to improve the effectiveness with which they 'act locally', that is to say that they are concerned with strategies of 'glocalization'.

In order to illustrate some of the crucial issues of local and global knowledge management, our study represents a stripped down version of the complexities facing multinational firms. We have only a single parent and affiliate. We examine distinct, individual processes within each firm, reflecting only a part of any firm's overall activity, but each of which is an exemplar of larger issues. Parents and affiliates are respectively from either the USA and the UK or the reverse, so that we have only two (broadly similar) cultures and one language (almost!) of operation. We have only two industries. This eliminates many extraneous effects and allows us to concentrate on the process in a pure form. The conclusion attempts to relate this simple analysis to more complex situations.

Creating value from localized knowledge

Knowledge and uncertainty

Knowledge may be conceived as a resource that can be used to create gains out of the uncertainty facing the firm. In the entrepreneurial view of the firm (Casson, 1982, 1997), it is superior knowledge about areas of uncertainty that enables the firm to create and maintain profitable applications of physical and human resources. Uncertainty results from volatility: random fluctuations and difficult-to-predict economic and technical change, and agents with better information are able to respond more effectively to changes than less well-informed competitors.

Firms face several kinds of uncertainty (Buckley and Carter, 1999). The first is *primary uncertainty*, resulting both from volatility outside the firm, including exogenous shocks, changes in consumer's preferences and external technological change, and also from endogenous change due to the firm's internal or collaborative research and development activities.

Primary uncertainty comes from many sources, and the firm's knowledge about these sources needs to be synthesized and integrated. Large firms must rely on a division of knowledge-synthesizing labour (Casson, 1985; Carter, 1995), and this is the source of *secondary uncertainty*, described by Koopmans (1957) as '... uncertainty arising from a lack of communication, that is from one decision maker having no way of finding out the concurrent decisions and plans made by others ...' (pp. 162–3).

Secondary uncertainty arises if managers are *unable* to combine their knowledge in ways that are beneficial to the firm though ineffective communication or lack of access to knowledge resources. A third type of uncertainty, *tertiary uncertainty*, might arise from *opportunism*, 'self-interest seeking with guile' (Williamson, 1996, p. 56) if managers *choose* not to reveal this knowledge that they hold, or if they divulge incorrect or misleading information.

The focus of this study is on the processes and structures that a firm deploys for the synthesis and integration of knowledge, and it is therefore concerned with the firm's response to secondary uncertainty. The three types of uncertainty facing the firm present it with three organizational problems (Buckley and Carter, 1996): acquiring *information* (primary uncertainty), *coordination* (secondary uncertainty) and *motivation* (tertiary uncertainty). The processes described here are those for *coordinating* the activities of the corporation. The coordination problem, in particular, highlights the local and global aspects of the organization of multinational firms. The sources of both external and internal volatility can be in many different locations, but knowledge synthesis must form combinations that are coherent for the corporation as a whole and that also match the local needs of each of its activities. While knowledge acquisition and its application are both local in character, the processes and organizational structures for resolving secondary uncertainty and coordinating the application of knowledge must promote communications between locations where needed and, if necessary, must ensure that location-specific knowledge is made globally available. This is indicated schematically in Figure 8.1.

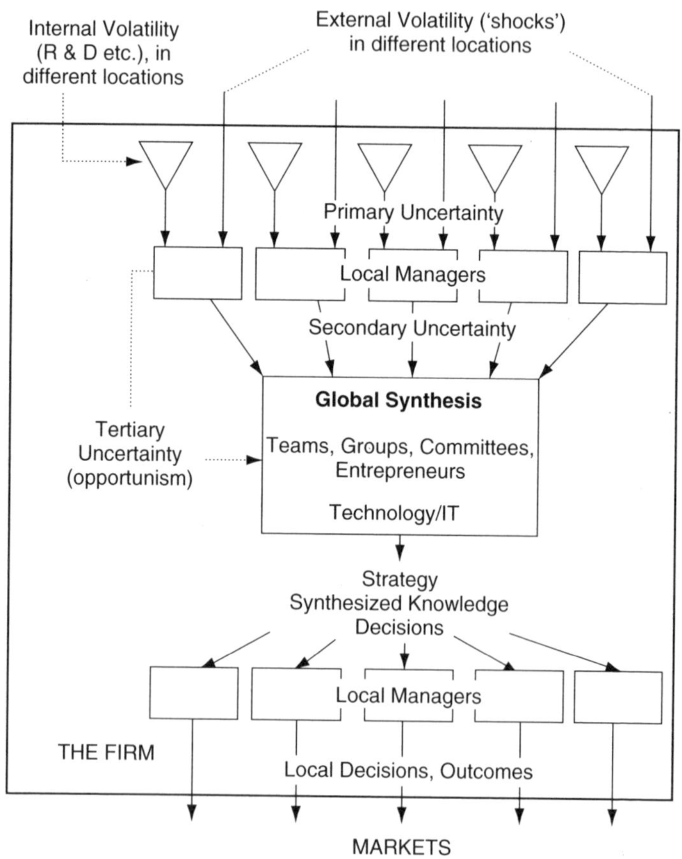

Figure 8.1 Spatial aspects of knowledge management

Uncertainty and complementary knowledge

Combining knowledge from geographically separated sources reduces secondary uncertainty. The process of knowledge synthesis indicated in Figure 8.1 depends on identifying those items of knowledge that provide additional value on combination – that is, items of knowledge that are *complementary*.

Complementarity between items of knowledge can take a number of alternative forms (Buckley and Carter, 1999). 'Additive' complementarity refers to the situation in which current knowledge, which is available in different places within the firm, may be combined to facilitate the firm's actions in one of these locations. For example, in Figure 8.2, K_1 may represent knowledge of particular local market conditions and K_2 might be a new technology developed by the firm in another place. Application of the new technology is dependent on combining both kinds of knowledge so that its exploitation is adapted to conditions pertaining in the local market.

'Sequential' complementarity arises when new knowledge is created or acquired by the firm in response to knowledge of local conditions, such as when knowledge about consumer tastes or competition in a particular market might stimulate the choice of new areas of product research and development (Figure 8.3).

Complementarity of a different kind arises when there are interactions or externalities between the activities of a firm in different geographical or product areas. These interactions may be positive (complementary) or negative in their impact on the outcome for the firm. Examples include the coordination of pricing in different countries, coordinating services to global customers who buy in more than one market, ensuring that product development activities in one country do not duplicate activities in other areas and do not inhibit their use in other countries, for example, by disqualifying them from patent protection. In such cases, it may be important to coordinate the actions to ensure the best combined outcome (Figure 8.4). We will call this *complex* complementarity.

This classification of types of complementary knowledge suggests differences in the geographic focus that might arise for each type. Additive complementarity reflects the situation in which the firm has knowledge of some particular product or service or technique of manufacture (K_2 in Figure 8.2)

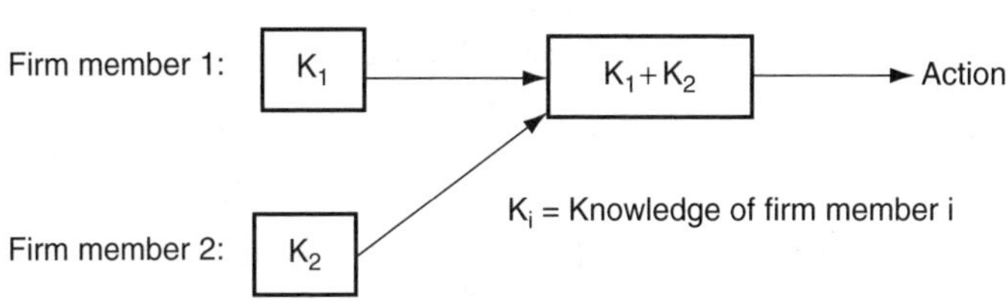

Figure 8.2 Additive complementarity

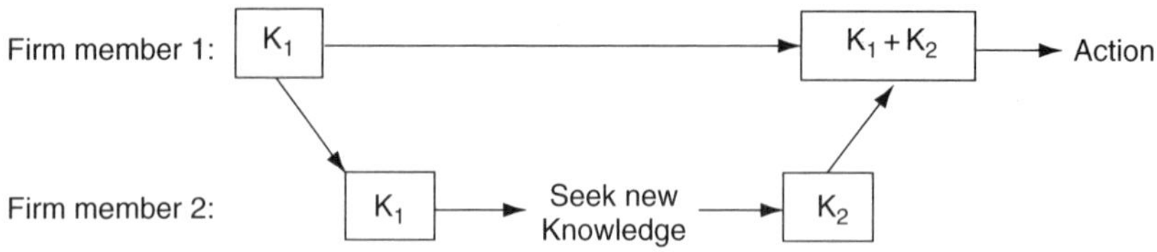

Figure 8.3 Sequential complementarity

with the potential to be used in a number of distinct local markets, so that the focus is likely to be on multiple transfers of core expertise to each distinct market, and ensuring that local management structures are able to integrate both local knowledge, K_1, and the global knowledge asset, K_2. In contrast, sequential complementarity suggests a more concentrated geographic focus, since the knowledge that is created (K_2 in Figure 8.3) is specific to a particular market application. The creation of K_2 may of course be spatially separated from the location of its intended application. The structures required to facilitate the creation of K_2 will depend on characteristics of K_1 and K_2, such as their degree of tacitness or codifiability. It may be that the transfer of the input K_1 can be a distinct stage that precedes the search for K_2. Alternatively, Firm Member 2 may need to draw on K_1 continually *during* the search for K_2. These differences will influence the organizational structures and communication channels needed between the participants. In the case of complex complementarity, coordination inevitably implies some form of centralized governance, as the nature of the interdependence is such that the independent actions of the separate agents will be suboptimal for the firm as a whole.

Our approach represents something of a break with existing literature because we have moved away from conceptualizing knowledge *flows,* particularly unidirectional flows (Gupta and Govindarajan, 2000; Foss and Pederson, 2000). Our suggestion is that, in most cases, more complex interactions will occur. One particular extension is to make explicit the spatial dimension, allowing links to be made with global and local issues in the analysis of the strategy of multinational enterprises.

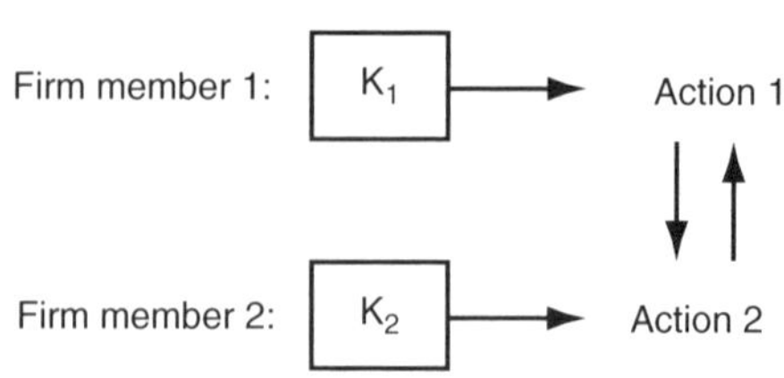

Figure 8.4 Complex complementarity

Global and local knowledge strategies

We have already suggested that the multinational enterprise engages in the synthesis and integration of knowledge, which is originally localized and which the enterprise seeks to apply more broadly. This activity may be described as the globalization of local knowledge, but there are several distinct approaches that firms may adopt, which we will indicate here. In order to do so, it will be helpful to provide clear interpretations of the terms local knowledge and global knowledge for the present discussion. We will use these terms to indicate the spatial *availability* of knowledge within the corporation. Thus, local knowledge has limited availability within the firm and is typically confined to one place. This may often be knowledge within an operating subsidiary, perhaps concerning local market conditions or possibly a technique or process that has been developed locally. However, the term may equally refer to knowledge that is confined to the administrative headquarters of a corporation. Examples might include knowledge of particular strategic plans such as expansions, mergers, acquisitions or disposals, as well as more general know-how concerning corporate finance expertise in multinational managing.

We use the term global knowledge to indicate knowledge that is generally available across the corporation, accessible to all operating subsidiaries, as well as to the administrative centre. Global knowledge is available to all within the firm, the point to emphasize being the accessibility of knowledge rather than its location. Access depends on factors that are not solely spatial, although spatial proximity may often be important. Access to knowledge depends on a number of factors, including awareness of its existence and potential, the presence of channels for communicating knowledge and the absorptive capacity (Cohen and Levinthal, 1990) of the potential users. These are the outcomes of intermediation within the firm in identifying knowledge – using opportunities and organizing access accordingly.

Thus, the knowledge that is localized within the firm and the knowledge that it chooses to make globally available are characteristics of the firm's deliberate knowledge exploitation strategy. There are a number of global/local strategic configurations that firms may display, which depend significantly on the particular circumstances of the market opportunities available to the firm. The first and simplest orientation is that of the firm that has an established home market and seeks to exploit the knowledge developed there by international expansion into other national markets. Typical examples of such knowledge are technological or marketing know-how and expansion as a multinational is preferred when internal transfer of knowledge is more efficient than the alternatives of licensing the use of that knowledge to others or of international trade in the firm's output (Buckley and Casson, 1976). In such a case, each foreign subsidiary of the parent company has access to technological or market know-how that the enterprise intends to apply in the new markets, so that this constitutes part of the firm's global knowledge. However, complementary knowledge in operating subsidiaries concerning the market conditions affecting that subsidiary remains local in character insofar as it has no value to other subsidiaries. In this case, global knowledge is confined to that which originates in the corporate parent.

A second configuration can arise when local knowledge from operating subsidiaries is valuable to other parts of the enterprise. For example, an adaptation in one country of the firm's basic technology for customers in that country might have wider applications in subsidiaries operating in other countries. The enterprise then has reason to provide all subsidiaries with access to both the know-how from the original home market and also to knowledge developed in other operation units. The firm's global knowledge comprises the original parental know-how supplemented by complementary knowledge from operating subsidiaries.

A third pattern is the firm that acts more explicitly as an intermediator in disseminating throughout the enterprise knowledge acquired by any of its subsidiaries. In this role, the parent may be less concerned with acting as the originator of the knowledge that the enterprise treats as global and rather more with facilitating global knowledge exchange within the corporation.

The patterns described here are not mutually exclusive alternatives, nor do they make an exhaustive list of possibilities. However, they do indicate alternative strategic orientations, which can be discerned in different firms for creating value by combining complementary knowledge globally and locally.

The third section of this chapter will explore the connection between these global/local knowledge-related strategies pursued by firms and the processes required and structures that firms might adopt.

The theory of the strategy-active subsidiary

The relation between global and local knowledge provides the basis for the theory of the creative subsidiary (Pearce, 1999) or of subsidiary strategies, as distinct from a single, centralized MNE strategy (Otterbeck, 1981). To some extent, the idea of subsidiary initiatives (Birkinshaw and Ridderstrale, 1999) is set up against a straw man, that of the centralized, single centre of control hierarchical MNE. However, there is virtue in looking at the MNE subsidiary as the interface between two knowledge communities – the firm itself and its local science base. Thus, MNE subsidiaries can become 'knowledge brokers' and form distinctive competencies. Such organizational strengths of subsidiaries can be measured by internal factors such as capabilities and patents residing in the unit and in their business network relationships (Forsgren et al., 1999).

The concept of an MNE as a differentiated network of distinctive knowledge communities is encompassed by the notion of heterarchy. 'This entails a geographical diffusion of core strategic activities and coordinating roles, a break with the notion of one uniform hierarchy of decisions as well as organisational positions, and an increased focus on normative control mechanisms' (Hedlund and Rolander, 1990, p. 15).

As Birkinshaw and Ridderstrale (1999) point out, there is little empirical evidence for the phenomenon of subsidiary initiative – a factor they suggest is due to the deadening effect of 'the corporate immune system' on local subsidiary initiatives. This they attribute to the structural and resource-based power of corporate headquarters. Our evidence, below, does suggest that the model of low power and low visibility of subsidiaries is not a uniform phenomenon and that dynamic factors suggest significant changes over time (the case of 'Frecknall' is a prime example). This fits well with Kogut's (1990) notions of sequential strategy and network flexibility and, in a link with the knowledge management literature, accords with Nonaka's (1990) concepts of continuous information creation and the role of subsidiaries in global self-renewal. The strategy-active subsidiary may not fit well with modern approaches to resource allocation in multinational enterprises (Buckley and Casson, 1998). As Mudambi (1999) points out, granting strategic independence to subsidiaries may limit the ability of headquarters to control resources and may reduce the efficiency of the internal capital market of MNEs. Our suggestion here is that spatial knowledge strategy need not be a choice between polar opposites. It is quite feasible for a subsidiary to be differentiated in the sense of deploying particular local knowledge in combination with knowledge that is global within the corporation. At the same time, the subsidiary exists within, draws upon and contributes to the internal knowledge market of the firm.

These balances, global versus local, and multiple strategy sources versus central capital allocation are examined below in the context of knowledge management practices. This analysis suggests that the strategy-active subsidiary may be a special case of the management of spatially distributed knowledge. Moreover, it may be a particular stage in the evolution of a global knowledge management system.

Strategy, process and structure

Strategy and process

Differences in strategy of the kind discussed above imply differences in the business processes of the enterprise, particularly in the types of knowledge management process. In the first situation, in which a firm seeks to establish new national markets for pre-existing products and services, the process is the most straightforward. In this case, parental and subsidiary knowledge are additive, and there are three principal knowledge management activities, comprising the transfer of parental knowledge to the overseas subsidiary, the acquisition of local knowledge by the subsidiary and the combined application of these two sets of knowledge. The process may be replicated in different subsidiaries and in each case may be carried out separately, without special measures for coordination between separate markets.

Greater complexity arises – with additional knowledge management requirements – when significant research and development activity is needed in order to expand into a new market (sequential complementarity). Two broad requirements need to be considered by the firm. The first of these is in managing the knowledge creation process itself, since at least two distinct sets of localized expertise must contribute to the development activities. This entails a significant mutual exchange of information to specify development requirements, together with monitoring and evaluation of the results for the new market. The firm must allocate responsibilities for these activities in the appropriate location or locations and must establish channels of communication and suitable incentives for the participants.

The second broad requirement that comes out of such development activities is to fit the knowledge creation for any particular market with the potential for its application in other markets. It may be worthwhile to broaden the goal of development activity by taking into account the potential for more widespread use. Or it may be desirable to prioritize and restrict development activities to certain markets. Local developments are thus not strictly separable processes in a firm that operates in multiple markets: it is often desirable that local development activity takes place within a company-wide coordination process.

In firms whose strategy approaches the global intermediation of knowledge from its various separate subsidiaries, coordination and communication are likely to be central to the modus operandi of the corporation. Several additional knowledge management activities can be expected in such a coordination process. For example, firms will need to facilitate contact between specialists in each knowledge area in each location. They may establish a systematic register of knowledge in key areas in order to enable access to expertise by potential users. They may also establish systems to actively maintain knowledge and expertise, establishing a corporate 'memory', both for the purpose of improving access and also as an insurance against the turnover of knowledge-holding staff.

Process and structure

In order for processes to be carried out effectively, firms require some degree of structural organization. Structures signify several functional aspects of an organization. For example, they identify who may carry out what activities, they allocate the division of responsibilities and they specify how individuals are grouped together within boundaries of control. Structures can formally indicate and facilitate connections and communications between individuals both within and across these boundaries, although connections may also arise spontaneously and informally. Structures may also place *limits* on communications or create intentional or unintentional obstacles.

The firm should establish structures that economize on the costs of combining process inputs (combining knowledge) and that can also optimize the process output. The dependence of output on complementarity is the defining characteristic of team production, in which common control of the process can help to optimize output (Alchian and Demsetz, 1972; Buckley and Carter, 1996, 1998). Control can also be affected by the costs of combining inputs, and we will consider two potential sources of cost, which may be barriers to the combination of knowledge.

One possible type of barrier is that due to geographic distance. Von Hippel (1998) characterizes the costs of transferring knowledge from one place to another in terms of 'sticky information' and draws a strong relationship between sticky information and the locus of problem solving. 'We define the stickiness of a given unit of information in a given instance as the incremental expenditure required to transfer that unit of information to a specified locus in a form usable by a given information seeker' (p. 61). As discussed earlier, tacitness, context and complementary knowledge are key dimensions of this cost. There are several structural strategies available to deal with stickiness:

1. Carry out the problem solving at the locus of the sticky information.
2. Iterate problem solving between sites (where there is more than one source of sticky information).
3. 'Task partitioning' where the problem is split into subproblems where each draws on one sticky source.
4. Invest in 'unsticking' information. Examples of unsticking information include: expert systems, easily transferable software, a centrally accessible database.

This general issue that needed information and problem-solving capacity have to be brought together physically (or virtually) at a given point to solve a problem is central to knowledge management and reflects the facts that information is costly to acquire, transfer and use – and that it is sticky.

The other type of potential barrier is that due to 'knowledge boundaries'. We will use this term broadly to cover differences in individuals' cognitive knowledge and specialization, and also differences of language, social norms and identities, type of sense making and so on. Within such boundaries, where individuals already have a significant degree of shared knowledge, as well as language and other norms, transfer of new knowledge will incur relatively low costs. Transmission of knowledge across such boundaries is expected to be relatively costly, as well as not fully effective. It will frequently be most effective to group together members with shared knowledge and a collective understanding of a particular field or problem and also so that communications across boundaries require relatively little of the specialist knowledge and remain limited to the information that is necessary for other specialist groups to apply their own knowledge to the common problem.

Structures within firms should therefore be capable of both economizing on knowledge and facilitating its effective application. The structures and organization of knowledge processes are chosen to create value by combining complementary knowledge, but are constrained by costs, reflecting characteristics of process participants – their expertise and locations – and by the technologies that are available for communication. We will now examine how these factors are exemplified in the structural choices made by three firms for three contrasting knowledge combination processes. The first of these is described at some length. The second and third are treated more briefly, as aspects of these have already been discussed elsewhere (Buckley and Carter, 2000). The discussion here focuses on spatial and global/local aspects of each of the cases.

Case studies[1]

'Frecknall': transfer of parent knowledge to overseas subsidiaries

The first example concerns the transfer of commercial expertise to new affiliates in emerging markets. The company, which we will refer to as Frecknall, is a US-owned research-based ethical pharmaceutical manufacturer. During the 1980s and 1990s, the company established new subsidiaries in developing markets throughout the world. By the late 1990s, it had established a four-stage process, which was in use in Eastern Europe and in Africa. The developments in these territories were administered through the UK/Europe subsidiary rather than directly from the US parent. The discussion here will examine both the process of knowledge transfer to the new subsidiaries and the organization of this process from the US parent and the UK/European regional HQ.

Frecknall conceives the stages of establishing a new subsidiary in terms of a sequence of four 'affiliate business models' (Figure 8.5). The transfer of expertise takes place over an extended period, and each phase represents an increase in the degree and scope of local control and responsibility. These become possible as the number of individuals with appropriate expertise becomes larger over time, as the depth of knowledge grows and as local operations become more established and aligned both with local conditions and market requirements and with the strategic direction established by the corporation.

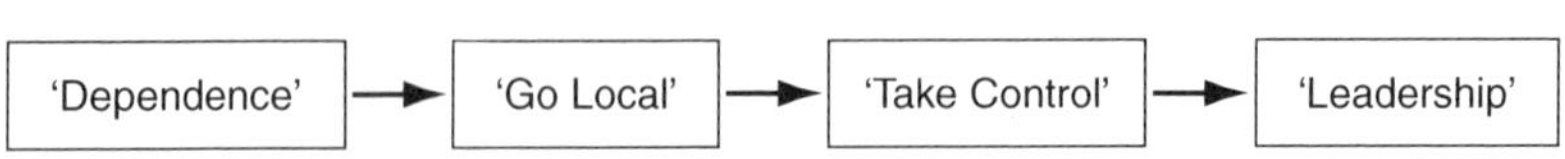

Figure 8.5 Frecknall's sequential affiliate business models

In the earliest stage, the subsidiary is directed and monitored in a directive hierarchical relationship by specialists in the regional headquarters. By the final stage, the subsidiary is integrated into Frecknall's matrix form of organization in which geographical reporting is combined with reporting in product-based 'global business units'. The organizational and knowledge-process characteristics of each stage can be briefly summarized as follows.

Dependence

In the first stage that a local company is established, these activities are limited to the sales and distribution of Frecknall products. Management of this business is the responsibility of an experienced Frecknall manager, who is therefore almost always an expatriate from the US or Europe. The subsidiary manager reports to the unit in regional headquarters, which is responsible for developing markets within its designated region. This unit is responsible for the marketing strategy for all products handled by the 'dependent' subsidiary and is accountable for its profit. Registration of medicines for sale in the new market is carried out by staff at the regional headquarters with the subsidiary manager and staff in the developing markets unit acting as mediators with the regulatory authority and healthcare providers in the target country. The subsidiary manager recruits sales personnel and sets up a distribution network, typically by contracting with an established local business. He or she, and the staff recruited for sales, are the main channel through which the developing market unit in HQ acquires knowledge of local market conditions and requirements.

At this stage, the principal requirements for knowledge transfer into the target country are product knowledge, selling experience and good distributional practice concerning the control of medicines. This knowledge is provided through training courses, provided both locally by division staff visiting the subsidiary and centrally by subsidiary staff visiting regional headquarters and where appropriate through monitoring visit audits by staff from regional headquarters.

Go local

This stage is structurally and operationally similar to the previous one, and characterized by the appointment of *local* managers to carry the day-to-day responsibility of the business rather than expatriate managers. Marketing decisions continue to be the responsibility of the development market unit in regional headquarters, which is also still the profit centre for the operation. During this phase, it is also possible that local managers may take over the direct responsibility for product registration and medical liaison with the country authorities and health providers. The individuals who take these senior positions in the developing market have usually benefited from 'switch programme' training, in which they are relocated to an established Frecknall subsidiary for a period to gain operating experience and improve their understanding of and 'alignment' with Frecknall custom and practice. An important mechanism for raising local awareness of Frecknall's corporate perspectives and aims is linking the subsidiary into the company intranet. This provides ready access to technical information, information about market developments and perspectives on corporate priorities and strategy. It not only provides information but also enhances the degree in which local managers identify with the corporation and not simply their own subsidiary, for example, through receiving directly regular statements from the chairman. At this stage, there continues to be close supervision from staff at regional headquarters, who are likely to visit the subsidiary frequently. Headquarters staff must still approve many aspects of local activity. For example, they may wish to ensure that low price decisions are not inconsistent with global pricing policy across the corporation.

Take control

This is the stage in which the subsidiary becomes a profit centre and local management take over formal responsibility for product registration, marketing and sales. Operationally, there continue to be 'dotted line' links to functional managers for each activity in the regional headquarters. Headquarters staff continue to pay regular visits to audit both financial and medicinal good practice. They will also review major contracts.

Coherence with corporate aims is further developed through the subsidiary's participation in the corporate planing process. Two annual meetings consider 3-year strategic business plans and 1-year operating plans. These meetings bring together subsidiary and corporate managers from several levels of organization. The forum promotes alignment by the subsidiary with the corporation practice and permits dialogue and exchange of understanding in both directions. The subsidiary continues to be accountable to the regional headquarters for its activities and control of the subsidiary is centralized in unitary form through functional managers reporting to the subsidiary CEO.

Leadership

The final stage brings about a significant structural change. The organization switches from a functional basis in which the CEO provides central control of the subsidiary to a more decentralized product-based organization. Product strategies are determined by specialists who now communicate directly with product-based global business units in the US parent. The subsidiary managers continue to oversee sales and distribution and may now be permitted to establish local manufacturing if this is the most cost-effective means to supply the local market. This form of organization, with a network of communication channels between product and functional specializations globally and operational managers locally, is the normal structure adopted by Frecknall for operating in mature country markets.

The stages outlined briefly here indicate several ways in which the company overcomes knowledge combination barriers of the kind discussed earlier. For example, the responsibility for new market development is given to a specialist group. This group is located in Europe, a regional headquarters where there is plenty of mature experience, but from where travel to and communication with the new market is easier than it would be for the US parent. The development from 'dependence' to 'go local' to 'take control' illustrates the gradual transfer of expertise into the subsidiary – 'unsticking' the expertise. While the expertise is located mainly in the regional headquarters, profit responsibility lies there, but it is transferred as the knowledge is progressively transferred. In the final mature form of organization, corporate expertise and practices are sufficiently diffused within the subsidiary that it is possible to decentralize the combination of local and global knowledge from its focus in the subsidiary CEO and the development unit of the regional HQ to separate product managers and global business units. This sequence of changes is indicated in Figure 8.6. In terms of the literature on the strategy-active subsidiary, we can see a temporal sequence of transferring to the subsidiary the rights and abilities to set its own strategic parameters. In examining issues of the spatial location of decision making, we should not neglect temporal factors. Examining the subsidiary in its 'leadership' phase gives a very different picture than that of 'dependence'. Analysts who have identified the strategy-active subsidiary may be focusing on a particular phase in the development of global knowledge management practices as they evolve over time.

'Devonian': capturing bidding expertise

Devonian is a large British telecommunications multinational. This firm bids for 'big ticket' projects on a global scale. These bids require the assembly of multilocational, multiskilled teams, which come together to formulate and progress a bid for a single project. The key knowledge management question here is how best to retain the relevant knowledge from each individual project, whether successful or not. Each team generates useful information, and there is a pressing need to recover all the relevant information and to store it in a recoverable form. Devonian's solution to this problem is to create 'flexible teams', which introduce new entrants to the process while retaining key members of past teams, under the management of 'the major bids department' (see Figure 8.7).

The spatial aspects of this configuration are important. Through video conferencing and other means, the virtual teams are brought together to focus on a bid that may be anywhere in the world. 'Local' specialists are key parts of each bid team, but they will revolve off the bid team when the spatial focus of the next bid shifts. Local expertise and contacts are thus key foci, but are constantly shifting within the virtual team.

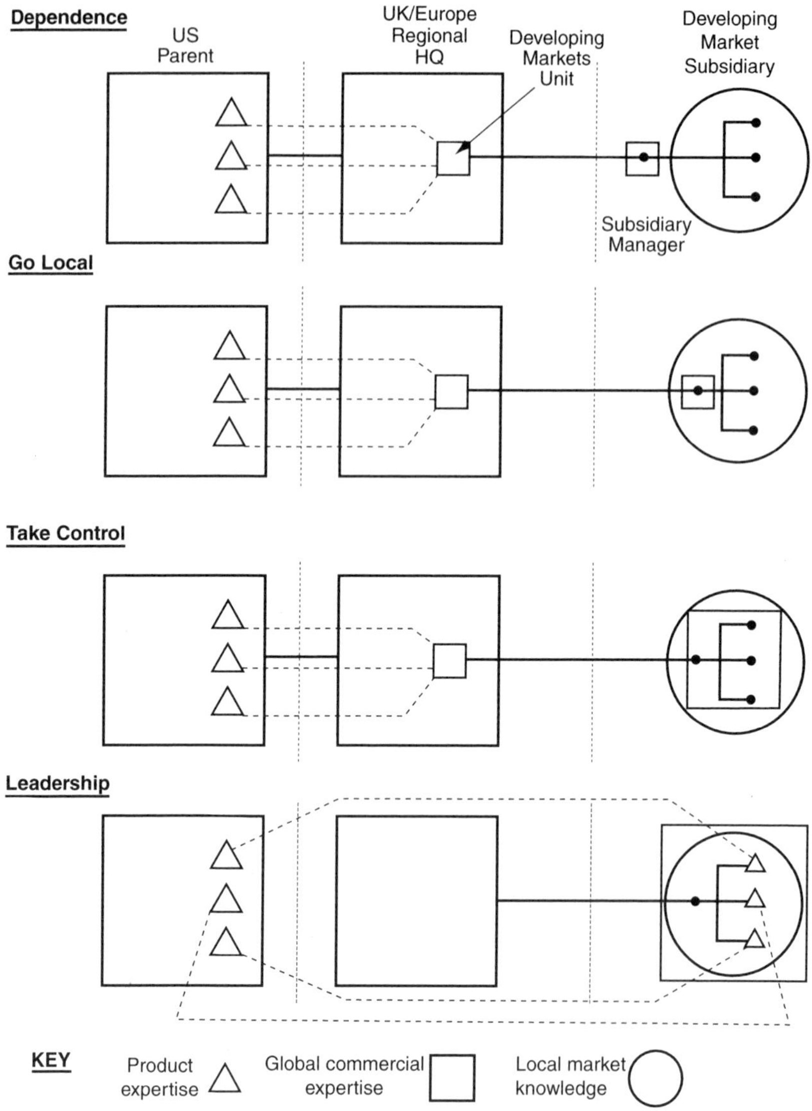

Figure 8.6 Sequential development of knowledge transfer processes in Frecknall

The global/local structure of the bid teams is complex. Some teams will have large numbers of local membership where political, cultural, social and local business practice matters are important. In other cases, local membership is a vital component but will be numerically small in comparison with

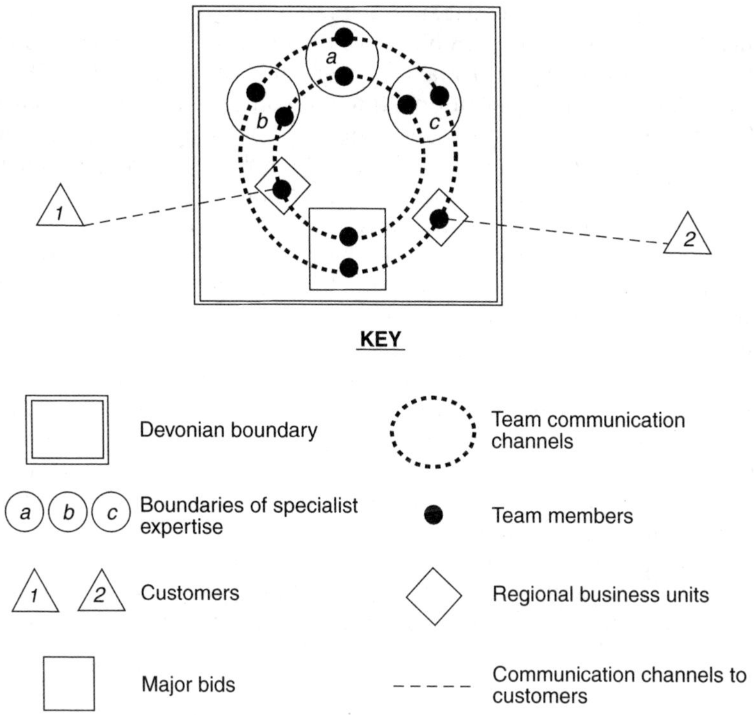

Figure 8.7 Devonian's 'virtual teams'

technology specialists. Regional units of Devonian also play a coordinating role where multiple local representation is required, e.g. in a bid for a spatially diversified multinational's telecommunication requirements. The 'virtual team' enables local elements to be integrated and reconfigured as the particular situation requires.

'Braxia': global capability for licensing externally sourced technology

The large-scale project in Braxia, a UK-owned global pharmaceutical company, is an international system for the evaluation of external technology for inward licensing or exploitation. Braxia has created a system of interactive software that enables the management of opportunities external to the firm on a worldwide scale. The system enables the evaluation, decision making (rejection or acceptance of the proffered technology) and retention of knowledge from new contacts or traditional sources of new developments. It acts as a repository of knowledge on past and ongoing decisions. (Has Braxia evaluated or rejected this piece of technology before?)

The software acts as a spatial attractor and international disseminator. In principle, it removes spatial problems for the technology supplier because it is a single point entry into Braxia's internationally dispersed R&D, production and marketing operations. Internal connections between Braxia's different therapeutic areas and the imported knowledge are made within Braxia's system, thereby obviating the need for the technology supplier to know an individual contact person or contact point.

The introduction of this system caused a radical change in the organization and power structure of the firm. The system both replaces a specialist licensing unit and integrates it within the therapeutic areas, making the knowledge available to all the relevant managers (who have automatic access to the system) (see Figure 8.8).

This both removed the central position of the old 'inward licensing' unit and took away the power of individual managers' 'personal contacts', with whom they, and only they, dealt. The system was carefully managed and introduced over time to show its value in the everyday working experience of managers, and it has proven a successful interface between Braxia and its external technology providers.

This example shows the power of a 'virtual department', as embodied in carefully designed software to collapse spatial problems by making a single entry point in Braxia available to spatially dispensed outsiders. The system

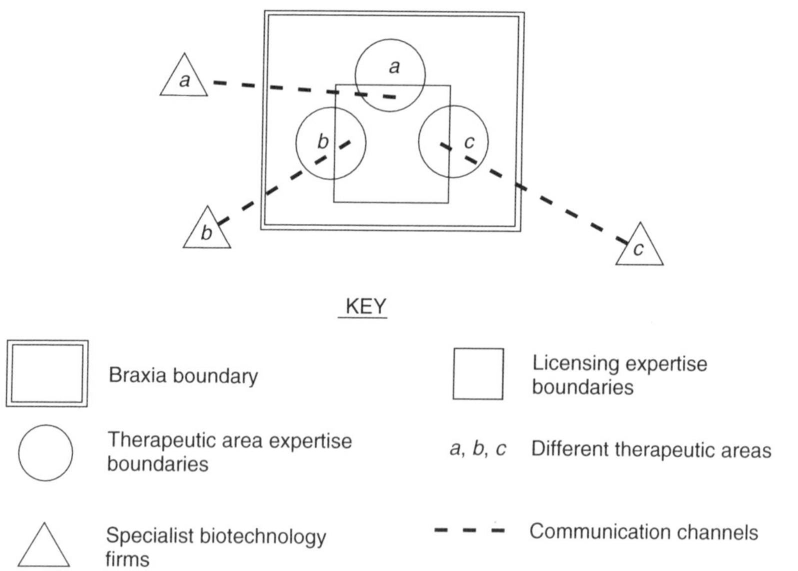

Figure 8.8 Hybrid structure: Braxia's virtual department

also enables the information to be dispensed effectively across a multilocational, multinational firm.

Spatial issues and knowledge management

Problems in the organization of multinational enterprise are often presented as oppositions. Typical are global/local, centralize/decentralize, standardization versus adaptation and efficiency versus responsiveness. These dimensions are frequently embodied in models or descriptions of the different organizational structures within the MNEs such as multidomestic versus global (Harzing, 1998) 'heterarchy' (Hedlund, 1986) and in works on 'the transnational firm' (Bartlett and Goshal, 1989). Our concern is for the relationship between the organization of the firm and knowledge management and, hence, unpacking these oppositions in the terms that we have developed in our theorizing and case studies can shed light on our study of practice.

The global/local opposition has implications for flows of knowledge and physical product. Global organization is often taken to imply that knowledge flows freely throughout the company, from each unit to every other unit (this is what transnational organization implies), whereas local organization, in its multidomestic form, is 'centre-out' in knowledge flows, the headquarters being the source of most of the company-specific knowledge, flowing out to combine with spatially fixed knowledge in the subsidiaries. As our work shows, the 'global' model ignores the cost of managing the flows and the local model contains a rigid assumption that there is a division between general 'company-wide' knowledge and separable, spatially fixed local-specific knowledge. Both of these positions, except as ideal types, are not helpful in designing knowledge processes in real companies, real space and real time.

A second opposition is that between centralization and decentralization. This is an organizational, decision-making-based description of companies. If centralization implies central control, then the implementation is likely to be inimical to free flows of knowledge and to combining knowledge in all but centre outwards types of processes (refer to our model and cases). However, extreme decentralization would inhibit knowledge combination and so it is inevitable that elements of both extremes are present in successful knowledge combination strategies.

Issues of standardization versus adaptation are clearly dependent on the external market. Where individual (national) markets are differentiated by regulation, culture, pattern of demand or other factors, then the company will be forced down the adaptation end of the spectrum. If markets are homogeneous across national boundaries (perhaps as a result of economic integration as in the EU), then standardization becomes more feasible. Standardization gives rise to *efficiency* (cost) gains, whereas the benefit of adaptation to local demand should give rise to revenue gains. These oppositions are knowledge management issues in themselves as the firm has to obtain 'second-order' knowledge on what knowledge it needs to serve international markets in an optimal fashion. Knowledge on 'how to service markets' is a key overarching question in combining and separating individual national markets and marketing strategy.

These issues are therefore not independent of knowledge management. Spatial questions are one part of dealing with knowledge organization, but spatial issues are bound up with a whole set of temporal, organizational, strategic and process issues.

Conclusion

All three case studies illustrate the importance of spatial issues in knowledge management. In all three multinational firms, there was not one unique source of knowledge, but the resources were dispersed, and each firm had to find a way of combining their knowledge assets in a dynamic process with changing parameters. Moves towards an organizational structure that facilitated knowledge sharing could be on a planned incremental, almost staged, basis (Frecknall) or in an evolutionary format (Devonian) or in the creation of a particular new structure (Braxia). The strategies all had both a spatial and temporal dimension. Furthermore, all strategies had both global and local components. These examples indicate that knowledge strategies which are both dynamic and 'glocal' are likely to be widespread, although their detailed forms may be rich and varied.

Our research suggests that conceptualization of knowledge management should move away from thinking of unidirectional flows of knowledge towards much more complex interactions, which, nevertheless, can be captured within a conceptual framework such as what we put forward in the second and third sections. Spatial and temporal issues also interact in an interesting fashion and the age of a firm and of a subsidiary needs to be factored into any spatial analysis of knowledge management practices. The analysis of the input into strategy of the Frecknall subsidiaries would be very different, depending on the time at which it was examined. The 'window of observation' is crucial in coming to clear conclusions on appropriate knowledge management structures.

The limitations of our approach are clear. We provide three illustrations of spatial issues in knowledge management, but in order to generalize, a wider study is necessary. Such a study would move from a relatively 'stripped down' context to problems set in a greater degree of complexity, including wider cultural differences and firms chosen explicitly to illustrate the impact of overt company strategy (hierarchical control, internal capital market operations, multiple sources of strategic direction). However, our limited study shows great scope for extension, conceptually, in practice, and in guiding management thinking.

Acknowledgements

This research was conducted with a financial support from the Carnegie Bosch Institute for Applied Studies in International Management, Carnegie Mellon University, Pittsburgh, PA, USA. The authors would like to thank the editor and two anonymous referees for their incisive and helpful comments.

Note

1. Personal interviews were conducted in each of the three multinational firms. Multiple interviews were conducted with a number of executives in each firm. These multiple interviews were supplemented by participant observation in Braxia, by participant observation and by an internship in Devonian and by extensive long-term liaison with a sponsoring executive in Frecknall. In all cases, company documentation was provided to verify the results. The longitudinal studies covered a period of not less than a year in each case.

References

Alchian, A. and Demsetz, H. (1972) 'Production, Information Costs and Economic Organisation'. *American Economic Review*, vol. 62, pp. 777–95.

Bartlett, C. A. and Goshal, S. (1989) *Managing across Borders: the Transnational Solution*. Boston: Harvard Business School Press.

Birkinshaw, J. and Ridderstrale, J. (1999) 'Fighting the Corporate Immune System: a Process Study of Subsidiary Initiatives in Multinational Corporations'. *International Business Review*, vol. 8, no. 2, pp. 149–80.

Buckley, P. J. and Carter, M. J. (1996) 'The Economics of Business Process Design: Motivation, Information and Coordination within the Firm'. *International Journal of Economic Business*, vol. 3, pp. 5–25.

Buckley, P. J. and Carter, M. J. (1998) 'The Economics of Business Process Design in Multinational Firms'. In R. Mudambi and M. Ricketts (eds), *The Organisation of the Firm: International Business Perspectives*. London: Routledge, pp. 56–78.

Buckley, P. J. and Carter, M. J. (1999) 'Managing Cross-border Complementary Knowledge: Conceptual Developments in the Business Process Approach to Knowledge Management in Multinational Firms'. *Organization of International Business*, vol. 29, no. 1, pp. 80–104.

Buckley, P. J. and Carter, M. J. (2000) 'Knowledge Management in Global Technology Markets: Applying Theory to Practice'. *Long-Range Planning*, vol. 33, no. 1, pp. 55–71.

Buckley, P. J. and Casson, M. C. (1976) *The Future of the Multinational Enterprise*. New York: Macmillan.

Buckley, P. J. and Casson, M. C. (1998) 'Models of the Multinational Enterprise'. *Journal of International Business Studies*, vol. 29, no. 1, pp. 21–44.

Carter, M. J. (1995) 'Information and the Division of Labour: Implications for the Firm's Choice of Organisation. *Economic Journal*, vol. 105, pp. 385–97.

Casson, M. C. (1982) *The Entrepreneur: an Economic Theory*. Oxford: Martin Robinson.
Casson, M. C. (1985) 'Entrepreneurship and the Dynamics of Foreign Direct Investment'. In P. J. Buckley and M. C. Casson (eds), *The Economic Theory of the Multinational Enterprise*. London: Macmillan, pp. 172–91.
Casson, M. C. (1997) *Information and Organisation: a New Perspective on the Theory of the Firm*. Oxford: Clarendon Press.
Cohen, W. M. and Levinthal, D. A. (1990) 'Absorptive Capacity: a New Perspective on Learning and Innovation'. *Administrative Science Quarterly*, vol. 35, pp. 128–52.
Forsgren, M., Pedersen, T. and Foss, N. J. (1999) 'Accounting for the Strengths of MNC Subsidiaries: the Case of Foreign-owned Firms in Denmark'. *International Business Review*, vol. 8, no. 2, pp. 181–96.
Foss, N. J. and Pedersen, T. (2000) 'Transferring Knowledge in MNCs: the Role of Sources of Subsidiary Knowledge and Organizational Context'. LINK Discussion Paper, Copenhagen Business School.
Gupta, A. K. and Govindarajan, V. (2000) 'Knowledge Flows within Multinational Corporations'. *Strategic Management Journal*, vol. 21, pp. 473–96.
Harzing, A.-W. (1998) 'Integration within MNCs: from Multidomestic to Global and Transnational Firms?' In H. Mirza (ed.), *Global Competition Strategies in the New World Economy: Multilateralism, Regionalisation and the Transnational Firm*. Cheltenham: Edward Elgar, pp. 313–26.
Hedlund, G. (1986) 'The Hypermodern MNC – a Heterarchy?' *Human Resource Management*, vol. 25, no. 1.
Hedlund, G. and Rolander, D. (1990) 'Action in Heterarchies – New Approaches to Managing the MNC'. In C. A. Bartlett, Y. Doz and G. Hedlund (eds), *Managing the Global Firm*. London: Routledge, pp. 15–46.
Kogut, B. (1990) 'International Sequential Advantages and Network Flexibility'. In C. A. Bartlett, Y. Doz and G. Hedlund (eds), *Managing the Global Firm*. London: Routledge.
Koopmans, T. C. (1957) *Three Essays on the State of Economic Science*. New York: McGraw-Hill.
Krugman, P. (1994) 'Location and Competition'. In R. P. Rumelt, D. E. Schendel and D. J. Teece (eds), *Fundamental Issues in Strategy: a Research Agenda*. Boston: Harvard Business School Press, pp. 69–94.
Mudambi, R. (1999) 'MNE Internal Capital Markets and Subsidiary Strategic Independence'. *International Business Review*, vol. 8, no. 2, pp. 197–211.
Nonaka, I. (1990) 'Managing Globalization as a Self-renewing Process: Experiences of Japanese MNCs'. In C. A. Bartlett, Y. Doz and G. Hedlund (eds), *Managing the Global Firm*. London: Routledge.
Otterbeck, L. (ed.) (1981) *The Management of Headquarters–Subsidiary Relationships in Multinational Corporations*. London: Gower.
Pearce, R. D. (1999) 'Evolution of Technology in Multinational Enterprises: the Role of Creative Subsidiaries'. *International Business Review*, vol. 9, no. 2, pp. 125–48.
Von Hippel, E. (1998) '"Sticky Information" and the Locus of Problem Solving: Implications for Innovation'. In A. D. Chandler Jr, P. Hagström and Ö. Sölvell (eds), *The Dynamic Firm: the Role of Technology, Strategy, Organisation and Regions*. Oxford: Oxford Univ. Press, pp. 60–77.
Williamson, O. E. (1996) *The Mechanisms of Governance*. Oxford: Oxford Univ. Press.

9

Governing Knowledge Sharing in Multinational Enterprises

with Martin J. Carter

Key results

- A variety of knowledge governance problems are encountered in four case studies and all involve resolving global/local issues. The coordination methods employed need to take account of this and other trade-offs (e.g. specialization versus integration) and their resolution involves attention to the processes of knowledge sharing, the incentive structure within the firm and knowledge frontiers. These trade-offs are examined using the notions of partition and integration as architectural forms.
- Achievement of both application strategies (uses of a given portfolio of knowledge) and discovery strategies (new combinations of knowledge) are important goals of knowledge governance structures.

Introduction

The chapter examines knowledge-sharing processes in four high technology multinational enterprises. It derives five propositions on governing knowledge processes and utilizes these propositions in an examination of the four firms.

Knowledge and knowledge sharing in multinational enterprises

The starting-point of this chapter is that knowledge is the converse of uncertainty. Shifts in demand and technology cause trade-inhibiting uncertainty in firms that lack relevant knowledge, but present opportunities for trade in firms who possess such knowledge (Buckley and Carter, 1999). Just as uncertainty is a state of the human mind, so can effective knowledge only reside in the minds of people. Knowledge is a *quality* possessed by people, literally a *state of mind*.

The organization's knowledge is an aggregation of the individual knowledge of its members (Grant, 1996, pp. 112 et seq.). No individual possesses all the knowledge within a firm. Division of knowledge within the firm results in 'secondary' uncertainty, if individuals do not know what is in the mind of others. Koopmans claims that '[in] a rough and intuitive judgement the secondary uncertainty arising from a lack of communication, that is from one decision maker having no way of finding out the concurrent decisions and plans made by others ... is quantitatively at least as important as the primary uncertainty arising from random acts of nature and unpredictable changes in consumers' preferences' (1957, pp. 162 et seq.). Secondary uncertainty can be reduced by sharing knowledge. The purpose of this chapter is to examine the means which firms employ to achieve knowledge sharing amongst their members. Firms are communities of practice (Brown and Duguid, 1991, 1998) which undertake 'the integration of knowledge fragmented in various parts of the firm ... confronting within the context of the firm Hayek's problem of utilizing knowledge not known to anyone in its entirety...' (Fransman, 1998, p. 189). Our particular concern is with bringing together complementary knowledge. In multinational enterprises (MNEs) this includes, for example, knowledge of different national markets and knowledge of existing technologies within and outside the enterprise. The firm must understand how technology can be adapted or developed to meet the changing requirements of these markets. Such knowledge transfers are rarely one-way flows and involve global/local interactions which have important implications for the governance of the firm (Buckley and Carter, 2002).

The governance of knowledge

A fundamental tenet of received theory is that knowledge is shared more efficiently (at less cost) within the firm than between firms (Buckley and Casson, 1976). Firms internalize the governance of knowledge by combining knowledge which is dispersed amongst individuals and applying it collectively towards a common purpose. The division of knowledge in a multi-person firm reflects the bounded rationality of individuals (Simon, 1945). Internal governance is motivated by several sources of gain in collective action. First are gains due to *complementarity* (*inseparability*), in which the value of the knowledge of in one part of the organization is only realized when combined with knowledge held in another part of the firm (Buckley and Carter, 1996, 2000). Second, there are gains from collective knowledge *processes*, particularly involving tacit knowledge, due to social characteristics of groups. These characteristics have been described as 'higher order organizing principles' and 'tacit procedural knowledge' by Kogut and Zander (1992, 1996) and have also been discussed by Nonaka and Takeuchi (1995). Third are gains from internal *contracting* of which the classic example is the labour contract in Coase's (1937) rationale for the existence of the multi-person firm. These gains include monitoring and incentive allocation to overcome moral hazard (Alchian and Demsetz, 1972), internalizing the appropriation problem (Arrow, 1962), avoiding complex price-setting problems (Rosen, 1991) and providing better incentives than the market for individuals to develop co-specific human capital (Williamson et al., 1975; Williamson, 1985, p. 249).

However, there are knowledge frontiers where an individual firm will find it more efficient to purchase inputs which embody the knowledge rather than internalize the knowledge transfer. Opportunities arise to economize on the transfer of knowledge when knowledge can be unambiguously codified or embodied in physical commodities. For example, a steel fabricator buys specified grades of metal rather than internalizing the knowledge required for steel production (Demsetz, 1991). Inseparability, processing, pricing and contracting problems diminish and market contracting is more attractive.

> *Proposition 1.* Firms will recognize that some knowledge processes are better organized by another organization and purchased through the market than by their organization. Therefore, they will specialize in knowledge activities in a discrete but changing area. Specialized firms are separated from each other by the agency of the market.

The intra-firm governance of knowledge

The frontiers of knowledge specialization *between* firms are drawn where uncertainty can be effectively borne by market contracting. Specialization *within* firms produces internal knowledge frontiers between separate cognate areas, often corresponding to functional or divisional boundaries. Within each area, individuals specialize in knowledge of a broadly similar content, so that workers can interact and managers can monitor and guide their subordinates: integrated knowledge and 'organic' governance. Communication between specialized areas cannot depend on the full transfer of specialized knowledge, but requires the development of a sufficiently rich common code or language to allow each group to transmit and receive the messages which enable them to play their part in advancing the collective goals of the firm but which economizes on knowledge transfer. This language, its knowledge content and the associated mechanics of communication, must allow senior managers to supervise and direct the firm's activities, even though no individual or small group holds, or could hold, all the firm's strategic knowledge.

Knowledge governance structures within firms must pay attention to the:

1. Boundaries between different knowledge holders (individuals, departments, functional areas);
2. Coordination and sharing of knowledge across frontiers;
3. Incentives to individuals for sharing knowledge.

A potentially important boundary within MNEs is that between individuals from different countries. Our study focuses on two culturally close countries, the USA and the UK, and so reduces some of the factors that increase psychic distance (Hallen and Wiedersheim-Paul, 1979). This enables us to isolate more distinctly the factors that arise from physical and time differences and from the need for adaptation to individual local markets. It is, however, possible that differences in managerial practice, style and linguistic nuances may exacerbate the separation of head office and affiliate.

> *Proposition 2.* Governing knowledge within the firm requires attention to knowledge frontiers, to mechanisms of knowledge sharing and to the means of encouraging individuals to pool knowledge.

Knowledge architectures in the firm

Groups within the firm can coordinate their activities by sharing complementary knowledge. There is, however, a further problem concerning the coherence and reliability of knowledge exchanged in this way. An important dimension of knowledge intended for practical application is its degree of reliability or truth. A widely used shorthand in the business literature is that knowledge is 'a justified true belief'. Fransman (1998) points out that whenever there is uncertainty then firms do not act on 'justified true beliefs' but simply on their *beliefs*, based on incomplete information, combined with insight, creativity and misconception. He suggests the term 'vision' for the *dominant* set of beliefs which guide its actions in the face of uncertainty. In an *organization* different members of the firm can hold different beliefs. Furthermore, there may even be a lack of awareness that this is so as some individuals may keep their beliefs secret yet still base their actions upon them. This is potentially problematic, especially in the case of procedural norms and routines. A gap between the 'vision' adopted by top management and beliefs in other parts of the firm may result at the least in incoherence between parts of the organization, and further in confusion, incomprehension, disaffection and even conflict. How routines and habits often embody hidden beliefs and assumptions is illustrated in Scott-Morgan (1994). This has radical implications for the governance of knowledge in firms. The firm might respond in two ways. One solution is *integration*, based on 'heedful interrelating' (Weick and Roberts, 1993) in which managers have an understanding of the knowledge possessed by those with whom they work. The alternative arrangement is *partition* in which the firm's structure is designed so that it is not necessary for managers to have a detailed understanding of the work of others or even the same beliefs. This has parallels with organic and mechanistic governance structures in managing the dynamics of knowledge development (Burns and Stalker, 1961). The choice between integration and partition depends on a trade-off between breadth and depth in the domain of knowledge governance, so that some groupings are based on coherence of beliefs and widening the scope of collective action whereas other are based on specialization and depth of knowledge. Partition and integration will coexist in the architecture of any firm in so far as some knowledge remains within knowledge frontiers and some is shared across frontiers.

One important aspect of hidden beliefs is Williamson's concept of opportunism as 'self-seeking with guile' (Williamson, 1975, 1985). Incentives need to be created at the individual or group level to encourage actions to conform to the objectives of the firm. Such incentives can be individual rewards or benefits to the group. The culture of the firm can be engineered towards collective goals which override opportunistic behaviour. The incentive structure must ensure that group goals are consistent with the firm's goals and that individual goals are consistent with group goals. Observation of an individual's behaviour may lead to the view that his action is inconsistent with the firm's objectives. However, this could only be verified by examining the intermediate level of the group. The hierarchy of incentives may provide a coordinating mechanism which brings individuals' 'deviant' behaviour into line with the collective purpose of the firm. We would expect to observe different incentive structures in the two architectural forms of integration and partition.

In multinationals based on high technology, professionalism and a common educational background may be factors around which groups cohere which can overcome cultural differences, nuances of language and other barriers to knowledge sharing. This shared background and language transcends local differences in the internal knowledge markets where employees are highly educated individuals sharing a common training based on the natural sciences. This may create internal knowledge frontiers and foster partition along the lines of particular scientific sub-disciplines.

The next proposition we derive is:

> *Proposition 3*. Two ways to achieve coherence and coordination are architectural forms which we designate as *integration* and *partition*. Both may be present in a single firm as firms seek solutions to problems of uncertainty.

New knowledge configurations

Overconcentration on perceived current capabilities may well lead management astray (Bercovitz et al., 1997). Over time, other producers can learn what the firm already knows, or learn other ways to achieve the same capabilities, or capabilities that will supersede them. Over time rents will dissipate. Firm-specific advantages must be defined over a given time period (and possibly over a given cultural space) before they atrophy (Buckley, 1983).

Protection of existing knowledge can include finding new capabilities based on *new combinations* of knowledge, redeploying and extending existing assets, including by the acquisition of or joint venture with the owners of other, complementary, assets. Existing knowledge assets with multiple applications are similar to the 'core competencies' discussed by Prahalad and Hamel (1990). Strategies concerned with applying and protecting rents from existing knowledge might be termed *application strategies*. When the firm has developed multiple applications, this an *application portfolio strategy*. The internal structures of firms reflect the need to facilitate the application of specialized knowledge and the collaboration between firm members with complementary knowledge. Von Hippel (1998) draws a strong relationship between 'sticky information' and the locus of problem solving. There are several strategies available to deal with stickiness:

1. Carry out the problem solving at the locus of the sticky information.
2. Iterate problem solving between sites (where there is more than one source of sticky information).
3. 'Task partitioning' where the problem is split into sub-problems where each draws on one sticky source.
4. Invest in 'unsticking' information. Examples of unsticking information include: training and the replication of existing knowledge, expert systems, easily transferable software, a centrally accessible database.

This general issue, that needed information and problem-solving capacity have to be brought together physically or virtually at a given point to solve a problem, is central to knowledge management and reflects the facts that information is costly to acquire, transfer and use – and that it is sticky. This helps to determine the information structure within the firm, in which knowledge is partitioned to meet the requirements of each distinct applications and communication channel designed for the supervision of and development of the applications portfolio. The divisional type of organization has the advantage that knowledge that is specialized to divisions can stay within divisional boundaries, allowing each group of specialists to increase their division-specific knowledge and avoid the overload which would arise if all specialists were expected to be cognizant of all application areas. The divisionalized organization is particularly well adapted for the delivery of a *portfolio of applications*.

As Langlois (1991) has pointed out, whether a firm can avoid the complete diffusion of capabilities into the market place depends on the relative learning abilities of the market and of the firm. The search for new applications of existing knowledge can only take the firm so far, and sooner or later it must engage in the development of new capabilities based on new knowledge. Failure to engage in the 'creative destruction' of existing competencies can result in the choice of an incorrect growth path for the firm. Decision-making biases may come from bounded rationality in which managers preserve erroneous beliefs or theories of the world. According to North (1990), erroneous beliefs are a failure of 'instrumental rationality', representing the impact of information costs on individual or group decision making. When information feedback is inadequate to convey to the participants in a process the correct theory of how their world operates, this will impact upon the individual's decision and in turn the outcome of the process and the further information which it generates (Dixit, 1996, p. 45). This can take place even in the face of information which would suggest revision if it were not for the common practice of deselecting information which does not support our established beliefs (Fransman, 1998). There is a connection here with the notion of scientific paradigms and research programmes, which may only be revised some time after the evidence which first challenges them (Kuhn, 1962; Lakatos, 1970). Core capabilities become *core rigidities* (Leonard-Barton, 1992). Furthermore there is path dependency of knowledge creation, so that experience gained in the past may reduce the cost of developing knowledge in areas with similarities or with complementarities (Dierickx and Cool, 1989). The resulting increasing returns to knowledge creation can provide significant first mover advantages for knowledge-intensive firms, although simultaneously they carry the risk for firms to be 'locked in' to technologies which may be superseded (Arthur, 1989).

A possible term to use for strategies which seek new capabilities based on new knowledge is *discovery strategies*. The forms of organization adopted for application strategies may present some constraints to the pursuit of *discovery* strategies. Of course, there is no obstacle to the development of new capabilities using the expertise within a particular division, and many diversified companies have long experience of research and development. But an implication of divisionalization is that discovery activities are either centralized, or are conducted independently in separate divisions. In either case, discovery capabilities of the firm are constrained in particular locations within the firm. This does not prevent innovation, but it places some limits on the scope of the innovation that is likely to take place. It is likely to be restricted to particular areas of application drawing on a subset of the expertise within the firm. Furthermore, it may be hard to disseminate any discoveries which have potential applications in other divisions of the firm. Therefore, a divisionalized firm may engage in a *portfolio of applications* and some individual discovery, but will have difficulties if it wishes to develop a strategy comprising a portfolio of discoveries.

The recent developments in global knowledge sharing provide responses to these limitations. MNEs thus provide channels of communication and planning and policy formation between functional specialists in different application areas. As a result, new specialist knowledge is disseminated across application boundaries, so that new capabilities can be integrated across the portfolio of the firm's activities. Furthermore, if ideas for innovation arise in one part of the organization, perhaps derived from contact with a particular customer, this offers better access to the full range of knowledge and expertise in other parts of the corporation which may be able to contribute to the innovative development. Thus these forms of organization offer the potential for a firm to move from a strategy based around an *application portfolio* to one based around a *discovery portfolio*.

> *Proposition 4.* Long-run success depends on processes of knowledge sharing that encompass both *application* and *discovery* strategies. The implementation of the latter will be crucial to sustained success.

Furthermore, the architectures (combination of partition and integration) which are adapted for application strategies may not be well suited for discovery strategies.

> *Proposition 5.* Governance structures for application strategies may obstruct discovery strategies.

Applying the propositions to four multinational enterprises

The following section confronts these *propositions* with material drawn from repeated interviews with a number of executives in each of four multinational companies. These longitudinal studies covered not less than a year in each case. This research uses multiple case design, the results of which can be extended to a wider context based on 'analytical generalisation' (Yin, 1994, p. 10). This is an appropriate method for our purposes because we are engaged in an exploratory theory-building exercise rather than theory testing. The choice of cases was determined by the wish to reduces influences of extreme cultural and language difference and therefore the four companies are all US or UK owned. Company names are disguised.

Braxia PLC: buying technology in a global market

The Braxia case is an example of the development of a new capability to buy technology by embodying valuable organizational knowledge in a new process architecture. This not only facilitated the company-wide dissemination of a nascent organizational capability, but incorporated a degree of continual learning.

Braxia is a UK-owned firm with a long history of developing ethical pharmaceuticals in the traditional whole-cycle method from basic research and development through trials, registration, production and marketing. Scientific knowledge deepens continuously, and there is an increase both in the number of technologies that can be applied in a particular therapeutic area and a widening of potential therapeutic applications of particular technologies. A single firm can no longer internalize all the knowledge relevant to even a selected group of strategically chosen therapeutic areas. One result is that the basic research for novel therapies is increasingly carried out by independent biotechnology firms who then offer their discoveries to be licensed and marketed by the large pharmaceutical companies. Independent firms provide a greater variety of approaches by each specializing in their particular technology, and can rely on the large pharmaceuticals to provide production, marketing and distribution capabilities. Furthermore, these technology suppliers are spatially dispersed in various locations around the world. Similarly, final markets are globally distributed. Braxia and other MNEs provide the means of linking disparate consolidating technologies and adapting them to the particular needs of individual markets. Thus, there is a need for access to information on both internal and external technological developments and on market needs in a managed fashion. The domain of internalized knowledge needs to be integrated with the external across the interface with other firms.

This trend creates a requirement for a new organizational capability for buying technology in large pharmaceutical firms. Such a capability needs to combine alertness to potential developments with technological and commercial assessments of prospective 'purchases' and with legal and commercial expertise in drawing up agreements. Its application must be integrated with the strategic goals of the firm as a whole, with its continuing research plans and its market strategy. Expertise in buying (licensing) is complementary to detailed technological knowledge and marketing knowledge of relevant therapeutic areas. The firm must somehow strike a balance between benefits of increased specialization, through a division of expertise between specialists, and the difficulties that such division of expertise creates in then combining one area of expertise with other complementary expertise.

A mechanism for knowledge sharing is therefore essential. One form of the 'partition' solution to achieving coherence (*Proposition 3*) is to locate all the firm's licensing expertise together in a separate specialist group which would provide a service for the corporation. This arrangement would facilitate the development of expertise and the deepening of knowledge in this area. This would have the advantages which functional groups provide: advantages of managing and monitoring performance, as managers have expertise in common with their team; mutual support through flexibility of individuals amongst tasks; exchange of ideas and experience; consistency of practice and coordination of activities. Appropriate communication channels would be needed between the licensing group and the therapeutic groups in order to combine licensing expertise with specialist technical and marketing knowledge. Such communications take time and often use summarized information, which can result in delays and misunderstandings. It may be difficult for members of the licensing group to internalize all the knowledge that would be desirable of the different therapeutic areas and the different national markets in which products would be sold. Furthermore, even though this group is formally providing a service to the other groups, there is a risk of competing strategic goals between therapeutic area groups and the group with licensing responsibility.

An alternative 'partition' is for responsibility for licensing to be allocated to specialists within each therapeutic or marketing unit. That is, for expertise to be combined within each therapeutic area. This would help to overcome difficulties of combining knowledge of licensing with that of therapeutic strategy and marketing, because licensing experts in each group concentrate on the needs of the group. But different experience in different groups may lead to different practices and different capabilities dispersed through the organization. Furthermore, there is now a problem of coordination. Both Braxia and the independent suppliers of new technologies are geographically dispersed as well as representing a wide range of scientific and therapeutic applications. One part of the organization may be unaware of actions taken by another operating unit. For example, a biotechnology company may approach more than one group and be rejected by one part of the organization and yet be accepted by another.

Braxia's chosen solution resulted in the establishment of a 'virtual department', which provides benefits of both specialization of expertise and of combination of expertise. This solution also creates a clear division of knowledge between Braxia and outside organizations as in *Proposition 1*. Expertise in buying is developed collectively by individuals who are located in each therapeutic area but who are also able to share their knowledge as though they were in a distinct unit specialized in licensing. This is made possible by adopting a common process of knowledge sharing for evaluating prospective offers and a management and information system which is embodied in customized computer software. This is accessible to all firm members who have responsibilities for licensing. The 'virtual department' is made up of a group of specialists, who support and manage the system, together with members of operating groups who have responsibility for licensing. The expertise of licensing specialists is available to all operating groups as needed while the decision-makers in each client group comprise a 'virtual' licensing group while continuing to be fully integrated members of their own operating unit. The arrangement provides benefits of both forms of knowledge partition.

This form of organization successfully overcomes trade-offs in knowledge specialization, paying attention to perceived knowledge frontiers as suggested by *Proposition 2*. The incentives to knowledge sharing are not individual monetary rewards but collective returns from 'making the job easier and more rewarding' (Braxia senior manager). Managers in Braxia were dismissive of using monetary incentives to individuals because it is deemed to devalue the process and the team ethic. This might otherwise require a greater division of labour amongst more specialized individuals, but is overcome through the application of a piece of organizational knowledge. This knowledge is the recognition that all acquisitions of products and technologies (including companies) could be achieved through the same process in all therapeutic areas and all countries. Furthermore, this process could be embodied in computer software which would automate many of the administrative requirements, and facilitate the required information flows, record keeping and documentation.

The embodiment of organizational knowledge, together with some licensing knowledge, in an information technology system provides an alternative to the internalization of such knowledge in the minds of separate specialists. This improves the firm's ability to exploit the complementarities between its therapeutic-marketing knowledge and developing licensing expertise and to move on to integrating separate knowledge flows in a discovery process (*Proposition 4*). The Braxia case provides a good example of a governance structure for knowledge management which facilitates discovery strategies (*Proposition 5*).

Devonian PLC: the sale of technology in a global market

Devonian is a UK-owned global telecommunications company which owns and operates cable systems, fibre-optic networks and satellite earth stations. It is a leading supplier of global communications services to international firms such as banks, information technology companies, oil and gas companies and shipping companies. Two aspects of this business which strongly affect the nature of the knowledge creation requirements are firstly the rapid rate of innovation in telecommunications technology and secondly the wide local variations in the needs of individual customers. Designs must be tailored to customer requirements and bidding is intensely competitive. Integration of Devonian's internalized knowledge governance processes with its clients' needs are key elements in a successful strategy (*Proposition 1*). Bids often comprise several rounds. The client may use the first round to select two or three competitors who submit more detailed bids. Bidders can be asked to carry out partial or pilot projects in competition with one another.

The preparation of bids is a complex process drawing on many specializations within Devonian including: general and specialized network design work, costing and pricing, commercial and financial appraisal, legal services, sales and service contacts with client, liaison with third-party suppliers, project management for implementation of successful bids. Due to economies of specialization, these skills are located in different groups. Furthermore, Devonian is a global corporation, serving international customers with headquarters in many different parts of the world and with international service requirements. Therefore customer contacts and Devonian's own sales and customer service personnel may be widely dispersed geographically as well as being members of different regional business units. Like Braxia, Devonian must find the balance between the architectural forms of partition and integration for coherence and coordination (*Proposition 3*).

Devonian needs to direct many diverse knowledge resources towards each potential client, when the needs vary between clients. Different clients have different technical problems and different geographical distributions of their head offices and operating divisions. Devonian has to call on whatever specialized resources are required, and also to align the sales and service communication channels with those of the client. The number of possible governance structures is very large, with some areas of expertise separately specialized and others combined. The ideal structure is likely to be different for different clients, particularly for high-value projects for large international clients. Thus there is a variable domain of internalized knowledge with heavy reliance on information in the (potential) client base.

Devonian's solution to the problem of governance of knowledge is a flexible form of organization which matches the organization to the requirements of individual bids. This knowledge sharing is achieved by assembling 'bid teams' under the control of a specialist section called 'Major Bids'. Rewards are psychic returns from successful team working and a higher number of bids won, which feeds directly into the firm's pay structure via individual bonuses (*Proposition 2*). A 'virtual team' (the bid team) is appointed with membership from each of the key areas of expertise required for the bid. The Major Bids section supplies the lead design engineer, called the 'bid consultant' and the most appropriate regional business unit provides the sales account manager, who forms the primary channel of communication with the client. Knowledge sharing is thus within the team across functional areas and across teams by retaining key personnel in sequential bids (*Proposition 4*). However, this potential for discovery is sometimes negated by the phenomenon which the company describes as 'executive burn-out'. The pressure on individual managers of the bid process can be so great that over a period of two to three years the managers have to be replaced because they simply cannot function effectively in subsequent teams. Discovery strategies over time are inhibited by this excessive pressure. This represents a confirmation of *Proposition 5*.

Verona Inc.: global supply

The global supply arrangements of Verona (a US-owned MNE) are similar to those of most large pharmaceutical manufacturers. The corporation has a network of approximately 30 manufacturing facilities which are distributed throughout the world. Supply management in Verona is concerned with both the short-term, tactical realization of the current operating plan and the long-term, strategic planning and construction of production capacity for future market expectations. On both timescales supply adopts a following rather than a leading role. Its senior managers perceive that its function is to make happen what has been determined elsewhere. In our terms, the supply function is separately partitioned and works to given objectives (*Proposition 3*). Nevertheless, both strategic planning and operational planning must allow for supply constraints. Therefore, in practice there are flows of knowledge both into the supply function as an output of the planning processes and from the supply function as one of the inputs into planning.

In common with many corporations, Verona has deployed enterprise resource planning (ERP) software at the heart of its global supply management in order to achieve coordination between its spatially distributed supply network in meeting the global market plan. Consequently, a large part of the information which must be captured and transferred is collected and disseminated through its ERP system. The system provides ready-defined relations between marketing, manufacturing and distribution and captures knowledge supplied by the supply system as parameters for the capacities and capabilities of the global supply network. This is both internalized and external knowledge from outside suppliers covering the interface with the market (*Proposition 1*). When the forecast is generated from marketing, the responses of purchasing, manufacturing, sales and distribution are therefore determined by processes which have been rationalized and are effectively standardized. The value-creating knowledge relating to supply is thus embodied in its planning software. Knowledge is codified in a form which turns its use into a set of *routines*. Data processing and data transfer are automated wherever possible.

This codification of operating knowledge enables the corporation to maximise the value achieved on the tactical, operational timescale. It provides real-time monitoring and control of inventories, production schedules and distribution. Changes can be made with minimal response times if there are changes in the market environment in order to capture advantages, or minimize disadvantages. Standardization eliminates many costs and time delays of knowledge transfer which would result from differences in understanding, selective capture of data, different mental models of business processes by the individuals concerned, differences in priorities and so on. Operational effectiveness requires many complementary activities to be coordinated in concert, with separate but related activities often taking place simultaneously, providing a challenge to the firm to go further to identify knowledge frontiers across which knowledge sharing is to take place. These activities must be based on mutually consistent understandings of the immediate goals and of the prevailing circumstances. The ERP system is central to achieving this common operational world-view within the business for controlling concurrent operations. However, this process of knowledge sharing is imperfect, because some kinds of knowledge are less susceptible to codification and quantification, and may depend wholly on judgement and on trust of the judgement of others.

Frecknall Inc.: pharmaceutical product development

Frecknall Inc. is a US-owned global research-based pharmaceutical company. In the last two years it deployed a set of related computer-network based tools in its efforts to increase the success rate of its product development activities and reduce the product development cycle time. Several factors prompted the development of these tools, including cost and competitive pressures in the industry and the complexity of global product development. The aim of the network systems it developed is to facilitate communication amongst all those engaged in product development. There are four systems, which are intended to achieve knowledge sharing. These are: portfolio information for senior management, project management system for project managers and participants, team communication system and an expertise support tool for members of individual functions.

Compared with the previous cases, the correspondence between the structure of these systems and the product development process itself is less transparent. This is partly because of the relative complexity of product development in a globally dispersed pharmaceutical company. At least 21 distinct functional specializations can contribute to any given project, and many of these have further geographical sub-specialization.

The absence of a clear identification between process and structure is reflected in an internal evaluation conducted by Frecknall itself. In an appraisal of the system, there is a significant variation between systems in the perceptions of their users. The Expertise Support system (which is *not* cross-functional) is assessed the most positively across all dimensions and the Portfolio Information system the least positively. Most notably, the contribution to an identifiable business process is the lowest or equal lowest rated characteristic in all cases, and the technology is the highest rated characteristic. The significance of this result for the discussion here is that technology appears to have been the leading influence in designing all these systems, and the contribution to business processes has played a smaller part.

Frecknall's system has the objective of creating a coordinated product development process, but it has paid little attention to knowledge frontiers within and across the boundaries of the corporation and its methods of knowledge sharing are unsystematic and patchy (*Proposition 2*). Although designed to achieve new combinations of knowledge (discovery strategies as in *Proposition 4*), there is little evidence that this top-down approach has yet achieved consistency in governing knowledge across the firm. There is as yet little evidence of discovery strategies as outcomes of the knowledge governance process (*Proposition 5*).

Conclusion

A variety of knowledge governance problems are encountered in the four case studies and all involve resolving global/local issues. The coordination methods employed need to take account of this and other trade-offs (e.g.

specialization versus integration) and their resolution involves attention to the processes of knowledge sharing, the incentive structure within the firm and knowledge frontiers. These trade-offs are examined using the notions of partition and integration as architectural forms. Achievement of both application strategies (uses of a given portfolio of knowledge) and discovery strategies (new combinations of knowledge) are important goals of knowledge governance structures.

Examination of the cases suggests optimism in the applicability of our five propositions to the governance of knowledge sharing in multinational firms (see Table 9.1). Our suggestion that 'integration' and 'partition' are separate and identifiable architectural forms of achieving this requires more research. The specialization of firms around particular knowledge domains is a product of past research to which our cases contribute additional support. Mechanisms of knowledge sharing are found to be diverse, even within such a small sample of firms. The achievement of both application strategies (uses of a given portfolio of knowledge) and discovery strategies (new combinations of knowledge) are found to be important goals of knowledge governance structures, and our findings provide preliminary evidence that controlling information may, in certain circumstances, conflict with discovery strategies. Top-down approaches to governing knowledge sharing seem to be inappropriate and the phenomena of executive burn-out are examples of unsuccessful attempts to control information. The introduction of sophisticated IT systems for storing and sharing information is not necessarily successful in rectifying problems of the knowledge architecture of the firm unless they are introduced with great care, consultation and in accord with appropriate incentives.

Possible extensions of this research include extending the case study method to include cases with wider cultural and psychic distance between units of the firm in order to refine the propositions and derive hypotheses which will then be testable by the use of survey methodology. The results can also be refined by further longitudinal studies at the level of the individual managers and groups within firms. The incentive structures implied by our findings need further investigation together with their implications for the methods of knowledge sharing.

Acknowledgements

This research was conducted with financial support from the Carnegie Bosch Institute for Applied Studies in International Management, Carnegie Mellon University, Pittsburgh, PA, USA.

The authors would like to thank the editors and three anonymous referees for their insightful and helpful comments on earlier drafts.

Table 9.1 The propositions in practice

Propositions		*Braxia*	*Devonian*	*Verona*	*Frecknall*
Proposition 1	Internalized knowledge versus the market	Licensing in specialized knowledge and combining with internal skills	Integration of internalized knowledge with clients' needs	Combining internal knowledge with external market/ supply information	Little attention to boundaries
Proposition 2	Knowledge frontiers, knowledge sharing. Global/local issues	Worldwide sources of technology combined and disseminated to global markets	1. Bid specialization and experience versus local and technical expertise. 2. Loss of information from each separate bid team versus executive 'burn-out'. Local bids/ clients. Globally distributed expertise	Global primacy over local conditions. Hierarchical decision-making	Unsystematic approach. E.g. status of local knowledge inputs is unclear
Proposition 3	Knowledge architectures. Integration-partition. Trade-offs resolution. Implications for incentives	Integrating through a company-wide licensing system which coordinates the partitioned therapeutic areas. Specialized licensing department versus therapeutic expertise.	Integration across functional areas by means of flexible teams, partitioned for each client. Major Bid team acts as a repository of information and same people on repeat teams.	Enterprise resource planning system. Codified knowledge in short term leading to operational efficiency versus inflexibility in planning system.	Portfolio information system. Global information system loses (local) detail. Insufficiently developed and unclear to participants

		Virtual department liaises with individual therapeutic areas. Psychic rewards across organization	Both individual incentives and psychic rewards for members of successful teams	Loss of autonomy, local control and flexibility. Partial feedback of knowledge from supply function into plan. No obvious integration of knowledge sharing with incentive structure	
Proposition 4	Need for application and discovery	Exploiting complementarities between therapeutic marketing knowledge and inward licensing expertise	Knowledge sharing within team across functional areas		Top-down software development process
Proposition 5	Application/discovery conflicts	Governance structure for knowledge management facilitates discovery	Successive creation of appropriate teams. Knowledge maintained across teams by retaining key personnel in sequential bids		Little evidence of discovery strategies as outcomes of the knowledge governance process

References

Alchian, A. and Demsetz, H. (1972) 'Production, Information Costs and Economic Organisation'. *American Economic Review*, vol. 62, no. 5, pp. 777–95.

Arrow, K. J. (1962) 'Economic Welfare and the Allocation of Resources for Invention'. In *The Rate and Direction of Inventive Activity*, National Bureau of Economic Research, Princeton University Press, pp. 609–26.

Arthur, B. (1989) 'Competing Technologies, Increasing Returns and Lock-in by Historically Small Events'. *Economic Journal*, vol. 99, pp. 106–13.

Bercovitz, J. E. L., de Figueiredo, J. M. and Teece, D. J. (1987) 'Firm Capabilities and Managerial Decision Making: a Theory of Innovation Biases'. In R. Garad, P. R. Naygar and Z. B. Shapira (eds), *Technological Innovation: Oversights and Foresights*. Cambridge, UK: Cambridge University Press.

Brown, J. S. and Duguid, P. (1991) 'Organizational Learning and Communities of Practice: Towards a Unified View of Working, Learning and Innovation'. *Organization Science*, vol. 2, pp. 40–57.

Brown, J. S. and Duguid, P. (1998) 'Organizing Knowledge'. *California Management Review*, vol. 40, no. 3, pp. 90–111.

Buckley, P. J. (1983) 'New Theories of International Business: Some Unresolved Issues'. In M. Casson (ed.), *The Growth of International Business*. London: George Allen and Unwin.

Buckley, P. J. and Carter, M. J. (1996) 'The Economics of Business Process Design: Motivation, Information and Coordination within the Firm'. *International Journal of the Economics of Business*, vol. 3, pp. 5–25.

Buckley, P. J. and Carter, M. J. (1999) 'Managing Cross-Border Complementary Knowledge: Conceptual Developments in the Business Process Approach to Knowledge Management in Multinational Firms'. *International Studies of Management and Organisation*, vol. 29, no. 1, pp. 80–104.

Buckley, P. J. and Carter, M. J. (2000) 'Knowledge Management in Global Technology Markets: Applying Theory to Practice'. *Long Range Planning*, vol. 33, pp. 55–71.

Buckley, P. J. and Carter, M. J. (2002) 'Process and Structure in Knowledge Management Practices of British and US Multinational Enterprises'. *Journal of International Management*, vol. 8, pp. 29–48.

Buckley, P. J. and Casson, M. C. (1976) *The Future of the Multinational Enterprise*. London: Macmillan.

Burns, T. and Stalker, G. M. (1966) *The Management of Innovation*. London: Tavistock.

Coase, R. H. (1937) 'The Nature of the Firm'. *Economica*, New Series, vol. 4, pp. 386–405.

Demsetz, H. (1991) 'The Theory of the Firm Revisited'. In O. E. Williamson and S. G. Winter (eds), *The Nature of the Firm: Origins, Evolution and Development*. Oxford: Oxford University Press.

Dierickx, I. and Cool, K. (1989) 'Asset Stock Accumulation and the Sustainability of Competitive Advantage'. *Management Science*, vol. 35, no. 12, pp. 1504–11.

Dixit, A. K. (1996) *The Making of Economic Policy*. Cambridge, Mass.: MIT Press.

Fransman, M. (1998) 'Information, Knowledge, Vision and Theories of the Firm'. In G. Dosi, D. J. Teece and J. Chytry (eds), *Technology, Organization and Competitiveness: Perspectives on Industrial and Corporate Change*. Oxford: Oxford University Press.

Grant, R. M. (1996) 'Toward a Knowledge-based Theory of the Firm'. *Strategic Management Journal*, vol. 17, Winter Special Edition, pp. 109–22.

Hallen, L. and Wiedersheim-Paul, F. (1979) 'Psychic Distance and Buyer–Seller Interaction'. *Organisasjon, Marked og Samfund*, vol. 16, no. 5, pp. 308–24.

Kogut, B. and Zander, U. (1992) 'Knowledge of the Firm, Combinative Capabilities and the Replication of Technology'. *Organization Science*, vol. 3, pp. 383–97.

Kogut, B. and Zander, U. (1996) 'What Do Firms Do? Coordination, Identity and Learning'. *Organization Science*, vol. 7, no. 5, pp. 502–18.

Koopmans, T. C. (1957) *Three Essays on the State of Economic Science*. New York: McGraw-Hill.

Kuhn, T. S. (1962) *The Structure of Scientific Revolutions*. Chicago: University of Chicago Press.

Lakatos, I. (1970) 'Falsification and the Methodology of Scientific Research Programmes'. In I. Lakatos and A. Musgrave (eds), *Criticism and the Growth of Knowledge*, vol. 4 of Proceedings of the International Colloquium in the Philosophy of Science, Cambridge: Cambridge University Press.

Langlois, R. N. (1991) 'Transaction Costs in Real Time'. *Industrial and Corporate Change*, vol. 1, no. 1, pp. 99–127.

Leonard-Barton, D. (1992) 'Core Capabilities and Core Rigidities: a Paradox of Managing New Product Development'. *Strategic Management Journal*, vol. 13, pp. 111–25.

Nonaka, I. and Takeuchi, H. (1995) *The Knowledge-creating Company*. Oxford: Oxford University Press.

North, D. (1990) *Institutions, Institutional Change and Economic Performance*. Cambridge: Cambridge University Press.

Prahalad, C. K. and Hamel, G. (1990) 'The Core Competence of the Corporation'. *Harvard Business Review*, vol. 66.

Rosen, S. (1991) 'Transaction Costs and the Internal Labor Market'. In O. E. Williamson and S. G. Winter (eds), *The Nature of the Firm: Origins, Evolution and Development*. Oxford: Oxford University Press.

Scott-Morgan, P. (1994) *The Unwritten Rules of the Game*. New York: McGraw-Hill.

Simon, H. A. (1945) *Administrative Behaviour*. New York: Free Press.

Von Hippel, E. (1998) '"Sticky Information" and the Locus of Problem Solving: Implications for Innovation'. In A. D. Chandler, P. Hagström and Ö. Sölvell (eds), *The Dynamic Firm: the Role of Technology, Strategy, Organisation and Regions*. Oxford: Oxford University Press.

Weick, K. E. and Roberts, K. H. (1993) 'Collective Mind in Organisations: Heedful Interrelating on the Flight Deck'. *Administrative Science Quarterly*, vol. 38, no. 3, pp. 357–81.

Williamson, O. E. (1975) *Markets and Hierarchies*. New York: Free Press.

Williamson, O. E. (1985) *The Economic Institutions of Capitalism*. New York: Free Press.

Williamson, O. E., Wachter, M. L. and Harris, J. E. (1975) 'Understanding the Employment Relation: the Analysis of Idiosyncratic Exchange'. *Bell Journal of Economics*, vol. 6, pp. 350–80.

Yin, R. K. (1994) *Case Study Research: Design and Methods* (2nd edn). London: Sage.

Part IV

Empirics

10
Evolution of FDI in the United States in the Context of Trade Liberalization and Regionalization

with Jeremy Clegg, Nicolas Forsans and Kevin T. Reilly

Introduction

As the world economy has become globalized, the simultaneous move towards regionalization has been a striking feature of the past decade. Europe, Asia, and North America, among others, have developed a wide range of institutionalized arrangements to formalize the rising economic integration that has occurred between countries on a regional basis. The link between globalization and the growth of trade blocs is foreign direct investment (FDI). FDI represents a major strategic weapon for multinational enterprises (MNEs) in their struggle for the world's appropriable surplus (Buckley, 1996). It is an important reality of the regionalized world economy that firms based outside trade blocs are highly discriminated against.

Regional economic integration (REI) is therefore a way of increasing discrimination against firms outside the area of integration and, crucially, of raising the preference of MNEs for local production within the integrating area. Indeed, the literature, largely focused on the European experience, would suggest that MNEs should react differently to the formation of free trade areas (FTA) according to whether they are based in the integrated area ('insiders') or outside ('outsiders') (UNTCMD, 1993).

In this chapter, we focus on the strategic responses of Canadian, European, and Japanese MNEs to the Canada–United States Free Trade Agreement (CUSFTA), which started in 1989, and then to the North American Free Trade Agreement (NAFTA) among Canada, the United States, and Mexico, which took effect in 1994. The second section attempts to characterize economic integration in North America. The third section focuses on the reactions of 'insiders' and 'outsiders' to these agreements. In the fourth section, we present the results of an econometric model aiming at differentiating the separate effects of CUSFTA and NAFTA on the FDI strategies of MNEs by their location of origin. Our results suggest that the asymmetric strategic positions of 'insider' and 'outsider' firms are capable of explaining some of the contrasts in their FDI behaviours.

Characterization of REI in North America

In comparison with economic integration within Europe, REI in North America has been more driven by pressure from private sector firms rather than public policy initiatives (Buckley et al., 2001). The incentives to reduce trade and investment barriers within the CUSFTA and the NAFTA are primarily those of reducing the artificial barriers that burden the considerable trade already conducted between the member countries. Unlike the European Union and its precursors, the NAFTA is a free trade agreement in which each member country retains its own tariff on imports, and other regulations regarding trade with third countries. The bases of this agreement are the rules of origin that aim to prevent trade deflection from occurring. The required local content of goods for liberal treatment in the NAFTA was initially set at 50 per cent but with an increase to 62.5 per cent in 2002. Also, the CUSFTA and NAFTA framework of integration leaves important areas untouched; subsidies, labour markets, and agriculture (Jovanovic, 1998) are, for the most part, not addressed in these treaties. Indeed, as Krugman (1996, p. 165) has pointed out, NAFTA represents a method of trying to help the Mexican economic reform process, which is in effect a precondition for starting the process of REI for Mexico. Given the fact that the entire economy of Mexico is equal to that of Massachusetts, it becomes clear that 'economics' (large market, economies of scale, jobs, and growth) has not played a primary role in this integration. The United States is very concerned about stability at its southern border. Hence, the NAFTA needs to be seen as a tool that is supposed to help a friendly Mexican government succeed in its reform and development process, as Krugman (1996, p. 165) points out. The striking feature of the NAFTA is that it is an arrangement that brings together countries with significant differences in per capita income. This is why Mexico was permitted a transition period of seven years for the elimination of tariffs, i.e. longer than under the CUSFTA. The initial economic impact of NAFTA is not large, but paves the way for integration of a deeper character in the future.

A framework for the impact of REI on FDI-based strategic responses

While REI may be seen as a further step towards the liberalization of trade and investment, institutionalized agreements bring with them a package of discriminatory weapons against outsiders (e.g. rules of origin). The contrasts between the strategic reactions of insiders and outsiders in the context of regionalization are a major theme of this chapter. We shall first focus on the impact of REI on outsiders, especially on European and Japanese MNEs (who are the major investors in North America), and then consider the possible effects on insiders (Canadian MNEs).

North American integration's impact on inter-bloc strategies

One of the primary purposes of REI is to shift locational attractiveness – to encourage investment diversion (switching from extra-bloc to intra-bloc investment). It attempts to induce a switch in the market-servicing strategies of extra-trade bloc firms from exporting to inward investment. In addition to diverting investment into the bloc by non-bloc multinationals, regional integration is also expected to affect the investment location decisions of both insider and outsider firms. In principle, the creation of an FTA from a number of separate markets may make a central production site for the region more attractive. This provides incentive for firms to create a 'hub-and-spoke' system where central facilities (research, manufacturing) are combined with a set of dispersed distribution outlets radiating from the central facility. This location strategy combines 'global' (economies of scale) with 'local' advantages (adaptation of product). It can be combined with an ownership strategy that keeps the central facilities under total control by being wholly owned, while the distribution outlets can be joint ventures, reducing the firm's risks by involving local capital and therefore gaining access to local marketing expertise (Buckley and Casson, 1998).

It could also be argued that the formation of an FTA provokes firms to move from a multidomestic strategy (where firms can treat competition in each country as separate) to a 'regional' strategy, where strategy becomes inextricably intertwined across the newly integrated market (Porter, 1986). For example, following regional integration, a UK firm that had formerly invested in Canada to service the Canadian domestic market might now consider switching its investment to the United States or Mexico. New investors face the same choice among more flexible options. Indeed, the nature of firms' adjustments in the wake of NAFTA depends on the starting position of the investor. For firms newly entering North America, location in one market may indeed be employed as a platform for expanding into the rest of NAFTA. For established investors, more harmonized legislation on standards is more likely to stimulate the replacement of subsidiaries with representative offices than to generate increased cross-border business. The rationalization of manufacturing facilities between Canada and the United States may be possible, with the caveat that local representation through sales and marketing will still be necessary.

However, the sheer size of the North American market and the fact that barriers such as legislative differences arising out of historical developments continue to segment Canada, the United States, and Mexico mean that a single strategic approach to North America is unlikely to be appropriate for many firms. These considerations explain why many firms have continued to pursue separate organizational developments in each of the national markets.

Intra-bloc effects

The integration of the North American market is marked by a long-standing collaboration between Canada and the United States – one that predates both the CUSFTA and the NAFTA. Direct investment by US firms in the Canadian economy, and by Canadian firms in the US economy, has historically been substantial and has continued to grow during the NAFTA years. The 1965 Auto Pact forged a strong alliance between auto manufacturers and has resulted in this particular sector's being well integrated 30 years later. This early movement toward closer linkages was furthered by both the CUSFTA and the NAFTA.

Although a significant part of US FDI into Canada has been raw materials-oriented, consistent with the traditional comparative advantage-based view of FDI, the bulk of US FDI into Canada clearly has been market-seeking and import-substituting. Because of the historically high Canadian tariffs, foreign firms wanting to gain access to the Canadian market have typically been forced to build plants in Canada. This has applied in the greatest measure to United States firms. The primary mission of these plants was to serve the Canadian market, and it was often cheaper to produce in Canada than to export from the home country and pay the tariff (Rugman, 1990).

In the 1970s, when Canadian tariffs began to be reduced in earnest, two predictions were made regarding the way US MNEs' affiliates would adjust to trade liberalization. First, there was great concern among opponents of free trade that US 'tariff factories' would leave Canada, only to serve the Canadian market through exports originating in the United States. Second, it was also predicted that, due to the high Canadian unit cost of production, firms would adjust to trade liberalization by rationalizing their production, i.e. specializing production at the plant level by reducing the number of product varieties produced in each plant. However, as Rugman (1990) points out, even if protectionism were the initial impetus to FDI, MNEs accrue intangible benefits from operating in host markets over time, which confer advantages on foreign-owned firms, fuelling future competitiveness, and expansion of their operations in the host country.

Finally, North American FDI in Mexico, although very small before the NAFTA started in 1994, consisted mainly of efficiency-seeking FDI aimed at a greater exploitation of comparative advantage (in this case, low-wage labour). The immediate pre-NAFTA period saw favourable macroeconomic conditions for US investment in general and investment in Mexico in particular. These conditions account, to some extent, for the increases in US FDI in Mexico prior to 1994 (USITC, 1997).

A framework for North American integration's impact on FDI

Following UNTCMD (1993) and Buckley et al. (1998), four kinds of FDI strategies related to REI can be identified. The first is a defensive import-substituting investment in which the outsider firm, to maintain market share in the newly integrated area, switches from an export-orientated strategy aimed at individual countries to production within the area. This follows from REI changing the balance of locational advantages between the rest of the world and the region.

The second is reorganization investment, in which insider firms reorganize production within the integrated area in accordance with member countries' comparative advantages. This is likely to result in fewer production locations within the regionally integrated area.

The third form of investment is that of rationalization, in which insider firms take advantage of the newly created returns to scale possibilities in the REI area. Member countries with established production units enjoying (or potentially enjoying) scale economies, will expect to see increases in investment as facilities expand to capture the reduced production costs. The rationalization strategy is likely to generate the 'hub-and-spoke' system of organization discussed earlier.

The final form of investment is that of offensive import substitution, employed by insider and outsider firms alike. This arises from business expectations about the dynamic effects (i.e. growth augmentation effects) of the creation of the regionally integrated area. As a result of NAFTA's dynamic effects, the size of the barrier-free market within which a firm operates expands. These growth-enhancing and market-augmenting effects of NAFTA give rise to FDI whose motivation is to take advantage of growing demand and the opening up of new markets.

These strategic responses affect both the geographical and sectoral distributions of FDI within the FTA, as well as the level of FDI. The relationship between trade and investment is very complex, and these four FDI strategies do not necessarily replace trade; some can complement a trade-based strategy, especially the cases of rationalization and reorganization FDI (Buckley et al., 2000).

The impact of North American economic integration on FDI-based strategic responses of multinational firms

The data used in this study are from the US Bureau of Economic Analysis, Department of Commerce, and consists of annual estimates of the inward FDI stock in the US for 1960–97. We concentrate on Canada, five main European investors in the United States for which data are available for the whole period, i.e. the UK, the Netherlands, Switzerland, France and Germany, and Japan. Table 10.1 shows that Canada's share in total inward

Table 10.1 Share of FDI in the United States by Canada, Europe, Japan, and the rest of the world (ROW)

Years	*1960*	*1970*	*1980*	*1985*	*1990*	*1995*	*1996*	*1997*
Canada	27.99	23.49	14.74	9.28	7.48	8.52	9.22	9.39
Europe	68.12	72.00	66.91	65.77	62.63	62.06	62.00	62.38
Japan	1.27	1.73	6.18	10.46	21.04	19.61	19.28	18.12
ROW	2.62	2.79	12.17	14.49	8.85	9.81	9.50	10.11
Total	100	100	100	100	100	100	100	100

Source: US Bureau of Economic Analysis.

FDI in the United States has fallen by around two-thirds over the last three decades, from 28 per cent of the total stock of FDI in the United States to just 7.5 per cent in 1990. It is of interest that Canada's share only started to increase again after this long-term decline from 1990, i.e. in the wake of the CUSFTA and NAFTA, to represent an overall figure of 10 per cent in 1997. Table 10.2 shows that European countries are the main investors in the United States; in 1997, Europe was responsible for 62 per cent of the total FDI stock in the United States – slightly less than their 1960 percentage of 68 per cent. Japanese FDI, although little over 1 per cent in 1960, is now approaching 20 per cent; between 1985 and 1990, Japan's share doubled.

To model the growth in the FDI we have selected a parsimonious constant growth curve. The intercept term in this equation represents base (or starting point) natural log FDI (ln FDI) and the parameter on the time trend (t) represents the growth rate of FDI. Both parameters have an expected sign of greater than zero. To measure the policy effects in this equation, we introduce two dummy variables that correspond for the time periods when the CUSFTA and NAFTA were implemented. The literature suggests these agreements will affect the FDI decision. Indeed, Clegg and Scott-Green (1999) argue that when considering the effect of economic integration on FDI decisions, you should allow for the fact that firms will make decisions on

Table 10.2 Share of FDI in the United States by European countries

Years	*1960*	*1970*	*1980*	*1985*	*1990*	*1995*	*1996*	*1997*
UK	32.53	31.10	17.91	23.59	24.99	21.71	20.42	19.01
Netherlands	13.70	16.21	24.74	20.07	16.38	12.16	12.51	12.45
Switzerland	11.19	11.64	7.42	5.72	4.48	5.13	5.12	5.66
France	n.a	n.a	5.46	3.61	4.72	6.75	6.92	6.91
Germany	n.a	n.a	11.11	8.03	7.15	8.59	10.08	10.23
Europe	68.12	72.00	66.91	65.77	62.63	62.06	62.00	62.38

Source: US Bureau of Economic Analysis.

the assumption that the agreement will be reached prior to actual implementation given the time lags for the returns. In this context, we have turned on the CUSFTA dummy in 1987 and turned off this dummy when we assume the NAFTA agreement becomes effective in 1992. This rather than the actual implementation dates of 1989 and 1994 for CUSFTA and NAFTA, respectively. The expected signs on these variables are positive, in that we propose the alternative hypothesis that North American integration has resulted in a significantly greater level of inward FDI into the United States. The interpretation of the actual coefficient is that it represents the effect on natural log of base FDI. Therefore, the equation for country *i* in period *t* is

$$\ln \mathrm{FDI}_{it} = \alpha_i + \beta_{1i}t + \beta_{2i}\mathrm{CUSFTA}_{it} + \beta_{3i}\mathrm{NAFTA}_{it} + \mu_{it} \qquad (10.1)$$

The 'countries' of interest are 'all countries', Europe, and individual countries Canada and Japan over the 38 years of data that are available.

Table 10.3 reports our results for estimating equation (10.1) separately for Canada, Europe and Japan. We tested for a common model for three regions and individually using a standard *F*-test. The results suggest that we should not pool the data for Canada, Europe, or Japan in any combination. The coefficients for the time trend and the constants are all highly significant and positive, as the theory would predict, and four of the six coefficients for the North American integration variables have significant positive signs as expected.

The CUSFTA dummy is positive and significant in each case. For Japan, the level of significance is lower, but the strength of the coefficient for CUSFTA is perceptibly higher. An interpretation of this result is that Japanese firms reacted more strongly earlier on to regional integration as a defensive

Table 10.3 Determinants of the natural logarithm of FDI into the United States by Canada, Europe, and Japan

	Year	*CUSFTA*	*NAFTA*	*Constant*	*Adjusted R^2*
Canada	0.034[a]	0.357[a]	0.467[a]	8.820[a]	0.952
	[11.349]	[4.737]	[5.588]	[196.641]	
Europe	0.080[a]	0.327[a]	0.078	9.535[a]	0.981
	[24.433]	[3.909]	[0.839]	[191.463]	
Japan	0.190[a]	0.607[b]	−0.609	4.779[a]	0.952
	[15.531]	[1.943]	[−0.199]	[25.267]	

Number inside brackets is the *t* ratio.
[a] The parameter is significant at the 99% level of confidence.
[b] The parameter is significant at the 95% level of confidence.

import-substituting response, as befits firms with large export shares in the period previous to integration.

Europe also responded strongly to the CUSFTA, with a magnitude similar to that of the insider Canada. The theory of international business suggests that the insider differs from the outsider: the former is likely to develop rationalized FDI as a response to the cost reduction effects and efficiency gains brought about by FTAs, while FDI by the latter will tend to be driven by import-substitution motives. At the aggregate level, one cannot distinguish these two theoretically different effects.

The NAFTA variable fails to reach significance for Europe and Japan, attaining significance only for investment from Canada. The lone significance of NAFTA for Canada is likely to be the result of the unique position of Canada in this enquiry vis-à-vis the United States, i.e. that of the only insider as opposed to the outsider countries. Within the context of North American integration, NAFTA's primary role is to enable Mexico to catch up in terms of liberalization. As noted earlier, although the economic impact of this alone for the North American economy is not large, the NAFTA paves the way for integration of a deeper character in the future. This may be part of the reason why the NAFTA coefficient is insignificant for the outsider countries of Europe and Japan, in that the outsider can wait, while the insider cannot – a point which we now consider further. Buckley et al. (1994) note that Canadian firms, spurred by NAFTA, seemed to have intensified their investments in the United States and were characteristically market-seeking in their motives. This offers some explanation for the amplified response of Canadian firms to NAFTA compared with CUSFTA. Canadian firms appear to have adopted an outward-looking strategy in response to NAFTA.

Given the extremely simple nature of the model, our main conclusion is that the modelling of United States' inward FDI needs in the future to consider the insider–outsider distinction, since our modest results suggest differential reactions to the implementation of REI agreements.

Conclusions

North American REI, on the evidence of this study, has resulted in an increase in the level of inward FDI to the United States above the level that would otherwise have prevailed. This provides support for the theory that regional integration should exert a positive impact on FDI and of findings from earlier work on FDI into the European Union and its precursors. The evidence in this chapter indicates that outsider firms, in the form of the European countries and Japan, responded more via FDI to CUSFTA than to NAFTA. There is some suggestion that outsider firms engaged in defensive import-substituting FDI. In contrast, the insider country in this study, Canada, responded more to NAFTA. Canadian firms are without exception insiders, whereas only a proportion of non-North American inward investors (or potential investors) into the United States would fall into this category by virtue of substantial existing investments within North America. Canadian firms appear to have engaged most energetically in offensive import-substituting FDI, very much along the lines of our earlier theoretical analysis for insider firms.

Further research is desirable, but the statistical hurdles to employing more desegregated data (especially by industry) are extremely high. Despite these obstacles, the results of this study show that there are differences in the strategic responses between insider and outsider firms, to the extent that these follow country of origin. Our findings also demonstrate that these differences can be interpreted within the framework of international business theory.

References

Buckley, P. J. (1996) 'Government Policy Responses to Strategic Rent-seeking Transnational Firms'. *Transnational Corporations,* vol. 5, no. 2, pp. 1–17.

Buckley, P. J. and Casson, M. C. (1998) 'Models of the Multinational Enterprise'. *Journal of International Business Studies,* vol. 29, no. 1, pp. 21–44.

Buckley, P. J., Pass, C. L. and Prescott, K. (1994) *Canada–UK Bilateral Trade and Investment Relations.* London: Macmillan.

Buckley, P. J., Clegg, J. and Forsans, N. (1998) 'Foreign Market Servicing Strategies in the NAFTA Area'. *Canadian Journal of Regional Science,* Special Issue on North American Trade and Investment, vol. XXI, no. 2, pp. 255–75.

Buckley, P. J., Clegg, J., Forsans, N. and Reilly, K. T. (2001) 'Increasing the Size of the "Country": Foreign Direct Investment and Regionalisation in a Globalized World Economy'. *Management International Review* (March).

Clegg, J. and Scott-Green, S. C. (1999) 'The Determinants of New Foreign Direct Investment Capital Flows into the European Community: a Statistical Comparison of the USA and Japan'. *Journal of Common Market Studies,* vol. 37, no. 4, pp. 597–616.

Jovanovic, M. N. (1998) *International Economic Integration* (2nd edn). London: Routledge.

Krugman, P. (1996) *Pop Internationalism.* Cambridge, Mass.: MIT Press.

Porter, M. E. (1986) *Competition in World Industries.* Cambridge, Mass.: Harvard Business Press.

Rugman, A. M. (1990) *Multinationals and Canada–United States Free Trade.* Columbia, SC: University of South Carolina Press.

United Nations Transnational Corporations and Management Division (UNTCMD) (1993) *From the Common Market to EC 92: Regional Economic Integration in the European Community and Transnational Corporations.* New York: United Nations, Department of Economic and Social Development.

United States International Trade Commission (USITC) (1997) *The Impact of the North American Free Trade Agreement on the US Economy and Industries: a Three-year Review.* Investigation no. 332–381. Washington, DC.

11

The Impact of Inward FDI on the Performance of Chinese Manufacturing Firms

with Jeremy Clegg and Chengqi Wang

Introduction

Recent years have witnessed the emergence of China as one of the most important destinations for foreign direct investment (FDI), which reached US$403.98 billion by the end of 1999 (MOFTEC, 2000). China is now the largest recipient of FDI in the developing world. However, the amount of FDI will underestimate its overall consequences if spillover effects are significant (Murphy, 1992; O'Malley, 1994; Buckwalter, 1995). This study investigates the impact of FDI on the performance of Chinese locally owned firms in manufacturing.

Prior research on spillovers from foreign to locally owned firms shows mixed results (Blomström and Kokko, 1997). Evidence to show that the productivity of local firms is enhanced because of FDI-induced spillovers (Caves, 1974; Globerman, 1979; Liu et al., 2000) is balanced by other studies finding negligible spillovers (Haddad and Harrison, 1993), or a negative correlation between FDI and the performance of the host country economy (Singh, 1992). These results may reflect the omission of important variables, such as the level of R&D expenditure and employees with technical degrees (Diankov and Hoekman, 2000). Spillovers are generally measured as the impact of the presence of foreign multinational enterprises (MNEs) on productivity in domestic firms. Mixed findings may result from the fact that these studies use different proxies for foreign presence (Görg and Strobl, 2001). In addition, these studies do not investigate non-productivity spillovers.

At the national level, the importance of FDI for China's economy has been demonstrated by empirical research (Kueh, 1992; Zhan, 1993; Wang, 1995; Chen et al., 1995; Wu, 1999). At the micro level, studies examine technology transfer by MNEs (Lan and Young, 1996) and linkages between foreign subsidiaries and Chinese local firms (Li and Yeung, 1999). The results are generally qualitative and support the view that the entry and operation of MNEs promote the development of Chinese indigenous firms. Zhu and Tan (2000) find that the intensity of FDI inflow is positively correlated with labour productivity in several Chinese cities.

Few industry-level analyses examine how far MNEs influence the performance of indigenous Chinese firms. One exception is Liu (2001), whose results indicate that FDI is positively associated with higher total factor productivity in an industry. Liu's study regresses total factor productivity on the ratio of FDI to total capital in the same industry. However, spillover effects are usually measured as the impact of foreign share of capital or employment on the productivity of the domestically owned sector in each industry (Caves, 1974; Liu et al., 2000). Indeed, the observed improvements in total factor productivity might be largely a result of the growth within the industry of the foreign sector itself.

Our research differs from existing work in three respects. First, it examines not only productivity, but also non-productivity spillovers. Second, it explores the possibility that different types of ownership advantage of MNEs from the overseas Chinese (OC) and from non-Chinese (NC, i.e. Western countries and Japan) might lead to contrasting effects on local firms. Third, it differentiates between the types of locally owned Chinese firms, to examine whether their absorptive capabilities differ, and the extent to which they are able to benefit from the effects of spillovers.

Hypotheses

Productivity spillovers take place when the entry or presence of MNE affiliates lead to productivity benefits in local firms, and the MNEs are not able to internalize the full value of these benefits (Blomström et al., 2000). Kokko (1992) points out that the term 'spillover' has a broader meaning than 'imitation' or 'technology diffusion'. It is primarily associated with productivity – hence the interchangeable use of the terms 'productivity' and 'technology' spillover in much of the literature. According to Eden et al. (1997), MNE technology can spill over to host country firms in the following ways: (1) demonstration effects; (2) backward and forward linkages between MNEs and their local suppliers and buyers; (3) training of local employees by the MNE; (4) competition effects between foreign and local firms (Blomström et al., 2000). The existence of such spillovers should benefit domestic firms, as low-cost access to leading-edge technologies should be productivity-enhancing (Feinberg and Majumdar, 2001).

Large multinationals such as Microsoft, IBM, Lucent Technologies, Intel, have recently established laboratories in China to benefit from employing the most promising Chinese scientists and technologists available at low cost. In the process of generating research results that are proprietary to the multinational, cooperation with local companies and research institutes supported the development of China's high-tech sector (Gelb, 2000). Interaction between local and foreign firms through component supply, subcontracting, licensing, and technical cooperation, can serve to upgrade the operations of Chinese firms. When cooperation occurs, normally the MNE provides training and technical services to Chinese partners.

MNEs that are export-oriented may act as export catalysts to local firms by producing externalities which enhance their export prospects (Rhee and Belot, 1990). These 'market access spillovers' may arise through the employment of local firms as suppliers and subcontractors to MNEs. These linkages provide knowledge about product and process technologies and foreign market conditions. Indirect channels exist through which local export performance can be improved. Local firms may learn how to succeed in foreign markets by copying MNEs. MNEs may also train local employees in export management and foreign market knowledge. Local firms acquire this knowledge if MNEs' employees move to local firms.

There is considerable empirical evidence showing that foreign MNEs help the exports of local firms (Aitken et al., 1994; Kokko et al., 1997). With respect to China, Thoburn (1997) concludes that foreign MNEs have played a significant role in China's export growth. In 1994, foreign MNEs accounted for 41 per cent of China's overall exports (Mok, 2000). This may be primarily due to the growth in export-oriented FDI. Learning from their foreign counterparts may stimulate exports by local Chinese firms.

> *Hypothesis 1:* The higher the foreign capital participation, the greater the (a) productivity, (b) development of high-tech products, (c) development of new products, and (d) access to international markets.

FDI in China originates from OC and NC. In this study OC comprises FDI from Hong Kong, Macau and Taiwan, representing 72 per cent of the total value of accumulated FDI by year-end 1995 (Luo, 1999). NC refers to Western FDI which includes all other countries, notably the USA, Western Europe and Japan. OC FDI is primarily export-oriented (Zhang, 2000) – an orientation which is encouraged by China's cheap labour and incentive policies and by OC MNEs' advantages in labour-intensive production. By contrast, NC FDI tends to be local market oriented, motivated by China's potentially huge market, by external trade barriers and by Western attempts to internalize technological advantages. Anand and Delios (1996) suggest that superior technology and management inflows accompany export-oriented FDI. One reading of this is that the productivity spillovers from OC capital should exceed those of Western capital. However, the industrial concentration of OC firms in standardized goods market segments within industries means that the scope for technological spillovers is reduced.

MNEs' ownership advantages consist of technological skills, organizational skills and marketing skills (Luo, 1999). NC MNEs are superior to OC firms (typically conglomerates) in product and process innovation and in technological development (Yeung, 1997). NC MNEs have been more innovative, transferred more technologies to local firms, and have made greater commitments to quality control and adapting technologies to suit the needs of Chinese consumers (Luo, 1999). In contrast, OC MNEs use what is referred to as 'appropriate technology' – technologies that are generally standardized and mature (Davis, 1996; Lee and Plummer, 1992), to compete with local and foreign firms by occupying a niche market. The performance of OC MNEs in China is therefore not based on ownership advantages in state-of-the-art technology and patented products (Shi, 1998).

Compared with OC MNEs, the managerial expertise of Western investors is more attractive to Chinese enterprises (Luo, 1999). NC MNEs are more likely to transfer organizational skills to local operations because they tend to pursue long-term market growth (Luo, 1999). In contrast, OC MNEs have less experience in organizing mass production, and do not enjoy the same level of organizational skills as their Western counterparts. OC MNEs are less motivated to transfer organizational skills since their operations tend to be short-term and less technologically sophisticated. OC MNEs' advantages are more likely to include marketing skills that enable the delivery of timely and uniform quality products to Western markets (Wells, 1993), or the ability to adapt mature technologies to more labour-intensive contexts and to local raw materials.

This means that the presence of both Western and OC MNEs should positively impact upon the performance of Chinese local firms. However, OC capital may transfer a relatively low level of technology of older vintages. This may result in modest levels of spillover benefits for indigenous firms. Foreign presence may even reduce the productivity of domestic firms, particularly in the short run. This could happen when FDI occurs in industries where MNEs are strong (not necessarily in technology) and locals are weaker and dependent on a protected local market. This gives rise to crowding out of local firms.

This suggests the following hypotheses:

Hypothesis 2: The higher the OC capital participation, the greater the (a) productivity, (b) development of high-tech products, (c) development of new products, and (d) access to international markets.

Hypothesis 3: The higher the NC capital participation, the greater the (a) productivity, (b) development of high-tech products, (c) development of new products, and (d) access to international markets.

Hypothesis 4: The magnitude of the effect of NC capital participation is greater than that of OC capital participation in terms of (a) productivity, (b) development of high-tech products, (c) development of new products, and (d) access to international markets.

A number of studies stress that the extent of spillovers depends largely on the ability of recipient firms to absorb information. Cohen and Levinthal (1989) and Cantwell (1993) emphasize that a firm's ability to acquire innovative skills depends on its existing technological capabilities. Wang and Blomström (1992) point out that the majority of spillovers do not arise automatically from the presence of foreign firms. Instead, to benefit, indigenous firms need to invest in 'learning activities'. Ostry and Gestrin (1993) argue that the interaction of foreign affiliates and host country firms might become less effective if local firms cannot adjust to the higher organizational and technological requirements of participation in the new corporate structures associated with the development of new technologies. We might speculate that firm-specific differences in the ability to absorb spillovers may explain some of the contradictory findings in the empirical literature, and that the cost of learning activities may be likely to differ with the type of knowledge involved.

Chinese industries consist of state-owned enterprises (SOEs) and non-state-owned enterprises. Collectively owned enterprises (COEs) are non-state-owned,[1] and they include rural township, village enterprises and urban collective firms. SOEs are tightly controlled by the government, and operate bureaucratically mandated plans. In contrast, COEs are collectively owned by the managers and employees, have much greater decision-making autonomy, secure resources and dispose of outputs through markets. The central government has a soft budget constraint on SOEs, so that they constantly rely on financing from central government regardless of performance, whilst COEs have to be financially self-reliant. SOEs' goals are not simply the production of goods, but also political support for the government, expansion of employment, and provision of various social services and benefits, which conflict with productive efficiency. In contrast, COEs focus entirely on economic objectives.

One previous finding is that COEs outperformed SOEs (Huang and Meng 1997). Whilst SOEs are owned by the state, control rights are divided or shared between government bureaucrats and enterprise managers (Zhu, 1999). There are no well-defined property rights in SOEs, so neither managers nor government are responsible for SOEs' performance. SOEs are not strongly committed to long-term technology development through learning from foreign technologically advanced firms. This contributes to the low absorptive capabilities of SOEs. Consistent with these arguments, we suggest:

> *Hypothesis 5:* The magnitude of the effect of (a) (overall) foreign capital participation, (b) OC participation, and (c) NC capital participation is greater for collectively owned firms than for state-owned firms.

Methodology and data

Following Kokko (1992) and Liu et al. (2000) we assume that labour productivity (Y) is a function of foreign presence (FP). Görg and Strobl (2001) argue that it is preferable to use alternative measures of foreign presence when measuring spillover effects. Improving on previous studies, we measure FP in six dimensions: the share of foreign owned firms' capital in total capital in each industry (FP_1); the share of employment in foreign owned firms in total employment in each industry (FP_2); the share of investment by OC firms in total investment in each industry (FP_3); the share of investment by NC firms in total investment in each industry (FP_4); the share of foreign capital in total capital of the state-owned sector in each industry (FP_5) and the share of foreign capital in total capital of the collectively owned sector in each industry (FP_6).

Other variables that influence labour productivity are included as controls: capital intensity (KL), the capital labour ratio; R&D intensity (RI), R&D expenditure per employee; labour quality (LQ), the share of college graduates in total employment, which reflects human capital; firm size (FS), the value of assets per firm, to capture firm size effects (Liu, 1999; Luo, 1997, 1998). This yields the following multi-equation model:

$$(Y)^{(\mathrm{p,\,h,\,n,\,e})}_{(\mathrm{d,\,s,\,c})} = \alpha_0 + \alpha_1(\mathrm{KL})_{(\mathrm{d,\,s,\,c})} + \alpha_2(\mathrm{RI})_{(\mathrm{d,\,s,\,c})} + \alpha_3(\mathrm{LQ})_{(\mathrm{d,\,s,\,c})} + \alpha_4(\mathrm{FP})_i + \alpha_5(\mathrm{FS})_{(\mathrm{d,\,s,\,c})} + \varepsilon \quad (i = 1, 2, \ldots 6) \qquad (11.1)$$

where p, h, n and e represent the form of spillovers – p denotes productivity, h development of high-tech products, n development of new products, and e export intensity, while d, s and c represent all Chinese domestically owned firms, SOEs and COEs respectively. In model (11.1) all variables are in logarithmic form, and ordinary least square (OLS) is employed throughout. Given that small, medium, and large-sized firms or industrial branches are sampled together in our cross-sectional data set, heteroscedasticity is expected to be widespread, and this was confirmed in pre-testing. Consequently, all variance-covariance matrixes have been estimated according to White's (1980) method.

Inward FDI is expected to have a positive effect on the performance of domestic firms. On the other hand, foreign MNEs are more likely to be attracted to industries where domestic productivity is higher and above average profits are realized. The estimation of model (11.1) with respect to productivity using OLS will lead to spurious results in situations where a two-way relationship between foreign presence and productivity exists. To examine the possibility of simultaneity between $Y^{\mathrm{p}}_{\mathrm{d}}$ and FP_1, the Hausman test (Hausman, 1976) is employed. This requires a two-equation model:[2]

$$Y^{\mathrm{p}}_{\mathrm{d}} = \alpha_0 + \alpha_1(\mathrm{KL})_{\mathrm{d}} + \alpha_2(\mathrm{RI})_{\mathrm{d}} + \alpha_3(\mathrm{LQ})_{\mathrm{d}} + \alpha_4(\mathrm{FP})_1 + \alpha_5(\mathrm{FS})_{\mathrm{d}} + \phi \qquad (11.2)$$

$$(\mathrm{FP})_1 = \beta_0 + \beta_1(\mathrm{EI})_{\mathrm{d}} + \beta_2(\mathrm{RI})_{\mathrm{d}} + \beta_3(\mathrm{LQ})_{\mathrm{d}} + \beta_4(\mathrm{MS}) + \beta_5(\mathrm{GP}) + \beta_6 Y^{\mathrm{p}}_{\mathrm{d}} + \psi \qquad (11.3)$$

Equation (11.2) is derived from model (11.1), and in equation (11.3) EI is export intensity (exports/total sales) and MS is market size, proxied by the sales in each sector. GP is a dummy variable, which takes a value of one in sectors where inward investment is encouraged by government policy, and zero otherwise (MOFTEC, 1996).

Following the Hausman procedure, we then estimate the following equation:

$$Y_{\mathrm{d}}^{\mathrm{p}} = \alpha_0 + \alpha_1(\mathrm{KL})_{\mathrm{d}} + \alpha_2(\mathrm{RI})_{\mathrm{d}} + \alpha_3(\mathrm{LQ})_{\mathrm{d}} + \alpha_4(\mathrm{FP})_1 + \alpha_5(\mathrm{FS})_{\mathrm{d}} + \lambda R + u \tag{11.4}$$

where R is the residual from the reduced form of the OLS estimate of equation (11.3). If λ is not statistically significant, then there is no simultaneity between $Y_{\mathrm{d}}^{\mathrm{p}}$ and FP_1, justifying the estimation of unidirectional equation (11.1).

Our empirical inquiry is based on industry level data from the Third Industrial Census, published by the State Statistical Bureau of China (SSB) in 1997. The Census reports data for 1995 on a cross-section of branches of Chinese industry. It is the latest and most comprehensive industrial survey published. The industry boundaries are similar to the SIC employed in the USA. There are 191 sectors in the Census (19 mining, 165 manufacturing, 7 public utilities). Our study includes 130 sectors because of missing data.

Table 11.1 documents the top 20 industries with the largest foreign presence (FP) according to four of the six measures. Foreign presence varies when different measures are used. Overall, foreign capital is concentrated in low-technology industries, e.g. textile and toys, and in electronics-related industries, such as computers and office machinery. Foreign presence in terms of employment share (FP_2) shows a similar pattern. OC capital (FP_3) is concentrated in industries characterized as low technology, such as textile-related industries, while NC-owned capital (FP_4) has a larger presence in high-tech industries, especially electronics-related industries.

Table 11.2 displays the correlation matrix and descriptive statistics for the main independent and dependent variables. Only two correlations between the independent variables are fractionally higher than 0.50, indicating no serious multi-collinearity problems. The relevant FP variables show high correlations in the expected direction.

The panel for dependent variables shows, first, that foreign-owned firms enjoy productivity on average twice that of Chinese locally owned firms, which partially reflects the industry distribution of inward FDI. Second, COEs' productivity is twice that of SOEs, signalling differences in absorptive capability between the two types of firms.

Table 11.1 Top 20 industries in terms of foreign presence in Chinese manufacturing

Industry	FP_1	FP_2	FP_3	FP_4
22 Other food processing	0.442	0.374	0.211	0.136
23 Cakes and sugar confectionery	0.466	(*0.221*)	0.211	0.127
24 Dairy products			(*0.034*)	0.228
26 Fermentation products			(*0.049*)	0.164
28 Other food products			(*0.128*)	0.160
30 Soft drinks	0.352	(*0.267*)	0.186	(*0.128*)
32 Other drinks	(*0.326*)	0.366	0.209	(*0.047*)
41 Knitting	0.341	0.288	0.225	(*0.076*)
42 Other textile products	0.391	0.258	0.278	0.138
43 Clothes	0.398	0.477	0.239	(*0.098*)
44 Hats	(*0.313*)	0.368	0.202	(*0.068*)
47 Leather manufacturing	(*0.170*)	0.622		
48 Leather products	(*0.283*)	0.259	0.173	(*0.063*)
65 Toys	0.559	0.624	0.397	(*0.058*)
76 Household chemical products	0.372	(*0.165*)	(*0.072*)	0.254
84 Fishing tools and associated materials	0.405	0.379	0.273	(*0.091*)
85 Rubber tyres	0.324	0.237	(*0.077*)	0.170
86 Rubber tyres for man-powered vehicles			0.322	(*0.021*)
88 Rubber spare parts			(*0.139*)	0.162
93 Other rubber products			0.220	(*0.086*)
95 Rubber boots and shoes			0.185	(*0.064*)
97 Plastic board, tubes and bars	(*0.314*)	0.302		
100 Household plastic grocery	0.459	0.363	0.268	(*0.077*)
107 Pottery products			0.229	(*0.047*)
123 Heavy metals smelting			(*0.081*)	0.196
142 Other ordinary machinery			(*0.072*)	0.199
147 Medical machinery			(*0.057*)	0.253
148 Other special equipment	0.339	(*0.104*)		
152 Motorcycles			(*0.027*)	0.194
156 Traffic equipment repairing	0.339	(*0.239*)		
159 Communications equipment	0.417	0.308	(*0.101*)	0.173
162 Computers	0.480	0.433	(*0.158*)	0.217
164 Electronic devices	0.412	0.318	0.191	0.161
165 Household electronic apparatus	0.393	0.427	0.190	0.172
166 Other electronic equipment	0.581	0.455	0.223	0.254
170 Measuring instrument			(*0.070*)	0.179
171 Office machinery	0.566	0.381	(*0.158*)	0.359
172 Clocks and watches	0.406	0.281	0.254	(*0.041*)
Mean (all 180 industries)	0.4221	0.376	0.234	0.195
Std Dev.	0.077	0.108	0.054	0.055

Note: Italic figures in brackets show industries which are not among the top 20 industries.
Source: Third Industrial Census, the State Statistical Bureau, Beijing: China Statistical Publishing House, 1997. The foreign shares of various measures are the authors' own calculation.

Table 11.2 Descriptive statistics and correlation matrix for selected variables ($n = 130$)[a]

Variables	*Mean*	*SD*	*2*	*3*	*4*	*5*	*6*	*7*	*8*	*9*	*10*	*11*	*12*	*13*	*14*
1. KL_d	3.05	2.67	−01	−39	36	52	30	−21	−18	06	−21	80	59	81	04
2. RI_d	0.10	0.19		−49	46	−02	19	−17	−17	−20	00	11	27	13	50
3. LQ_d	0.07	0.03			−40	−17	−27	38	52	41	−14	−46	−46	−52	−42
4. FS_d	0.27	0.51				33	22	−23	−19	−05	−27	46	17	47	26
5. MS	269.42	345.89					09	−34	−32	−03	−17	40	30	49	04
6. GP	0.42	0.49						−01	−02	−10	−05	35	23	35	04
7. FP_1	0.20	0.13							82	29	22	−09	02	−27	−06
8. FP_2	0.14	0.13								36	03	−03	−05	−23	−18
9. FP_3	0.31	0.13									−66	01	−21	−07	−11
10. FP_4	0.23	0.13										−08	10	−07	−01
11. Y^p_d	1.58	0.85											49	89	11
12. Y^{p}_f[b]	3.44	3.20												50	25
13. Y^p_s	1.31	0.85													06
14. Y^p_c	2.93	6.91													

[a] Decimal points are omitted from the correlations.
[b] For comparison, Y^p_f, productivity of foreign-owned firms and the counterpart of Y^p_d, is shown here, though this variable does not appear in any of the regressions throughout the study.

Empirical results

We estimate equation (11.4) in the first instance and find that λ is statistically insignificant at the 1 per cent level. We infer that there is no evidence of a two-way link between productivity and foreign presence, justifying the OLS method to estimate equation (11.1). This result confirms Liu (2001) who reached the same conclusion using a similar methodology and the same data set (but with 180 industries). Tables 11.3–11.5 report the results of estimation of model (11.1) when collapsed to single equations. Table 11.6 summarizes the findings for each of the hypotheses set out in section two of the chapter.

Table 11.3 presents the results for the impact of total foreign capital on the performance of Chinese domestically owned firms in terms of productivity, the development of high-tech and new products, and export performance. Results in regressions (3.1) and (3.2) show that foreign presence, whether measured as capital (FP_1) or employment (FP_2), is significantly positively correlated with the productivity of Chinese local firms, although the size of the coefficient is low. This finding corroborates H1(a), and agrees with Zhu and Tan (2000) regarding the positive role of FDI in enhancing labour productivity.

Regressions (3.3) and (3.4) show that that foreign capital participation has significantly contributed to the development of high-tech and new products

Table 11.3 Foreign presence and the performance of Chinese domestic firms

Dependent variable	*Hypothesis*	*Expected sign*	Y_d^p *Domestic labour productivity*		Y_d^h *Domestic high technology*	Y_d^n *Domestic new products*	Y_d^e *Domestic export intensity*
			(3.1)	*(3.2)*	*(3.3)*	*(3.4)*	*(3.5)*
Constant			1.720	1.759	−2.679	−7.676	−0.320
			(4.05)***	(4.21)***	(−0.78)	(−3.26)***	(−0.24)
KL_d		+	0.530	0.509	−2.045	−1.842	−1.401
(Capital intensity)			(7.66)***	(7.64)***	(−2.77)***	(−3.40)***	(−3.94) * **
RI_d		+	−0.022	−0.021	1.094	1.002	−0.045
(R&D intensity)			(−1.37)	(−1.30)	(5.46)***	(6.30)***	(−0.49)
LQ_d		+	0.507	0.520	2.602	−0.374	−0.510
(Labour quality)			(4.87)***	(4.93)***	(3.43)***	(−0.78)	(−1.90)*
FP_1	H1	+	0.076		0.427	0.313	0.477
(Capital share)			(3.18)***		(2.05)**	(2.96)***	(4.90)***
FP_2	H1	+		0.053			
(Empl. share)				(2.42)**			
FS_d		+	0.055	0.058	0.415	0.465	0.624
(Size)			(1.39)	(1.51)	(1.18)	(2.24)**	(4.00)***
$\bar{R}^2$			0.710	0.705	0.529	0.589	0.315
F-statistic			64.26***	62.55***	30.01***	37.93***	12.76***

(1) Figures in parentheses are *t*-statistics (two-tailed tests); *, **, and *** denote significance at the 10, 5 and 1% levels respectively; (2) while regression estimates were obtained using both FP_1 and FP_2 in regression (3.1) and (3.2), because they are very similar, only the estimates using FP_1 are reported in all other regressions in this and other tables throughout this study.

Table 11.4 FDI origins and the performance of Chinese domestic firms

Dependent variable	*Hypothesis*	*Expected sign*	Y_d^p *Domestic labour productivity*		Y_d^h *Domestic high technology*		Y_d^n *Domestic new products*		Y_d^e *Domestic export intensity*	
			(4.1)	*(4.2)*	*(4.3)*	*(4.4)*	*(4.5)*	*(4.6)*	*(4.7)*	*(4.8)*
Constant			1.658	1.892	−4.048	−315	−8.623	−5.914	0.209	1.137
			(3.72)***	(4.41)***	(−1.26)	(−0.09)	(−3.59)***	(2.55)***	(0.15)	(0.80)
KL_d		+	0.525	0.513	−2.007	−2.205	−1.817	−1.960	−1.486	−1.519
(Capital intensity)			(7.97)***	(8.59)***	(−3.48)***	(−4.27)***	(−3.27)***	(−3.83)***	(−4.04)***	(−4.22)***
RI_d		+	−0.025	−0.037	0.989	0.949	0.929	0.895	−0.022	−0.156
(R&D intensity)			(−1.66)	(−2.21)**	(4.51)***	(4.67)***	(6.05)***	(5.79)***	(−0.23)	(−1.70)*
LQ_d		+	0.550	0.556	2.698	2.915	−0.295	−0.144	−0.393	−0.204
(Labour quality)			(4.99)***	(5.27)***	(3.84)***	(4.08)***	(−0.59)	(−0.32)	(−1.37)	(−0.715)
FP_3	H2, H4	+	0.006		−0.827		−0.558		0.416	
(OC capital share)			(0.10)		(−1.38)		(−1.89*		(3.92)***	
FP_4	H3, H4	+		0.044		0.505		0.376		0.354
(NC capital share)				(2.42)**		(2.90)***		(4.28)***		(3.36)***
FS_d (Size)		+	0.025	0.061	0.262	0.652	0.352	0.643	0.639	0.718
			(0.66)	(1.70)*	(0.76)	(1.64)*	(1.77)*	(2.92)***	(3.91)***	(4.49)***
$\bar{R}^2$			0.679	0.692	0.521	0.544	0.577	0.607	0.303	0.271
F-statistic			55.57***	59.07***	29.07***	31.72***	36.18***	40.84***	12.13***	10.52***

Figures in parentheses are *t*-statistics (two-tailed tests); *, **, and *** denote significance at the 10, 5 and 1% levels respectively.

Table 11.5 Foreign presence, type of Chinese domestic firms and their performance

Dependent variable	*Hypothesis*	*Expected sign*	Y_s^p *SOEs' labour productivity*			Y_s^e *SOEs' export intensity*	
			(5.1)	*(5.2)*	*(5.3)*	*(5.4)*	*(5.5)*
Constant			−0.909	−0.782	−0.996	1.107	2.154
			(−1.93)*	(−1.59)	(−2.09)**	(0.71)	(1.29)
KL_s		+	0.703	0.698	0.691	−1.714	−1.666
(Capital intensity)			(8.85)***	(9.19)***	(9.84)***	(−3.75)***	(−3.92)***
RI_s		+	0.041	0.053	0.059	−0.143	−0.169
(R&D intensity)			(1.54)	(1.93)*	(2.19)**	(−1.33)	(−1.64)*
LQ_s		+	0.046	0.056	0.042	−0.072	0.058
(Labour quality)			(0.47)	(0.56)	(0.42)	(−0.17)	(0.132)
FP_1	H5	+/−				0.198	
(Capital share)						(0.67)	
FP_3	H5	+/−	−0.132				
(OC capital share)			(−2.07)**				
FP_4	H5	+/−		0.001			
(NC capital share)				(0.04)			
FP_5	H5	+/−			−0.032		0.235
(Capital share in SOEs)					(−1.59)		(1.33)
FS_s (Size)		+	0.081	0.084	0.078	0.644	0.578
			(2.32)**	(2.39)**	(2.31)**	(4.65)***	(3.22)***
$\bar{R}^2$			0.651	0.639	0.646	0.185	0.205
F-statistic			49.21***	46.71***	47.98***	6.86***	7.667***

Table 11.5 (Continued)

Dependent variable	*Hypothesis*	*Expected sign*	Y_s^p COEs' labour productivity			Y_s^e COEs' export intensity	
			(5.6)	*(5.7)*	*(5.8)*	*(5.9)*	*(5.10)*
Constant			1.179	1.124	1.378	0.485	1.340
			(2.59)***	(2.88)***	(2.90)***	(0.39)	(1.03)
KL_c		+	0.633	0.693	0.595	0.069	0.018
(Capital intensity)			(4.48)***	(6.83)***	(4.15)***	(0.51)	(0.10)
RI_c		+	−0.10	−0.081	−0.088	−0.136	−0.154
(R&D intensity)			(−2.31)**	(−2.54)***	(−2.42)**	(−2.31)**	(−2.65)***
LQ_c		+	0.078	0.070	0.075	0.241	0.209
(Labour quality)			(2.04)**	(1.81)*	(2,28)**	(1.85)*	(1.17)
FP_1	H5	+				0.301	
(Capital share)						(1.79)*	
FP_d	H5	+	−0.019				
(OC capital share)			(−0.29)+				
FP_4	H5	+		0.098			
(NC captial share)				(1.95)**			
FP_6	H5	+			0.075		0.254
(Capital share in COEs)					(1.91)*		(2.00)**
FS_c (Size)		+	0.063	0.030	0.024	0.274	0.270
			(1.11)	(0.58)	(0.50)	(1.27)	(1.11)
$\bar{R}^2$			0.661	0.698	0.676	0.156	0.118
F-statistic			51.40***	60.74***	54.72***	5.78***	4.44***

Figures in parentheses are *t*-statistics (two-tailed tests); *, **, and *** denote significance at the 10, 5 and 1% levels respectively; as the data for R&D intensity is not available, to keep comparison between the SOEs and COEs results, RI_c is assumed to take the same value as RI_d.

Table 11.6 Hypotheses and the estimated results

Hypotheses	*Regressions*	*Support (S)/not support (N) hypotheses*
H1: (a)	(3.1), (3.2)	S
(b)	(3.3)	S
(c)	(3.4)	S
(d)	(3.5)	S
H2: (a)	(4.1)	N
(b)	(4.3)	N
(c)	(4.5)	N
(d)	(4.7)	S
H3: (a)	(4.2)	S
(b)	(4.4)	S
(c)	(4.6)	S
(d)	(4.8)	S
H4: (a)	(4.1), (4.2)	N
(b)	(4.3), (4.4)	S
(c)	(4.5), (4.6)	S
(d)	(4.7), (4.8)	N
H5:(a)	(5.3), (5.4),(5.5), (5.8), (5.9), (5.10)	S
(b)	(5.1), (5.6)	S
(c)	(5.2), (5.7)	S

in the domestic sector, supporting (H1(b) and H1(c)). This implies that the presence of foreign technologically advanced firms has improved the competitiveness of local Chinese firms. As expected H1(d) also receives a high level of support in the form of the statistically significant foreign presence variable in regression (3.5), indicating that foreign capital participation improves the export performance of Chinese local firms.

The elasticities for the effect of foreign capital participation (FP_1) on non-productivity spillovers are found to significantly exceed those on productivity spillovers, and this requires some discussion. One possibility is that the resource costs to beneficiary firms of assimilating knowledge may be higher for productivity as compared with non-productivity spillovers. The literature emphasizes the role of learning activities, principally with regard to productivity spillovers. This implies the widespread and deep embodiment of knowledge in human and physical capital. However, competent firms which have already engaged in appropriate learning activities to acquire innovative skills may be able to reverse engineer and emulate high-technology and new products through inspection, so avoiding heavy feasibility and development costs. Similarly, the beneficiary does not have to pay the large initial costs of identifying of export markets, only those of the exporting process. This interpretation suggests that learning activities are important in explaining these marked differences in impacts.

Our findings are enhanced through the use of other theoretically relevant variables as controls. Capital intensity is statistically significant throughout, but only positively so with productivity. Firm size is only important for the development of new products and for exports. R&D only exerts a positive effect on the development of high-tech and new products in the domestic sector, having no role in domestic Chinese firms' productivity improvements. The Chinese R&D : GDP ratio is low, and limited R&D activities are concentrated in government research institutes and universities, not in companies. At least one of the control variables, labour quality and R&D, are significant and correctly signed in each equation, except for equation (3.5) where LQ is incorrectly signed for exports, suggesting that cheap labour promotes exports.

Table 11.4 exhibits regression results for the effects of OC and NC capital on the performance of Chinese local firms. Regression (4.1) reveals that OC capital does not have a statistically positive impact on the productivity of Chinese firms, not supporting H2(a), while NC capital does (regression (4.2)), corroborating H3(a).

The OC capital participation variable (FP_3) in regression (4.3) registers an unexpected sign, contradicting H2(b), while the positive and statistically significant NC capital participation variable (FP_4) in regression (4.4) indicates that FDI from Western countries exerts a positive impact on the development of high-tech products in domestic firms, providing support for H3(b). This contrasting effect is consistent with the sectoral distribution of foreign capital by source country (Table 11.1). NC MNEs are technology intensive and in a strong position to transfer technologies to local firms. Per contra, the ownership advantages of OC firms lie in their marketing skills and knowledge of China (Luo, 1999), which does not generate significant spillovers of a technological kind. A similar finding applies to regressions (4.5) and (4.6) where the dependent variable is the development of new products by domestic firms. The data supports H3(c) but not H2(c). Export performance is found to benefit from both OC and NC capital (regressions (4.7) and (4.8)), corroborating both H2(d) and H3(d). This implies that both OC and NC capital provide a stimulus to potential or modest Chinese exporters, indirectly enabling domestic Chinese firms to identify target markets in the West, or by the transfer of marketing knowledge from Sino–foreign joint ventures back to the Chinese parent. A similar pattern of results is obtained in Table 11.4 for KL, RI, LQ and FS, as in Table 11.3.

In order to evaluate the relative magnitudes of the coefficients for FP_3 and FP_4 the data for NC and OC capital were pooled, and dummy variable tests were conducted. In regressions (4.1) and (4.2), although FP_4 is significant, this coefficient is not significantly larger than the insignificant coefficient for FP_3. Whilst in this case the differential is statistically insignificant, it remains true that NC capital exerts a positive effect while OC capital exerts none. More clear-cut results are obtained for regressions (4.3) and (4.4), also for regressions (4.5) and (4.6), which show that NC capital exerts a significantly greater impact on high-tech and new product development in local firms than does OC capital. The effects of both types of capital on the export intensity of local firms is of the same magnitude (regressions 4.7 and 4.8), where in both cases the impact is significant at the 1 per cent level.[3] These results support hypotheses 4(b) and 4(c), but not 4(a) and 4(d). Overall, the results in Table 11.4 indicate that NC capital generates both technological and market access spillovers, while OC capital confers only market access benefits.

The contrasts between SOEs and COEs as beneficiaries of spillovers are presented in Table 11.5. The results for the SOEs' panel indicate that the presence of foreign MNEs does not positively affect the productivity and export performance of SOEs, regardless of which definition of foreign presence is adopted. In contrast, the matching results for all regressions in the COEs panel, except (5.6), record significant positive coefficients for the FP variables, indicating that NC capital participation (FP_4) improves productivity while total foreign capital participation (FP_1) enhances the exports of COEs, and FP_6 promotes both the productivity and export performance of COEs. Following the same procedure as for Table 11.4, we conduct dummy variable tests for the relative magnitude of the FP coefficients in Table 11.5. We found that the effect of foreign capital participation on labour productivity and export of COEs is significantly greater than that for SOEs. This significant result is uniform across the equations.[4] These findings lend support for H5(a), H5(b), and H5(c). Taken together, the results indicate a lower level of competitiveness, absorptive capability and motivation to learn on the part of SOEs compared with COEs.

The statistically negative FP_3 in regression (5.1) in the SOEs panel merits discussion. This finding implies that OC capital impedes the productivity of SOEs. The expansion of OC firms' output appears to have 'crowded out' SOEs, particularly in industries where their products compete directly, e.g. food and textiles. In such industries, the market share of SOEs has fallen considerably following the entry of OC firms. Moreover, the lesser proclivities on the part of OC versus NC MNEs to form joint ventures and backward linkages with SOEs reduces the opportunities for SOEs to participate in industrial development. This finding is consistent with our discussion in the second section.

R&D is found to have a significantly positive effect on productivity of SOEs in regressions (5.2) and (5.3), which is at variance with the generality of the results in Tables 11.3 and 11.4 with respect to domestic firms as a whole. In China, though corporate R&D is low, it is still heavily concentrated in the state-owned sector and our findings generally support the view that it brings productivity benefits to the most research-intensive SOEs. In contrast, research intensity shows a significantly negative impact on COEs' productivity. This is not surprising as COEs' productivity derives from mature technologies.

Labour quality seems to be important for the performance of COEs but not of SOEs. An explanation for this result is the employment and personnel management system in SOEs. First, the lifetime employment system in SOEs means managers and workers experience no pressure from the labour market. Second, SOEs' personnel management is notoriously rigid, which prevents well-educated employees from contributing fully to the firm's performance (Liu, 2001). Third, China's SOEs are overstaffed with white-collar workers. This causes bureaucratization and red tape, leading to lower productive efficiency. In contrast, COEs are unencumbered by those management and personnel practices that are the legacy of central planning. Staff are deployed more often according to ability, signalled by college education.

There are more unexpected signs in the export regressions, and this is particularly true for the capital intensity and R&D intensity variables. The pattern of significance of capital intensity suggests that Chinese firms' product development is principally in labour-intensive goods, in which China has a comparative advantage. The impact of R&D intensity is negative and sometimes statistically significant. The effect of R&D is seen to be marginal, as exported goods rely either on mature technologies, or on innovation derived from Western firms, e.g. through subcontracting and imitation. This is likely to be true for COEs in particular. This shows the complex role of R&D as an explanatory variable.

Explaining the export performance of domestic firms is difficult given the absence of relevant data in China. Where the dependent variable is the export performance of domestic firms, in Tables 11.3, 11.4 and 11.5, all the $\bar{R}^2$ values, and a number of *F*-statistics are low. Economic theory holds that productivity and export intensity, both indicators of economic performance, have a wide set of determinants, not all of which we were able to include.

Conclusions

This investigation has found evidence of both productivity and non-productivity spillovers – notably the development of high-tech and new products and market access spillovers, each of which contributes to the upgrading of Chinese industry. Chinese policy towards FDI since 1979 has been predicated upon appropriating Western technology, either directly or indirectly, and our findings demonstrate the existence of the indirect route.

We find that non-Chinese firms' advantages, and the spillovers they confer, differ from those of overseas Chinese firms, as generally shown by the pattern of results and the magnitude tests. This shows that the character of spillover effects follows that of MNEs' ownership advantages, which differ by nationality of origin. This illuminates the issue of the appropriability of the returns on intangible assets by MNEs in host markets. The economic losses and disincentive effects that externalities pose for foreign investors are exactly congruent with the role that FDI plays in domestic industrial and economic development. This is a transition from a preoccupation with the source country perspective on gains and losses, to a position that accommodates host country development aspirations and priorities.

We find that the segments of locally owned industry that are best able to internalize spillover benefits are those with the greatest absorptive capacity – paralleling the findings of the technology transfer literature that centre on formal transfers. In our study, COEs enjoy this superior capability to absorb external spillover benefits, as confirmed by the uniformly significant results of our magnitude tests. The pattern of results is consistent with market interactions between foreign and domestic firms. These appear to be negative in the case of SOEs and OCC inward investment, arising from competition in low-tech light-industry markets. The spillover benefits that are enjoyed by COEs arise through interactions in final, intermediate and factor markets. These include learning within network relationships formed with Western firms, subcontracting, training by Western firms of local employees, and the transfer of technical skills to upgrade the services provided to the MNE by local industry.

Our study sheds light on the complexity of spillover effects in an emerging host economy. In doing so, it exposes some of the possible methodological weaknesses in the existing literature on these effects for all types of host. Apart from the shortcomings of existing studies noted in the Introduction, it is now clear that inconclusive findings can result from a failure to identify either or both the nationality of foreign investors and the forms of ownership of the beneficiary host firms. Conflicts between existing studies may arise on account of differences between the distributions of foreign investors, or in the forms of ownership in the host economy.

The findings in this chapter add to the state of knowledge in the literature in three respects. First, the existence of non-productivity spillovers, e.g. notably in the form of the development of high-tech and new products by local firms. Second, clear evidence is presented that different types of ownership advantage of MNEs, linked to nationality, confer contrasting spillover effects on local firms in the host country. Third, the results suggest that absorptive capacities differ between the types of locally owned firm, and that form of ownership has a strong influence on how far, if at all, local firms are able to benefit from spillovers.

Each of these new findings has implications for policy. The Chinese authorities have long put a premium on the transfer of technology to local industry to generate productivity gains. Our results suggest that while the productivity gains are important to locally owned industry, the value of non-productivity benefits should not be underestimated. These may be available even in modest technology industries. Therefore, policy to encourage diversity in inward investment may lead to improved export performance, and the development of high-tech and new products by a wide range of locally owned firms. Under the WTO agreement China is bound to follow a policy of non-discrimination towards inward investors, and this study provides substantiation for the benefits of the full implementation of this. The Chinese authorities can expect that the range of spillover benefits, in products and in technical and management processes, that are available to local firms should be at least as extensive as the different ownership advantages of the investing nationalities.

The association between absorptive capacity and ownership form has implications for the policy of reform in the state-owned sector. Our results suggest that, wherever possible, SOE reform should precede inward FDI in order to mitigate the possibility of negative spillovers. These are detrimental not only to SOEs, but also to the welfare of the local economies. This suggests that the reform of SOEs should be a priority – especially in the regions where both the foreign and the state-owned sector are particularly large. While this reform is costly in terms of economic adjustment, the prospect of positive spillovers is a benefit of which policy makers need to be aware.

Notes

1. COEs are industrial enterprises in which the means of production are owned collectively. COEs are not cooperative in the normal sense of the word. Rather they resemble state enterprises, with the 'state' being the local community.
2. We only examine empirically the possible two-way relationship between Y_d^p and FP_1, not between any other productivity and FP measures. We justify this by reference to the fact that foreign firms are attracted to China by market size and low cost labour, not by other factors likely to induce bidirectional causal relationships. For instance, the recent vintage of high-tech and new product development by domestically owned firms is unlikely to be the cause of inward foreign investment. Similarly, the recent export performance of domestic Chinese firms is unlikely to attract export-oriented FDI, which is far more likely to be attracted by indigenous cheap labour.
3. The *t*-ratios for the dummy variables are, respectively: 0.59, 2.38**, 2.67***, and 1.12.
4. The *t*-ratios for the dummy variables are, respectively: 1.79*, 3.37***, 1.72*, 2.59***, and 2.04**.

References

Aitken, Brian, Hanson, Gordon H. and Harrison, Ann E. (1994) 'Spillovers, Foreign Investment, and Export Behavior'. National Bureau for Economic Research Working Paper No. 4967, New York.

Anand, Jaideep and Delios, Andrew (1996) 'How Japanese MNCs have Matched Goals and Strategies in India and China'. *Columbia Journal of World Business*, vol. XXXI, no. 3, pp. 50–62.

Blomström, Magnus and Kokko, Ari (1997) 'How Foreign Investment Affects Host Countries'. Policy Research Working Paper No. 1745. International Trade Department, World Bank, Washington, DC.

Blomström, Magnus Kokko, Ari and Zejan, Mario (2000) *Foreign Direct Investment: Firm and Host Country Strategies*. Macmillan.

Buckwalter, D. W. (1995) 'Spatial Inequality, Foreign Direct Investment, and Economic Transition in Bulgaria'. *The Professional Geographer*, vol. 47, pp. 288–98.

Cantwell, John A. (1993) 'Technological Competence and Evolving Patterns of International Production'. In H. Cox, J. Clegg and G. Ietto-Giles (eds), *The Growth of Global Business*. London: Routledge.

Caves, Richard E. (1974) 'Multinational Firms, Competition and Productivity in Host Country Markets'. *Economica*, vol. 41, pp. 176–93.

Chen, Chung, Chang, Lawrence and Zhang, Yimin (1995) 'The Role of Foreign Direct Investment in China's Post-1978 Economic Development'. *World Development*, vol. 23, no. 4, pp. 691–703.

Cohen, Wesley M. and Levinthal, Daniel A. (1989) 'Innovation and Learning: the Two Faces of R&D'. *The Economic Journal*, vol. 99, pp. 569–96.

Davies, Howard (1996) 'High IQ and Low Technology: Hong Kong's Key to Success'. *Long Range Planning*, vol. 29, no. 5, pp. 684–90.

Diankov, Simeon and Hoekman, B. (2000) 'Foreign Investment and Productivity Growth in Czech Enterprises'. *The World Bank Economic Review*, vol. 14, no. 1, pp. 49–64.

Eden, Lorraine, Levitas, Edwin and Martinez, J. Richard (1997) 'The Production, Transfer and Spillovers of Technology: Comparing Large and Small Multinationals as Technology Producers'. *Small Business Economics*, vol. 9, pp. 53–66.

Feinberg, Susan E. and Majumdar, Sumit K. (2001) 'Technology Spillovers and Foreign Direct Investment in the Indian Pharmaceutical Industry'. *Journal of International Business Studies*, vol. 32, no. 3, pp. 421–37.

Gelb, Catherine (2000) 'Software Research in – and for – China'. *The China Business Review*, July–August, pp. 40–3.

Globerman, Steven (1979) 'Foreign Direct Investment and "Spillover" Efficiency Benefits in Canadian Manufacturing Industries'. *Canadian Journal of Economics*, vol. 12, pp. 42–56.

Görg, Holger and Strobl, Eric (2001) 'Multinational Companies and Productivity Spillovers: a Meta-Analysis'. *The Economic Journal*, vol. 111 (November), pp. 723–39.

Haddad, Mona and Harrison, Ann (1993) 'Are There Positive Spillovers from Direct Foreign Investment? Evidence from Panel Data for Morocco'. *Journal of Development Economics*, vol. 42, pp. 51–74.

Hausman, J. A. (1976) 'Specification Tests in Econometrics'. *Econometrics*, vol. 46, pp. 1251–71.

Huang, Yiping and Meng, Xin (1997) 'China's Industrial Growth and Efficiency: a Comparison between the State and the TVE Sectors'. *Journal of the Asia Pacific Economy*, vol. 2, no. 1, pp. 101–21.

Kokko, Ari (1992) *Foreign Direct Investment, Host Country Characteristics and Spillovers*. Stockholm: Stockholm School of Economics.

Kokko, Ari, Tansini, Ruben and Zejan, Mario (1997) 'Trade Regimes and Spillover Effects of FDI: Evidence from Uruguay'. Mimeo, Stockholm School of Economics, Stockholm.

Kueh, Y. Y. (1992) 'Foreign Investment and Economic Change in China'. *China Quarterly*, vol. 131, pp. 637–90.

Lan, Ping and Young, Stephen (1996) 'Foreign Direct Investment and Technology Transfer: a Case-Study of Foreign Direct Investment in North-East China'. *Transnational Corporations*, vol. 5, no. 1, pp. 57–83.

Lee, K. and Plummer, M. G. (1992) 'Competitive Advantages, Two-Way Foreign Investment, and Capital Accumulation in Korea'. *Asian Economic Journal*, vol. 6, pp. 93–114.

Li, Xiaojian and Yeung, Yue-man (1999) 'Inter-Firm Linkages and Regional Impact of Transnational Corporations: Company Case Studies from Shanghai, China'. *Geografiska Annaler*, vol. 81b, no. 2, pp. 61–72.

Liu, Xiaming (1999) 'Comparative Productivity of Foreign and Local Firms in Chinese Industry'. Paper presented at the 26th Annual Conference of the Academy of International Business United Kingdom Chapter, University of Strathclyde, Glasgow.

Liu, Xiaming, Siler, Pamela, Wang, Chengqi and Wei, Yingqi (2000) 'Productivity Spillovers from Foreign Direct Investment: Evidence from U.K. Industry Level Panel Data'. *Journal of International Business Studies*, vol. 31, no. 3, pp. 407–25.

Liu, Xiaohui (2001) 'Total Factor Productivity and Foreign Direct Investment in Chinese Industries'. Paper presented at the 28th Annual Conference of the Academy of International Business United Kingdom Chapter, Manchester Metropolitan University Business School.

Luo, Yadong (1997) 'Performance Implications of International Strategy: an Empirical Study of Foreign-invested Enterprises in China'. *Group & Organization Management*, vol. 22, no. 1, pp. 87–116.

Luo, Yadong (1998) 'Industry Attractiveness, Firm Competence, and International Investment Performance in a Transitional Economy'. *Bulletin of Economic Research*, vol. 50, no. 1, pp. 73–82.

Luo, Yadong (1999) 'Dimensions of Knowledge: Comparing Asian and Western MNEs in China'. *Asia Pacific Journal of Management*, vol. 16, pp. 75–93.

MOFTEC (1996) 'The Orientation Directory of Industries for FDI'. In *Regulations Towards Foreign Direct Investment*. Beijing: Social Science Publishing House.

MOFTEC (2000) Website: http://www.moftec.gov.cn/moftec/official/html/statistics data

Mok, Vincent (2000) 'Post-Mao Economic Transition: the Role of Non-State Enterprises'. *Issues & Studies*, vol. 36, no. 2, pp. 1–31.

Murphy, A. B. (1992) 'Western Investment in East-Central Europe: Emerging Patterns and Implications for State Stability'. *The Professional Geographer*, vol. 44, pp. 249–59.

O'Malley, Eoin (1994) 'The Impact of Transnational Corporations in the Republic of Ireland'. In P. Dicken and M. Quevit (eds), *Transnational Corporations and European Regional Restructuring*. Utrecht: NGS.

Ostry, Sylvia and Gestrin, Michael (1993) 'Foreign Direct Investment, Technology Transfer and the Innovation-Network Model'. *Transnational Corporations*, vol. 2, no. 3, pp. 7–30.

Rhee, Y. W. and Belot, T. (1990) 'Export Catalysts in Low-Income Countries'. World Bank Discussion Paper No. 72, Washington, DC.

Shi, Yizheng (1998) 'Technological Assets and the Strategy of Foreign Firms to Enter the China Market'. *Journal of International Marketing and Marketing Research*, vol. 23, no. 3, pp. 129–38.

Singh, R. (1992) 'Government Introduced Price Distortion and Growth, Evidence from Twenty Nine Developing Countries'. *Public Choice*, vol. 73, pp. 83–99.

Thoburn, John (1997) 'Enterprise Reform, Domestic Competition and Export Competitiveness: the Case of China'. *Journal of the Asia Pacific Economy*, vol. 2, no. 2, pp. 166–77.

Wang, Jian-Ye and Blomström, Magnus (1992) 'Foreign Investment and Technology Transfer: a Simple Model'. *European Economic Review*, vol. 36, pp. 137–55.

Wang, Z. Q. (1995) *Foreign Investment and Economic Development in Hungary and China*. Avebury: Aldershot.

Wells, Louis T. (1993) 'Mobile Exporters: New Foreign Investors in East Asia'. In K. A. Froot (ed.), *Foreign Direct Investment*. Chicago: University of Chicago Press.

White, Halbert (1980) 'A Heteroscedasticity Consistent Covariance Matrix Estimator and a Direct Test for Heteroscedasticity'. *Econometrica*, vol. 48, pp. 817–38.

Wu, Yanrui (1999) *Foreign Direct Investment and Economic Growth in China*. Cheltenham, UK: Edward Elgar.

Yeung, H. W. (1997) 'Cooperative Strategies and Chinese Business Networks: a Study of Hong Kong Transnational Corporations in the ASEAN Region'. In P. W. Beamish and J. P. Killing (eds), *Cooperative Strategies: Asian Pacific Perspectives*. San Francisco: New Lexington Press.

Zhan, Xiaoning J. (1993) 'The Role of Foreign Direct Investment in Market-Oriented Reforms and Economic Development: the Case of China'. *Transnational Corporations*, vol. 2, pp. 121–48.

Zhang, H. Kevin (2000) 'Why is U.S. Direct Investment in China So Small? *Contemporary Economic Policy*, vol. 18, no. 1, pp. 82–94.

Zhu, Gangti and Tan, Kong Yam (2000) 'Foreign Direct Investment and Labor Productivity: New Evidence from China as the Host'. *Thunderbird International Business Review*, vol. 42, no. 5, pp. 507–28.

Zhu, Tian (1999) 'China's Corporation Drive: an Evaluation and Policy Implications'. *Contemporary Economic Policy*, vol. 17, no. 4, pp. 530–9.

12

FDI, Regional Differences and Economic Growth: Panel Data Evidence from China

with Jeremy Clegg, Chengqi Wang and Adam R. Cross

Introduction

Development economists have long argued that countries pursuing externally oriented development strategies are more likely to achieve higher rates of economic growth than those that are internally focused. A number of studies have examined the relationship between inward FDI and economic growth in the developing host countries.[1] A generally accepted conclusion is that FDI has played a significant role in promoting economic growth in host countries because FDI represents 'the transmission to the host country of a package of capital, managerial skills, and technical skills' (Johnson, 1972, p. 2). An interesting finding of previous studies is that the economic and technological conditions of a recipient economy influence the extent to which FDI contributes to growth.

FDI in China is one of the most palpable outcomes of China's Open Door Policy, which was adopted in December 1978. Already in 1993, China held a position second only to the United States as the largest host country for FDI (UNCTAD, 1994). By the end of 1998, China had attracted $267 billion worth of FDI, and had approved 324,712 foreign-invested projects (*Almanac of China's Economy*, 1999, p. 81).

The geographical distribution of FDI in China is characterized by its concentration in the eastern coastal area. As shown in Table 12.1, between 1989 and 1998 the eastern region has attracted most FDI. The central and western regions attracted only 9 and 3 per cent of the total FDI inflows, respectively. In terms of per capita FDI, the central and western regions achieved only $8.63 and $1.67, respectively, far behind the level of the eastern region's $45.98 and the national average of $21.19.

Considerable qualitative evidence on the positive effects of inward FDI on the Chinese economy has been found in recent years (Kueh, 1992; Lardy, 1995; Henley et al., 1999). Shang-Jin Wei (1995) finds statistical evidence

Table 12.1 Geographical distribution of FDI in China by region,[a] 1989–98

Year	*FDI inflows ($100 million)*			*FDI inflows per person ($)*		
	Eastern region	*Central region*	*Western region*	*Eastern region*	*Central region*	*Western region*
1989	28.12	1.17	1.22	5.54	0.46	0.28
1990	29.72	1.22	0.72	5.91	0.45	0.16
1991	38.88	1.68	0.68	7.78	0.61	0.16
1992	97.94	7.25	1.96	19.75	2.64	0.46
1993	236.83	23.80	10.14	48.40	8.79	2.38
1994	290.89	25.99	14.03	59.93	9.71	3.32
1995	324.58	33.24	11.42	67.45	12.57	2.73
1996	365.20	39.21	8.13	76.58	15.01	1.97
1997	385.65	47.90	11.68	81.76	18.55	2.86
1998	394.96	44.21	9.42	86.73	17.52	2.39
Total[b]	2,193 (88%)	226 (9%)	69 (3%)	45.98	8.63	1.67

[a] The geographical grouping of the provinces is as follows: eastern region: Beijing, Tianjin, Hebei, Liaoning, Shanghai, Jiangsu, Zhejiang, Fujian, Shangdonh, Guangdong and Guangxi; central region: Shangxi, Neimenggu, Jilin, Heilongjiang, Anhui, Jiangxi, Henan, Hubei and Hunan; western region: Sichuan, Guizhou, Yunnan, Shanxi, Gansu, Qinghai, Ningxia and Xinjiang.
[b] The bottom row shows the total FDI inflows and percentages and average per capita FDI.
Source: Authors' own calculations from *China Statistical Yearbook* (various issues).

that FDI is positively associated with cross-city differences in growth rates in China. In his comment on Wei's work, Wing Thye Woo (1995) argues that FDI is correlated with total factor productivity (TFP) growth because the incidence of FDI is a good proxy for the degree of economic liberalization; and the greater the degree of liberalization, the higher the TFP growth. Other studies draw a conclusion similar to Wei (1995). For example, Stephane Dees's (1998) evidence supports the view that FDI affects China's growth through the diffusion of ideas; Chung Chen et al. (1995) find that FDI has been positively associated with economic growth and the increase of total fixed assets investment in China; Peter J. Buckley et al. (2001) find that FDI improves the performance of Chinese indigenous firms. The above empirical findings point to the collective importance of the elements in the package of resources associated with FDI (Dunning, 1977, 1993).

The vast land area of China is inevitably associated with enormous contrasts in conditions, both natural and artificial, between provinces. The degree of economic development is substantially different across the provinces of China, and the geographic distribution of FDI is characterized by its concentration in coastal areas. Whilst an overall positive impact of FDI on growth is supported by the empirical literature, China's large absolute size and economic diversity may mean that this finding masks wholly mixed impacts between geographic and economic areas. The aim of this chapter is to shed some light on how the FDI–growth relationship is affected by regional differences in China at the provincial level.

The chapter proceeds as follows: the following section reviews the literature; data and methodology are briefly explained next; the empirical results are presented in the subsequent section; and concluding remarks are offered in the last section.

FDI and growth

Many studies discuss the ways in which inward FDI can contribute to the growth of a host country economy (see, for example, Wei, 1995; Balasubramanyam et al., 1996; de Mello, 1997). In general, these studies argue that the impact of FDI on growth is complex. First, through capital accumulation in a recipient economy, FDI is expected to be growth enhancing by encouraging the incorporation of new inputs and technologies into the production function of a host economy. Second, FDI improves the efficiency of locally owned host country firms via contact and demonstration effects, and their exposure to fierce competition. Last and most importantly, FDI is believed to be a leading source of technological change and human capital augmentation in developing countries. Technological progress takes place through a process of 'capital deepening' in the form of the introduction of new varieties of knowledge-based capital goods. It also proceeds via specific productivity-increasing labour training and skills acquisition promoted by transnational corporations (TNCs). A recent embellishment in the growth literature is to highlight the dependence of the domestic growth rate on the state of technology relative to that in the rest of the world (de Mello, 1999).

The basic shortcoming of conventional neo-classical growth models, as far as FDI is concerned, is that long-run growth can only be achieved by technological progress, which is considered to be exogenous. FDI would only affect output growth in the short run and, in the long run, under the conventional assumption of diminishing returns to capital inputs with a given technology, FDI would have no permanent impact on output growth. Within the new growth framework, FDI is treated as one of the factor inputs along with labour and (domestic) capital and is expected to promote growth in the long run. Whether or not technological progress is best described as exogenous to the world as a system, the role of FDI in diffusing technology (both hard and soft) to developing countries appears clear.[2] Under either interpretation, technology created in the developed world is exogenous to a developing country. Consequently, a positive relationship between FDI and long-run growth in a developing host country should be expected.

The lessons from developed economies are that the productivity of foreign capital is dependent on initial conditions in a host country. Eduardo Borensztein et al. (1998) highlight the twin roles of the introduction of advanced technology and the degree of absorptive capability in the host country as determinants of economic growth. Luiz R. de Mello (1997) argues that an increase in the productivity of FDI can only be achieved if there is already a sufficiently high level of human capital in a recipient economy. These authors agree that preconditions in recipient economies help convert new capital effectively into higher levels of output in the host countries.

It is also important to evaluate the extent of complementarity between domestic investment and FDI. Under complementarity, innovations embodied in FDI may create, rather than reduce, rents accruing to older technologies (Young, 1993). If FDI is expected to affect growth positively, some degree of complementarity with domestic investment needs to be at work.

It should be pointed out that the direction of causation may run either way. FDI may be drawn to regions of faster growth or greater potential because their growth prospects have made it more attractive to foreign TNCs. De Mello (1997) envisions a case in which the size of the consumer market in a recipient economy is getting larger, as a result of faster growth leading to rapid increases in the potential purchasing power of consumers in a host country. Consequently, it is tenable that growth itself may be an important determinant of FDI in addition to those listed above.

Within an evaluation of the impact of FDI-induced technological change on growth in developing countries, Magnus Blomström et al. (1994) find that the positive and statistically significant impact of FDI is stronger, the higher the level of development in a host country. Pursuing the effects of preconditions in a developing host country, Borensztein et al. (1998) find that FDI is more productive than domestic investment only when the host country has a minimum threshold stock of human capital. However, de Mello (1999) found a positive impact for FDI on output growth regardless of the technological status of a host country as a technological leader or follower, but this result did not apply when growth was replaced by technological change (measured by TFP). In this case, FDI exerted a positive impact on TFP only for technological leaders, while a negative relationship arose between FDI and TFP for technological followers.

The findings reviewed above collectively suggest that the way in which FDI affects growth is likely to depend on the economic and technological conditions in a host country. The evidence to date points to an increasing relationship between the level of development in a recipient economy and the productivity benefits associated with inward FDI.

Empirical findings have so far not offered clear-cut conclusions with respect to the causality between FDI and growth. The surge of FDI might be associated with domestic policy variables, and this was evidenced in the case of Latin America (Elias, 1990). De Mello (1996) finds that FDI plays a determinant role in increasing both output and TFP in Chile, while capital accumulation and TFP growth precede FDI in Brazil. In both cases the direction of the relevant causalities cannot be determined. The direction of causality between FDI and growth may well depend on the determinants of FDI. If the determinants have strong links with growth in the host country, growth may be found to cause FDI, while output may grow faster when FDI takes place in other circumstances (de Mello, 1997).

The model and data

The conventional approach to investigating the relationship between growth and FDI involves running regressions for the rate of output growth on the rate of FDI growth. Often, additional explanatory variables (for example, the rate of growth of the domestic capital stock, domestic labour force growth) are included in order to control for other influences upon the rate of economic growth. As we have noted, such models are often presented in terms of a production function-type of framework that treats FDI (foreign capital) as a factor input.

Conventional neo-classical growth models in the Solovian tradition predict that the elasticity of output with respect to capital should be equal to the share of capital in total output. However, empirical estimations of this relationship have commonly been flawed. As is well known, in the case of cross-country and time-series estimations, the correlation between the error term and the regressors in standard growth accounting-based time-series production function estimations leads to simultaneity and omitted variables biases. Owing to these biases, cross-sectional estimates frequently point to a much higher value of capital elasticity than is predicted on the basis of the growth models. For example, the correlation between capital per capita and the error term leads to capital elasticity estimates that are well above the capital share in output (Young, 1992, 1995). By including more theoretically germane explanatory variables in our equation, the biases associated with the omission of variables can be substantially reduced.

For these reasons we eschew a growth accounting exercise, and construct our model as follows. Let province *i* and time *t* operate within the following equation, so enabling the impact of FDI on growth to be estimated:

$$Y_{it} = \alpha + \beta_1 K_{dit} + \beta_2 K_{fit} + \beta_3 L_{it} + \beta_4 H_{it} + \beta_5 M_{it} + \beta_6 E_{it} + \beta_7 I_{it} + \varepsilon_{it} \quad (12.1)$$

The estimation of equation (12.1) without due consideration of possible region-specific or time-specific effects could generate misleading results. In the context of panel data, the existence of unobservable growth determinants that are specific to regions can be acknowledged and taken into account in the estimation procedure. Therefore, we estimate equation (12.1) in the form of what is usually referred to as a fixed effect (FE) model. We do not use a random effects model here since this would require that the omitted variables are uncorrelated with the specified right-hand-side variables – an unrealistic assumption in the context of our model.[3] The FE model is as follows:

$$Y_{it} = \alpha_i + \gamma_1 K_{dit} + \gamma_2 K_{fit} + \gamma_3 L_{it} + \gamma_4 H_{it} + \gamma_5 M_{it} + \gamma_6 E_{it} + \gamma_7 I_{it} + \phi_{it} \quad (12.2)$$

where Y is the growth rate of GDP,[4] K_d the growth rate of the domestic capital stock (proxied in the usual way by the share of investment in output) and K_f the growth rate of the stock of FDI,[5] L the growth rate of the labour force and H human capital (proxied by the share of university and college students in the population). In contrast with previous studies, our model includes some supplementary variables that have been introduced into the above equation, to capture the determinants of the Solovian type of residual, and thus improve the quality of our estimations. These variables are: the level of marketization, M (proxied by the share of number of employees in private enterprises and self-employed individuals in total employment); the growth rate of provincial exports (E); and the growth rate of provincial imports (I). Finally, α captures province-specific unobserved inputs, which are assumed to be constant over time, and ϕ is a white noise error term.[6]

Positive relationships are expected between the dependent variable and all explanatory variables. If the model specification is reasonable, the estimated coefficient of K_f (i.e. γ_2) will indicate the direction and magnitude of the impact of FDI on economic performance.

It would be of great interest to experiment with a lag structure in this model, although this would be unusual with panel data in circumstances such as our own. We have 261 observations in the full sample, but a relatively short time series covering 1989–98. If we were to employ lags, this would adversely affect the number of usable observations particularly in the subsamples, which are the focus of our analysis. Furthermore, there is no prima facie evidence to suggest that lags would yield a benefit, as argued in UNCTAD (1999, p. 332): 'Current growth in a period is always positively and significantly related to FDI inflows in the same period ... there is much stronger evidence that the growth rate and FDI inflows coincide in time.'

Before the data are described and the estimates reported, a few remarks concerning the model are necessary. It is not the purpose of this chapter to offer either a new theory or specification of the linkages between FDI and growth. Rather, the main objective is to shed fresh light on these linkages at the provincial (sub-national) level by extending a model that is already familiar from studies at the national level. However, our study does employ additional and theoretically pertinent variables, thereby enabling us to focus on a broader range of issues. Although our model cannot be considered to be perfect, it can claim to be well justified in the light of our discussion above.

While equation (12.2) captures the impact of most of the important variables, it does not account for the possibility of bidirectional relationship between growth and FDI highlighted in the recent literature. To capture these possible temporal causality relationships, the technique of Granger causality can be employed (Granger, 1969, 1980). The test involves estimating the following regressions:

$$Y_t = a_0 + \sum_{j=1}^{8} a_j Y_{t-j} + \sum_{j=1}^{8} b_j K_{\mathrm{f},\, t-j} + u_t \tag{12.3}$$

$$K_{\mathrm{f}t} = c_0 + \sum_{j=1}^{8} c_j K_{\mathrm{f},\, t-j} + \sum_{j=1}^{8} d_j Y_{t-j} + \nu_t \tag{12.4}$$

where $K_{\mathrm{f}t}$ and Y_t are stationary time series and u_t and v_t are uncorrelated error terms. By equation (12.3), K_f Granger causes Y if $b_j \neq 0$. By equation (12.4), Y Granger causes K_f if $d_j \neq 0$. Bidirectional Granger causality is obtained if $b_j \neq 0$ and $d_j \neq 0$.

The estimation of equations (12.2)–(12.4) is based on a panel of data for 29 out of 31 of China's provinces over the period 1989–98 for realized FDI.[7] Tibet was excluded because of a lack of reliable data, while Chongqing and Sichuan provinces were included as one combined province, as they were aggregated together in the source data for most of the period. The panel data set yields a total of 261 observations when growth rates are calculated. The data were compiled from various volumes of the *Chinese Statistical Yearbook, China Foreign Economic Statistical Yearbook* and *China Industrial Statistical Yearbook*.

The first part of our investigation of the FDI–growth relationship involves testing equations (12.3) and (12.4) to examine the causal relationship between FDI and growth. The second part of our analysis then analyses the bidirectional effects using the full sample of 29 provinces to obtain parameter estimates for China as a whole. The third part of our analysis groups the full sample of provinces into sub-samples based on differences in characteristics between the provinces. These characteristics are:

1. Membership of geographic region;
2. Economic development levels, proxied by GDP per capita;
3. Levels of technological capability, proxied by R&D/GDP;
4. The level of infrastructure, employing the rankings of Amy Y. Liu et al. (1999), which use electricity usage per capita, number of telephones per capita, road-to-land ratio and wage level to measure infrastructure conditions;
5. The degree of inward FDI concentration (FDI intensity), proxied by FDI/total domestic investment);

6. The degree of state-owned enterprise (SOE) concentration (SOE intensity), proxied by the share of SOEs' sales in total sales in the manufacturing sector;
7. The degree of competition from Chinese locally owned firms, proxied by the growth rate of sales by domestically owned firms.

This measure follows Blomström et al. (1994), on which we have improved by calculating the sales of only locally owned firms. This involves removing the sales of all foreign affiliates, including international joint ventures and wholly owned affiliates, which gives us a pure measure of Chinese locally owned sales.

The provinces in the sample are differentiated; in the case of the economic criteria, this involves assigning a rank. Following ranking, the provinces are divided into various pairs of mutually exclusive groups: provinces with high and low income per capita; provinces with high and low technological capability; provinces with better and poorer infrastructure; provinces with high and low levels of FDI intensity; provinces with high and low SOE intensity; and, finally, provinces with high and low degrees of domestic competition. The analysis of these contrasting sub-samples serves to determine how these differences affect the FDI–growth relationship across provinces.

Empirical results

We first employ the Granger causality test to examine the relationship between FDI and growth. Equations (12.3) and (12.4) were estimated by ordinary least square (OLS) procedure. We chose two year-long lag periods based on the final-prediction-error (FPE) criterion (Akaike, 1969). All the variables were found to be covariance stationary.

We first test if FDI (K_f) Granger causes growth (Y) by estimating the unrestricted equation (12.3), and restricted equation (12.3) by dropping lagged K_f. The F-statistic yields a value of 11.548,[8] which exceeds the critical value of $F_{0.01} = 5.53$. Thus, we can reject the null hypothesis ($b_j = 0$) and conclude that adding lagged values of K_f does improve the statistical results. This signals that FDI Granger causes growth. The same procedure was carried out with respect to equation (12.4) and the result indicates that growth Granger does not cause FDI (F-statistic 3.25, below the critical value of $F_{0.01} = 5.53$).

We now analyse the effects of FDI on growth. Table 12.2 presents the results for the broad panel from the estimation of equation (12.2) in which the growth of GDP is generated by growth in domestic investment, FDI, employment, exports and imports, as well as the level of human capital and degree of marketization. In regressions (2.3) to (2.8) various interaction terms are added into the equation to examine whether some variables exert a joint effect on growth.

Table 12.2 FDI and growth of GDP, full sample, 1990–98

Variable	*(2.1)*	*(2.2)*	*(2.3)*	*(2.4)*	*(2.5)*	*(2.6)*	*(2.7)*	*(2.8)*
K_d	0.049	0.046	0.046	0.045	0.023	0.029	0.046	0.047
	(3.60)***	(3.45)***	(3.32)***	(3.38)***	(1.65)*	(1.64)*	(3.58)***	(3.63)***
K_f	0.007	0.008		0.005		0.002		−0.005
	(4.09)***	(4.32)***		(1.77)*		(0.52)		(−1.08)
L	0.057	0.096	0.106	0.099	0.119	0.114	0.071	0.061
	(0.39)	(0.66)	(0.73)	(0.68)	(0.83)	(0.79)	(0.50)	(0.43)
H	12.77	−1.889	−3.874	−2.684	−2.228	−2.17	−2.79	−3.121
	(2.25)**	(−0.26)	(−0.53)	(−0.37)	(−0.31)	(−0.30)	(−0.39)	(−0.44)
M		0.312	0.315	0.319	0.312	0.314	0.241	0.199
		(3.63)***	(3.63)***	(3.70)***	(3.65)***	(3.67)***	(2.91)**	(2.18)**
E		0.017	0.015	0.017	0.016	0.016	0.018	0.017
		(1.19)	(1.08)	(1.18)	(1.14)	(1.16)	(1.28)	(1.26)
I		0.023	0.025	0.023	0.023	0.023	0.022	0.022
		(3.76)***	(3.99)***	(3.78)***	(3.79)***	(3.75)***	(3.58)***	(3.58)***
$K_f H$			2.810	1.059				
			(4.02)***	(0.87)				
$K_d K_f$					0.025	0.019		
					(4.57)***	(1.51)		
$K_f M$							0.186	0.270
							(5.33)***	(3.19)***
N	261	261	261	261	261	261	261	261
$\bar{R}^2$	0.34	0.41	0.41	0.41	0.42	0.42	0.44	0.44

Note: Figures in parentheses are *t*-statistics (two-tailed tests); ***, ** and * denote significance at the 1, 5 and 10% levels, respectively.
Source: Authors' calculations.

Table 12.2 reveals several interesting results concerning the effects of FDI on economic growth. Regressions (2.1) and (2.2) indicate that FDI has a positive impact on economic growth. The addition of some ancillary variables, i.e. the level of marketization, and the growth rates of exports and imports in regression (2.2) does not reduce, but rather increases, the significance of the FDI variable. The level of human capital, proxied by the ratio of number of college students to the total population, does not seem to contribute to growth in regressions (2.2)–(2.8). This variable, although commonly employed in empirical research, might not perform as expected as a proxy for human capital in the case of China. It might be argued that in China the efficiency with which the stock of technical knowledge is translated into technologies in the market, via the higher education system, is very low. This is likely to be a legacy of central planning, which is well known to have been inimical to the commercialization of ideas. Another possible reason is that the rigidity of personnel management systems in state-owned firms prevents well-educated employees from contributing fully to the firm performance. In additional regressions that were run using average wages in each region, in place of the student-population ratio, the results do not change significantly. The insignificant role of human capital in growth found here appears to be consistent with the studies by Wei (1995) that investigated the role of FDI and human capital in economic growth in China. In contrast with the result for human capital, we find as expected that investment (especially domestic investment) and marketization have a positive impact on growth.

The specification in regression (2.3) replaces the FDI variable with the product of FDI and human capital, and yields a coefficient that is positive and statistically highly significant. While this specification follows closely from the framework developed in the second section, the significance of the interaction term may be the result of the omission of other relevant factors, in particular, the FDI variable by itself. Thus, it is necessary to include FDI and human capital individually alongside their product. In this way, we can test jointly whether these variables affect growth by themselves or through the interaction term. This specification is adopted in regression (2.4), which shows that the coefficient on FDI is still positive and significant, while the interaction term is no longer significant. This means that the significance of the interaction term is likely to be the result of the omission of the FDI variable itself. Thus, we are unable to link the significance of the K_fH variable in regression (2.3) to the so-called 'threshold' effect, i.e. we need to be cautious in averring that in China FDI might promote growth only when human capital reaches a certain level, at least on the basis of our data. However, this does not necessarily mean that the effect of FDI on economic growth has nothing to do with conditions in the host country or local economy. In fact, as we will see later, the effect of FDI on growth in this study is closely associated with provincial differences with respect to technological and market, or industry, conditions.

Domestic investment has been one of the most important factors supporting the continuous economic growth in China since the Open Door Policy. This is reflected throughout Table 12.2 where the K_d variable is positive and statistically significant in all the equations. Similar to the results in columns (2.3) and (2.4) with respect to the FDI-human capital variable, the interaction term between domestic and foreign investment is significant in equation (2.5) where the FDI variable is absent, but insignificant in equation (2.6) where the FDI variable is also included. This casts doubt on the existence, as is usually assumed in the literature, of a complementary relationship between the two types of investment. The insignificance of the K_dK_f variable may be related to the structure of domestic investment in China. Investment in infrastructure has been extensive and should, in principle, serve to enhance the role of FDI in promoting growth. However, in practice a substantial share of investment in fixed assets in China is accounted for by industrial projects and real assets that have been state-funded and which have relatively little opportunity to interact positively with incoming foreign capital.

We find that market-oriented reform has been one of the major forces driving economic growth in China. This is reflected in Table 12.2 where the marketization variable in all the equations is positive and statistically significant. It is interesting to see the role of the interaction between FDI and marketization. In contrast to the cases of K_fH and K_dK_f, the positive and significant performance of the interaction variable K_fM is invariant of whether the FDI variable is included or excluded in the relevant equations. In addition, the increased value of $\bar{R}^2$ in equations (2.7) and (2.8) also justifies our inclusion of the marketization variable and of the interaction term K_fM in these regressions.

Of the two trade variables, only that for imports attains significance. These two variables should be interpreted with caution as they refer to trade at the level of the province. As such they are not exclusively concerned with trade in the international sphere – they include inter-provincial trade – and so do not measure only the international trade that brings the Chinese host economy and foreign economies into contact. This dilution of the variables may account for the lack of significance of exports. However, the across-the-board significance of imports is perhaps best understood as a special aspect of market liberalization. Provinces of China have customarily been segmented by restrictive local distribution monopolies. Those provinces with the fastest growth in imports are likely to be those that have embraced liberalization in trade, and that have also provided environments most conducive to economic growth. Our results indicate that the Chinese economy is still at a stage in which growth for the country as a whole has been mainly driven by the expansion of domestic investment and by market-oriented reform, rather by imported technology and the stock of human capital.

As discussed in the preceding section, the FDI–growth relationship may vary across provinces due to various differences specific to the characteristics of these regions. The impact of these differences can be explored by dividing the full sample into sub-samples. Tables 12.3–12.5 show the results from the estimation of equation (12.2) for subsamples to investigate how provincial differences affect the FDI–growth relationship.

Table 12.3 examines the difference in the way in which our standard model performs between the regions of China. The designation of China on such a regional basis underpins the Open Door Policy, and so the contrasts that arise in Table 12.3 essentially arise from the timetable for the rolling out of that policy, as well as from the underlying economic attractiveness of the provinces within the regions. It is therefore not surprising that, within each of the three classes of region, there is limited variation in economic and policy characteristics. The result is that all but one of the explanatory variables supplementary to domestic investment and FDI fail to reach significance.

Government development policy has managed to foster economically convergent provinces by region. Within these regions the driving force behind growth is confirmed as springing from domestic and foreign investment.

Table 12.3 Geographical regions and the FDI–growth relationship, 1990–98

Variable	*Eastern region* (3.1)	*Central region* (3.2)	*Central region* (3.3)
K_d	0.045	0.061	0.015
	(2.63)**	(1.80)*	(0.78)
K_f	0.041	0.010	0.002
	(7.14)***	(3.08)*	(1.84)*
L	0.385	0.241	−0.127
	(1.38)	(0.97)	(−1.04)
H	2.295	20.53	25.93
	(0.26)	(0.62)	(1.71)*
M	0.318	0.305	−0.045
	(0.13)	(1.37)	(−0.26)
N	108	81	72
$\bar{R}^2$	0.50	0.37	0.27

Note: Figures in parentheses are *t*-statistics (two-tailed tests); ***, ** and * denote significance at the 1, 5 and 10% levels, respectively.
Source: Authors' calculations.

Moreover, the significance of these relationships rises in the geographical movement from west to east, as does the size of the adjusted R^2. Therefore, domestic investment contributes insignificantly to growth in the provinces of the western region, significantly in the central region and yet more significantly and strongly in the east. Across the regions, the significance of the impact of FDI parallels that of domestic investment, but is somewhat higher within each region. The strength of the FDI–growth relationship clearly rises from west to east. This suggests that FDI in some way is differentiated from domestic investment. On the basis of theory, we can interpret this as being the result of FDI conferring a package of new resources, in which the elements are qualitatively and quantitatively different from domestic investment.

Although the size of the coefficients on FDI lies below that for domestic investment (where both are significant), it attains its zenith in the eastern region. The key conclusion from the equations in Table 12.3 is that the importance of FDI in driving growth rises in step with the development policy programme of the government of China. Accordingly, FDI should be expected to become still more important to China's development aspirations in the future. The pattern of significance and strength that we observe in the coefficients suggests that domestic investment leads chronologically in creating growth. Surprisingly, this leadership does not apply in the least-developed provinces of the eastern region. It is possible that in these provinces the quality (and perhaps also the quantity) of domestic investment is so low that its impact on growth is negligible.

The human capital variable is unique among the supplementary variables in attaining significance for the provinces of the western region. This signals that between the most economically backward provinces, increases in investment in human capital make a positive contribution to economic growth.

For a deeper understanding of the true impact of the economic and policy variables, we must reclassify the provinces by their economic characteristics, rather than by simple membership of geographical region. Proceeding along these lines we are able to produce Tables 12.4 and 12.5. The results in equations (4.1) and (4.2), which divide the sample of provinces by GDP per capita, bear a strong resemblance to those in Table 12.3 precisely because development levels rise in the movement from the western region to the eastern region. Thus, we find again that domestic investment is of primary importance in driving economic growth in the less developed provinces. What can be considered as a standard result is obtained for the FDI variable, i.e. that its growth-promoting effects are evident in the developed rather than in the less developed provinces, which is in line with the result in Table 12.3. This is analogous to the common finding for export-led growth in the development literature. Here, the FDI variable captures an interaction between the domestic and the international sectors, analogous to exporting, and the results show that this interface promotes growth but contingent upon local development being in the higher end of the distribution. The

Table 12.4 Provincial economic differences and the FDI–growth relationship: sub-sample results, 1990–98

Variable	*GDP per capita*		*R&D expenditure/GDP*		*Level of infrastructure*	
	High (4.1)	*Low (4.2)*	*High (4.3)*	*Low (4.4)*	*High (4.5)*	*Low (4.6)*
K_d	0.049	0.060	0.035	0.066	0.028	0.093
	(2.60)***	(2.76)***	(2.26)***	(3.19)***	(1.56)	(4.13)***
K_f	0.009	0.001	0.007	0.010	0.005	0.001
	(2.47)***	(1.37)	(3.28)***	(3.30)***	(2.96)***	(0.89)
L	0.331	−0.112	−0.075	0.394	0.064	0.359
	(1.33)	(−0.67)	(−0.52)	(1.45)	(0.33)	(1.53)
H	0.614	6.563	1.466	0.212	−0.223	−23.28
	(0.06)	(0.35)	(0.21)	(2.47)***	(−0.03)	(−0.74)
M	0.195	0.279	0.25	0.334	0.157	0.464
	(1.50)	(1.85)*	(2.49)***	(3.14)***	(1.30)	(2.19)**
N	126	135	126	135	126	135
$\bar{R}^2$	0.31	0.33	0.38	0.39	0.37	0.31

Note: Figures in parentheses are *t*-statistics (two-tailed tests); ***, ** and * denote significance at the 1, 5 and 10% levels, respectively.

Source: Authors' calculations.

degree of marketization appears as a significant variable in the low, but not in the high, GDP per capita regions. This result underscores the role played by the movement towards private sector economic activity in the growth process in the poorest provinces. It appears that, in the rich provinces, where the degree of marketization is already very high, the variation in this variable is no longer critical to the growth process, i.e. the main part of the benefits have already been reaped.

In equations (4.3) and (4.4) the provinces are reclassified by provincial research-and-development capability (R&D effort), producing some fresh results. Domestic investment and FDI promote growth in both high and low-research provinces and, at this point, it might be helpful to reflect upon the nature of the data on research. Pure and applied research will be conducted by domestic and foreign-invested firms, and by government research institutes. There is a well-understood relationship between R&D and growth in locations in which research levels are considerable. But where R&D is low, both in intensity and in absolute terms, our results call to mind that the presence of a relatively few provinces, with effort at the higher end of the low distribution, might be sufficient to lead to a positive relationship with growth.

The human capital variable assumes significance for the subsample of provinces with low – but not high – research effort. It appears that growth is promoted by an expansion in the number of tertiary students at the lower end of the distribution, i.e. in the relatively large quantum leap from low participation rates to moderate rates. From this we can infer that an increase in human capital in the low-research provinces has a synergistic effect with such meagre provincial resources as there are, to stimulate an expansion in growth. In contrast, we find that within the high-research provinces an increase in the abundance of human capital is no longer critical for growth.

The key policy finding from equations (4.3) and (4.4) concerns the influence of marketization. In both high and low-research provinces, marketization augments economic growth. This implies that this policy is of commensurate value whatever the research status of the province, and therefore that it can be pursued with universal benefit to growth. This benefit may derive from the way that private enterprise pursues more aggressively the exploitation of research outputs than does state enterprise.

Turning to equations (4.5) and (4.6), in which provinces are classified by level of infrastructure, we see that some sharp contrasts emerge between the high and low subsamples. Growth is promoted by domestic investment in the low infrastructure group, but not in the high group. This points to the conclusion that it is domestic investment in infrastructural projects that is playing a leading role in the early stages of the growth process. These projects may well lie in the state sector and, accordingly, this hints at the pivotal part played by the state in raising socially productive capital. For its part, foreign (and therefore also private) capital and knowledge, conferred via FDI, furthers growth in high – but not low – infrastructure provinces.

This leads one to believe that, to be productive, FDI calls for an adequate level of infrastructure to be in place. Lastly, in equation (4.6), we find that marketization promotes growth where infrastructure levels are low, suggesting that this policy can be pursued with benefit notwithstanding impoverished provincial foundations. In provinces that are well founded in this respect, marketization has no impact (in equation 4.5), it being probable in these cases that marketization rates have probably already converged, and may lie reasonably close to an upper boundary.

The data by province can also be investigated in terms of regional differences in industrial characteristics that relate primarily to the activities of enterprises. This is the purpose of Table 12.5. Equations (5.1) and (5.2) reclassify provinces by the share of FDI in provincial capital formation. In this way we can discern how the determinants of growth contrast between highly invested provinces and low FDI intensity provinces. Domestic investment remains a powerful factor in both categories of province, though attaining a higher significance in the highly invested provinces. This hints at the possibility of a complementary relationship with FDI at the provincial level. In equation (5.1), where provincial FDI intensity is high, the impact of FDI on growth is significantly positive, but there is no such effect where FDI intensity is low. This indicates that FDI's contribution to growth is contingent upon there being a sufficient share of FDI in economic activity. This might

Table 12.5 Provincial differences in industrial characteristics and the FDI–growth relationship: subsample results, 1990–98

Variable	*FDI/total investment*		*SOE's sales/ total sales*		*Growth of sales by domestically owned firms*	
	High (5.1)	*Low (5.2)*	*High (5.3)*	*Low (5.4)*	*High (5.5)*	*Low (5.6)*
K_d	0.051	0.048	0.048	0.044	0.047	0.082
	(2.79)***	(2.29)**	(2.84)***	(1.99)**	(2.66)***	(3.50)***
K_f	0.016	0.001	0.018	0.001	0.010	0.0004
	(4.92)***	(0.85)	(5.87)***	(0.63)	(3.88)***	(0.63)
L	0.529	−0.166	0.469	−0.001	0.348	0.023
	(2.06)**	(−1.12)	(1.67)*	(−0.01)	(1.31)	(0.14)
H	−3.406	32.99	−0.948	18.79	−3.856	21.43
	(−0.35)	(1.94)*	(−0.10)	(1.20)	(−0.39)	(1.29)
M	0.466	0.0048	0.357	0.106	0.307	0.068
	(3.07)***	(0.04)	(2.95)***	(0.76)	(1.83)*	(0.53)
N	126	135	126	135	126	135
$\bar{R}^2$	0.38	0.33	0.41	0.27	0.38	0.29

Note: Figures in parentheses are *t*-statistics (two-tailed tests); ***, ** and * denote significance at the 1, 5 and 10% levels, respectively.

Source: Authors' calculations.

be in the same industry – in which case the need for critical mass is implicated – or in different industries, in which event a network of suppliers may be present. This suggestion, that a critical foreign competitive mass is needed to realize the growth benefits of FDI, might link to the incentive for rapid technology and knowledge transfer that comes with effective competition between foreign-owned producers.

There are two further significant variables in equation (5.1), namely the growth rate of the labour force and the degree of marketization. The labour force variable captures increases in the abundance of labour of working age. There are two sources of domestic labour growth, one is natural population growth and the other is immigration. The first lies outside the policy domain in the time frame of our study, but not so the second source. The inference is that immigration into highly foreign-invested provinces should be promoted for its positive impact on growth.

The remaining significant variable in equation (5.1) is marketization. Marketization promotes economic growth in high, but not low, foreign-invested provinces. From this we can infer that when the provincial economy is highly foreign-invested, then the expansion of private enterprise contributes significantly to growth. The precise process through which this occurs cannot be elucidated through this present research. It may involve the stimulation, through various means, by foreign affiliates of local private firms' value-adding activities. Again, the competitive process may be pivotal in this finding. The greater the presence of foreign affiliate competitors the more keen the competition, and the more beneficial market reform may be for all producers in the Chinese market.

In equation (5.2), apart from the domestic investment variable, the only significant variable is that for human capital. This significance, in the context of a low foreign-invested environment, suggests a pattern of economic growth drawing on improvements in the quality of labour, and echoes our earlier finding for the western region provinces. It appears that modest improvements in human capital have value in encouraging the early stages of economic growth.

In equations (5.3) and (5.4), the data are reordered according to the proportion of state-owned enterprise sales in total sales. This procedure separates provinces in which most of the economic activity is still in state hands from those in which the private sector is now very considerable, owing to the rapid growth of private enterprise. While the domestic investment variable attains significance in both equations, we find that the two equations otherwise contrast markedly. There are four significant variables in equation (5.3), but just one in equation (5.4). Counter to intuition, we find that the FDI variable exerts a significant positive effect on economic growth in those provinces in which state-owned activity is high, rather than where it is low. Here we must reflect on the pattern of inward FDI into China. Typically, much foreign capital has been directed to joint ventures with state-owned enterprises rather than with enterprises spawned in the private sector. The largest foreign-invested projects in China conform to this characterization. This provides a tenable account of why the contribution of FDI to growth has been greatest where SOE activity has been highest, but we cannot conclude that this is the true basis for this finding.

The two further significant variables in equation (5.3) shed more light. The growth rate of the labour force and the degree of marketization both promote economic growth in high state-sector provinces. This again points to the importance of increases in the stock of labour, and possibly of migration, for growth and to the general benefits to be derived from marketization. As this latter variable is based on the proportion of employees who are not in the state sector, we can infer than the movement towards employment in private enterprise in provinces dominated by state enterprise brings considerable benefits for economic growth. The sole significance of the domestic investment variable in equation (5.4) suggests that most of the growth in private enterprise in provinces with low SOE shares has been Chinese-owned enterprise.

The final two equations in Table 12.5 (equations 5.5 and 5.6) divide provinces into those with high and low growth rates of sales by domestically owned firms, which is intended to reflect the degree of competition from Chinese locally owned firms. The reasoning is that, where sales by local firms are growing fastest, this will be the result of the growth of Chinese-owned enterprise, which produce substantial volumes of output for the local market. Equation (5.5) duly reports that the FDI variable contributes significantly to growth when domestic competition in local goods markets is keenest. Once again, competition is seen to associate with a positive FDI–growth relationship, this time within the context of domestic competition. Marketization also, within the same environment, promotes growth. In contrast, equation (5.6) reveals that where the degree of Chinese-owned competition is least, no variable, apart from that for domestic investment, records a significant effect on economic growth. The inference to be made here is that, in the absence of effective local competition, the economic factors and policies that would otherwise be relied upon to generate growth are rendered ineffective. This again points to the importance of promoting competitive market structures.

Conclusions

We find two main strands in our conclusions arising from this study of the FDI–growth relationship in China. Firstly, conditions in the host economy profoundly impact upon the growth relationship. This applies to China at the national as well as at the provincial level. The role of the market reform process deserves special attention, as it pervades the growth process, enabling resources, whatever quality or quantity, to be employed with an efficiency superior to that under state planning and control. Secondly, the quality and quantity of resources are crucial to promoting growth, as witnessed by the significance of domestic and foreign investment and, on occasion, labour growth and human capital.

In agreement with earlier research, our results support the view that externally oriented development strategies promote economic growth. We have specifically found support for FDI as a channel in this process. The imperative to treat China as a country of discrete provinces is evident from the pattern of results in our estimations. In the full sample, the lack of significance of human capital obscures a subtle relationship which differs between the provinces. We find no evidence of the human capital threshold effect for FDI, as posited in the development literature. However, we do find that human capital appears to be significant for growth in the less developed western provinces, and in provinces with low research capability. In other words, the effect of human capital is to favour growth in the economically weaker provinces, i.e. it is independent of FDI. The finding that, in contrast, FDI favours growth in the economically stronger provinces, may partly account for the belief in a 'threshold effect'.

The findings for each of the variables employed, to some extent, carry some implications for policy; in the context of this study, the implications point to ways to maximize the growth benefits of FDI. It is clear that policy needs to be crafted to suit the characteristics of provinces. However, some policies are more generally applicable than others. Firstly, there is no indication in these data that a stage has been reached in which the growth of domestic investment has become secondary in the growth process, although the contribution of inward FDI can be considerable. Foreign investment appears to be supportive of market reform and growth, but specifically in provinces that have already attained greater development. We find that the full benefits of FDI are felt when competition in the local market is keen from both foreign and domestic firms. We can no more than surmise that competition, from whichever source, is likely to reduce the incentive to incoming firms to exploit market power, thereby increasing the likelihood of technology and knowledge transfer.

Where it attains significance, the labour variable points to the value of expansion in the workforce, and possibly of inward migration, for economic growth. As we have noted, human capital plays a subtle role in promoting growth. On the basis of our findings, it seems clear that the economically weaker provinces should follow an education policy to raise the stock of human capital, as the greatest returns to growth from such a policy accrue to this group.

Market reform emerges as a successful general policy that betters growth in a wide range of circumstances and which, our results suggest, is bolstered in its effects by FDI in the more developed provinces. The view that inward FDI and the level of marketization are complementary in their action on growth is supported in our study. Accordingly, FDI can be viewed as an integral part of the market reform process towards the promotion of growth. The explicit policy of the government of China has been to develop first the eastern coastal provinces, and subsequently to roll the programme of reform and marketization westwards through the interior towards the western provinces. The Western Region Development Programme of the government of China (*Almanac of China's Economy*, 1999) has placed emphasis on investment in infrastructure, the attraction of inward FDI and the upgrading of human capital through education and inward migration. Our results lend support to the FDI and human capital policies, in view of the fact that growth has been responsive to the appropriate variables targeted by the government.

The key role of liberalization appears to be reinforced by our findings for the variable on the growth of imports. We argue that it is probable that imports reflect an underlying process of liberalization in the host economy, and capture the movement to more effective competition in final markets.

Provinces in China are comparable in economic size to large sovereign developing countries. The political unity of China has meant that a unique opportunity exists to manage the development process, while learning from the experience of the more advanced provinces. China is moving from a command economy based on central planning and state-owned enterprise towards a market economy in most sectors of activity. This gives the government of China an unusual degree of control over the market reform process, at least as compared with the many developing countries that have never employed comprehensive state ownership. Perhaps for this reason, our findings reveal especially clear-cut effects on growth arising from market reform policy and the degree of competition in final markets.

Amongst our findings there have been no contrary signs, nor statistical problems that would call into question the reliability of the results. We should, however, note the limitations of this research. The study relies on a small sample. Although the number of provinces is given, the number of years for which suitable data are available must be considered the crucial limiting factor. The FDI–growth relationship is inevitably investigated over a short period of time. On the other hand, in a country such as China in which conditions have changed rapidly, estimation over a longer period would require a thorough exploration of the stability of the relationship. We should also note that there is believed to be a degree of overlap, but not a high degree, between the data on the provinces. The variables employed in this study are, however, believed to be robust and trustworthy, drawing in their construction on a lineage of comparable variables that appears in earlier studies on the FDI–growth relationship in developing countries. One advantage for our study in researching China using these variables is that it is reasonable to have more confidence in the comparability of data collected within one developing country than between a number of separate developing countries.

The low level of FDI in services in China to data justifies the focus on the manufacturing sector in this article. Services FDI has been customarily restricted owing to the official view that the services sector is less productive than manufacturing, and that domestic Chinese enterprises have been far too weak to bear foreign competition. In the future, it will be increasingly the case that research on FDI in services will be needed to investigate the growth process in a comprehensive fashion.

Our findings point collectively, and strongly, to the importance of competition in output markets for the realization of the full growth benefits of FDI. The reform process has clearly borne fruit, but it is naturally bounded when very high degrees of marketization are achieved. At this upper boundary, the barriers to efficiency that we have been unable to address in this chapter may become of key importance to future growth. In our study, we cannot capture the full range of factors that impede foreign business in China. Such factors would relate to bureaucratic and discriminatory obstacles, poor intellectual property protection, as well as discretionary measures towards foreign investors. These are substantial issues, and ones that must be addressed in the implementation of China's membership of the World Trade Organization.

Notes

1. For a literature survey, see de Mello (1997).
2. The development literature does not much concern itself with the motive for FDI. However, there are reasons for believing that FDI should not be regarded as homogeneous to the degree to which it bears technology. This is likely to be influenced by the motive for FDI. For instance, it is expected that the greater the extent to which market power is a motive, then the lower the incentive for technology transfer. This motive would be more prominent in markets where competition is lower (Buckley and Clegg, 1991).
3. There is considerable debate regarding the choice between the fixed effects (FE) model and random effects (RE) model. A common and convenient way forward is to regard the FE regression as a better and less biased one (Griliches, 1984).
4. The reliability of Chinese statistics is open to question (*Financial Times*, 2002a, b). There appears to be an upward bias in the GDP data arising from over-reporting, and in the FDI data arising from 'disguised FDI'. This latter can arise where investment ostensibly from, for example, Hong Kong (China) in fact has a mainland Chinese ultimate beneficial owner (Lan and Young, 1996). These inflationary tendencies may mitigate each other to some extent.
5. The definition of domestic investment is investment in fixed assets, which contribute the greatest part of the capital invested in Chinese-owned firms. This can be considered commensurable with the Chinese data on FDI, which are defined differently from the IMF definition (IMF, 1977), as all expenditures that add to the capital of a firm. The Chinese FDI data have the benefit of not being influenced by the financial positioning between the parent firms and affiliates.
6. See, for example, Hsiao (1986) for a discussion of panel data methods.
7. Realized FDI is investment that has been made, as opposed to planned FDI.

8. The *F*-statistic can be calculated using:

$$\frac{(\text{RSS}_{\text{R}} - \text{RSS}_{\text{UR}})/m}{\text{RSS}_{\text{UR}}/n - k}$$

where m in the present case is equal to the number of lagged K_f terms and k is the number of parameters estimated in the unrestricted regression.

References

Akaike, H. (1969) 'Fitting Autoregressive Models for Prediction'. *Annals of the Institute of Statistical Mathematics*, vol. 2, pp. 243–7.

Almanac of China's Economy (1999) Beijing: Almanac of China's Economy Press.

Balasubramanyam, V. N., Salisu, M. and Sapsford, D. (1996) 'Foreign Direct Investment and Growth: New Hypotheses and Evidence'. Discussion Paper C7/96, Department of Economics, Lancaster University, mimeo.

Blomström, Magnus, Kokko, Ari and Zejan, Mario (1994) 'Host Country Competition, Labour Skills, and Technology Transfer by Multinationals'. *Weltwirtschaftliches Archiv*, vol. 130, pp. 521–33.

Blomström, Magnus, Lipsey, Robert and Zejan, Mario (1994) 'What Explains Growth in Developing Countries'. NBER Discussion Paper No. 1924, Cambridge, Mass., mimeo.

Borensztein, Eduardo, de Gregorio, José and Lee, Jong-Wha (1998) 'How Does Foreign Direct Investment Affect Growth'. NBER Working Paper No. 5057, Cambridge, Mass., mimeo.

Buckley, Peter J. and Clegg, Jeremy (1991) 'Introduction and Statement of the Issues'. In Peter J. Buckley and Jeremy Clegg (eds), *Multinational Enterprises in Less Developed Countries*. London: Macmillan, pp. 3–23.

Buckley, Peter J., Clegg, Jeremy and Wang, Chengqi (2001) 'The Impact of Foreign Direct Investment on the Performance of Chinese Locally Owned Firms'. Paper presented in the 27th Annual Conference of European International Business Academy, Paris, ESCP–EAP, mimeo.

Chen, Chung, Chang, Lawrence and Zhang, Yimin (1995) 'The Role of Foreign Direct Investment in China's Post-1978 Economic Development'. *World Development*, vol. 23, no. 4, pp. 691–703.

Dees, Stephane (1998) 'Foreign Direct Investment in China: Determinants and Effects'. *Economics of Planning*, vol. 31, pp. 175–94.

De Mello, Luiz R., Jr (1996) 'Foreign Direct Investment, International Knowledge Transfers and Endogenous Growth: Time Series Evidence'. Canterbury: Department of Economics, University of Kent, mimeo.

De Mello, Luiz R., Jr (1997) 'Foreign Direct Investment in Developing Countries and Growth: a Selective Survey'. *The Journal of Development Studies*, vol. 34, no. 1, pp. 1–34.

De Mello, Luiz R., Jr (1999) 'Foreign Direct Investment-led Growth: Evidence from Time Series and Panel Data'. *Oxford Economic Papers*, vol. 51, pp. 133–51.

Dunning, John H. (1977) 'Trade, Location of Economic Activity and the Multinational Enterprise: a Search for an Eclectic Approach'. In Bertil Ohlin, Per-Ove Hesselborn and Per Magnus Wijkman (eds), *The International Allocation of Economic Activity*. London: Macmillan, pp. 395–418.

Dunning, John H. (1993) *Multinational Enterprise and the Global Economy*. Wokingham, Berks.: Addison-Wesley.

Elias, V. J. (1990) *Sources of Growth: a Study of Seven Latin American Economies*. San Francisco: ICS Press.

Financial Times (2002a) 'Report Casts Doubt over Chinese Data'. 28 February, p. 14.

Financial Times (2002b) 'Pyramid of Power behind the Numbers Game'. 28 February, p. 14.

Granger, C. W. J. (1969) 'Investigating Causal Relations by Econometric Models and Cross Spectral Methods'. *Econometrica*, vol. 37, pp. 47–55.

Granger, C. W. J. (1980) 'Testing for Causality'. *Journal of Economic Dynamics and Control*, vol. 2, pp. 32–52.

Griliches, Zvi (1984) 'R&D and Productivity Growth at the Firm Level'. In Z. Griliches (ed.), *R&D, Patents and Productivity*. Chicago: University of Chicago Press, pp. 339–74.

Henley, John, Kirkpatrick, Colin and Wilde, Georgina (1999) 'Foreign Direct Investment in China: Recent Trends and Current Policy Issues'. *The World Economy*, vol. 22, no. 2, pp. 223–43.

Hsiao, Cheng (1986) *Analysis of Panel Data*. Cambridge: Cambridge University Press.

International Monetary Fund (IMF) (1977) *Balance of Payments Manual*, 4th edn. Washington, DC: IMF.

Johnson, Harry G. (1972) 'Survey of the Issues'. In Peter Drysdale (ed.), *Direct Foreign Investment in Asia and Pacific*. Toronto: University of Toronto Press, pp. 1–17.

Kueh, Y. Y. (1992) 'Foreign Investment and Economic Change in China'. *The China Quarterly*, vol. 131, pp. 637–90.

Lan Ping and Young, Stephen (1996) 'Foreign Direct Investment and Technology Transfer: a Case-study of Foreign Direct Investment in North China'. *Transnational Corporations*, vol. 5, no. 1, pp. 57–83.

Lardy, R. Nicolas (1995) 'The Role of Foreign Trade and Investment in China's Economic Transformation'. *The China Quarterly*, vol. 144, pp. 1065–82.

Liu, Amy Yingli, Li, Shaomin and Gao, Yuxian (1999) 'Location, Location, Location'. *The China Business Review*, March–April, pp. 20–5.

United Nations Conference on Trade and Development (UNCTAD) (1994) *World Investment Report 1994: Transnational Corporations, Employment and the Workplace*. New York and Geneva: United Nations, United Nations publication, Sales No. E.94.II.A.14.

UNCTAD (1999) *World Investment Report 1999: Foreign Direct Investment and the Challenge of Development*. New York and Geneva: United Nations, United Nations publication, Sales No. E.99.II.D.3.

Wei, Shang-Jin (1995) 'Foreign Direct Investment in China: Sources and Consequences'. In Terutomo Ito and Anne O. Krueger (eds), *Financial Deregulation and Integration in East Asia*. Chicago: University of Chicago Press, pp. 77–101.

Woo, Wing Thye (1995) 'Comment'. In Terutomo Ito and Anne O. Krueger (eds), *Financial Deregulation and Integration in East Asia*. Chicago: University of Chicago Press, pp. 102–5.

Young, Alwyn (1992) 'A Tale of Two Cities: Factor Accumulation and Technical Change in Hong Kong and Singapore'. *NBER Macroeconomics Annual*, pp. 13–54.

Young, Alwyn (1993) 'Substitution and Complementarity in Endogenous Innovation'. *Quarterly Journal of Economics*, vol. 108, pp. 775–807.

Young, Alwyn (1995) 'The Tyranny of Numbers: Confronting the Statistical Realities of the East Asian Growth Experience'. *Quarterly Journal of Economics*, vol. 110, pp. 641–80.

Incentives to Transfer Profits: a Japanese Perspective

with Jane Frecknall Hughes

Introduction

The intense interest in transfer pricing problems shown by academics and tax practitioners alike has deepened with the publication (on 8 October 1997) of the UK Inland Revenue's consultative document and draft legislation on transfer pricing. In particular there has been a spate of professional commentary and queries (for example, see Atkinson and Tyrrall, 1997; Bunn, 1997; Taylor, 1997; Antzcak, 1998; Fairpo, 1998). The prevailing tone of many articles is an agreement that something needed to be done in this area to address a perceived problem in the growth and development of multinational corporations.

> The removal of international trade barriers has created a global economy with unprecedented world trade. World trade has increased by a factor of 16 since 1950 while total world output increased only 5.5 times. Intra-group transfers are a large proportion of this trade. Tax authorities are acutely aware of the need to protect their tax base by policing transfer pricing more actively than in the past. (Atkinson and Tyrrall, 1997, p. 18)

> Goods which may be subject to transfer pricing account for about half of world trade. (Adams, 1997)

Much of the academic research on transfer pricing has concentrated on the global aspects of income shifting (for example see Harris, 1993; Harris et al., 1993; Klassen et al., 1993; Jacob, 1996). There has been a general feeling, mostly in recent press reports (see Buckley and Frecknall Hughes, 1997), that global companies, especially Japanese multinationals, have operated transfer pricing policies to the deliberate disadvantage of host countries by artificially locating profits in jurisdictions where a tax advantage could be obtained (see also Emmanuel and Mehafdi, 1994, p. 40). The ethical considerations of such activities are not usually highlighted in academic research (though Hansen et al., 1992 do consider them). However, Jacob (1996), after examining a sample overall of 495 US companies, does comment in his conclusion (p. 312) 'that firms with substantial intrafirm sales pay lower global taxes.... This result is consistent with global tax minimization through transfer prices.' He explicitly suggests earlier that some of the effects he examined may be 'most likely due to the manipulation of transfer prices for tax reasons' (p. 311). There is thus some empirical evidence now in support of the general feeling expressed above.

However, in the case of Japanese companies[1] this study feels that it has been demonstrated that this view is mistaken. This study has argued that a fundamentally different approach to pricing has the result that profits are located in the companies' home bases in Japan (see Buckley and Frecknall Hughes, 1997). There are several ways in which multinational firms may transfer profits to their home base – by means of dividends, management charges, and by manipulating prices for goods transferred between group companies, etc., all of which are dealt with under the different national tax rules which apply according to the location of payer/recipient. Here, however, this study is concerned especially with the effects of the target costing approach, which is a common feature of Japanese operations – it is used, for example, by 80 per cent of major Japanese companies in assembly-type operations (see Sakurai, 1989, 1990). Where this method is operated, the transfer of profits to a home base is almost an inevitable and natural result. First a price for the sale of a good into a market is set according to the price that market will bear (see Drury, 1996, pp. 333). Second an examination of the costs is done, and if these absorb too much of the desired contribution margin, pressure is exerted on suppliers/subcontractors to produce and supply at lower costs (see Sparkes et al., 1987; Carr and Ng, 1995). The contribution margin is protected by this approach. Sparkes et al. show that this margin is split into net contribution, a contingency element and administrative expenses, the various elements of which can be sacrificed if there is fierce competition in the market place, thus giving rise to different prices for different markets, if required. Where goods manufactured overseas by companies under the control of the multinational parent are exported to the UK, say, for sale via a distribution-type operation, then it is easy to see that the input price to the UK can be controlled (see Buckley and Frecknall Hughes, 1997): sales can be made (effectively) at marginal cost plus a minimal contribution to cover local running costs. Such sales will still be profitable to the home-based company if all other overheads are recovered from the home market, especially if this is protected against foreign investment. Recent problems experienced by Kodak (see Graham, 1997) in trying to export film to Japan suggest that this may still be the case. (Japan's four largest distributors of photographic film and paper all have exclusive contracts with Fuji Film, the dominant Japanese maker.)

Ohmae (1995) explicitly refers to the protection of its home market by the Japanese government. Several examples are given. For instance, it is illegal for Japanese companies to post items into the country from an overseas jurisdiction, despite the fact that it is cheaper than using domestic postal services. Government subsidies for farming, air travel and weaker industries, coupled with severe restrictions on foreign investment into Japan, have meant that Japanese consumers have paid high prices for goods and services within their own country. Such prices may have seemed artificially high when compared with the prices of Japanese goods sold outside Japan. In these circumstances, it is easy to see how allegations may arise of price manipulation and acting to the tax disadvantage of a host country, which may be left with little, if any, profit in its own jurisdiction to tax.

It is not surprising that, in circumstances such as those outlined above, Revenue authorities worldwide should be concerned about the activities of Japanese multinational corporations within their respective jurisdictions. The USA has been a leader in developing transfer pricing regulations and has a more structured framework than most countries. Many European countries (e.g. the Netherlands, Germany, France, Italy, Spain and Portugal) are tightening up their transfer pricing regulations. The Ukraine enacted its first transfer pricing law on 1 July 1997, and the new tax code which Russia hoped to adopt by 1999 (originally scheduled for January 1998), is expected to include transfer pricing provisions. Nations are thus seeking to minimize tax leakage (Atkinson and Tyrrall, 1997), that is, they are endeavouring to tax profits deemed to arise from activities undertaken within their jurisdictions. Ernst & Young's third annual survey (see also Bunn, 1997) suggests that multinationals regard transfer pricing as the most important international tax issue facing their organizations while the Inland Revenue (per Ernst & Young) views it as an 'avoidance issue'. Further professional opinion (see Taylor, 1997) suggests that transfer pricing is by far the most effective way of collecting some of the extra tax which the Revenue seeks to collect as part of its 'Spend to Save' campaign, though there is now empirical evidence which clearly shows that tax evasion or avoidance is not the primary reason for transfer pricing policies adopted by certain multinationals. For example, Cravens (1997) lists a number of possible strategic objectives, such as: managing the tax burden; complying with tax regulations; managing tariffs; promoting equitable performance evaluation; motivating managers; promoting goal congruence; maintaining competitive market position; mitigating cash transfer restrictions; minimizing inflation risk; managing foreign currency exchange; addressing social or political concerns; and reflecting actual costs and income consistently. Of her sample of 542 firms, 28 per cent only operated their particular policies specifically for tax reasons: maintaining competitive position, promoting equitable performance evaluation, promoting goal congruence and motivating employees also scored relatively high percentages (17 per cent, 11 per cent, 10 per cent and 10 per cent respectively). She also points out that the same transfer pricing policy could be undertaken by two different firms for entirely different reasons, and comments that academic interest in the past has mostly centred on how to determine transfer pricing methods, rather than why the methods are used. There is also evident an interest in the overall results of transfer pricing policies (see Jacob, 1996).

However, it is also easy to perceive why Japanese multinationals may feel that they are being particularly targeted. Profits in Japan are taxed at rates of 50 per cent or more – much higher than rates prevailing in the UK (see Chennels and Griffith, 1997, pp. 146–53). The effective marginal and average rates of tax also operate at this or a similarly high level (see Chennels and Griffith, 1997, pp. 150). Thus if higher tax is paid at home in any case, it is hard to see why there is not a reversal of the procedures outlined above, such that profits are left in lower-rated jurisdictions: this would be seen, perhaps, from a Japanese viewpoint as true manipulation! It is the underlying purpose of this chapter to consider reasons why such a change is not made and why profits continue to be generated for the home company when it may appear less than tax effective to do so.

Incentives to foreign direct investment

The majority of work done on foreign investment by one country into another examines the reasons why a company will invest in a foreign jurisdiction; the incentives that are offered by a foreign jurisdiction to attract inward investors (see, for example, Higson and Elliott, 1994; Coyne, 1995; Mason and Encarnation, 1995; Conklin and Robertson, 1996; van Eenennaam and Brouthers, 1996); and related topics such as how businesses actually become global (see Clegg et al., 1993). Such work deals with the establishment and process of growth of such investments, but once a foreign investment has been established, and is making profits, what happens to those profits? Traditionally profits have two major functions: (i) to pay dividends to shareholders and (ii) to reinvest in the business. The international dimension complicates this scenario – which seems to be one which no one has examined, as far as can be ascertained, hence this study attempts to address it here with particular reference to Japanese corporations. This study shall only consider reasons for foreign investment here in so far as they are relevant to trying to provide answers to this question as this area is already considered in depth by others.

Reasons to transfer profits

There can be no doubt that profits are transferred across national boundaries in the way we have outlined (or, indeed, in others). Adams (1997), for instance, reports that in 1993, Nissan paid nearly Y17 billion in penalty taxes to the US Internal Revenue Service after an IRS ruling that the company avoided US taxes 'by transferring part of its income from the US to Japan'. Such alleged avoidance need not, of course, be intentional. Indeed there is a considerable body of work which examines the legitimate planning procedures available to businesses to minimize tax (see for example, Scholes and Wolfson, 1992). Considering the use of such devices does not fall within the scope of this chapter, as this study is looking at a situation that appears to run counter to the notions of minimizing tax. This study considers that the possible reasons for transferring profits fall under three headings – control, need and business consciousness, and we shall examine each of these in turn.

Control

By this is meant measures whereby profits earned overseas can be kept under the jurisdiction of the home-based company. This may be done because a foreign investment is perceived to be 'risky' for various reasons – which may be political instability of a particular regime; instability of currencies in terms of exchange rate (which may, or may not, be connected with any political instability); uncertainty of resources in the foreign jurisdiction; inability to transfer cash physically or pay dividends because of restrictions imposed by the foreign government, etc. The desire to have one's profits at home also may be no more than an owner's wish to have property where it can be seen and be within personal grasp. There may also be a consequent, perceived need (and to some extent this falls also into the two categories discussed below) to demonstrate to one's peers that business operations are functioning well, in an environment where directors and managers actually are resident, and this is considered socially important. Thus far these reasons are not peculiar to Japan: rather they are common-sense type reasons with which anyone who owns any asset can identify.

Need

Japanese corporate structures themselves may suggest reasons why such corporations may actually need to ensure that profits return to Japan.

In the first place it is well documented that there is a multiplicity of cross-shareholdings between the major Japanese global companies or *keiretsu* (see Brown and Stickney, 1992; Miyashita and Russell, 1996, pp. 66–70 and 81–2; Jinnai, 1997), as well as within the individual groups. As Miyashita and Russell comment, the cross-shareholdings provide the 'glue' which keeps the *keiretsu* together. The simplified diagram below illustrates this in theory.

The hypothetical groups in Figure 13.1 present a very different structure for the operation of businesses on a national level in Japan when compared with the 'pyramid' group structures familiar to Western business, which are not typically characterized by the same type of cross-shareholdings, or, consequently, intergroup activity.

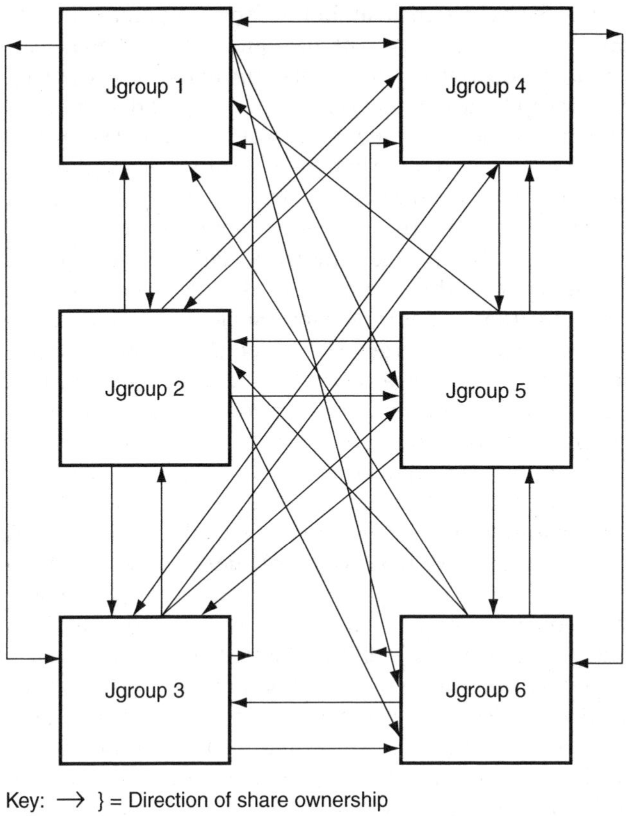

Figure 13.1 Theoretical intra-group shareholdings

Therefore if profits are transferred back to Japan, to enable dividends to be paid to shareholders, then they are paid to a small number of entities. In the above diagram then, Jgroup 1 pays dividends to Jgroup 2 and Jgroups 3, 4, 5 and 6. Jgroup 2 pays them to Jgroup 1, and to Jgroups 3, 4, 5, and 6 – and so on. Thus to keep other shareholders happy, the profit has to be returned home – and thus it is retained within the country: all groups participate in this profit retention and circulation. Jinnai (1997) (drawing on Japanese statistics for 1992) notes that the percentage of personal shareholders for all Japanese listed companies was only 23.2 per cent. He also comments that the structure of the corporate shareholdings has affected the dividend policy of the large corporations: 'In 1992, the average ratio of dividends to earnings (dividends/income after tax) was 30.3 per cent for Japanese listed companies, while it was 54 per cent in the USA, 66 per cent in the UK, and 50 per cent in Germany' (Jinnai, 1997, p. 73). Thus while profit is being retained at home, and corporate shareholders are being paid dividends, the level of pay-out is not as high as elsewhere: the instinct to retain one's own profits still remains. 'In Japan, the view has arisen that capital accumulation for the "corporation itself" is regarded as the ultimate end of each capital' (Jinnai, 1997, p. 73). In this context, capital is regarded as including retained earnings. That the large corporations share this same underlying business philosophy would explain their acceptance of this apparently reduced pay-out. (There will obviously be wide-reaching implications regarding the circulation of capital, but these lie outside the scope of this present discussion.)

To recap briefly from earlier this chapter suggested that it was the desire to locate profits in their home base which made target costing so popular with Japanese corporations (not vice versa), thus this element 'drove' the pricing structure. The Japanese multinational operates as one entity, the aim being to make profit centrally. Subsidiary companies do not exist to make profits in their own right (which would be dysfunctional according to this analysis), but for the parent, thus transcending any notion of individual company and national boundaries. Whatever legal form they take, overseas operations are agents in this – no more or less. To repeat the earlier analogy, they can be seen more as the arms or legs of a body, carrying out particular functions, rather than as offspring of a mother company. This 'arms and legs' analogy for individual groups is extremely relevant if one extends it and look at the entire country's business groups in the same way: they are the arms and legs of business carried out on a national scale. In this context the cross-shareholdings make more sense. All structures are set up with one common aim (see Buckley and Frecknall Hughes, 1997, 1998). This chapter shall return to discuss this later when considering cultural issues.

The opinion that Japanese industries are 'globalized' is a common one. Any company which operates in jurisdictions in addition to its own may be said in some respect to be a global company, but the suggestion of overseas operations acting as agents, not as independent entities, in our opinion, undercuts this concept. The level of control from the home base for Japanese entities is so great as to negate the effect of a national border between them and Japan, which could be argued is an effect consciously targeted.

There is a strong suggestion that Japanese companies are more highly geared than their Western counterparts with a heavy reliance on short-term debt (see Brown and Stickney, 1992), thus there will be a need to pay interest to the providers of the loan finance. To ensure that there is enough profit to do this, and to prevent losses being made, it may thus be desirable to transfer (via target costing) adequate amounts of profits earned overseas. One also needs to consider the position of the loan providers: often they are banks owned by, or closely associated with (because of the cross-shareholdings), one of the *keiretsu*: thus the need to pay interest to maintain one's business reputation is clear.

In this context too, it must be remembered that any Japanese company's losses cannot be offset under current Japanese law against the profits of another company in the group (see *The Economist*, 17 February 1996) so there is an added incentive to ensure profitability.

Business consciousness

This study already touched on this in the above comments about group structures. The idea of the group of companies as a single entity, and the groups in total serving collectively the national interest seems central to Japanese consciousness: individual contributions are valuable only so far as they assist in achieving this wider objective. This idea permeates the whole of Japanese life. Many articles on different aspects of Japanese business refer to a deep cultural basis in groupism and group-consciousness which is all-pervading (for example see Srinivasan, 1992) on the decreased significance (compared with the West) of individual rights in Japan, vis-à-vis data protection; Cutchergershenfield et al. (1994) on team-based work; Nussbaum-gomes (1994) on culture as a control mechanism; Saha (1994) on the relation to technology of Zen Buddhism, Confucianism and Shintoism; Vandenhoven et al. (1994) on the influence of Japanese company culture (as regards information systems) in companies in Holland and Belgium; and Jun and Muto (1995) on public administration. This attitude can be said to derive from the central concept of *ie*. This is often translated as 'household' or 'family', which is a central familial concept in Japanese life (see Nakane, 1973) and is frequently examined and interpreted from a sociological perspective. However, it may be argued that the concept (which is continually evolving) has much wider application and ramifications and should comprise consideration also of other sociological effects such as a similar educational background ('old school tie' ideals), aspiration to an ideal or idealized life-goal, common appreciation of lifestyle, etc. This study would argue that it should also include an appreciation of issues which would typically be covered outside the specific field of sociology, such as religion, law, history and agriculture (the pooling of resources necessary to produce effectively in wet rice farming have reinforced such cooperative strategies – see Smith, 1959). This is why it is such a difficult concept to grasp when looked at from one dimension. If this argument can be sustained, then *ie* is a multi-faceted, multi-dimensional concept the roots of which lie very deep in Japanese society: their growth would necessarily be affected by the passage of time, the physical and geographical isolation of Japan as a group of islands, and, indeed, the conscious realization that effects of such a concept (given common daily expression in family and social contexts) had produced a unique nation, and which should therefore be deliberately fostered. Thus the strong bonds formed by membership of a family (the typical sociological expression) find a direct analogy with managers' adherence to a company, which is the business expression of the same concept. The existence of this group consciousness within the *kaisha* ('my' company, 'our' company) will thus be a powerful force in Japanese organization, because derived from fundamental principles. As Nakane says (1973, p. 3): 'Kaisha does not mean that individuals are bound by contractual relationships into a corporate enterprise, while still thinking of themselves as separate entities; rather, kaisha is "my" or "our" company, the continuity to which one belongs primarily, and which is all important in one's life' (see Clark, 1979; Abegglen and Stalk, 1985). It is common to speak of the *transfer* of this group consciousness to a business context, but no conscious transfer is necessary. As Nakane's words quoted above also suggest, it is only a different expression of the same underlying concept.

In view of this, it would not be surprising that reinvestment and dividend payment is 'centrally directed' and decisions are not made by individual subsidiaries, because those notions are alien to *ie* based decision processes. Rewards to managers are not on a stand-alone basis but are on the basis of a contribution to the collectivity. This is reinforced by the system of transfer of executives within the Japanese company. What counts is the position in the central, that is, home-based hierarchy. A period out of Japan, even in a prestigious post, may not confer the seniority of a post in the home base. This is gradually changing, as Japanese companies become more internationally orientated, but overseas postings do not carry the prestige, even now, that they do in 'Western' companies (Buckley and Mirza, 1985).

Conclusion

It can be demonstrated clearly that Japanese corporations not only transfer profits to their home base, but do so for a variety of reasons and using a variety of methods. Where target costing (relatively common) is used to price products into overseas markets, the profits transferred home become a natural part of the home company's profits (they are not, for example, transferred to Japan by means of a subsidiary paying a dividend to its parent or by means of management charges). Manipulation of pricing to obtain tax advantages need not be a reason for so locating profits. Indeed, profits in Japan are (often) taxable at higher rates than if left in jurisdictions where earned. It is not easy with any method of transfer pricing to analyse costs/prices into component parts (see Buckley and Frecknall Hughes, 1998), but where the head office is 'the heart not the head' of the company, it becomes almost impossible, and yet, this is the course followed by most Revenue authorities, when they examine transfer pricing in attempts to get a 'fair' or 'arm's length' price for goods transferred in or out of their jurisdictions. In a Japanese context this study has suggested that reasons for transferring profits to the home base may be threefold – need, control and business consciousness. This study deliberately refrains from referring to this latter reason as business 'culture' because, as an explanatory term, the use of the word 'culture' in this context might be misleading and open to misinterpretation. The whole concept should be looked at from a much wider perspective, as it is, in our opinion, by far the most pervasive and far reaching of the reasons this study suggests – and one that has not been considered before in this way.

Acknowledgements

The authors wish to thank Yoshiaki Jinnai, Professor of Accounting, Tokyo Keizai University, Japan, for his kind and helpful comments on an earlier version of this chapter, also participants at the 1998 British Accounting Association Conference, the 8th Institute of Chartered Accountants in England and Wales Sponsored Tax Workshop, and the *Accounting, Organizations and Society* International Accounting Symposium, City University of Hong Kong, 4–5 January 1999.

Note

1. It would be simplistic and incorrect to assume that all Japanese companies operate in exactly the same way, and this study does not make such an assumption when it speaks generally of 'the Japanese company' or of 'Japanese companies'. However, this study feels that there is sufficient distinction between them and their Western counterparts, such that this manner of description will not be misleading within the context of this chapter, as we are, in fact, attempting to distinguish in some way defining and diacritical characteristics.

References

Abegglen, J. C. and Stalk Jr, G. (1985) *Kaisha, the Japanese Corporation*. New York: Basic Books.

Adams, C. (1997) 'Transfer Pricing: Confusion over Tax Treatment'. *Financial Times*, 2 September.

Antzcak, G. (1998) 'Conference Report: AIC Conference on Transfer Pricing 22/23 June 1998'. *The Tax Journal*, Monday, 3 August, pp. 20–2.

Atkinson, M. and Tyrrall, A. (1997) 'International Transfer Pricing'. *Taxation Practitioner*, December, pp. 18–20.

Brown, P. R. and Stickney, C. P. (1992) 'Instructional Case: Tanaguchi Corporation'. *Issues in Accounting Education*, vol. 7, pp. 57–9.

Buckley, P. J. and Frecknall Hughes, J. (1997) 'Japanese Transfer Pricing: a Note'. *Applied Economics Letters*, vol. 4, pp. 13–17.

Buckley, P. J. and Frecknall Hughes, J. (1998) 'Transfer Pricing and Economic Functions Analysis: the Japanese Paradigm'. *Applied Economics*, vol. 30, pp. 621–9.

Buckley, P. J. and Mirza, H. (1985) 'The Wit and Wisdom of Japanese Management: an Iconoclastic Analysis'. *Management International Review*, vol. 25, pp. 16–32.

Bunn, J. (1997) 'Confusion Reigns on Transfer Pricing'. *Accountancy Age*, 4 September, p. 4.

Carr, C. and Ng, J. (1995) 'Total Cost Control: Nissan and its UK Supplier Partnerships'. *Management Accounting Research*, vol. 6, pp. 347–65.

Chennels, L. and Griffith, R. (1997) *Taxing Profits in a Changing World*. London: ICAEW/IFS.

Clark, R. (1979) *The Japanese Company*. New Haven: Yale University Press.

Clegg, L. J., Cox, H. and Ietto-Gillies, G. (eds) (1993) *The Growth of Global Business*. London: Routledge.

Conklin, D. W. and Robertson, R. (1996) 'Tax Havens as a Determinant of International Investment'. Working Paper Series No. 96–14, Western Business School, The University of Western Ontario, Canada.

Coyne, E. J. (1995) *Targeting the Direct Foreign Investor*. Boston, Mass.: Kluwer Academic Publishers.

Cravens, K. S. (1997) 'Examining the Role of Transfer Pricing as a Strategy for Multinational Firms'. *International Business Review*, vol. 6, pp. 127–45.

Cutchergenshenfield, J., Nitta, M., Barrett, B., Belhedi, N., Bullard, J., Coutchie, C., Inarba, T., Ishino, I., Lee, S., Lin, W. S., Mothersell, W., Rabine, S., Ramanand, S., Strolle, M. and Wheston, A. (1994) 'Japanese Team-based Work Systems in North America – Explaining Diversity'. *California Management Review*, vol. 37, pp. 42–64.

Drury, C. (1996) *Management and Cost Accounting*, 4th edn. London/Boston: International Thomson Business Press.

The Economist (1996) 'The Ties That Bind'. vol. 74, 17 February.

Emmanuel, C. and Mehafdi, M. (1994) *Transfer Pricing*. CIMA/Academic Press.

Ernst & Young (1997) *Transfer Pricing 1997 Global Survey*.

Fairpo, A. (1998) 'Already Behind the Times?' *The Tax Journal*, Monday 27 April, pp. 12–14.

Graham, E. M. (1997) 'Kodak Reveals WTO Limits'. *The Journal of Commerce*, 11 December.

Hansen, D. R., Crosser, R. L. and Laufer, D. (1992) Moral Ethics v. Tax Ethics – the Case of Transfer Pricing among Multinational Corporations'. *Journal of Business Ethics*, vol. 11, pp. 679–86.

Harris, D. G. (1993) 'The Impact of US Tax Law Revision on Multinational Corporations' Capital Location and Income Shifting Decisions'. *Journal of Accounting Research, Supplement*, vol. 31, pp. 111–40.

Harris, D. G., Morck, R., Slemrod, J. and Yeung, B. (1993) 'Income Shifting in US Multinational Corporations'. In A. Giovannini, R. Hubbard and J. Slemrod (eds) *Studies in International Taxation*. Chicago: University of Chicago Press, pp. 277–302.

Higson, C. and Elliott, J. (1994) 'The Incentive to Locate a Multinational Firm: the Effect of Tax Reforms in the United Kingdom'. *International Tax and Public Finance*, vol. 1, pp. 81–97.

Inland Revenue (1997) *Modernisation of the Transfer Pricing Legislation – a Consultative Document*. 8 October.

Jacob, J. (1996) 'Taxes and Transfer Pricing: Income Shifting and the Volume of Intrafirm Transfers'. *Journal of Accounting Research*, vol. 34, pp. 301–12.

Jinnai, Y. (1997) 'The Concept of Capital in Theorising about the Firm: Discussions in Japanese Critical Accounting'. *Tokyo Keidai Gakkaishi*, vol. 204, pp. 59–77.

Jun, J. S. and Muto, H. (1995) 'The Hidden Dimension of Japanese Administration – Culture and Impact'. *Public Administration Review*, vol. 55, pp. 125–34.

Klassen, M., Lang, M. and Wolfson, M. (1993) Geographic Income Shifting by Multinational Corporations in Response to Tax Rate Changes'. *Journal of Accounting Research, Supplement*, vol. 31, pp. 141–73.

Mason, M. and Encarnation, D. (eds) (1995) *Does Ownership Matter? Japanese Multinationals in Europe*. Oxford University Press.

Miyashito, K. and Russell, D. (1996) *Keiretsu – Inside the Hidden Japanese Conglomerates*. McGraw-Hill, USA.

Nakane, C. (1973) *Japanese Society*. Harmondsworth: Pelican Books.

Ohmae, K. (1995) 'Letter from Japan'. *Harvard Business Review*, vol. 73, pp. 154–5.

Nussbaumgomes, M. (1994) 'The Subconscious in Organizational Control – the Case of MITS Heavy Industry'. *International Journal of Comparative Sociology*, vol. 35, pp. 105–30.

Saha, A. (1994) 'Culture and the Development of Technology in Japan'. *Technology in Society*, vol. 16, pp. 225–41.

Sakurai, A. (1989) 'Target Costing and How to Use it'. *Journal of Cost Management*, Summer, pp. 39–50.

Sakurai, A. (1990) 'The Influence of Factory Automation on Management Accounting Practices: a Study of Japanese Companies'. In R. Kaplan (ed.), *Measures for Manufacturing Excellence*. Cambridge, Mass.: Harvard Business School Press.

Scholes, M. S. and Wolfson, M. A. (1992) *Taxes and Business Strategy: a Planning Approach*. Englewood Cliffs, NJ: Prentice-Hall, Inc..

Smith, T. C. (1959) *The Agrarian Origins of Modern Japan*. Stanford, Calif.: Stanford University Press.

Sparkes, J. R., Buckley, P. J. and Mirza, H. (1987) 'A Note on Japanese Pricing Policy'. *Applied Economics*, vol. 19, pp. 729–32.

Srinivasan, S. (1992) 'Privacy and Data Protection in Japan'. *Government Information Quarterly*, vol. 9, pp. 121–33.

Taylor, A. (1997) 'Coming of Age?' *The Tax Journal*, 16 January, pp. 4–6.

Vandenhoven, P. T., Vanvalkenburg, F. P. A. and Heng, M. S. H. (1994) 'Managing Information Systems within Japanese Companies in Europe – Empirical Study'. *Information and Management*, vol. 27, pp. 315–25.

Van Eenennaam, F. and Brouthers, K. D. (1996) 'Global Relocation: High Hopes and Big Risks!' *Long Range Planning*, vol. 29, pp. 84–93.

14

A Survey-based Investigation of the Determinants of FDI in Portugal

with Francisco B. Castro[1]

Introduction

A long-established recipient of FDI, Portugal has all the characteristics of a small open economy of recent industrialization. In 1960 Portugal became a member of EFTA and industrialization was finally made a policy objective, putting an end to several decades of restrictions to foreign and domestic investment. EFTA membership represented a radical change in the country's geopolitical orientation. For the first time in its 850 years as an independent nation, Portugal was engaged in a process of integration in Europe. The collapse of economic relations with Africa after the independence of the colonies, in 1975, only consolidated this trend.

FDI flows can also be said to be characteristic of a recently industrialized nation, albeit one fast approaching a stage of development close to that of the most developed countries (Buckley and Castro, 1998a). During the 1960s and early 1970s, FDI inflows averaged 0.5/0.6 per cent of GDP, but were reduced to about half that value in the years that followed the 1974 democratic revolution. They picked up again after 1980, to reach the highest values ever in the late 1980s and early 1990s (Figure 14.1). Membership of the European Union, in 1986, certainly helps to explain this evolution.

In recent years, however, the flows decreased sharply and in 1999 registered the lowest level since the 1950s. The average flows of the 1990s were much lower than those in other countries of similar or smaller size, such as The Netherlands, Belgium, Ireland or Sweden (OECD, 1997). Buckley and Castro (1998b, c) suggested that the end of the cold war was part of the explanation. Portugal lost much of its attractiveness as a low cost location, which may have been amplified by its small domestic market if compared with some of the emerging markets in Central and Eastern Europe.

Given that this chapter is centred on manufacturing and commercial firms, it is important to add a brief note on the industry distribution of

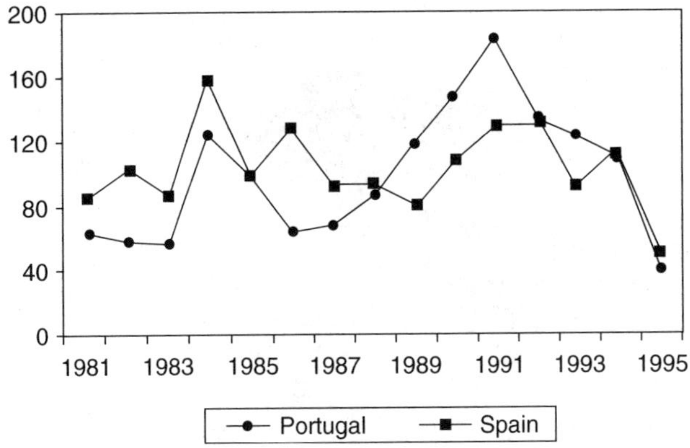

Figure 14.1 Inward FDI flows, 1965–99 (% of GDP)

Source: Own calculations based on Banco de Portugal (1997a, b, 2000a various)

FDI. According to Banco de Portugal (1998b, p. 28), the manufacturing industries represented in 1996 about one-third of the stock of inward FDI in Portugal, while commerce was responsible for a further 17 per cent. The primary sector represented no more than 1 per cent (Figure 14.2).

In terms of the distribution of the stock of manufacturing FDI (Figure 14.3), transport equipment and electric machinery concentrated, in 1996, respectively, 19 and 17 per cent of the stock of manufacturing FDI in Portugal. Forest products, chemicals, and food and beverages were the other

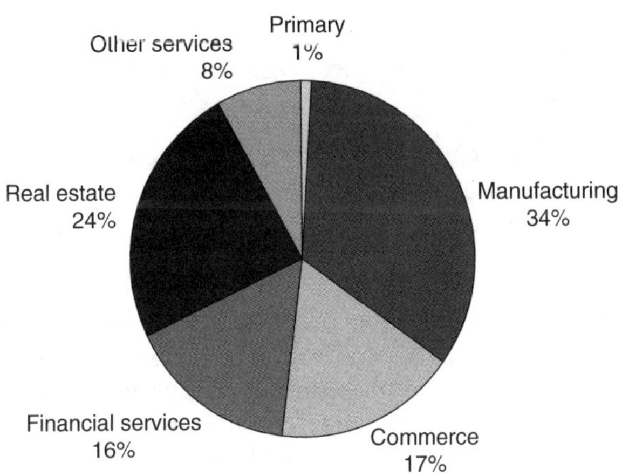

Figure 14.2 Stock of inward FDI in Portugal, 1996

Source: Banco de Portugal (1998b)

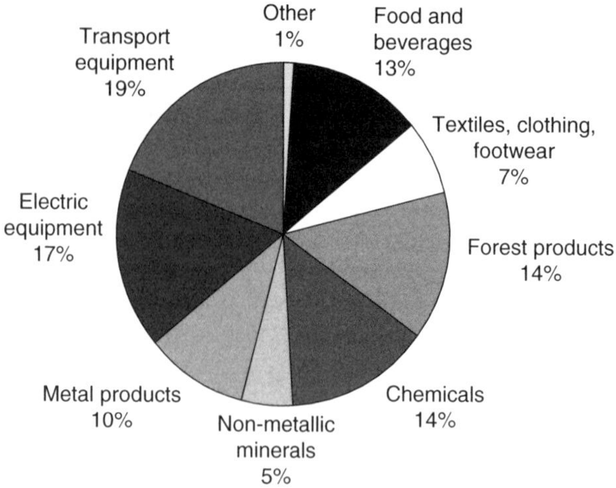

Figure 14.3 Stock of manufacturing FDI in Portugal, 1996

Source: Banco de Portugal (1998b)

industries with a share above 10 per cent. This distribution confirms that inward FDI is in Portugal essentially concentrated in capital-intensive industries. Gonçalves and Guimarães (1996, p. 10) compared this with the distribution of domestic investment (more concentrated in labour-intensive industries) to conclude that FDI has been an important contributor to the diversification of the local industrial structure.

Brief survey of previous empirical research on the determinants of FDI in Portugal

In the first study ever published of FDI in Portugal, Matos (1973) identified several reasons why foreign firms chose to invest in Portugal. Access to the local market was considered the most relevant. The size of the market did not make it very attractive, but after investing in more promising markets, expansion to Portugal and other small markets could be considered a logical step for any MNE. Access to the markets of Angola and Mozambique, then Portuguese colonies, was also a motivation for some industries.

Low wages and access to natural resources were other determinants of FDI. Portugal was at the time (and to a certain extent remains today) in an intermediary position in terms of production costs. Wages were in the early 1970s five to seven times lower than in the most developed countries (Matos, 1973). But the quality of the labour force and infrastructure were superior to those of developing countries. Natural resources, mining, tourism, and forest products were examples of sectors where Portugal seemed to have a comparative advantage. Other determinants of FDI listed by Matos (1973) were the access to the market of other EFTA members, low interest rates, and low corporate and personal income taxes. The last two vanished in the crises that marked the 1970s.

Taveira (1984) used regression analysis to test the determinants of FDI in Portugal. She also concluded that market-related variables were more important than those associated with production costs or natural resources. Other significant determinants were the level of concentration of the industry, government intervention (a negative influence), and quantitative barriers to trade. When only the export-oriented industries were being analysed, however, production costs were a relevant determinant. Nevertheless, market-related variables remained highly significant. This suggests that access to the local market played a role even in the case of FDI that was apparently export-oriented.

Fontoura (1995) also found little relevance of labour costs with an econometric model that used aggregate FDI flows in 1991/1992. She claimed that Morais (1993) obtained similar results with a different methodology. Labour skills, however, were found by Fontoura (1995) to be significant in that period. With a survey of 37 firms, Santos (1997) found both labour costs and access to the local market critical determinants of FDI in Portugal. Other relevant variables were the international image of Portugal, labour skills, stability and proximity.

Finally, Buckley and Castro (1998b) found market-related variables to be the most strongly associated with inward FDI in Portugal between 1980 and 1995. But labour costs were also significant, as was a dummy variable for the aftermath of the fall of the Berlin Wall.

Method, population and sample

A major limitation of existing studies of the determinants of FDI in Portugal was the data used. Not only was it of poor quality but it was limiting in terms of the disaggregation available. The use of alternative methods of data collection was, therefore, highly advisable. In order to obtain the information at the firm level a questionnaire was devised and distributed to the subsidiaries of foreign firms operating in Portugal. Appendix A presents the section of the questionnaire relevant for this chapter.[2]

The population for this study was defined as comprising the subsidiaries of foreign firms operating in Portugal in manufacturing (including the agro-industries) and commercial activities. A number of sources were used to identify the population: the National Institute of Statistics (INE), the Institute for Foreign Trade and Investment (ICEP), national chambers of industry and commerce operating in Portugal, and assorted publications by leading business newspapers and magazines.

Due to the poor quality of some of the databases obtained, firms were selected if: (a) they were not known to have less than 50 per cent of foreign capital; and (b) they were not known to have less than 10 employees. The latter was a pragmatic criterion: it generated a sample of 1517 firms, which was considered viable on the face of the resources available. As a result of the way the sample was selected, as many as 253 firms were excluded during the fieldwork period. They should not have been included in the population.[3] The fieldwork was conducted between June and October 1998. It produced 237 valid questionnaires,[4] which represented 18.8 per cent of the adjusted sample.

Brief description of the sample

The sample distribution per industry is presented in Figure 14.4. Given the way the sample was obtained, it can be expected to reflect the distribution of the stock of inward FDI in Portugal. But the representativeness of the sample is difficult to assert. The Bank of Portugal's data (see the first section of this chapter) is not directly comparable because the average size of firms in different industries can be expected to vary substantially.

Most firms in the sample were very recent (Figure 14.5). Over two-thirds were created or acquired after Portugal joined the (then) EEC, in 1986. However, the most recent years may be expected to be over-represented in the sample. Older firms still operating in Portugal are the ones that survived the changes in the Portuguese and international markets, the evolution of relative costs

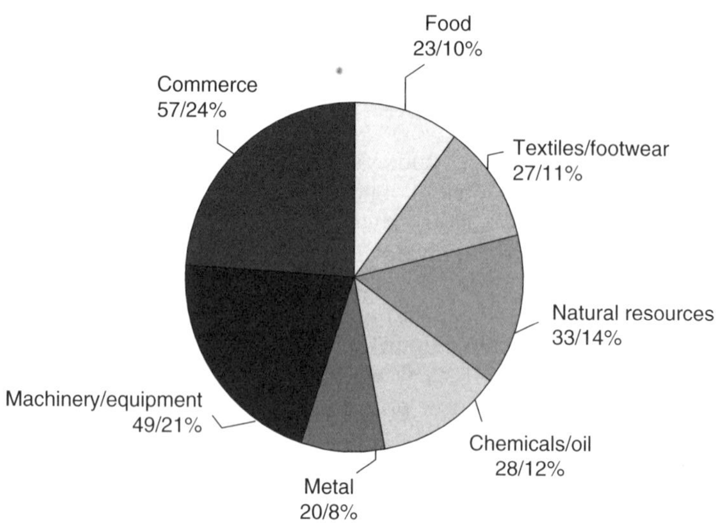

Figure 14.4 Distribution of the sample per industry

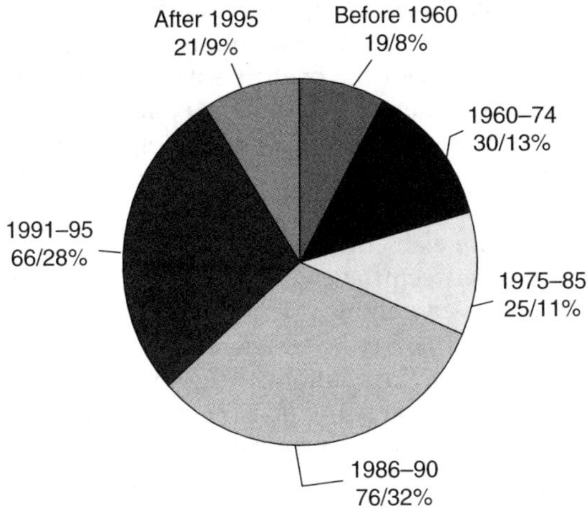

Figure 14.5 Distribution of the sample per year of investment

across the world, and the transformations in the structure, competitiveness and strategy of the parent companies. The most recent firms, on the other hand, were not yet submitted to the sieve of time.

In terms of country of origin (Figure 14.6), Germany alone accounted for 24 per cent of all firms in the sample. Overall, Germany is only the fifth foreign investor in Portugal, but German investment is largely concentrated

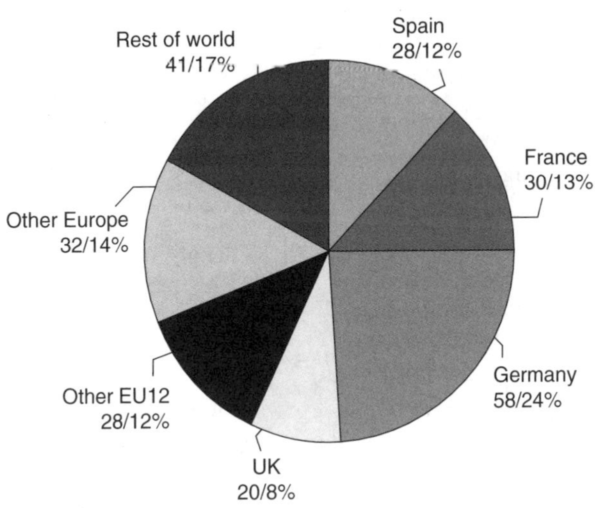

Figure 14.6 Distribution of the sample per country of origin

on manufacturing industries (Simões, 1989; Câmara de Comércio e Indústria Luso-Alemã, 1996). Henceforth, the importance of German investors in the sample was likely to represent the country's true weight in the Portuguese economy when services are excluded. France, Spain, the UK and the US were the other countries with a significant representation in the sample. With the exception of Spain, the only country with a border with Portugal, these are the main foreign investors worldwide. Only Japanese firms, with a negligible presence in Portugal, were absent from this list.

The confrontation between the country of origin and the year of investment (Table 14.1) revealed a more or less predictable pattern. Spanish subsidiaries were younger than the average, which shows how recent the phenomenon of economic integration in the Iberian peninsula is. Other recent investors in Portugal were the non-EU12 European countries (which included the three most recent EU members), who seem to have 'discovered' Portugal in 1986. The older firms in the sample were those from the UK, Portugal's main economic partner until 1974. But even in this case two in five investments took place in the 1990s.

Table 14.2 presents the industry distribution for different countries of origin. One immediate observation was the weight of machinery and equipment manufacturing in the investment by non-European, German, and French firms. This translated those countries' worldwide position in the sector. However, the inability of Portugal to attract Japanese investors was here particularly apparent. Despite many of the biggest machinery and equipment producers in the world being Japanese, few of the non-European

Table 14.1 Country of origin versus year of investment

Country		*Before 1975*	*1975–85*	*1986–90*	*1991–98*	*Total*	*Mean*
Spain	no.	3	2	10	13	28	1987
	%	10.7	7.1	35.7	46.4	100.0	
France	no.	8	3	9	10	30	1981
	%	26.7	10.0	30.0	33.3	100.0	
Germany	no.	13	5	18	22	58	1984
	%	22.4	8.6	31.0	37.9	100.0	
UK	no.	6	2	4	8	20	1963
	%	30.0	10.0	20.0	40.0	100.0	
Other EU12	no.	8	4	8	8	28	1980
	%	28.6	14.3	28.6	28.6	100.0	
Other Europe	no.	4	3	9	16	32	1987
	%	12.5	9.4	28.1	50.0	100.0	
Rest of the world	no.	7	6	18	10	41	1984
	%	17.1	14.6	43.9	24.4	100.0	
Total	no.	49	25	76	87	237	1982
	%	20.7	10.5	32.1	36.7	100.0	

Table 14.2 Country of origin per industry

Country		*Food and beverages*	*Textiles, clothing, footwear*	*Natural resources*	*Chemicals and oil*	*Metal industries*	*Machinery + equipment*	*Commerce*	*Total*
Spain	no.	4		6	1	4	4	9	28
	%	14.3		21.4	3.6	14.3	14.3	32.1	100.0
France	no.	5	3	5	3	3	7	4	30
	%	16.7	10.0	16.7	10.0	10.0	23.3	13.3	100.0
Germany	no.	1	11	4	8	4	16	14	58
	%	1.7	19.0	6.9	13.8	6.9	27.6	24.1	100.0
UK	no.	2	3	6	2	1	1	5	20
	%	10.0	15.0	30.0	10.0	5.0	5.0	25.0	100.0
Other EU12	no.	8	2	3	4	3	4	4	28
	%	28.6	7.1	10.7	14.3	10.7	14.3	14.3	100.0
Other Europe	no.	1	6	8	4	3	3	7	32
	%	3.1	18.8	25.0	12.5	9.4	9.4	21.9	100.0
Rest of the world	no.	2	2	1	6	2	15	13	41
	%	4.9	4.9	2.4	14.6	4.9	36.6	31.7	100.0
Total	no.	23	27	33	28	20	50	56	237
	%	9.7	11.4	13.9	11.8	8.4	21.1	23.6	100.0

Table 14.3 Turnover and employment: descriptive statistics

Descriptive statistics		*Turnover 1997 (million PTE)*	*Labour force 1997*
Mean		7,918	304
Std deviation		19,403	795
Minimum		0	2
Maximum		160,000	7,455
Percentiles	25%	560	30
	50%	1,678	98
	75%	6,901	267

investors in the sample were from Japan (most were from the US). The fact that all the other dominant powers in those industries were well represented in the sample only made the absence more noticeable.

Among the remaining industries, textiles, clothing and footwear were particularly important for German and non-EU12 European investors (of which Switzerland represented a substantial proportion). The percentage assumed by the food industries in the investment by 'other EU12 countries' was to a big extent due to Dutch firms. Finally, the high percentage of commercial subsidiaries among Spanish firms probably reflects geographic proximity. In many industries it is perfectly possible to supply efficiently the whole Iberian market from one single productive location (Buckley and Castro, 1999). However, non-European firms also included a big percentage of purely commercial subsidiaries, which seems contradictory.

In terms of turnover and number of employees the sample was quite diversified (Table 14.3). Turnover ranged from nil, corresponding to five firms that only started operations in 1998, to 160 billion PTE. Over half the firms in the sample had a turnover above 1.6 billion PTE, and one quarter above 6.9 billion PTE. As for the number of employees, the sample reflects the small scale of firms operating in Portugal. The median was 98 employees, and one quarter of the firms in the sample had a labour force of no more than 30.

The determinants of inward FDI in Portugal

Introduction

Regarding the determinants of foreign direct investment in Portugal, the participants in the survey were confronted with two different but interrelated questions. First, they were asked to classify 32 potential determinants using a 5-point Likert scale, where 1 corresponded to irrelevant and 5 to very important. Next, the participants were required to, out of the same 32 determinants, single out the one they considered the most important reason for their firm to have invested in Portugal (see Appendix A). Table 14.4

Table 14.4 Why invest in Portugal

Rank	*Reason*	*Mean*[1]	*Main reason*[2]	
			N	%
(a) Manufacturing firms				
1	Reduction of labour costs	3.49	41	25.8
2	Increase group's turnover	3.10	11	6.9
3	Economic stability	3.08	1	0.6
4	Political stability	3.07	1	0.6
5	Quality of labour force	3.02	5	3.1
6	Reaction to competitors	2.59	1	0.6
7	Market expected growth	2.55	8	5.0
8	Competition home market	2.51	2	1.3
9	Transport costs	2.50	2	1.3
10	Portugal's image	2.43	0	0.0
11	Public incentives	2.42	8	5.0
12	Follow customers	2.33	13	8.2
13	Local firm for sale	2.32	15	9.4
14	Establish sales network	2.32	11	6.9
15	Market diversification	2.23	0	0.0
16	European Single Market	2.19	0	0.0
17	Local infrastructure	2.11	1	0.6
18	EU market	2.10	4	2.5
19	Quality of local cluster	2.10	3	1.9
20	Market size	2.01	2	1.3
21	Cultural proximity	1.97	0	0.0
22	Invitation	1.96	6	3.8
23	Geographic proximity	1.95	3	1.9
24	Complementarity locals	1.87	1	0.6
25	Reduce dependency on agents	1.84	0	0.0
26	Access natural resources	1.82	8	5.0
27	International experience	1.68	1	0.6
28	Acquire technology	1.66	1	0.6
29	Avoid barriers	1.65	2	1.3
30	Reduce dependency on suppliers	1.61	1	0.6
31	Inefficiency of agents	1.55	1	0.6
32	Inefficiency of suppliers	1.29	0	0.0
(b) Commercial firms				
1	Establish sales network	3.71	14	29.8
2	Increase group's turnover	3.38	10	21.3
3	Follow customers	3.31	3	6.4
4	Market expected growth	3.24	2	4.3
5	Economic stability	3.11	1	2.1
6	Political stability	3.07	0	0.0
7	Market diversification	2.82	2	4.3
8	Reaction to competitors	2.81	1	2.1

Table 14.4 (Continued)

Rank	*Reason*	*Mean*[1]	*Main reason*[2]	
			N	%
9	Reduce dependency on agents	2.76	1	2.1
10	Market size	2.59	2	4.3
11	Portugal's image	2.58	1	2.1
12	Competition home market	2.33	0	0.0
13	Inefficiency local agents	2.26	0	0.0
14	International experience	2.24	0	0.0
15	Quality of labour force	2.08	0	0.0
16	Geographic proximity	2.06	1	2.1
17	European Single Market	2.04	0	0.0
18	Reduction of labour costs	1.98	1	2.1
19	Quality of local cluster	1.93	0	0.0
20	Local firm on sale	1.91	4	8.5
21	Complementarity locals	1.91	1	2.1
22	Invitation	1.85	1	2.1
23	Cultural proximity	1.83	1	2.1
24	Local infrastructure	1.82	0	0.0
25	EU market	1.74	0	0.0
26	Reduce dependency on suppliers	1.72	0	0.0
27	Inefficiency of suppliers	1.63	0	0.0
28	Acquire technology	1.57	0	0.0
29	Transport costs	1.53	0	0.0
30	Public incentives	1.53	0	0.0
31	Avoid barriers	1.47	0	0.0
32	Access natural resources	1.24	0	0.0

Notes:
[1] Mean of a scale that ranged from 1 (irrelevant) to 5 (very important).
[2] Number of respondents that chose it as the 'most important reason to have invested in Portugal'.

summarizes the results. Because the differences between manufacturing and commercial firms were substantial, two separate lists were produced.

In the case of manufacturing firms (Table 14.4a), five determinants were rated well above all the others. However, the reduction of labour costs was unquestionably the top answer – it presented the highest mean in the Likert scale and was chosen as the most important reason by over one quarter of the respondents. The quality of the labour force was also among the top five determinants, but it was chosen as the main reason by only 3 per cent of the participants. It seems that the location decision was mainly a response to labour costs, the quality of the labour being relevant but secondary.

The second most important determinant in terms of the overall mean was to increase the group's turnover. It was considered the top reason by 7 per cent of the respondents. This should be no surprise. It simply translates the notion that internationalization is a special case of the growth of the firm (Buckley, 1993).

Economic and political stability were the other top determinants. Although econometric tests normally fail to find any association between stability and FDI inflows, survey-based studies tend to show political and economic stability to be at the top of managers' concerns (see Chase et al., 1988, for a survey). Tu and Schive (1995) and Akhtar (1999) used both approaches and found that political and economic stability were ranked highly by the surveyed managers *despite* not being significant determinants in parallel econometric models.

The explanation for this contradiction when different methodologies are adopted has to do with what is exactly being tested in each case. Econometric tests investigate the relationship between the magnitude of the variables. However, as we argued before (Buckley and Castro, 1998c, 1999), only when risk is very high can political and economic stability be expected to affect foreign investment. Once a certain level of stability is attained, the impact on FDI will be minimal. That is, stability is a precondition for FDI, but has little relationship with the volume of investment (Tu and Schive, 1995).

This is precisely what is suggested in Table 14.4. Despite the high mean of political and economic stability in terms of the Likert scale, very few managers considered these determinants the main reason to have invested in the Portugal. For most managers, these were highly valued characteristics of the country, probably a precondition for their decision. But other determinants were more decisive to the location choice. Interestingly, there was a group of variables in the opposite situation: their overall rating was low but they were pointed out as the main reason by a substantial number of firms. These included the existence of a local firm on sale (10 per cent), to follow customers (8 per cent), to establish a distribution network (7 per cent), and access to natural resources (5 per cent).

As for purely commercial subsidiaries (Table 14.4b), the establishment of a distribution network was, not surprisingly, the main reason to invest in Portugal. Not only was its mean well above all the others, but it was singled out as the main reason by 32 per cent of the participants. It was followed by the need to increase the group's turnover (chosen as the main reason in 23 per cent of the responses), to follow customers, and market growth. As above, economic and political stability were among the top reasons but were rarely chosen as the main reason to invest in Portugal. Another similarity with manufacturing firms was that the existence of a local firm for sale was the main determinant of investment for 9 per cent of the commercial subsidiaries. But in overall terms its influence was mild.

The determinants of inward FDI in Portugal

Despite these preliminary conclusions, the analysis of the determinants of FDI was seriously hampered by the high number of variables involved. This called for the use of data reduction techniques, such as factor analysis (Hair et al., 1998, p. 90). Factor analysis allows us to reduce the number of dimensions to be used in further tests, simplifying the investigation. Normally, it implies the loss of some information, since the new factors do not fully represent the original variables. In this case, however, the aim was not to create new variables based on the factor loadings. Factor analysis was simply a tool to investigate the way the variables were grouped by the respondents.

The number of factors to extract was a difficult choice. Two common criteria are to select the factors with an eigenvalue above unity or to base the decision on the observation of the scree plot (Hair et al., 1998). This suggested nine and eight factors, respectively. However, factor cohesion was particularly critical for this study. If they were to represent the determinants of FDI in Portugal, the factors needed to be consistent with existing theory. The representativeness of the factors extracted (total variance explained) was of secondary importance but not irrelevant. Taking all these elements into account, the decision was to extract 10 factors, which accounted for more than two-thirds of total variance. With fewer factors some individually relevant determinants were combined, making the analysis confusing. With more factors the theoretical interpretation of some of the determinants was difficult.

It turned out, however, that the behaviour of 'transport costs' had little in common with any of the factors in the analysis. It presented a low communality and dispersed factor loadings irrespective of the number of factors extracted. This does not necessarily mean that transport costs were irrelevant. Table 14.4 showed they were important for some firms, in particular in manufacturing. Nonetheless, the association with any of the factors (factor 2 in this case) was spurious and an alternative model, without transportation costs, was adopted.

Interestingly enough, this new model differed very little from the original one. The ten factors extracted were exactly the same that were obtained before, with the obvious absence of transportation costs. These factors constitute a theoretically consistent list of the determinants of foreign direct investment in Portugal (Table 14.5). They include location determinants (stability, local market, labour conditions, proximity), internalization determinants (upstream and downstream integration, market diversification) and strategy determinants (home conditions, passive expansion). However, before they could be used in a more detailed analysis, some adjustments were needed.

It was particularly interesting that public incentives were consistently associated with labour costs and skills. This suggests that public incentives have attracted to Portugal essentially efficiency-seeking FDI and will be further exploited in a later section. However, if the aim is to investigate the relevance of labour conditions as a determinant of FDI the variable public incentives cannot be associated with labour quality and costs. A similar reasoning applies to the variable 'to increase the group's turnover'. Its association with the local market is easy to understand. It is only reasonable to admit that the host country's market size and growth are important variables

Table 14.5 Factors (determinants) associated with investment in Portugal

Factor	*Variables included*	*Factor*	*Variables included*
Political and economic stability	Political stability Economic stability International image	EU market	Access to the EU market Reaction to European Single Market Need to avoid barriers
Upstream integration	Acquisition of technology Reaction to suppliers' inefficiency Access to natural resources	Labour conditions	Reduction of labour costs Quality of labour force
	Reduce dependency on suppliers Local cluster Local infrastructure	Geographic and cultural proximity	Geographic proximity Cultural proximity Invitation
Downstream integration	Reduce dependency on agents Reaction to agents' inefficiency	Passive expansion	Local firm for sale Search complementarity with locals
	Establishment distribution network Following customers	Market diversification	Market diversification Acquisition of international experience
Local market	Market growth Market size	Home conditions	Increased competition at home Reaction to competitors' move

when (market) growth is a major motivation for internationalization. But the variable cannot be part of a proxy for the importance of the local market in attracting inward FDI. Henceforth, both 'public incentives' and 'to increase the group turnover' were excluded from the analysis that follows (the tables associated with this new model can be found in Appendix B).

The importance of the new determinants was assessed by computing the mean of the respective variables (cf. Table 14.4). Like the original ones, these new variables had a minimum of 1 (when all the variables of the determinant had received the lowest rating in the Likert scale) and a maximum of 5 (when all received the top rating). Table 14.6 presents the ranking of the ten determinants. The respective means can be found inside brackets in the first line.

As was already mentioned in the preliminary analysis, there were marked differences between commercial and manufacturing firms. For the former, downstream integration – the internalization of the sales function (Buckley and Casson, 1976) – was the main motivation. It was followed by access to

Table 14.6 Rank of the determinants of investment in Portugal: all firms and per industry

Determinants of FDI industry	*Labour conditions*	*Stability*	*Compe-tition*	*Local market*	*Down-stream*	*Market diversification*	*Passive expansion*	*EU market*	*Proxi-mity*	*Up-stream*
All firms	*1*	*2*	*3*	*4*	*5*	*6*	*7*	*8*	*9*	*10*
	*(2.87)**	*(2.81)*	*(2.54)*	*(2.39)*	*(2.25)*	*(2.05)*	*(1.95)*	*(1.90)*	*(1.88)*	*(1.72)*
Food, beverages (20)	1	4	7	2	3	6	5	10	9	8
Textiles, clothing, footwear (20)	1	2	3	5	10	9	8	4	7	6
Natural resources (19)	3	2	1	4	5	6	8	10	7	9
Chemicals and oil (23)	4	1	2	3	5	7	6	8	10	9
Metal industries (17)	1	3	2	4	7	9	5	8	6	10
Machinery/ equipment (42)	1	2	3	5	9	6	8	4	7	10
All manufacturing (141)	1	2	3	4	5	7	6	8	9	10
Commerce (39)	7	3	4	2	1	5	8	9	6	10

Notes: *Figures in parentheses are the mean of a scale that ranged from 1 (irrelevant) to 5 (very important).

the local market, economic and political stability, and the competitive conditions at home. Market diversification was also relatively important for purely commercial subsidiaries.

As for manufacturing FDI, labour conditions and economic and political stability were clearly the dominant determinants. Competition in the home country, access to the local market, and downstream integration were next in importance. This combination of determinants confirms the duality of motivations (efficiency seeking and market seeking). The differences between industries, however, were more important than is apparent in Table 14.6. The analysis of the determinants' mean for each industry presents a clearer picture. Table 14.7 shows that labour conditions and stability were even more important for textiles, clothing and footwear, and for machinery and equipment (the most export-oriented industries) than for the other industries in the sample. Access to the EU market was also above average in these industries, being in both cases the fourth most important determinant. The local market, on the other hand, was much less important in these industries than in any other group of firms, and downstream integration was completely irrelevant.

There was, nevertheless, an important difference between the two groups of firms. In the case of machinery and equipment, labour and stability can almost be considered the only relevant determinants. There was a very big difference for the next two determinants (competition and EU market). In textiles, clothing and footwear, however, competition was only slightly less important than stability, well above the EU market. In both cases we are in the presence of efficiency-seeking FDI. But the 'push' factors seemed to be very different. The competitive conditions in the home country were critical in the decision of textiles, clothing and footwear producers to invest in Portugal, a politically and economically stable low cost location that is part of the European Union. Machinery and equipment manufacturing are more global industries in which the competitive conditions are at a different level.

Naturally, this analysis at the industry level hides differences in terms of the strategies of individual firms. These differences are due to firm-specific characteristics, but also to the fact that the industries are not completely homogeneous. Figure 14.7 shows very clearly that most firms in textiles, clothing and footwear and in machinery and equipment fell in the fourth quadrant. This corresponds to an above average rating of the labour conditions and a below average rating of the importance of local market. In other words, their investment can be classified as efficiency seeking.

When local market was replaced with downstream integration (Figure 14.8), however, almost all firms in these export-oriented industries fell in quadrant 4. This suggests that the location determinants were more important than internalization. Even when the local market was an important determinant of FDI, to internalize the sales function was not a priority. As for the presence of firms from other industries in quadrant 4 of Figure 14.7, it

Table 14.7 The determinants of investment in Portugal per industry: mean values

Determinants of FDI	*Labour conditions*	*Stability*	*Compe-tition*	*Local market*	*Down-stream*	*Market diversification*	*Passive expansion*	*EU market*	*Proxi-mity*	*Up-stream*
Food, beverages	3.1	2.3	2.2	2.5	2.4	2.3	2.3	2.0	2.0	2.1
Textiles, clothing, footwear	3.9	3.0	2.9	1.9	1.5	1.6	1.6	2.1	1.7	1.8
Natural resources	2.4	2.7	2.8	2.3	2.3	2.3	2.1	1.7	2.2	1.8
Chemicals and oil	2.8	2.9	2.8	2.8	2.5	2.2	2.2	1.9	1.7	1.8
Metal industries	3.0	2.5	2.6	2.4	1.9	1.4	2.2	1.7	2.0	1.3
Machinery/ equipment	3.5	3.0	2.2	1.9	1.7	1.9	1.8	2.1	1.8	1.7
All manufacturing	3.2	2.8	2.5	2.3	2.0	1.9	2.0	1.9	1.9	1.8
Commerce	1.8	2.9	2.5	2.9	3.1	2.4	1.8	1.8	1.8	1.6

Note: Mean of a scale that ranged from 1 (irrelevant) to 5 (very important).

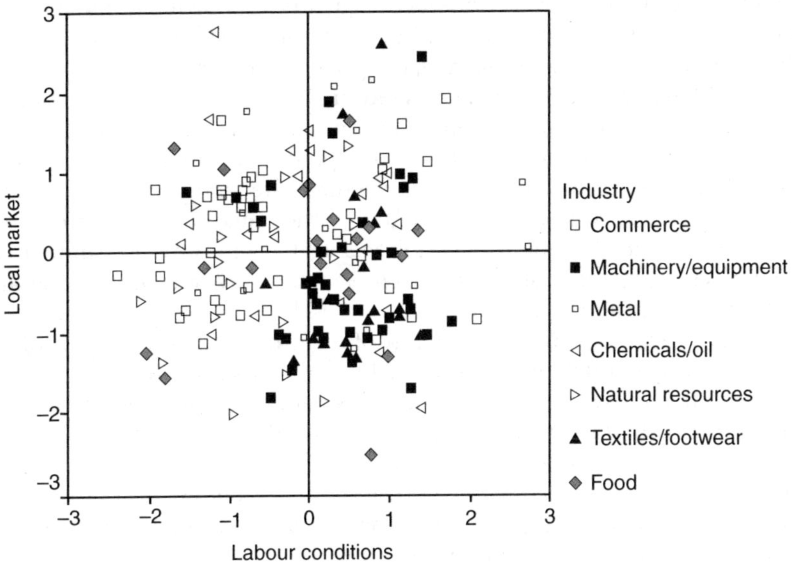

Figure 14.7 Labour conditions versus local market

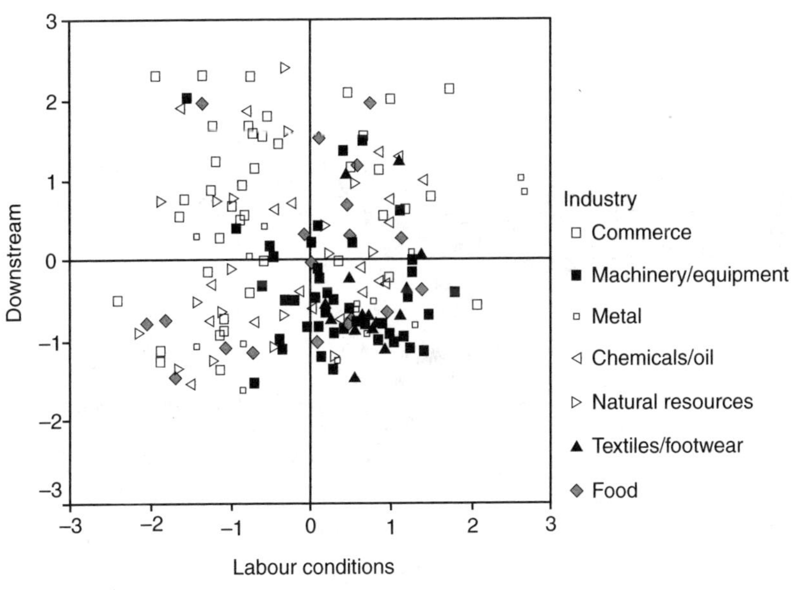

Figure 14.8 Labour conditions versus downstream

conveys that there are export-oriented segments (or individual strategies) in all industries. As an example, all firms in the oil and chemicals group in these conditions were manufacturers of plastic products.

The differences between textiles, clothing and footwear, and machinery and equipment were mentioned above and are illustrated in Figure 14.9. Almost all textiles, clothing and footwear producers appear in quadrant 2. Most machinery and equipment manufacturers are represented in quadrant 4. The difference corresponds to the role of the home country competitive conditions in the decision to invest in Portugal. Figure 14.9 also shows that textiles, clothing and footwear represent a much more homogeneous group than machinery and equipment.

The comparison of the determinants of investment in Portugal according to the country of origin is presented in Table 14.8. As could be expected, the biggest differences were found in the assessment of cultural and geographic proximity. This was the second most important determinant for Spanish firms, only behind the conditions in the local market. It was also relevant for French and Italian firms (included in 'other EU12'), but irrelevant for all the others.[5] Also very much predictable was that access to the EU market was more important for firms from outside the Union.

According to Table 14.8, Spanish firms were essentially market seekers. This was the only source country for which local market was the main determinant. Labour conditions, on the other hand, were of relatively little importance. As

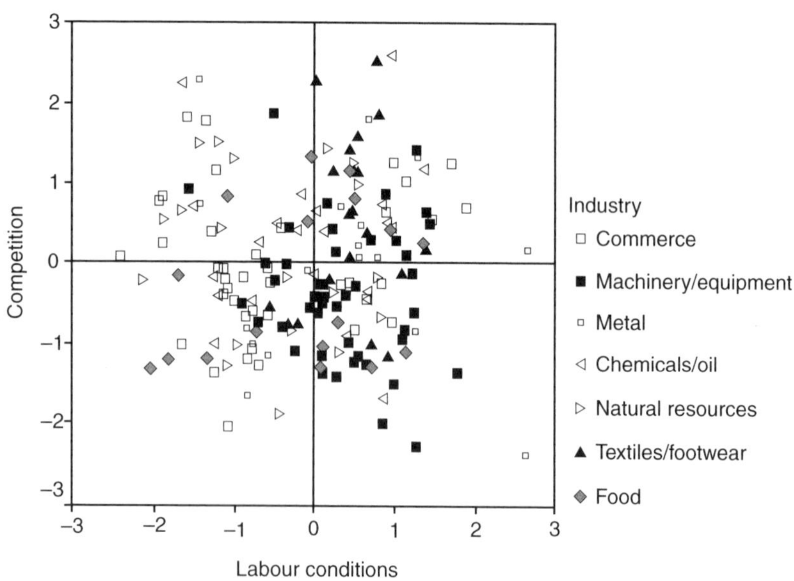

Figure 14.9 Labour conditions versus competition

Table 14.8 Rank of the determinants of investment in Portugal per country of origin

Determinants of FDI country	*Labour conditions*	*Stability*	*Compe-tition*	*Local market*	*Down-stream*	*Market diversification*	*Passive expansion*	*EU market*	*Proxi-mity*	*Up-stream*
All firms	*1*	*2*	*3*	*4*	*5*	*6*	*7*	*8*	*9*	*10*
Spain (21)	6	4	3	1	5	7	8	10	2	9
France (24)	3	1	2	5	6	8	7	10	4	9
Germany (48)	1	2	3	5	4	6	8	7	10	9
UK (16)	2 =	2 =	5	4	1	6	8	10	9	8
Other EU12 (19)	1	2	6	5	9	7	4	8	3	10
Other Europe (21)	1	3	2	4	7	8	5	6	10	9
Rest of the world (31)	2	1	3	4	6	8	8	5	10	9

for UK investors, they differed from the rest of the sample in the role of downstream integration. The UK was until 1974 the main trading partner of Portugal. This position is now less relevant, but the results obtained seem to translate a deeper involvement of British firms in Portugal, which over the years may have internalized their operations, replacing exports with FDI.

It should be noted, however, that the groups obtained using the firms' country of origin were very heterogeneous in terms of their motivations. Much more so than in the case of industries. That probably explains why so few differences were found in Table 14.8. The only determinants that seem to be country specific are those with geopolitical connections: proximity and access to the EU market.

Not many differences in the determinants of FDI can be attributed to the size of the subsidiaries (Table 14.9). In fact, the differences found reflect no more than different market orientations (Figure 14.10). Smaller firms (fewer than 50 employees) were particularly concerned with the conditions in the local market and with the sales function (downstream integration). For bigger firms the main determinant of FDI in Portugal was labour conditions. Rather interestingly, the importance of the local market and downstream integration decreased linearly with the size of the firm, while labour conditions registered a linear increase with size (all statistically significant at 10 per cent).

The differences in the determinants of FDI that could be associated with the year of investment were particularly interesting. Table 14.10 suggests that two periods in Portugal's recent history saw efficiency seeking being replaced by market seeking as the main motivation of inward FDI in Portugal. The first was the decade that followed the 1974 revolution, which also corresponds to a major economic crisis worldwide. The second was the period after 1995, which somehow seems to consolidate the trend of the first half of the 1990s. The latter is particularly worrying. It confirms that the recent decrease of inward FDI in Portugal (see first section) affected in particular efficiency-seeking FDI. This is further confirmed by the decreasing importance of competition as a determinant of FDI. Foreign investors seem to be searching in other locations the solution for stronger competition in the domestic market.

At face value, this trend is not necessarily negative for the Portuguese economy. Economic development and the resulting higher production costs tend to reduce countries' ability to attract these footloose investments. However, this evolution should translate into a growing importance of internalization variables over localization (Dunning, 1981). In terms of the determinants identified here, that would mean a growing importance of downstream and upstream integration, which was not the case.

Alternative locations

The decision to invest in a foreign country should normally involve the consideration of alternative locations. In the sample, however, only 42 per cent

Table 14.9 Rank of the determinants of investment in Portugal for firms of different sizes

Determinants of FDI labour force	*Labour conditions*	*Stability*	*Compe-tition*	*Local market*	*Down-stream*	*Market diversification*	*Passive expansion*	*EU market*	*Proxi-mity*	*Up-stream*
All firms	*1*	*2*	*3*	*4*	*5*	*6*	*7*	*8*	*9*	*10*
Less than 20 (31)	9	3	4	2	1	5	8	7	6	10
21 to 50 (28)	5	2	1	3	4	6	7	9	10	8
51 to 100 (30)	1	2	3	4	7	10	6	5	9	8
101 to 200 (34)	1	2	3	4	6	5	7	9	8	10
201 to 500 (32)	1	2	3	4	7	5	6	9	8	10
More than 500 (25)	1	2	3	5	10	6	7	4	8	9

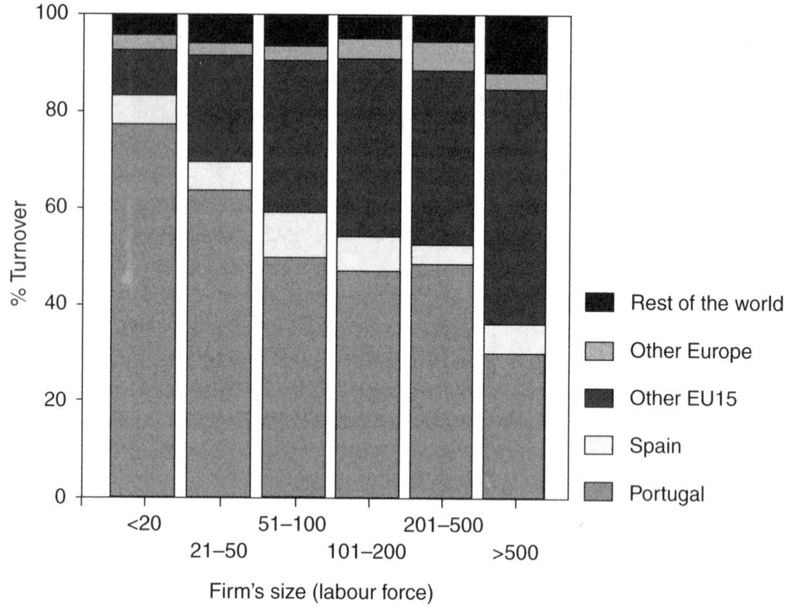

Figure 14.10 Market distribution versus firm's size

of the respondents (88 firms) claimed to have analysed other locations before investing in Portugal. Most of these, however, considered more than one alternative. Eastern Europe and Spain were the most common alternatives considered (46 and 44 firms, respectively), followed by the most developed EU members (considered by 40 of the respondents). Ireland and Greece were a hypothesis for a much smaller number firms (Table 14.11).

In general, the European locations were positively correlated, which suggests they were frequently considered simultaneously. The exception was the correlation coefficient (Spearman's rho) between Spain and Eastern Europe, which was negative and statistically significant at 10 per cent. That is, Spain and Eastern Europe did not seem to be, in general, alternatives to each other. Finally, non-European locations were positively correlated with Eastern Europe and negatively with Spain. But the level of statistical significance of these relationships was rather low, impeding further speculation.

The differences in the ranking of the determinants of FDI between firms that considered alternative locations and those that only considered Portugal for their investment were less marked than anticipated (Table 14.12). Nevertheless, labour conditions and EU market were much more important for firms that considered alternative locations than for those that did not. The opposite was true for local market and downstream integration. This

Table 14.10 Rank of the determinants of investment in Portugal per year of first investment

Determinants of FDI year of investment	*Labour conditions*	*Stability*	*Compe-tition*	*Local market*	*Down-stream*	*Market diversification*	*Passive expansion*	*EU market*	*Proxi-mity*	*Up-stream*
All firms	*1*	*2*	*3*	*4*	*5*	*6*	*7*	*8*	*9*	*10*
Before 1960 (11)	3	1	2	5	4	9	7	10	6	8
1960 to 1974 (25)	1	2	3	4	6	5	7	8	9	10
1975 to 1985 (15)	4	1	3	2	5	6	10	8	7	9
1986 to 1990 (58)	1	2	3	4	5 =	7	5 =	8	9	10
1991 to 1995 (51)	2	1	4	3	5	6	7	8	9	10
After 1995 (20)	4	1	5	2	3	7	10	8	6	9

Table 14.11 Alternative locations

		Strong alternative	*Considered*	*Total*
Eastern Europe	no.	33	13	46
	%	72	28	100
Spain	no.	35	9	44
	%	80	20	100
Ireland	no.	10	8	18
	%	56	44	100
Greece	no.	6	9	15
	%	40	60	100
Other EU	no.	24	15	39
	%	62	38	100
Other locations	no.	13	12	25
	%	52	48	100

suggests that efficiency-seeking investment was more common among firms that considered alternative locations, and market-seeking among those that did not. But the two types of investment coexisted in both groups.

Equally surprising was that only small differences were found in the determinants associated with firms that considered Spain as the alternative location and those that considered Eastern Europe (Table 14.12). The suspicion was that efficiency-seeking investment should be more common when Eastern Europe was the main alternative, and market-seeking investment dominant when the main alternative was Spain. However, the evidence to support this was weak. Firms that considered Eastern Europe the main alternative location did rate labour conditions higher and local market and downstream integration lower than those that considered Spain. But this is far from conclusive evidence.

Public incentives and the role of the government

It was seen above that, as a determinant of FDI, public incentives were consistently associated with labour costs and skills. This was interpreted as evidence that they have attracted essentially efficiency-seeking FDI – projects that exploited the relatively low Portuguese labour costs but reasonable labour skills. This idea was reinforced by the fact that public incentives were especially valued as a determinant of investment by the export-oriented industries: textiles, clothing and footwear, and machinery and equipment. In the sectors most oriented towards the local market, on the other hand (commerce and chemicals and oil), public incentives were completely irrelevant. Furthermore, there was a linear positive relationship (statistically significant at 1 per cent) between the importance of public incentives and

Table 14.12 Rank of the determinants of investment in Portugal

Determinants of FDI	*Labour conditions*	*Stability*	*Compe-tition*	*Local market*	*Down-stream*	*Market diversification*	*Passive expansion*	*EU market*	*Proxi-mity*	*Up-stream*
No alternative location considered	2 (2.58)	1 (2.76)	4 (2.51)	3 (2.54)	9 (1.74)	6 (2.14)	5 (2.50)	7 (2.00)	8 (1.96)	10 (1.71)
Alternative location considered	1 (3.36)	2 (2.93)	3 (2.61)	4= (2.21)	4= (2.21)	6 (1.99)	7 (1.96)	8 (1.92)	9 (1.76)	10 (1.75)
Spain considered	1 (3.04)	2 (3.02)	4 (2.51)	3 (2.53)	5 (2.21)	7 (2.14)	6 (2.19)	8 (2.06)	9 (1.74)	10 (1.72)
Eastern Europe considered	1 (3.61)	2 (3.16)	3 (2.83)	5 (2.29)	4 (2.39)	6 (2.22)	9 (1.84)	7 (2.11)	10 (1.69)	8 (1.92)

Note: Figures in parentheses are the mean of a scale that ranged from 1 (irrelevant) to 5 (very important).

firm size (no statistically significant differences were found when the firms were grouped by country of origin or year of investment).

These characteristics reflect very much the public policies towards FDI, particularly concerned with attracting big industrial projects with a stronger impact on employment and on public opinion. The official website of ICEP, the institution responsible for promoting Portugal as a location of FDI, is very clear about what Portugal can offer to foreign investors. 'Imagine a country with the lowest labour costs in Europe (...). Add to this a stable political environment (...) and low criminality' (ICEP, 2000).

As many as 38 per cent of the manufacturing firms in the sample that accepted examining this topic in more detail reported having received public incentives in their investment in Portugal. The figure was especially high in machinery and equipment, where 55 per cent of the subsidiaries received some sort of public support. On the other hand, in the natural resources-based industries only one in five firms were supported by the local authorities (Figure 14.11). Since foreign investment qualifies for support from the European Union's structural funds, the especial incidence of public support in the most recently created firms should be expected (Figure 14.12).

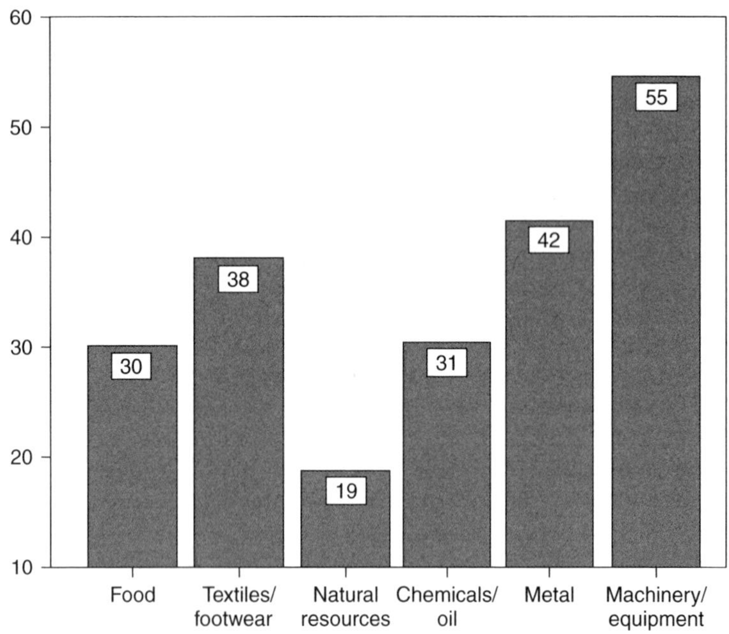

Figure 14.11 Percentage of firms that received public incentives, per industry

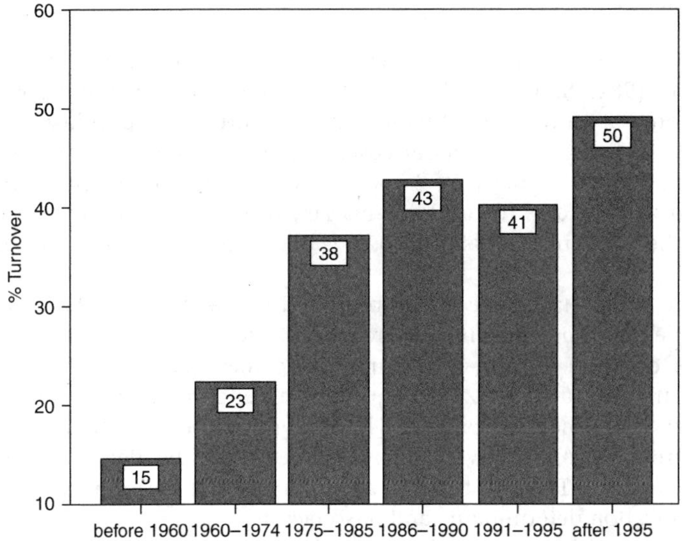

Figure 14.12 Percentage of firms that received public incentives, per year of investment

Despite the number of projects that received public support, only 11 per cent of the respondents claimed that without public incentives they would have not invested in Portugal; 54 per cent would have invested less than they did, but in 35 per cent of the cases public support was no more than a bonus for the investors: they claimed that the investment would have been exactly the same even without public incentives. Government intervention was, however, more important than these figures suggest. At least that is the inference that can be made from the opinion of the biggest firms (with more than 500 employees). One-third would not have invested in Portugal without incentives, and a further half would have invested but on a smaller scale.

The need for government intervention was, nevertheless, felt much more strongly at a different level. When asked about the main problems faced in Portugal, the managers that participated in the survey gave especial emphasis to bureaucracy and the legal system and to a shortage of skilled workers.[6] Both problems correspond to institutional failures. The failure to promote an efficient legal environment, and the failure to create advanced assets that may compensate for rising production costs. Successive governments seemed to have been aware of these difficulties. Investment in education and vocational training increased substantially in the last two decades, supported by the European Union structural funds. However, the dramatic fall of inward FDI in recent years suggests that not enough has yet been done.

Conclusion

Previous work on the determinants of FDI in Portugal (Matos, 1973; Taveira, 1984; Simões, 1985; Buckley and Castro, 1998b) suggested a dichotomy of motivations. Investment in export-oriented industries aimed to exploit Portugal's low labour costs and privileged access to some of the most developed markets in Europe. However, the dominant motivation seemed to be access to the local market; when aggregated data was analysed the relevance of labour costs was eclipsed by market-related variables.

Past research has, however, been limited by the poor quality of the data available and the deficient disaggregation in terms of industries and countries of origin. This firm level study overcomes that problem by using a questionnaire survey of 237 manufacturing and commercial foreign subsidiaries established in Portugal. The respondents' evaluation of a number of potential reasons to invest in Portugal permitted the identification of ten determinants of FDI, a list that is a combination of location variables with internalization determinants and push factors.

The dominant motivations were, for the manufacturing industries, labour costs and skills, political and economic stability, competition in the home country, and access to the local market. However, the determinants associated with the most export-oriented industries (textiles, clothing and footwear, and machinery and equipment) were substantially distinct from the others. Firms in these industries saw Portugal as a stable low cost location with easy access to the EU markets. Nonetheless, it was possible to confirm Simões's (1985) distinction between 'traditional' and 'modern' labour intensive industries. The former were especially sensitive to the competitive conditions in the home country, while the latter were more responsive to the global competitive conditions.

In the remaining manufacturing industries and in commerce market access was the dominant motivation. However, in all the manufacturing industries there seemed to be export-oriented segments (e.g. fabricated plastic goods in the chemicals and oil industries) or at least strategies of individual firms. An attempt to aggregate the subjects using cluster analysis produced fairly poor results. The clusters showed little homogeneity in terms of the industries represented in each cluster, which certainly constitutes an interesting element to be exploited in future research.

The country of origin of the investing firm was much less relevant than the industry in the definition of the determinants of FDI. Geographic and cultural proximity was, expectedly, the only determinant clearly country-related. The surprise was probably that proximity seemed to induce market-seeking investment, rather than efficiency-seeking FDI. However, the explanation may lay simply in the fact that the countries more engaged in the latter, notably Germany, Switzerland, the Nordic countries, are all rather 'distant' from Portugal.

Eastern Europe and Spain were, according to the participants in the study, the locations more likely to compete for foreign investments with Portugal. The two seemed to compete for different projects, but the evidence was not clear in terms of the expected differences despite hints that Spain was more commonly a competing location when market access was the main motivation, while Eastern Europe was more often considered in the case of efficiency-seeking FDI. The fact that the investigation did not cover firms that did not choose Portugal restricted the analysis.

Finally, the bigger firms in the sample considered that public incentives were of uttermost importance for their decision to invest in Portugal. Among smaller firms, however, the opinion was that incentives had little impact upon the investment decision. There was, nevertheless, a generalized concern with the difficulties created by bureaucracy and the unavailability of skilled workers. The sharp fall of inward FDI in Portugal in the past decade suggests that not enough has been done to overcome these problems.

Notes

1. This research was partially financed by Programa Parxis XXI, Fundação para a Ciência e Tecnologia.
2. The full questionnaire is available from the authors on request. For their suggestions in the elaboration of the questionnaire, we are indebted to a number of people: Vitor Corado Simões (ISEG, Universidade Técnica de Lisboa), Vasco Rodrigues and Leonor Sopas (Universidade Católica do Porto) and Ana Teresa Tavares (University of Reading and Faculdade de Economia do Porto). The formats were supplied by Madalena Araújo (Universidade Católica do Porto).
3. Many of these firms had ceased operations in Portugal. Others had merged or changed their name, and had been contacted twice. In others the foreign participation had been sold to Portuguese investors.
4. Of the 257 questionnaires received, 19 could not be used, either for not being correctly filled in or because they corresponded to firms that, contrary to the information previously available, did not meet all the criteria for sample selection. One questionnaire was excluded during the data analysis because several of the answers were strongly inconsistent.
5. Brazilian companies also ranked this determinant very high, but they were too few to exert a significant influence over their group's mean.
6. This is particularly ironic since ICEP (2000) publicizes Portugal as 'a flexible economy with little bureaucracy and low taxes'.

Appendix A Foreign firms' questionnaire

Table 14A.1 Sample of the questionnaire (page 3)

1. REASONS TO INVEST IN PORTUGAL: What was the influence of each of the following elements in the decision to invest in Portugal [1 – *irrelevant*... 5 – *very important*]?

1. Size of the Portuguese market	1	2	3	4	5
2. Expected growth of the Portuguese market	1	2	3	4	5
3. To increase the Group's turnover	1	2	3	4	5
4. To establish/acquire your own distribution network	1	2	3	4	5
5. Follow-up of customers in their entry into the Portuguese market	1	2	3	4	5
6. Reaction to competitors' move	1	2	3	4	5
7. Increased competition in the home market	1	2	3	4	5
8. Need to reduce dependency on sales agents	1	2	3	4	5
9. Need to reduce dependency on suppliers	1	2	3	4	5
10. Reaction to the inefficiency of sales agents	1	2	3	4	5
11. Reaction to suppliers' inefficiency	1	2	3	4	5
12. Need to reduce risk through market diversification	1	2	3	4	5
13. Reduction of labour costs	1	2	3	4	5
14. Quality of labour force	1	2	3	4	5
15. Transportation costs	1	2	3	4	5
16. Access to natural resources	1	2	3	4	5
17. Need to avoid tariff or non-tariff barriers	1	2	3	4	5
18. Quality of local infrastructure	1	2	3	4	5
19. Quality/density of the Portuguese *cluster* relevant to the firm	1	2	3	4	5
20. Acquisition of technology/ catch up with technological developments	1	2	3	4	5
21. Search for complementarity with local partners	1	2	3	4	5
22. Acquisition of international experience	1	2	3	4	5
23. Good opportunity to buy local firm	1	2	3	4	5
24. Invitation/suggestion of Portuguese individual or firm	1	2	3	4	5
25. Easier access to the European Union market	1	2	3	4	5
26. Reaction to the new conditions set by the European Single Market	1	2	3	4	5
27. Public incentives to foreign investment in Portugal	1	2	3	4	5
28. Cultural proximity between Portugal and the home country	1	2	3	4	5
29. Geographical proximity between Portugal and the home country	1	2	3	4	5
30. Economic stability in Portugal	1	2	3	4	5
31. Political stability in Portugal	1	2	3	4	5
32. International image of Portugal	1	2	3	4	5
33. Other	1	2	3	4	5

- Which of the previous elements would you single out as the most important? ☐☐

2. DID THE FIRM CONSIDER ALTERNATIVE LOCATIONS BEFORE INVESTING IN PORTUGAL?

No☐	Yes☐	1.	Spain	1	2	3
		2.	Ireland	1	2	3
		3.	Greece	1	2	3
		4.	Other European Union countries	1	2	3
		5.	Eastern European countries	1	2	3
		6.	Other	1	2	3

[1 – *not considered*; 2 – *considered*; 3 – *strong alternative*]

Appendix B The determinants of FDI

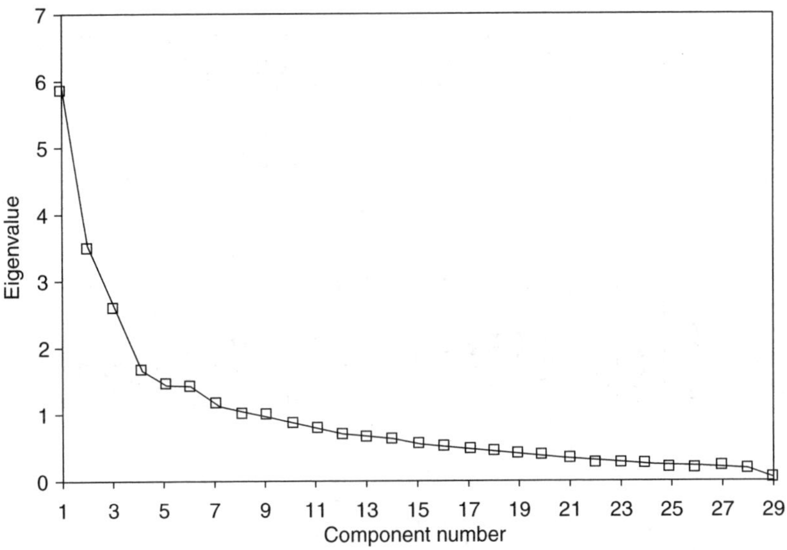

Figure 14B.1 Scree plot

Table 14B.1 Factors' loadings, rotated component matrix

	Component									
	1	*2*	*3*	*4*	*5*	*6*	*7*	*8*	*9*	*10*
Political stability	**0.904**	−0.014	0.001	0.084	0.071	0.052	0.160	0.083	0.075	0.044
Economic stability	**0.885**	−0.015	−0.007	0.103	0.079	0.163	0.159	0.080	0.065	0.043
International image	**0.791**	0.119	0.127	−0.014	0.073	0.203	−0.063	0.153	−0.040	0.128
Acquiring technology	0.050	**0.722**	0.036	0.159	0.013	0.071	0.081	0.132	0.086	0.227
Access natural resources	−0.117	**0.662**	0.052	−0.204	0.099	0.225	0.128	−0.091	0.155	−0.085
Inefficiency of suppliers	−0.003	**0.652**	0.261	0.010	0.076	−0.082	0.331	0.200	0.155	−0.037
Local cluster	0.326	**0.633**	0.011	0.252	0.183	−0.073	−0.231	−0.129	0.063	0.056
Local infrastructure	0.461	**0.553**	−0.111	0.057	0.196	0.008	−0.122	0.153	0.027	0.175
Reduce dependency on suppliers	−0.126	**0.546**	0.314	−0.044	0.080	−0.094	0.398	0.344	0.046	0.116
Reduce dependency on agents	0.015	0.176	**0.841**	0.015	0.078	−0.073	0.066	−0.100	−0.039	0.127
Inefficiency of agents	−0.005	0.178	**0.779**	0.056	0.049	0.023	0.039	−0.055	0.096	0.095
Establish network	0.056	−0.047	**0.698**	0.301	−0.020	0.162	0.093	−0.180	−0.032	0.035
Follow customers	0.058	−0.180	**0.594**	0.466	−0.067	−0.048	0.144	0.000	0.083	−0.046
Market growth	0.122	0.067	0.166	**0.831**	−0.007	0.110	0.055	−0.128	0.042	0.043
Market size	0.027	0.099	0.170	**0.825**	0.039	−0.004	0.055	−0.143	0.036	0.122
EU market	0.043	0.089	−0.032	0.015	**0.822**	0.061	0.128	0.106	−0.001	0.028
ESM	0.209	0.128	0.168	0.041	**0.703**	0.270	−0.126	0.202	0.166	0.047
Avoid barriers	0.111	0.178	0.010	−0.067	**0.612**	−0.205	0.376	−0.060	0.192	0.059
Geographic proximity	0.187	0.042	0.109	0.018	−0.006	**0.874**	−0.013	0.002	0.005	0.075

Cultural proximity	0.168	0.049	–0.088	0.076	0.121	**0.786**	0.207	0.018	0.092	0.037
Market diversification	0.282	0.094	0.216	0.098	0.031	0.089	**0.673**	–0.108	–0.067	0.095
International experience	0.010	0.116	0.045	0.104	0.248	0.210	**0.630**	0.028	0.178	0.233
Reduction of labour costs	0.113	0.064	–0.235	–0.229	0.064	0.016	–0.059	**0.835**	–0.056	0.073
Quality of labour	0.347	0.170	–0.128	–0.108	0.198	0.025	0.016	**0.727**	0.016	0.121
Invitation	0.088	0.011	0.062	0.089	0.337	–0.024	0.122	–0.044	**0.754**	–0.040
Local firm for sale	0.024	0.200	–0.030	–0.073	–0.111	0.064	–0.132	–0.050	**0.701**	0.246
Complementarity locals	–0.010	0.331	0.091	0.211	0.139	0.152	0.325	0.119	**0.588**	–0.132
Competition at home	0.091	0.095	0.038	0.014	0.110	0.153	0.137	0.087	–0.060	**0.818**
Reaction to competitors	0.146	0.088	0.223	0.162	–0.024	–0.054	0.099	0.077	0.200	**0.694**

Note: Rotation method: Varimax with Kaiser normalization; rotation converged in 14 iterations.

References

Akhtar, M. Hanif (1999) 'Foreign Direct Investment in Pakistan,' unpublished PhD thesis, University of Leeds.

Banco de Portugal (various years) *Relatório e Contas*. Lisbon: Banco de Portugal.

Banco de Portugal (1997a) *Séries Longas para a Economia Portuguesa – Pós II Guerra Mundial*. Vol. I: *Séries Estatísticas*. Lisbon: Banco de Portugal.

Banco de Portugal (1997b) *Boletim Estatístico*, March. Lisbon: Banco de Portugal.

Banco de Portugal (2000a) *Boletim Estatístico*, January. Lisbon: Banco de Portugal.

Buckley, Peter J. (1993) 'Barriers to Internationalization'. In L. Zan, S. Zambon and A. Pettigrew (eds), *Perspectives on Strategic Change*. Dordrecht: Kluwer Academic Publishers); reprinted in Peter J. Buckley (1995) *Foreign Direct Investment and Multinational Enterprises*. London: Macmillan, pp. 17–37.

Buckley, P. J. and Casson M. (1976) *The Future of the Multinational Enterprise*. London: Macmillan.

Buckley, Peter J. and Castro, Francisco B. (1998a) 'The Investment Development Path: the Case of Portugal'. *Transnational Corporations*, vol. 7, no. 1, pp. 1–15.

Buckley, Peter J. and Castro, Francisco B. (1998b) 'A Time-series Analysis of the Locational Determinants of FDI in Portugal'. Paper presented at the 25th Annual Conference of the Academy of International Business, Vienna, October.

Buckley, Peter J. and Castro, Francisco B. (1998c) 'The Locational Determinants of FDI in the European Periphery'. Paper presented at the 24th Annual Conference of the European International Business Academy, Jerusalem, December.

Buckley, Peter J. and Castro, Francisco B. (1999) 'Outward FDI in Manufacturing from Portugal: Internationalisation Strategies from a New Foreign Investor'. Paper presented at the 25th Annual Conference of the European International Business Academy, Manchester, UK, December.

Câmara de Comércio e Indústria Luso-Alemã (1996) *Empresas Alemãs em Portugal*. Lisbon: 16 Mass.

Chase, D. Carmen, Kuhle, L. James and Walther, Carl H. (1988) 'The Relevance of Political Risk in Direct Foreign Investment'. *Management International Review*, vol. 28, no. 3, pp. 31–8.

Dunning, H. John (1981) 'Explaining the International Direct Investment Position of Countries: towards a Dynamic and Development Approach'. *Weltwirtschaftliches Archiv*, vol. 117, pp. 30–64.

Fontoura, Maria Paula (1995) 'O Efeito do IDE na Composição das Exportações da Indústria Transformadora Portuguesa'. *Estudos de Economia*, vol. 15, no. 2, pp. 123–41.

Hair, F., Joseph Jr, E. Anderson, Rolph, Tatham, Ronald L. and Black, William C. (1998) *Multivariate Data Analysis*, 5th edn. Englewood Cliffs: Prentice-Hall International.

ICEP (2000) 'Investir em Portugal'. *Investimento Internacional*, http://www.icep.pt/portuagal/investimento.asp [15 March 2000].

Matos, Luís Salgado de (1973) *Investimentos Estrangeiros em Portugal*. Lisbon: Seara Nova.

Morais, H. (1993) 'Determinantes do investimento Directo Estrangeiro em Portugal: 1987–1992'. Unpublished Master's dissertation, ISEG.

OECD (1997) *International Direct Investment Statistics Yearbook*. Paris: OECD.

Santos, José de Freitas (1997) 'Localização da Empresa Estrangeira em Portugal (1990/94): Uma abordagem relacional'. Unpublished PhD thesis, Universidade do Minho.

Simões, Vitor Corado (1985) 'Portugal'. In John H. Dunning (ed.), *Multinational Enterprises, Economic Structure and International Competitiveness*. New York: Wiley.

Simões, Vitor Corado (1989) *German Direct Investment in Portugal: Report on the Empirical Study*. Lisbon: Instituto de Estudos para o Desenvolvimento.

Taveira, Elisa Ferreira (1984) 'Foreign Direct Investment in Portugal'. Unpublished PhD thesis, University of Reading.

Tu, Jenn-Hwa and Schive, Chi (1995) 'Determinants of Foreign Direct Investment in Taiwan Province of China: a New Approach and Findings'. *Transnational Corporations*, vol. 4, pp. 93–103.

Index

absorptive capacity
China, 3, 202, 215, 216
economic growth, 223
knowledge, 151, 202
spillovers, 202
adaptation
benefits, 133, 164, 191
local markets, 170
technology, 152
transaction costs, 104
adjustment costs, 23–4, 136
agency costs, 10
agents, 23–4
aggregation
e-commerce, 126, 127
levels, 38, 40–1
agriculture, 86
Aharoni, Yair, 9, 11
application strategies, 172, 173, 174
Asia
competition, 125
crisis, 90, 94, 96, 141
South-East, *see* South-East Asia
assets
developing countries, 90
investment, *see* foreign direct investment; investment
known value in use, 63, 65
monetary, 56, 57
options, 55, 56, 57
prices, 63–4, 65, 90
tradability, 56, 57, 58, 63–4, 80
Australia, 84

Bain, J. S., 9
banking, 92
bargaining power, 86, 88–91
Bartlett, Christopher A., 11
beliefs, 73–4, 170, 171, 173
Birkinshaw, J., 152, 153
Boersma, Margreet F., 2, 101–21
Bretton Woods system, 130
Buckley, Peter J., 10, 11, 12, 20, 25, 57, 67, 73, 75, 87, 88, 90, 91, 92, 96, 101, 103, 104, 119, 120, 128, 131, 146, 147, 149, 153, 156, 167, 168, 171, 189, 190, 191, 193, 196, 221, 243, 250, 256, 257, 265, 267, 282

call options, 55, 59, 64, 77, 78, 79
Canada–United States Free Trade Agreement (CUSFTA), 189, 190, 192, 194, 195, 196
capabilities
core rigidities, 173
knowledge, 171–2
licensing, 161–3
states, 94, 95
capital
accumulation, 222, 248
deepening, 222
elasticity, 224
human, *see* human capital
loss, 60
Carter, Martin J., 2, 96, 145–65, 149, 156, 167–83, 220–40
case studies
knowledge management, 146, 153, 156–63, 174–80
strategic management, 19
trust, 107–11
Casson, Mark, 1, 10, 11, 19–51, 54–81, 87, 90, 92, 101, 103, 104, 119, 120, 128, 131, 146, 147, 153, 168, 191, 267
Castro, Francisco B., 3, 256–87
Caves, Richard E., 9
Chandler, Alfred, 9, 84
chaos, 21
cheating, 102, 104, 137
China
collectively owned enterprises (COEs), 202, 203, 213, 215
country studies, 13
economic growth, 140, 220–40
R&D, 203, 212, 213, 214, 233
regional differences, 220–40

state-owned enterprises (SOEs), 202, 203, 213, 215, 216
WTO membership, 87, 140, 216
Chinese inward investment
absorptive capacity, 3, 202, 215, 216
economic growth, 220–40
empirical results, 227–36
footloose FDI, 140, 141
geographical distribution, 220, 221
incentives, 200
model and data, 224–7
non-Chinese (NC), 199–203, 212–13
Open Door Policy, 220
overseas Chinese (OC), 199–203, 212–13
panel data, 220–40
spillover effects, 3, 198–216
targeting, 93
volume, 97, 98, 198, 220
Chinese manufacturing
appropriate technology, 201
conclusions, 214–16
empirical results, 206–14
foreign presence (FP), 202–18
high-tech sector, 200, 201, 204
hypotheses, 199–202
labour-intensive projects, 140, 200, 201
labour productivity, 199, 203
labour quality, 214
methodology/data, 202–6
performance, 198–216
top industries, 205
Clegg, Jeremy, 189–97, 198–216, 245
Coase, Ronald, 10, 45, 168
commitment
FDI, 9, 72–3
trust, 105, 106, 107, 114–16
communication
barriers, 155
complementary knowledge, 150, 154
decision-making, 147
intermediation, 50, 151, 152, 154
internal communication, 50, 137
language, 169
organizational structure, 154–5
social networks, 21, 50
specialists, 173
subsidiaries, 76, 151
companies
corporate memory, 154
firms, *see* firms
Japanese, *see* Japan
MNEs, *see* multinational enterprises
subsidiary companies, *see* subsidiaries
TNCs, 222, 223
comparative management, 11
competencies
core, 172
creative destruction, 172
distrust, 116, 117, 118, 121
information processing, 137
local, 145, 146, 152
trust, 103, 106, 112, 113–14, 116, 117, 118, 120, 121
competition
alliances, 96
Asia, 125
competitiveness, 10–11, 90, 93
contribution margins, 243
decline, 95–7
developing countries, 92
diamond framework, 11
dynamic comparative advantage, 93
Eastern Europe, 3
globalization, 10–11, 95–7
initial entrants, 37
internal competition, 88
Portugal, 269
self-regulation, 1
shocks, 130
Spain, 3
system-wide optimum, 48–9
transfer pricing, 128, 244
complementary knowledge
additive, 149–50, 153
combination, 156
communication, 150, 154
complex complementarity, 149, 150, 154
inseparability, 168
knowledge sharing, 168, 170
local knowledge, 152
sequential, 149, 150, 154
uncertainty, 149–50
complexity
combinatorial, 22, 37
complementary knowledge, 149, 150, 154

complexity – *continued*
  confusion, 21–2
  global economy, 21
  knowledge flows, 150
  modelling, 20
  networks, 20–1, 37–8
  organic, 22
  popular perceptions, 21–2
  sources, 20–1
  strategic decisions, 1, 19–51
  systems theory, 22–4
  uncertainty, 20
Contractor, Farok, 11, 101
contracts
  formal/informal, 57
  IJVs, 103, 114, 115–16, 121
  internal contracting, 168
  linkages, 47
  options, 55, 56, 57, 63–6, 77
coordination
  knowledge management, 154, 170, 171
  linkages, 45
  uncertainty, 148
costs
  adjustment costs, 23–4, 136
  agency costs, 10
  communication, 21
  contribution margins, 243
  differentials, 41
  diversification, 54
  domestic production, 26, 256–7
  entry costs, 75
  errors/mistakes, 36, 76
  ex post costs, 104
  exit costs, 131
  flexibility, 131, 136, 137, 138
  foreign production, 26, 28–30, 32, 35, 42, 44
  information, *see* information costs
  integration, 125
  labour costs, 257, 278
  location, 42, 43, 45, 48
  Portugal, 256–7, 266, 278
  psychic costs, 75, 76
  R&D, 42, 129
  sunk costs, 42, 67
  switching, 131
  system structures, 46
  technology transfer, 42, 44, 48
  transactions, *see* transaction costs
  transport, 42, 266
Cross, Adam R., 220–40
culture
  domestic environment, 73
  IJVs, 107, 120
  Japan, 249, 250–1
  management, 73
  monopoly power, 130
  moral values, 138
  research agenda, 11–12

decision deferral
  accrued experience, 75
  foreign entry strategy, 31, 32, 33, 34, 35
  information collection, 76
  investment, 59, 64, 65, 71
  market growth, 67
  profitability, 66, 67–8, 71
decision trees, 30–1, 33, 59
decision-making
  bounded rationality, 168, 173
  communication, 147
  decision trees, 30–1, 33
  deferred, *see* decision deferral
  FDI, 9
  information collection, 28–9
  instrumental rationality, 173
  myopic, 23, 24
  new economy, 124–41
  non-contractual decisions, 58
  optimism, 36, 68, 74
  reversibility, 24, 31
  sophistication, 26, 76, 77
  strategic, *see* strategic decisions
  subjectivity, 73, 74
  uncertainty, 58
demand
  switching, 131–2, 137
  uncertainty, 66–8, 70
derivatives, 55
developed countries, 91–5, 222–3
developing countries
  asset prices, 90
  corruption, 91
  developed countries compared, 91–5
  industrialization, 85
  inward investment, 9
  less developed countries (LDCs), 9, 85, 93, 97–8

MNEs, 1, 85–7
myth of development, 86–7
privatization, 92–3
rents, 91
social assistance, 98
technological change, 223
technology dependence, 87, 222
discounting, 63
discovery strategies, 2, 173–4
discrete time models, 58
distribution
FDI, 47
globalization, 1, 97–8
information, 48–9
integration, 125
networks, 37, 38
distrust
incompetence, 116, 117, 118, 121
monopoly power, 130
diversification, 54, 134, 256
divestment, 131
division of knowledge, 2, 147, 168
division of labour, 50, 51, 84
domestic production, 26, 47, 256–7
dominant strategies
foreign entry strategy, 32, 34
investment, 64, 67, 71
Dunning, John H., 9, 10, 11, 89, 274
dynamic comparative advantage, 93
dynamic market entry, 31–6, 131–2, 139
dynamics optimized, 25, 31–6

e-commerce
aggregators, 126, 127
B2B, 126
disintermediation, 126–7
economies of scale/scope, 127
globalization, 124, 135–6
reach/richness, 127
reintermediation, 126–7
South-East Asia, 141
value chains, 126
Eastern Europe
competition, 3
FDI, 276, 278, 283
transition economies, 11, 63, 90
eclectic paradigm, 10
economic growth
absorptive capacity, 223
China, 140, 220–40
FDI, 220, 222–4
Granger causality test, 227
long-run growth, 222
markets, 67, 132
uneven, 84
economics
industrial economics, 8
international business (IB), 20, 40
rational action approach, 20
economies of scale
contract manufacturing, 138
e-commerce, 127
global operations, 133
IJVs, 120
location, 41, 92, 191
open internal markets, 128
economies of scope, 74, 75, 127
efficiency
complementarity, 168
FDI, 91, 222, 269, 274, 278, 282
global operations, 133
internal communication, 50
internal contracting, 168–9
knowledge sharing, 168
location, 42, 44
research, 42
standardization, 163
strategies, 49
emerging markets, 90, 92, 96
equilibrium, 22–3
errors/mistakes
beliefs, 173
costs, 36, 76
critical probability thresholds, 26, 55, 73
export strategy, 26–7, 28
marketing, 73, 74
rationalization, 73, 74
European Union (EU)
Portugal, 256, 258, 260, 269, 272, 282
regionalization, 88, 96
structural funds, 280, 281
exit costs, 131
exports
arm's length distribution, 47
foreign entry strategy, 26, 131
Portugal, 3
strategy, errors, 26–7, 28
transaction costs, 48

facilities
  levels of aggregation, 40
  location, *see* location
  long-run/short-run analysis, 41
  networks, 37, 38
  ownership, *see* ownership
  property, 63, 90
financial options, 55–6, 57, 61, 63, 80
firms
  behavioural theory, 9
  companies, *see* companies
  growth, 10, 84
  international, *see* internationalization
  MNEs, *see* multinational enterprises
  power, 89
  resource-based theory, 10, 19
  subsidiary companies, *see* subsidiaries
flexibility
  costs, 131, 136, 137, 138
  definition, 130
  IJVs, 77, 80, 132
  internal organization, 136–8
  manufacturing, 90, 138
  MNEs, 136–8
  ownership, 88, 125
  R&D, 129
  real options, 25, 66, 80
  small investments, 70
  strategies, 11, 88, 131
  volatility, 130, 136, 137
flows
  FDI, 7–9, 92, 98, 256, 257
  knowledge, *see* knowledge flows
  products, 37, 38, 39, 41, 45, 46, 47
footloose FDI, 140, 141, 274
footloose MNEs, 88, 90, 93
foreign direct investment (FDI)
  capital accumulation, 222
  China, *see* Chinese inward investment
  decision-making, 9
  determinants, 92, 256–7, 262–74
  distribution, 47
  economic growth, 220, 222–4
  efficiency, 91, 222, 269, 274, 278, 282
  fixed set-up cost, 32
  flows, 7–9, 92, 98, 256, 257
  footloose, 140, 141, 274
  foreign entry strategy, 26, 46
  human capital, 222, 223
  increasing commitment, 9, 72–3
  industrial economics, 8
  information collection, 36, 132
  integration, 267, 269
  international trade theory, 8
  inward, *see* inward investment
  Latin America, 223
  local earnings, 85–6, 87
  macro-economic determinants, 92
  markets, 91, 92, 257
  North/South, 92
  Portugal, 3, 256–87
  product cycle hypothesis, 9
  real options, 88
  REI, 190–6
  South-East Asia, 140, 141
  strategic decisions, 91
  synergy, 92
  total factor productivity (TFP), 221, 223
  transaction costs, 48, 92
  United States, 2–3, 7–9, 84, 85, 97, 189–97
foreign entry strategy
  customer loyalty, 37
  dominant strategies, 32, 34
  dynamic, 31–6, 131–2, 139
  errors/mistakes, 26–7, 28, 36
  exports, 26, 131
  FDI, 26, 46
  initial entry, 37, 71
  internally transferable advantage, 8
  profitability, 26, 32
  rational action approach, 25–8
  research, 28–35
  sequential entry, 74, 75, 76–7
  simultaneous entry, 54, 74, 75
  switching strategies, 29, 31, 32, 33, 34, 35–6, 131
  systems theory, 1
  uncertainty, 26, 27, 36
  Uppsala approach, 1
foreign exchange, 86, 130, 246
Forsans, Nicolas, 189–97
Fransman, M., 170, 173
free trade areas (FTAs)
  centralization, 191
  CUSFTA, 189, 190, 192, 194, 195, 196
  EU, 88, 96, 256, 258, 260, 269, 272, 282
  insiders/outsiders, 189, 190
  liberalization, 192

NAFTA, 2, 88, 96, 190–6
tariff factories, 192
fuzzy theories, 21, 131

gambler's earnings hypothesis, 83
Ganesan, S., 101, 102, 114
Ghauri, Pervez N., 1, 2, 83–91, 101–21
Ghoshal, Sumantra, 11
global economy, 21, 23
globalization
competition, 10–11, 95–7
differential speed, 135
distribution, 1, 97–8
e-commerce, 124, 135–6
Japan, 248
local knowledge, 151–2
markets, 74–5, 133
mass customization, 135–6
meaning, 2
oligopoly, 84, 95–6, 97
planned, 9
power of firms, 89
research agenda, 7, 8, 10–11
strategic management, 74
government policies
activism, 93, 95
bargaining power, 86, 88–91
collusion, 89, 91
equity related, 93, 95
externalities, 88, 93
government failure, 94
intervention, 88
Japan, 244
MNEs, 88, 91
Portugal, 278–81
protectionism, 92, 244
regulation, 94
state capabilities, 94, 95
tax, *see* taxation
Gulamhussen, Mohammed Azzim, 1, 54–81

Hennart, Jean-François, 10
heterarchy, 152–3, 163
hierarchies
incentives, 171
management, 9, 131, 137, 152
transaction costs, 10
Hofstede, Geert, 11
host countries
operations, *see* local operations; location
policies, *see* government policies
hub and spoke operations
global/local operations, 133–4
IJVs, 134–5
incentives, 191
location/ownership, 88, 134–5
South-East Asia, 140
Hughes, Jane Frecknall, 3, 242–51
human capital
China, 140, 199, 200, 201, 203, 214
FDI, 222, 223
Hymer, Stephen, 8–9, 84, 85, 92

IBRD, 94
import substitution, 84, 86, 92
incentives
China, 200
hub and spoke operations, 191
inward investment, 89, 200, 245, 266, 267, 278–81, 283
knowledge sharing, 169, 171
location, 88, 89
Portugal, 278–281, 283
profit transfer, 3, 245–50
trade/investment, 190
India, 13
information
distribution, 48–9
information sets, 28–31
initial information, 73
rents, 77
social networks, 50
sticky information, 145, 155, 172
information collection
decision deferral, 76
FDI, 36, 132
ownership/location strategies, 36
primary uncertainty, 147
real options, 70–3
switching, 131–2
uncertainty, 28–9, 73, 136
information costs
avoidance, 31
information collection, 28–9
rational action approach, 25, 51, 55
uncertainty, 73
information processing
competencies, 137

information processing – *continued*
division of labour, 50, 51
IT, 136
management, *see* knowledge management process
information technology (IT)
de-duplication of function, 136, 140
electronic commerce, *see* e-commerce
information processing, 136
outsourcing, 138
innovation, 129
insider status, 95, 96
integration
costs, 125
disintermediation/reintermediation, 126
distribution, 125
downstream, 267, 269, 274
FDI, 267, 269
horizontal, 124
knowledge, 167, 168, 170
operational, 119
regionalization, 189
supply chains, 138
upstream, 267, 274
vertical, 47, 124, 125
internal structure
centralization, 85, 145, 152, 163
communication, 50, 137, 154–5
competition, 88
contracting, 168–9
divisions, 9, 85, 128, 131, 172, 173
entrepreneurs, 137
flatter organizations, 137
flexibility, 136–8
knowledge management process, 145–6, 154–6
open internal markets, 128
R&D, 130–1
system structures, 45–6
internalization theory
internal markets, 128
knowledge flows, 41, 45, 46–7
levels of aggregation, 40
licensing, 46, 76, 131
linkages, 41, 46
MNEs, 10
ownership, 41, 45
Penrose effect, 75
pre-emptive advantage, 75
profitability, 76
takeovers, 45
international business (IB)
adjustment costs, 24
economics, 20, 40
levels of aggregation, 38, 40–1
long-run/short-run analysis, 41
networks, *see* networks
radical changes in theory, 22
research, *see* research
social sciences, 19, 20
softer theories, 20
theoretical challenges, 19–21
international joint ventures (IJVs)
asymmetric information, 77
business opportunities, 113
compromise, 132
contracts, 103, 114, 115–16, 121
culture, 107, 120
economies of scale, 120
equity trading, 77
financial investors, 77, 78
flexibility, 77, 80, 132
hub and spoke operations, 134–5
management, 101, 104
mergers, barriers, 109
negotiations, 77, 78, 104, 105, 106, 107, 112–14, 115, 118, 121
operational integration, 119
option value, 132
profitability, 78–9
quality assurance, 120
R&D, 78, 129
real options, 1, 66, 77–80, 132
research agenda, 11
sophisticated partners, 77
symmetrical, 109
transaction costs, 77, 101, 103–5
trust, *see* trust
international management, 11
international trade theory, 8
internationalization
classification of approaches, 75
creeping incrementalism, 9
markets, 75
real options, 54–81
research agenda, 7, 8, 9, 10–11
Scandinavian approach, 54
simultaneous/sequential, 74, 75
stages model, 9, 76

step-by-step model, 9
strategies, 54–81
transactions, 92
Uppsala approach, 9, 55, 73

investment
decision deferral, 59, 64, 65, 71
dominant strategies, 64, 67, 71
FDI, *see* foreign direct investment
import substitution, 84, 86
incrementalism, 9, 76, 80
information collection, 70–3
initial investment, 67, 71
inward, *see* inward investment
liquidation, 69
profitability, 64, 67–8
scaling up, 69, 71
small scale, 69–70, 71, 72
sophisticated investors, 76
timing, 63–5

inward investment
China, 2, 3, 93, 97, 98, 140, 141, 198–240
incentives, 89, 200, 245, 266, 267, 278–81, 283
less developed countries (LDCs), 9, 93, 97–8
Portugal, 3, 256–87

irreversibility, *see* reversibility

Japan
capital accumulation, 248
contribution margins, 243
corporate debt, 248
cross-shareholdings, 246, 247, 248
culture, 249, 250–1
dividend policy, 247–8, 250
families, 149
globalization, 248
government policies, 244
group consciousness, 149, 150
groups of companies, 246, 247, 248, 249
individual rights, 149
kaisha, 250
keiretsu, 246, 248
losses, 248, 249
MNEs, 3, 9
profit transfer, 3, 242–51
protectionism, 244
reinvestment, 248, 250
sociology, 249
subsidiaries, 248, 250
target costing, 243, 248, 250
taxation, 3, 245
transfer pricing, 3, 242–51

Jenkins, R., 89

joint ventures
complementary technologies, 129
fuzzy theories, 21
IJVs, *see* international joint ventures
internal trade, 128
networks, 128, 129
trust, *see* trust

Kindleberger, C. P., 8

knowledge
absorptive capacity, 151, 202
architectures, 170–1, 174
assimilation/verification, 11
boundaries/frontiers, 2, 146, 155, 169, 170
capabilities, 171–2
characteristics, 146
communities, 152–3
complementary, *see* complementary knowledge
corporate memory, 154
creation, 154, 173
hidden beliefs, 170, 171
justified true belief, 170
know-how, 37, 151, 152
local knowledge, 2, 8, 49, 147–53
networks, 37–8, 49, 152–3
new configurations, 171–4
privatization, 96
public good, 50, 75
public knowledge, 96
specialization, 169
state of mind, 167
sticky information, 145, 155, 172
uncertainty, 147–50, 167, 169
value creation, 147–53

knowledge flows
complexity, 150
externalization, 46–7
global networks, 37–9
global/local opposition, 163
internalization theory, 41, 45, 46–7
linkages, 45
transaction costs, 45, 47
unidirectional, 150

knowledge management
  application strategies, 2
  bidding expertise, 159–61
  case studies, 146, 153, 156–63, 174–80
  combination, 145, 146, 155, 156, 172
  coordination, 154, 170, 171
  discovery strategies, 2, 173–4
  global, 2
  integration, 167, 168, 170
  local, 2, 8, 49
  partition, 170, 171
  practices, 145–65
  real options, 1
  registers, 154
  spatial issues, 2, 145, 146, 148, 150, 151, 153, 163–4
  subsidiaries, 146, 151–3
  virtual teams, 159–61
knowledge management process
  constraints, 146
  determinants, 145
  drivers, 146
  organizational structure, 145–6, 154–6
  participants, 146
  pre-existing alignment, 145–6
  sequencing, 146
  strategies, 153–4
  synthesis, 147, 148, 151
knowledge processes
  division of knowledge, 2, 147, 168
  efficiency, 168
  governance, 2, 167–83
  intra-firm governance, 169–70
  market contracting, 169
  propositions, 169, 170, 171, 174–83
  tacit knowledge, 168
knowledge sharing
  complementary knowledge, 168, 170
  efficiency, 168
  governance, 2, 167–83
  incentives, 169, 171
knowledge transfer
  parent/subsidiaries, 156–9, 160
  sequential development, 156–9, 160
  specialized knowledge, 169
  technology, 146
Koopmans, T. C., 147, 168
Krugman, P., 88, 97, 146, 190
Larson, A., 105
Latin America, 223
lean retailing, 136
less developed countries (LDCs), 9, 85, 93, 97–8
Liberthal, K., 90
licensing
  cost differentials, 10, 41
  externally sourced technology, 161–3
  global capability, 161–3
  information collection, 36, 151
  internalization theory, 46, 76, 131
  transaction costs, 92
linkages
  contractual arrangements, 47
  coordination, 45
  internalization theory, 41, 46
  international, 41, 45
  MNEs, 126
  R&D, 46, 47
  transaction costs, 45
  value chains, 88
lobbying, 95, 96
local operations
  advantages, 133
  diversification, 256
  earnings reinvested, 85–6, 87
  'glocal', 131, 146
  knowledge, 2, 8, 49, 147–53
  local competencies, 145, 146, 152
  production costs, 26, 28–30, 32, 35, 42, 44
  representative offices, 191
location
  comparative advantage, 41
  costs, 42, 43, 45, 48
  determinants, 10
  economies of scale, 41, 92, 191
  efficiency, 42, 44
  emerging markets, 90
  factor intensities, 41
  footloose MNEs, 88, 90, 93
  greenfield projects, 45, 140, 141
  hub and spoke operations, 88, 134–5
  incentives, 88, 89
  information collection, 36
  network view, 41
  non-contractual options, 57
  research, 42, 44
  strategies, 36, 41–2, 44, 45–6

subsidies, 93–4
tournaments, 93
transport, 40, 41
volatility, 148
lock-in, 23–4, 173
long-term planning, 20
Lorange, Peter, 11, 101

McManus, J. C., 10
management
behaviour modelling, 54–5
beliefs, 73–4, 170, 171
case studies, 19
comparative management, 11
consultation, 137
culture, 73
downsizing, 136
flatter organizations, 137
hierarchies, 9, 131, 137, 152
IJVs, 101, 104
information processing, 137
internal entrepreneurs, 137
knowledge, *see* knowledge management
line responsibility, 10
local competencies, 145
networking, 137
personal integrity, 138
resources overstretched, 54, 75
strategic management, 19, 74
successful management, 23
vision, 170
manufacturing
China, *see* Chinese manufacturing
contract manufacturing, 138–9
diffusion, 85, 130
flexibility, 90, 138
Portugal, 256, 257–8, 272, 280, 282
shell factories, 138
market failure, 93, 94, 95
marketing, 73, 74
markets
decline, 131
disturbances, 130
emerging markets, 90, 92, 96
entry strategy, *see* foreign entry strategy
FDI, 91, 92, 257
global/local operations, 133–4
globalization, 74–5, 133
growth, 67, 132
interaction, 113–15
internal markets, 128
internationalization, 75
knowledge creation, 154
Scandinavian approach, 76
transaction costs, 10
transition economies, 11
unexpected growth, 132
withdrawal, 131
mass consumerism, 138
measurement, parameter values, 23
methodology, 111, 202–6, 257–8
Mexico, 189, 190, 191, 192
mistakes, *see* errors/mistakes
modelling
algebraic form, 58, 80
complexity, 20
continuous time models, 57–8
discrete time models, 58
disequilibrium behaviour, 23
format model, 20
managerial behaviour, 54–5
organizational behaviour, 50
process model, 2
product cycle model, 76
rational action approach, 19, 20, 23, 28, 54–5
real options, 36
recursive technique, 58
research agenda, 131
stages model, 9, 76
step-by-step model, 9
moral hazard, 160
moral values, 138
motivation, 148
multinational enterprises (MNEs)
antecedents, 84–5
Australia, 84
bargaining power, 86, 88–91
born globals, 11
continuous monitoring, 136
critical literature, 1, 83–7, 98
de-layering, 131
developing countries, 1, 85–7
divisions, 9, 85, 128, 131
education and training, 85, 86
flexibility, 136–8
footloose, 88, 90, 93
foreign exchange, 86

multinational – *continued*
  golden age, 124, 131
  government policies, 88, 91
  internal competition, 88
  internal organization, *see* internal structure
  internalization theory, 10
  Japan, 3, 9
  linkages, 126
  managers, *see* management
  multi-market operations, 129–31
  new economy, 2, 124–41
  North/South, 90
  outsourcing, 131, 138, 140
  profitability, 84, 87
  rents, 83–91
  research agenda, 7, 8, 9–10, 99
  resource seeking, 91
  sharing knowledge, *see* knowledge sharing
  single market operations, 124–9
  South-East Asia, 2
  strategies, 1, 87–8
  subsidiary companies, *see* subsidiaries
  tax, *see* taxation
  transfer pricing, *see* transfer pricing
  vertical integration, 124

negotiations
  bargaining power, 86, 88–91
  IJVs, 77, 78, 104, 105, 106, 107, 112–14, 115, 118, 121
networks
  complexity, 20–1, 37–8
  intangible flows, 37–8, 39, 41, 45, 46, 47
  joint ventures, 128, 129
  knowledge, 37–8, 49, 152–3
  linkage, *see* linkages
  social networks, 21, 49–50
  tangible flows, 37, 38, 39, 41, 45, 46, 47
  virtual networks, 129
new economy
  e-commerce, 124
  meaning, 124
  MNEs, 2, 124–41
  South-East Asia, 139–41
North America Free Trade Agreement (NAFTA), 2, 88, 96, 190–6
null strategy, 71, 74, 76, 80

oligopoly
  contract manufacturing, 138
  economies of scale, 92
  globalization, 84, 95–6, 97
  golden age, 131
opportunism, 102, 104, 147, 171
optimization
  dynamics, 25, 31–6
  initial decisions, 58
  initial investment, 67
  ownership, 44–8
option purchase
  decision rules, 61–2
  decision trees, 59
  graphical solution, 60–1
  prices, 56, 58, 60
options
  assets, 55, 56, 57
  call options, 55, 59, 64, 77, 78, 79
  classification, 56, 57, 66
  continuous time models, 57–8
  contractual, 55, 56, 57, 63–6, 77
  demand conditions, 66–8
  deposits, 63, 64
  financial options, 55–6, 57, 61, 63, 80
  non-contractual, 56, 57, 66
  put options, 55, 59, 77, 78, 79
  real, *see* real options
  speculation, 60, 65
  uncertainty, 65, 66–8
  valuation, 55, 62–3
outsourcing, 131, 138, 140
ownership
  contractual options, 57
  control, 125
  flexibility, 88, 125
  IJV case studies, 110
  information collection, 36
  internalization theory, 41, 45
  networks, 10
  optimization, 44–8
  transaction costs, 44–8

path-dependence
  agents, 23–4
  knowledge creation, 173
  lock-in, 23–4, 173
  non-explanation, 23–4
Penrose, Edith T., 11, 54, 75, 83
Porter, Michael E., 11, 24, 74, 93, 128, 191

Portugal
  alternative FDI locations, 274–8, 283
  competition, 269
  determinants of FDI, 262–74
  EFTA, 256, 257
  European Union (EU), 256, 258, 260, 269, 272, 282
  export industries, 3
  FDI, 3, 256–87
  government policies, 278–81
  incentives, 278–281, 283
  labour conditions, 274
  labour costs, 257, 278
  manufacturing, 256, 257–8, 272, 280, 282
  methodology, 257–8
  origin of FDI, 259–64, 282
  privatization, 109
  production costs, 256–7
  push factors, 3, 269
  sample, 258–62
  segments/clusters, 3
  transport costs, 266
Prahalad, C. D., 90, 135, 172
prices
  assets, 63–4, 65, 90
  hedging, 119
  manipulation, 243, 245, 250
  option purchase, 56, 58, 60
  transfer pricing, *see* transfer pricing
privatization, 89, 92–3, 96, 109
product cycle model, 76
production
  capacity expansion, 132
  cross-haul, 42
  domestic, 26, 47, 256–7
  facilities, *see* facilities
  foreign production costs, 26, 28–30, 32, 35, 42, 44
  location, *see* location
  product cycle hypothesis, 9
  product flows, 37, 38, 39, 41, 45, 46, 47
  standardization, 133
  vertical integration, 47, 124, 125
profit transfer
  business consciousness, 249–50
  control, 246
  incentives, 3, 245–50
  Japan, 3, 242–51
  need, 246–9
profitability
  decision deferral, 66, 67–8, 71
  divisions, 128
  foreign entry strategy, 26, 32
  IJVs, 78–9
  internalization theory, 76
  investment, 64, 67–8
  MNEs, 84, 87
  overhead recovery, 243
  volatility, 130
protectionism, 92, 244
psychic costs, 75, 76
put options, 55, 59, 77, 78, 79

rational action approach
  dynamics optimized, 25, 31–6
  economics, 20
  far-sighted agents, 23
  foreign entry strategy, 25–8
  game theory, 25
  information collection, 28–9
  information costs, 25, 51, 55
  international business strategy, 24–5
  long-term planning, 20
  modelling, 19, 20, 23, 28, 54–5
  real options, 25
  social networks, 49–50
  strategic decisions, 1, 24–8
  uncertainty, 26
rationalization, 73, 74, 80
real options
  exploitation, 55
  FDI, 88
  flexibility, 25, 66, 80
  IJVs, 1, 66, 77–80, 132
  information collection, 70–3
  internationalization, 54–81
  irreversibility, 55, 59, 63–4, 71
  knowledge management, 1
  modelling, 36
  non-tradable assets, 56, 63–4, 80
  rational action approach, 25
  rationalization, 80
  risk reduction, 55, 60, 66, 80
  strategic decisions, 1, 31, 36–7
  techniques of analysis, 57–63
regional economic integration (REI)
  discrimination, 189
  FDI, 190–6
  inter-bloc strategies, 191–2

regional economic – *continued*
intra-bloc effects, 192
North America, 190–7
regionalization
European Union (EU), 88, 96
integration, 189
NAFTA, 2, 88, 96, 190–6
Reilly, Kevin T., 189–97
rents
application strategies, 172
developing countries, 91
dissipation, 171
information, 77
intellectual property, 75
MNEs, 83–91
servicing strategies, 88
research
cross-haul, 42
decision trees, 30–1, 33
efficiency, 42
foreign entry strategy, 28–35
foreign production costs, 28–30, 32
information sets, 28–31
location, 42, 44
research & development (R&D)
China, 203, 212, 213, 214, 233
costs, 42, 129
flexibility, 129
IJVs, 78, 129
internal monopoly, 130–1
linkages, 46, 47
sequential complementarity, 154
research agenda
adverse scenarios, 131
big question, 1, 7, 12, 13
collective enterprise, 1
current agenda, 12–13
engagement, business world, 2
international business (IB), 7–13
internationalization, 7, 8, 9, 10–11
MNEs, 7, 8, 9–10, 99
modelling, 131
networks, 41–4
new/future, 13, 99, 131, 135
previous agenda, 7
stylized facts, 12, 13
resource seeking, 91
resource-based theories, 10, 19
reversibility
decision-making, 24, 31
irreversibility, 24, 55, 59, 63–4, 71
scale, 69–70, 71, 72
Ricardian theories, 41
Ridderstrale, J., 152, 153
Ring, P. S., 101, 105, 106, 111, 114
risks
capital loss, 60
contractual options, 64, 65, 66
profits, control, 246
reduction, 55, 60, 65, 66, 80, 132
subjective probability, 104
trust, 102, 104, 132
Rugman, Alan M., 11, 128, 192
rules of origin, 190

Sako, M., 102, 103, 106, 119
scale
economies, *see* economies of scale
reversibility, 69–70, 71, 72
Scandinavian approach
evaluation, 74–7
internationalization, 54
markets, 76
Schumpeterian theories, 97
self-interest
economic advantage, 113
goodwill, 103, 116, 118, 119
interests aligned, 115, 118, 120
opportunism, 102, 104, 147, 171
transaction costs, 105
shelter seeking, 95, 96
shock, 130, 134, 147, 148
social networks, 21, 49–50
social sciences, 19, 20
South-East Asia
dynamic market entry, 139
e-commerce, 141
expectations, 140
FDI, 140, 141
MNEs, 2
networks and clusters, 140–1
new economy, 139–41
takeovers, 140
volatility, 141
Spain
competition, 3
FDI, 260, 276, 278, 283
market seeking, 272, 278
subsidiaries, 262

spatial issues, knowledge management, 2, 145, 146, 148, 150, 151, 153, 163–4
speculation, 60, 65, 130
standardization, 133, 163
stock markets, 130
Strange, S., 89
strategic alliances, 19, 21
strategic decisions
  characteristics, 24–5
  complexity, 1, 19–51
  FDI, 91
  rational action approach, 1, 24–8
  real options, 1, 31, 36–7
strategic management, 19, 74
strategies
  dominance, *see* dominant strategies
  flexibility, 11, 88, 131
  foreign entry, *see* foreign entry strategy
  internationalization, 54–81
  knowledge management process, 1, 153–4
  location, 36, 41–2, 44, 45–6
  MNEs, 1, 87–8
  null strategy, 71, 74, 76, 80
  portfolio of applications, 172, 173
  sequential, 153
Streeten, P., 85, 86
structures
  IJV case studies, 11, 108, 109, 110
  MNEs, *see* internal structure
subsidiaries
  affiliate business models, 156
  arms and legs analogy, 248
  communication, 76, 151
  dependence, 157
  go local, 157–8
  independence, 153
  investment returns, 83
  Japan, 248, 250
  knowledge management, 146, 151–3
  knowledge transfer, 156–9
  leadership, 158–9
  replacement, 191
  shocks, 130
  strategy-active subsidiaries, 2, 152–3
  take control, 158
  transfer pricing, 3
sunk costs, 42, 67
supply
  indivisibility, 108, 109
  intermediate product trade, 129
  uncertainty, 66
Swedenborg, B., 10
switching
  costs, 131
  foreign entry strategy, 29, 31, 32, 33, 34, 35–6, 131
  hub and spoke operations, 134
  information collection, 131–2
  option strategy, 61
  shock, 134
  supply/demand source, 131–2, 137
system structures, 46
systems theory, 1

takeovers, 45, 96, 140
target costing, 243, 248, 250
taxation
  avoidance, 244
  Japan, 3, 245
  tax leakage, 244
  transfer pricing, 3, 85, 242–3, 244
  United States, 246
technology
  adaptation, 152
  capital deepening, 222
  complementary technologies, 129
  dependence, 87, 222
  electronic commerce, *see* e-commerce
  exogenous progress, 222
  IT, *see* information technology
  know-how, 37, 151
  knowledge transfer, 146
  licensed, *see* licensing
technology transfer, 42, 44, 48
transaction costs
  adaptation, 104
  bonding, 104
  ex ante/ex post, 104
  exports, 48
  FDI, 48, 92
  flexibility, 137
  haggling, 104
  IJVs, 77, 101, 103–5
  linkages, 45
  markets and hierarchies, 10
  ownership, 44–8
  process analyses, 101
  set-up, 104
  shared control, 104

transaction costs – *continued*
  theoretical debate, 19
  trust, 2, 77, 101, 103–5
transfer pricing
  competition, 128, 244
  developing countries, 85, 86
  income shifting, 242
  Japan, 3, 242–51
  objectives, 3, 244–5
  subsidiaries, 3
  taxation, 3, 85, 242–3, 244
  United Kingdom, 242, 244
transition economies, 11, 63, 90
transnational corporations (TNCs), 222, 223
transnational organizations, 133
transport, 40, 41, 42, 266
trust
  case studies, 107–11
  cheating, 102, 104
  commitment, 105, 106, 107, 114–16, 120, 121
  competencies, 103, 106, 112, 113–14, 116, 117, 118, 120, 121
  contractual, 103, 114, 115–16, 121
  cooperation, 101, 103, 104, 105, 114, 116, 120
  definition, 103
  dimensions, 102–3, 106
  egotistic/non-egotistic, 103, 119
  emergence, 101
  execution stage, 105, 106, 107, 116–17, 121
  explanation, 102
  financial investment, 116, 121
  forbearance, 101, 104, 114
  goodwill, 103, 106, 113, 114, 115, 116, 117, 118, 119, 120, 121
  IJVs, 2, 11, 77, 78, 101–21
  incompetence, 116, 117, 118, 121
  intuition, 113, 115
  negotiation stage, 105, 106, 107, 112–14, 115, 118, 121
  personal relationships, 112, 114, 115, 116, 117–18, 120, 137
  previous history, 105, 106, 107, 112, 121
  process model, 2, 101–2, 105–7
  professional skills, 114
  promissory-based, 102–3, 106, 113, 114, 115, 117, 118, 120, 121
  propositions, 107, 111–17
  reputation, 106, 107, 112, 113, 118, 121
  risks, 102, 104, 132
  self-interest, 103, 105, 113, 115, 116, 118, 119, 120
  sequential process, 107
  social networks, 21
  sources, 103
  stages, 105–6, 107, 121
  transaction costs, 2, 77, 101, 103–5

uncertainty
  beliefs, 170
  complementary knowledge, 149–50
  complexity, 20
  coordination, 148
  decision-making, 58
  demand, 66–8, 70
  ex post costs, 104
  foreign entry strategy, 26, 27, 36
  future asset price, 65
  graphical solutions, 36–7
  industrial property, 63
  information collection, 28–9, 73, 136
  knowledge, 147–50, 167, 169
  motivation, 148
  options, 65, 66–8
  primary, 147, 148, 149
  rational action approach, 26
  secondary, 147, 148, 168
  supply, 66
  tertiary, 147, 148
  trade-inhibiting, 167
  vision, 170
United Kingdom, 242, 244
United States
  CUSFTA, 189, 190, 192, 194, 195, 196
  FDI, 2–3, 7–9, 84, 85, 97, 189–97
  NAFTA, 2, 88, 96, 190–6
  taxation, 246
  transfer pricing, 243
Uppsala approach
  expansion, 76
  foreign entry strategy, 1
  internationalization, 9, 55, 73

value chains, 88, 126
van de Ven, A. H., 101, 105, 106, 111, 114
Vernon, Raymond, 9, 11, 76, 81, 89
vertical integration, 47, 124, 125

volatility
  flexibility, 130, 136, 137
  location, 148
  outsourcing, 138
  profitability, 130
  shock, 130, 147, 148
  South-East Asia, 141
  uncertainty, 147, 148

Von Hippel, E., 155, 172

Wang, Chengqi, 198–216, 220–40
Wilkins, Mira, 9
Williamson, Oliver E., 10, 46, 102, 104, 114, 147, 169, 171
World Trade Organization (WTO), 87, 140, 216